# How to access the supplemental online resource

We are pleased to provide access to an online resource that supplements *The Park and Recreation Professional's Handbook*. This resource offers activities and assignments, sample forms and documents from real recreation and leisure agencies, chapter overviews, key words, and more. We are certain you will enjoy this unique online learning experience.

## Accessing the online resource is easy!
## Follow these steps if you purchased a new book:

1. Visit **www.HumanKinetics.com/TheParkAndRecreationProfessionalsHandbook**.

2. Click the Sign In link on the left or top of the page. If you do not have an account with Human Kinetics, you will be prompted to create one.

3. If the online product you purchased does not appear in the Ancillary Items box on the left of the page, click the Enter Key Code option in that box. Enter the key code that is printed at the right, including all hyphens. Click the Submit button to unlock your online product.

4. After you successfully enter your key code, your online product will appear in the Ancillary Items box. On future visits to the site, all you need to do is sign in to the textbook's Web site and follow the link!

→ Click the Need Help? button on the textbook's Web site if you need assistance along the way.

## How to access the online resource if you purchased a used book:

You may purchase access to the online resource by visiting the text's Web site, **www.HumanKinetics.com/TheParkAndRecreationProfessionalsHandbook**, or by calling the following:

800-747-4457 . . . . . . . . . . . . . . . . . . . . . . . . . . . .U.S. customers
800-465-7301 . . . . . . . . . . . . . . . . . . . . . . . . . .Canadian customers
+44 (0) 113 255 5665 . . . . . . . . . . . . . . . . . . . . . European customers
08 8372 0999 . . . . . . . . . . . . . . . . . . . . . . . . . Australian customers
0800 222 062 . . . . . . . . . . . . . . . . . . . . . . . .New Zealand customers
217-351-5076 . . . . . . . . . . . . . . . . . . . . . . . .International customers

For technical support, send an e-mail to:
support@hkusa.com . . . . . . . . . . . . . . . . . . U.S. and international customers
info@hkcanada.com . . . . . . . . . . . . . . . . . . . . . . Canadian customers
academic@hkeurope.com . . . . . . . . . . . . . . . . . . . European customers
keycodesupport@hkaustralia.com . . . . . Australian and New Zealand customers

**HUMAN KINETICS**
*The Information Leader in Physical Activity & Health*

**Product:** The Park and Recreation Professional's Handbook online resource

**Key code:** HURD-FBISLB-OSG

HUMAN KINETICS ONLINE RESOURCE

# The Park and Recreation Professional's Handbook

Amy R. Hurd

Denise M. Anderson

Human Kinetics

**Library of Congress Cataloging-in-Publication Data**

Hurd, Amy R.
    The park and recreation professional's handbook  /  Amy R. Hurd, Denise M. Anderson.
       p.  cm.
    Includes bibliographical references and index.
    ISBN-13: 978-0-7360-8259-4 (hard cover)
    ISBN-10: 0-7360-8259-X (hard cover)
    1.  Recreation--Study and teaching--United States.  2.  Parks--Vocational
guidance--United States.   I.
Anderson, Denise M., 1970-  II.  Title.
    GV181.35.H87  2011
    790.06'9--dc22

                                                      2010032862

ISBN-10: 0-7360-8259-X (print)
ISBN-13: 978-0-7360-8259-4 (print)

The Web addresses cited in this text were current as of October 2010, unless otherwise noted.

**Acquisitions Editor:** Gayle Kassing, PhD; **Developmental Editor:** Ray Vallese; **Special Projects Editor:** Anne Cole; **Assistant Editor:** Derek Campbell; **Copyeditor:** Jocelyn Engman; **Indexer:** Sharon Duffy; **Permission Manager:** Dalene Reeder; **Graphic Designer:** Nancy Rasmus; **Graphic Artist:** Yvonne Griffith; **Cover Designer:** Bob Reuther; **Photographer (interior):** See page ix for a full list of photo credits. **Photo Asset Manager:** Laura Fitch; **Visual Production Assistant:** Joyce Brumfield; **Photo Production Manager:** Jason Allen; **Art Manager:** Kelly Hendren; **Associate Art Manager:** Alan L. Wilborn; **Illustrator:** © Human Kinetics; **Printer:** Sheridan Books

Printed in the United States of America          10  9  8  7  6  5  4  3  2  1

The paper in this book is certified under a sustainable forestry program.

**Human Kinetics**
Web site: www.HumanKinetics.com

*United States:* Human Kinetics
P.O. Box 5076
Champaign, IL 61825-5076
800-747-4457
e-mail: humank@hkusa.com

*Canada:* Human Kinetics
475 Devonshire Road Unit 100
Windsor, ON N8Y 2L5
800-465-7301 (in Canada only)
e-mail: info@hkcanada.com

*Europe:* Human Kinetics
107 Bradford Road
Stanningley
Leeds LS28 6AT, United Kingdom
+44 (0) 113 255 5665
e-mail: hk@hkeurope.com

*Australia:* Human Kinetics
57A Price Avenue
Lower Mitcham, South Australia 5062
08 8372 0999
e-mail: info@hkaustralia.com

*New Zealand:* Human Kinetics
P.O. Box 80
Torrens Park, South Australia 5062
0800 222 062
e-mail: info@hknewzealand.com

E4792

# contents

# preface

The Park and Recreation Professional's Handbook provides a road map to an understanding of the profession. The last chapter, which delves into professional development and certification, is really the beginning of this process. It culminates by telling readers that they have built a foundation of knowledge in the profession and explaining the importance of continuing their education and development and obtaining certification in their chosen profession. In order for this to happen, they need knowledge in marketing, programming, human resources, and other topics covered in the remaining chapters.

This book is designed with two purposes in mind. The first is to lay a foundation to help the reader comprehend the vastness of the parks and recreation profession from the point when it started to become a legitimate profession requiring a common educational basis. The second is to enhance the reader's knowledge base to become a Certified Park and Recreation Professional (CPRP) or obtain other certifications in the profession. By the end of this book, the reader should have the knowledge needed to be successful in the field and to pass the CPRP examination.

This text is designed to resonate with four distinct audiences:

1. Students preparing to graduate, begin their internship, and ultimately enter the profession
2. Professionals in the field who have recreation degrees but need a refresher course on the entire scope of the profession
3. Professionals in the field who have a degree in an area other than parks and recreation
4. Professionals in the field who have no college degree and know only information that applies to their current agency or who lack foundational knowledge of the profession

These audiences make The Park and Recreation Professional's Handbook somewhat unique in that it is designed to appeal to current students as well as to current practitioners. For this reason, the book uses many real-life examples to enhance the content. These examples help students put into perspective the concepts learned and allow practitioners to see how other agencies operate and gain ideas they can implement.

Because this book is designed to cover the entire profession in depth, it is essentially divided into four main areas: foundations and programming, planning and operations, administration, and professionalism. It is hoped that The Park and Recreation Professional's Handbook will remain in the reader's library of reference materials because it contains many discussions, forms, and examples that will be beneficial to both students and practitioners.

The book's chapters address the content as follows:

- Chapters 1 through 4 cover the history and foundation of the profession, programming, implementation, and evaluation. A unique feature of The Park and Recreation Professional's Handbook is the chapter on motor development. Much programming relies on an understanding of how people grow and develop. Chapter 3 provides an overview and shows the reader how individuals change and how programs need to change to meet their abilities.
- Chapters 5 through 7 cover operations management and encompass planning and management, maintenance management, and facility operations.
- Chapters 8 through 12 cover general administration and include budget and finance, hiring and employee management, marketing, and policy formulation and interpretation.
- Chapter 13 is the culminating chapter that outlines the next steps in the profession. It covers certification, professional associations, ethics, and professional development.

The Park and Recreation Professional's Handbook has online resources that provide an overview of each chapter, key terms, activities that allow application of the material covered, and sample resources. These resources are valuable for students and professionals. They are actual forms, policies, documents, plans, and other items that are used in the profession today. They can be used to reinforce content or help practitioners develop their own items. The online resource for *The Park and Recreation Professional's Hand-book* is located at www.HumanKinetics.com/TheParkAndRecreationProfessionalsHandbook.

It is hoped that this text will serve as a valuable resource during the student's formal education as well as during the practitioner's continuing education. There is a lot to learn about this exciting field, and *The Park and Recreation Professional's Handbook* will enhance this educational journey.

# acknowledgments

A textbook is a major undertaking that requires an incredible amount of support and guidance, both personally and professionally. We first must thank Illinois State University and Clemson University for their support of this project. Administrative and fellow faculty members offered encouragement, insight, and meaningful suggestions to make this book even stronger. A special thanks goes to Dr. Brent Beggs, Dr. Deb Garrahy, Dane Boudreau, Nancy Niebur, Dr. Barb Schlatter, and Dr. Melissa Zahl at Illinois State University and Tracy Mainieri, Teresa Tucker, and Brianna Clark at Clemson University. In addition to our universities, this book would not have been possible without the expertise and guidance received from Human Kinetics staff, including Gayle Kassing, Ray Vallese, Derek Campbell, Nancy Rasmus, Yvonne Griffith, Dalene Reeder, and many others.

On a personal note, I (Amy) would like to thank my family and support system—Dr. Deb Garrahy and my parents, Mike and Linda Hurd. The appreciation I have for your love, support, and encouragement is immeasurable. I also dedicate this book to Mr. Bill Vanderkolk, who lost his fight against cancer in 2009. He always pushed me to be a better writer and never let me settle for mediocrity.

And I (Denise) would like to thank those who got me here and still keep me laughing—my husband, Dan Anderson; my son, Hayden; and my mom, Jeanette Reifel. I also dedicate this book to the memory of my dad, Duane Reifel, who never quite understood what I study but never failed to be proud of me. Without each of you and your love, I would not be where I am today.

# photo credits

# chapter 1

# Introduction and Overview

## OUTCOMES

- Assess how the role of leisure has changed over time.

- Compare and contrast five philosophical approaches to leisure services.

- Identify your own philosophical approach to leisure services.

- Define six theories of play.

- Describe seven theories related to why people engage in leisure.

- Differentiate among the definitions of leisure as time, activity, or state of mind.

- Describe four theories related to recreation.

The field of parks and recreation has a long and rich history. From the games of the Greeks and Romans to the technological revolutions of today that have shaped how we play, parks and recreation has played a central part in Americans' lives. This chapter summarizes the history of the field of recreation and leisure as well as presents the philosophical foundation that guides what parks and recreation managers do today. This chapter also presents the theoretical foundations behind play, leisure, and recreation with respect to the physiological, psychological, sociological, and contemporary explanation for each.

The **leisure delivery system,** whether public parks and recreation agencies, nonprofit recreation providers, or commercial recreation businesses, has a long history in providing for the leisure needs of people across the globe. From the times of the ancient Greeks to the Middle Ages, from the Renaissance to the 21st century, the role of leisure in people's lives has fluctuated dramatically yet has always been present on some level. While parks and recreation professionals were not identified as such when Aristotle and Plato saw leisure as contemplation or when Michelangelo was painting the Sistine Chapel, there have always been individuals to whom we could point to as advocates for leisure. Starting in the late 1800s with playground supervisors, or "play ladies," the field quickly advanced to a full-fledged profession in the mid-1900s, when the Great Depression saw huge advances in the development of facilities and services with the establishment of both the Work Projects Administration and the Civilian Conservation Corps. Following World War II the field continued to grow and shift as people demanded more and more services and the National Recreation and Park Association (NRPA) was founded. The movement toward more professional recognition continued with a certification process that allows professionals in the field to earn the title of Certified Park and Recreation Professional after passing the certification examination. More specific certifications exist within the profession as well.

Without a doubt, today's parks and recreation professionals have many opportunities to engage people in leisure and to change lives. As the world faces growing challenges (and opportunities) related to equity, obesity, politics, technology, and other issues, the parks and recreation professional, through the provision of all aspects of leisure services, can continue to play a strong role in improving lives.

## History of the Field

The history of the field is rich and varied. From the ancient Greeks to modern day societies, perceptions of the field have changed dramatically and yet in some ways have stayed the same. This section looks at how our field has evolved over hundreds of years from the start of the Olympics in 786 BC, when only men were allowed to compete (naked at that), there were just a few events, and there was certainly no television coverage, to today's manifestation of leisure that runs the gamut from video games to youth sports to tourism around the world. As the world grows smaller through globalization, opportunities to engage in leisure loom larger than ever.

### Ancient Greeks

The idea of leisure has been around for centuries. The ancient Greeks saw leisure and play as essential to the development of the whole person, believing that these activities developed unity

Historically, leisure has reflected the culture of the participants.

of the mind and body. The Greeks saw these activities as a way to learn, especially when they involved time for contemplation. The Greeks' slave population allowed for the upper class, or leisure class, to engage in intellectual development, as they did not have to take time out of their days to labor.

Leisure was both aesthetic and spiritual and focused on the Athenian ideal of what made a balanced man, but only citizens (native men descended from a citizen father and native mother) had access to leisure. These men saw leisure as the balance of the virtues of mind, body, and character as represented through intellectual, cultural, physical, and political activities. The Greeks valued leisure more than work, but the only people who could realistically act on this value were the members of the aristocracy.

## Romans

The Romans also held leisure in high regard, but their leisure was more utilitarian—they used it to become and remain prepared for war. Roman citizens prepared for war through sport and gymnastics. They engaged in a great deal of leisure, attending hundreds of festivals, Roman baths, open-air theaters, amphitheaters, and gladiator fights at the Colosseum. The list of events was long and the leisure was plentiful, but again, leisure participation was dictated by social status. There were four social levels among the Romans: the senators, who were the richest; the curiae, who either owned 25 or more acres of land or were officeholders or tax collectors; the plebs, who were free common people who owned small properties or worked as tradesmen or artisans; and the coloni, who were land tenants. Over time, leisure moved away from preparing men for battle as less warfare made way for more entertainment. This entertainment often took the form of mass debauchery and was highly corrupt, leading to a weakened Roman state. In fact, many attribute the fall of the Roman Empire as being partly due to the lifestyle choices of the time.

## Middle Ages

The Middle Ages, which lasted from 400 AD to about 1500 AD, saw the Christian church strongly influencing what people engaged in during their free time. The church dictated the social values of the day. With the clergy and nobility in power, the leisure of peasants was greatly limited. However, while many assume that the church prohibited all

leisure during this period, it is more accurate to say that the church controlled it, particularly bringing a civilizing force to leisure after witnessing the effects of the debauchery that was prevalent in the Roman Empire. There was a social and political hierarchy in which states, or fiefs, were managed by lords while peasants worked the land. The status of people influenced their leisure. Members of the nobility engaged in leisure that focused on developing skills tied to survival as well as battle and included hunting, jousting, falconry, and sporting contests. Other popular amusements included children's games, gambling, sports, and entertainment in the form of minstrels.

## Renaissance

A resurgence of interest in art, music, science, and scholarship marked the end of the Middle Ages. This era is known as the *Renaissance,* meaning rebirth, as it brought advancements in the sciences and arts and held previously strict moral codes in contempt. Social power and influence shifted from the church to the nobility, who supported artists. In addition, society began to see play as an integral part of education and placed high importance on physical exercise and games. There was deliberate defiance of strict moral codes as the masses engaged in fencing, gambling, chess, bullfighting, tennis, carnivals, tournaments, castle entertainment including minstrels, and festivals; during this time women also became more involved in leisure. In addition, the Renaissance saw the beginning of park systems, with three types of parks in development: royal hunting preserves, formal garden parks, and English gardens. These allowed for restorative activities such as picnics.

## Colonial America

As our brief examination of the history of leisure moves to America, leisure again becomes influenced by religion, specifically by the Puritans, who felt that leisure holds the potential for evil and that work should be held in the highest regard—idleness is the devil's workshop. The Protestant Reformation, during which both Martin Luther and John Calvin professed that the purpose of work is to glorify God and thus idleness is a sin, certainly influenced this belief. In their move to America during their quest for religious freedom, the Puritans had little time for leisure and spent most of their energy surviving in the New World. Religion was the moral sanction for all laws that

With no parks in which to play, youth during the Industrial Revolution were relegated to playing in the streets.

suppressed amusements. This did not mean that they did not engage in any leisure activity at all but that the moral code of the religious strictly regulated the activity. For Puritans, appropriate leisure gave meaning to work and vice versa, and they engaged in activities such as hunting, fishing, bowling, reading, music, and swimming. Over time other leisure pursuits emerged, including country dances, sports, cockfighting, dice games, cards, racing, wrestling, logrolling, and watching traveling performers. During this time there was also recognition of the importance of maintaining open space, and the development of common areas became a priority.

## Industrial Revolution

The Industrial Revolution saw America's population moving from the countryside to the city as advancements in industry led to more job opportunities in the factories located in the cities. There was an ongoing transition from an agricultural society to an industrial society as well as an increase in the number of immigrants moving to the United States in search of a new life. With this urbanization and focus on factory work, life became more clock driven and less driven by the rise and fall of the sun (as it was on the farms). Unfortunately this focus meant long working hours for people of all ages and both sexes. Children worked 12- to 14-hour days alongside adults. After the government passed child labor laws, adults still worked long hours, leaving children to fend for themselves in their

free time, during which they often found trouble. This situation led to the youth movement, which was spearheaded by three individuals who have had a lasting influence on our field: Joseph Lee, Jane Addams, and Luther Gulick.

Joseph Lee, the president of the Playground Association of America for 27 years and the author of *Play in Education,* is known as the father of the playground movement. A lawyer and philanthropist, Lee identified that unstructured free time for youths was leading to trouble and therefore became an advocate for structured recreation programs for boys and girls during the mid- and late 1800s.

Jane Addams was a social worker in Chicago who in the late 1800s founded the settlement house Hull House. Addams worked tirelessly to improve the status of poor immigrants and citizens alike, including both youths and adults, through the development of recreational, social, and educational programs.

Luther Gulick, a physician by training, had a strong interest in physical education and recreation, particularly for girls and women, who up until the late 1800s had been largely ignored. In 1906, Gulick helped establish the Playground Association of America. He was deeply involved in the Young Men's Christian Association (YMCA) movement in both Canada and the United States, and he served as the first president of the Camp Fire Girls of America.

The social orientation of the field exemplified by Lee, Addams, and Gulick, particularly as it relates to youth development, is still reflected in the work our profession does today. Today's professionals embody the spirit of these three pioneers as they continue the work to enhance participants' quality of life.

## Great Depression

Our field continued to grow during the days of the Great Depression as President Franklin D. Roosevelt developed the Works Progress Administration, later renamed the **Work Projects Administration (WPA),** and the **Civilian Conservation Corps (CCC).** These two groups are responsible for much of the astounding progress the government made in developing community parks and recreation centers (WPA) and state parks and trails (CCC).

While no one would wish for the reoccurrence of the Great Depression, it and the efforts put forward by President Roosevelt advanced the field of leisure services far beyond what would have occurred naturally. Following are lists of well-known projects that were built or designed by the WPA and CCC.

### *WPA Projects*

- Merritt Parkway (Fairfield County, Connecticut)
- Timberline Lodge (Mount Hood, Oregon)
- Santa Monica City Hall (California)
- Lagoon Shelter House (University of Iowa)
- American Guides Series (Federal Writers' Project)
- Red Rocks Park and Amphitheatre (Denver, Colorado)

- Doubleday Field (Cooperstown, New York)
- Camp David (Maryland)
- Dealey Plaza (Dallas, Texas)
- LaGuardia Airport (New York)
- John Augustus Walker murals (Mobile, Alabama)
- Mathematical Tables Project
- *Aztec* statue by Donal Hord (San Diego State University, California)
- Outer Drive Bridge (Chicago, Illinois)

### *CCC Projects*

- Cleveland Metroparks (Ohio)
- Lost River State Park (West Virginia)
- Blue Ridge Parkway (Virginia and North Carolina)
- Devil's Den State Park (Arkansas)
- High Knob Fire Tower (Virginia and West Virginia)
- Red Rocks Park and Amphitheater (Colorado)
- Table Rock State Park (South Carolina)
- Balmorhea State Park (Texas)
- Yellowstone National Park (Wyoming and Montana)
- Shenandoah National Park (Virginia)
- Acadia National Park (Maine)
- Bandelier National Monument (New Mexico)
- Wind Cave National Park (South Dakota)
- Eliot Tower (Massachusetts)

## Dock Street Theatre

The Dock Street Theatre, located in Charleston, South Carolina, opened in 1736 but was destroyed by the city's famous fire in 1770. In the early 1800s a hotel was built at the theater site. It hosted many plantation owners over the next 50 years but was abandoned following the Civil War. The hotel remained untouched until the 1930s.

In the 1930s, due to public interest in preserving Charleston's history, the building was restored by the city as a WPA project. The building took the name of the previous theater located on Dock Street. The restorations, due to the WPA's involvement, resulted in the theater resembling those of 18th-century London. The theater includes pit, gallery, and box seating and was equipped with modern technology. As it stands today, the Dock Street Theatre has been named the oldest American theatrical building.

## Continued Advancements in the Modern Era

The field of leisure services continued to evolve. World War II brought more technological advances, including televisions, stereos, and computers. As the affluence of Americans grew, their interest in new forms of recreation also grew. This led to booms in all areas of the field, from commercial recreation services to municipal parks and recreation services. In addition, the desire for recreation fueled the demand for and appreciation of open spaces in the 1960s and 70s, particularly when suburbanization led to the loss of open space as the population starting moving from more centralized urban areas to housing developments outside the heart of the cities. Universities and colleges started offering curricula to prepare professionals to meet growing recreation needs, and in 1965 the NRPA was formed.

However, the 1970s saw the field taking a hit financially as governments cut budgets and thus reduced government-provided recreation services. A poor economy tied with an increasing resistance to high tax rates resulted in a backlash against funding for public parks and recreation services. This was exemplified by California's Proposition 13, which put a cap on the taxing power of government. These budget cuts brought to light the importance of entrepreneurism in the field during the early 1980s. The effects of the cuts are evident in today's standard operating procedures, which include the use of sponsorships, partnerships, grant funding, and **privatization** of services to meet the fiscal challenges agencies face and the recreation needs of participants and communities.

With the passage of the Americans with Disabilities Act, the 1990s started the trend of serving more diverse populations. While at the time public recreation had a bit longer history as a force for desegregation and equality of service provision, the changing landscape of the United States led to the demand for more diverse, as well as more inclusive, programming. Segments of the population, including older adults, people with disabilities, women, minorities, people currently unemployed, and gays and lesbians, demanded expanded services. The profession took notice not only because it was the right thing to do but also because it was the smart thing to do from a business perspective. This approach applied to the private nonprofit and commercial sectors as well as recreation providers competing for participants and funding.

As the United States enters the second decade of the 21st century, Americans face a growing number of new challenges for which recreation may provide answers. These include obesity, technological advances, demographic changes related to immigration and aging, environmental concerns, the provision of new opportunities for people with disabilities (particularly members of the armed forces as they return from war), poverty, and an increased interest in the arts. One example of the role that recreation can play in addressing current concerns involves the obesity epidemic. Research paints a grim picture of an increasingly overweight and unhealthy society in which children and adults consume more and move less. Recreation professionals are working hard to provide programs that can address physical inactivity as well as educational programs that can lead to other lifestyle changes. Though technological advances may be keeping youths and adults stationary in front of computers and televisions, they also allow recreation providers to take advantage of these advances to combat obesity.

A renewed emphasis on play, particularly outdoor play, is another initiative within the field. The US Play Coalition, for example, has a goal of promoting the importance of play for all ages through research and recognition of the positive outcomes of play. The coalition is working to achieve this goal by bringing together experts in the area of play in order to "begin the second great play movement" (U.S. Play Coalition 2010). An emphasis on play has multiple outcomes for people, including increased health, enhanced cognitive development, positive mental health, and appreciation for the natural environment.

In addition, the recreation field in the 21st century is experiencing the effects of economic stratification. Disparities in wealth continue to widen and the availability of leisure grows more and more elusive for certain populations. This became particularly true when unemployment numbers hit highs not seen in decades with the recession that began in 2009. This disparity has led many to support fiscally conservative social policies that ultimately affect all government provisions, including public parks and recreation services.

Thus at the beginning of the 21st century the leisure services field is facing great challenges but also ever-growing opportunities to influence all aspects of people's lives. By meeting these challenges and growing with each new opportunity, as we have done time and time again throughout history, recreation providers can continue to

Health concerns related to obesity may be combated through active recreation programming.

emphasize the role that leisure services play in improving quality of life.

# Philosophical Underpinnings

Philosophy is defined as a set of values, beliefs, and preferences that a person develops through reasoning in order to gain a guiding set of principles for navigating life. These principles not only influence a person's personal life but also affect the person's professional life and the decisions that the person makes. The following sections describe five of the most common philosophies that people embrace—**idealism, realism, pragmatism, existentialism,** and **humanism**—with the caution that there are numerous philosophical approaches beyond these.

## Idealism

An idealist focuses on his ideals, or his concept of what excellence or perfection entails. The ideal is what the person believes in regardless of what it would take to achieve the ideal in reality, what others think about the ideal, or what consequences might result from acting on that ideal. An idealist's values remain constant, and the idealist does what it takes to preserve those values. Idealist values within the field of recreation are related to

quality of life, preservation, youth development, or conservation. The leisure services professional who is an idealist focuses on ensuring that programs represent the ideal of what they should be (Edginton et al. 2006).

An idealistic leisure services programmer trying to combat youth involvement in gangs, for example, would approach this problem in a very discernible manner. The programmer would believe at heart that youths are inherently good and that they are not born bad and destined to become involved in gangs. The programmer would believe that the youths want to be good and succeed in life despite outside influences. The programmer would also believe that leisure inherently has valuable outcomes for youths, including learning, skill development, and leadership skills, that youths would choose to embrace if made available to them because they really do want to grow in positive ways. Therefore, the programmer would offer these programs with certainty that they would lead to reduced gang participation.

## Realism

A realist focuses on the natural order of the world, believing that objects are defined not only by the individual but also independently by reality. The realist focuses on the practical, not the ideal or the theoretical, and recognizes that change is natural. For the leisure services professional who is a realist, the focus is to use leisure to help people learn about the reality that is the world (Edginton et al. 2006).

Consider again the example of youth gangs. Contrary to an idealist, a realist dealing with this problem would believe that youths who want to be in gangs will do so, regardless of recreation programming. Having this belief does not mean that the realistic programmer would not offer the programs. Rather, the programmer would expect participation to mirror reality—that youths might participate and gain some of the benefits of the program but that the program is not likely to convince all youths that gangs are bad. If the programmer can get youths in the program to experience some of the benefits, even if the youths are in gangs, then she has made progress within a world that she sees from a realistic viewpoint.

## Pragmatism

The pragmatist determines the worth or value of something by its consequences. For instance, a practitioner who uses outcome-based measurements

Outcome-based programming may provide answers for reducing youth involvement in gangs.

to evaluate a program is likely a pragmatist. He would not believe in the program if it did not work. For the pragmatist, change is inevitable, and thus he must constantly test his ideas in order to determine if they are valid. The pragmatic leisure services provider, upon determining that a program is not producing the desired outcomes, would change it according to the evaluation results and not according to the ideal of what the program ought to be (Edginton et al. 2006).

Because a pragmatist basically does what works, the pragmatic youth programmer dealing with the example youth gang situation would constantly test the programming approaches used to addressing the gang problem. She would look for approaches that might improve upon the current approaches and would keep what works and discard what does not. While the program may not be ideal, the pragmatic programmer would live with that as long as she knows that the program is leading to change.

## Existentialism

The existentialist believes that reality is living and that individuals are responsible for developing themselves and are responsible only to and for themselves. Thus personal choice and freedom are given great importance. For the existentialist, leisure is not organized, prescribed play but an experience that focuses on the individual and on creating the individual's own rules and experiences. Change also plays a big role in what the existentialist views as reality (Edginton et al. 2006).

Believing that individuals are responsible for their own development, an existentialist youth programmer would not provide an organized program to combat gang involvement but would provide space within which this development can occur. Therefore, this recreation programmer would facilitate informal recreation opportunities that contribute to development, such as open-gym hours or a drop-in arts program.

## Humanism

Humanists focus on human interests and values and are not concerned with the idea of a divine being such as God. A humanist believes that humans are of the highest value in the universe and that we should therefore be concerned with their interests. A humanist leisure delivery professional is concerned with promoting and protecting human interests and capabilities within leisure pursuits. A humanist views leisure as a context for joy, mastery, uniqueness, self-actualization, and other higher outcomes (Edginton et al. 2006).

A humanist believes that leisure provides the context for people to reach their full potential and that every person is an individual with his own interests, beliefs, and desires. Therefore, the humanistic youth programmer who wants to address gang involvement would identify a mentoring program in which participants receive individual attention as an appropriate approach to providing the context in which participants can reach their potential.

# Definitions of Leisure, Play, and Recreation

Defining leisure, play, and recreation provides us as leisure professionals with a strong foundation for the programs, services, and facilities that we provide. While we might disagree on the standard definition of leisure, play, or recreation, we are all concerned with providing an experience for participants. Whether we work in the public, private nonprofit, or commercial sector, all three concepts are driving forces behind the experiences we provide. Table 1.1 outlines the basic definitions of leisure, play, and recreation.

## Definitions of Leisure

There is debate about how to define leisure. However, there is a general consensus that there are three primary ways in which to consider leisure: leisure as time, leisure as activity, and leisure as state of mind.

### Leisure as Time

By this definition leisure is time free from obligations, work (paid and unpaid), and tasks required for existing (sleeping, eating). Leisure time is residual time. Some people argue it is the constructive use of free time. While many may view free time as all nonworking hours, only a small amount of time spent away from work is actually free from other obligations that are necessary for existence, such as sleeping and eating.

### Leisure as Activity

Leisure can also be viewed as activities that people engage in during their free time—activities that are not work oriented or that do not involve life maintenance tasks such as housecleaning or sleeping. Leisure as activity encompasses the activities that we engage in for reasons as varied as relaxation, competition, or growth and may include reading for pleasure, meditating, painting, and participating in sports. This definition gives no heed to how a person feels while doing the activity; it simply states that certain activities qualify as leisure because they take place during time away from work and are not engaged in for existence. However, as has been argued by many, it is extremely difficult to come up with a list of activities that everyone agrees represents leisure—to some an activity might be a leisure activity and to others it might not necessarily be a leisure activity. Therefore, with this definition the line between work and leisure is not clear in that what is leisure to some may be work to others and vice versa.

### Leisure as State of Mind

Unlike the definitions of leisure as time or activity, the definition of leisure as state of mind is much more subjective in that it considers the

**Table 1.1** Definitions of Leisure, Play, and Recreation

| Concept | Definition |
| --- | --- |
| Leisure as time | Leisure is time free from obligations, work (paid and unpaid), and tasks required for existing (sleeping, eating). |
| Leisure as activity | Leisure is a set of activities that people engage in during their free time—activities that are not work oriented or that do not involve life maintenance tasks such as housecleaning or sleeping. |
| Leisure as state of mind | Leisure depends on a participant's perception. Perceived freedom, intrinsic motivation, perceived competence, and positive affect are critical to the determination of an experience as leisure or not leisure. |
| Play | Play is imaginative, intrinsically motivated, nonserious, freely chosen, and actively engaging. Play is typified by spontaneity, joyfulness, and inhibition and is done not as a means to an end but for its inherent pleasure. |
| Recreation | Recreation is an activity that people engage in during their free time, that people enjoy, and that people recognize as having socially redeeming values. The activity performed is less important than the reason for performing the activity, which is the outcome. |

individual's perception of an activity. Concepts such as perceived freedom, intrinsic motivation, perceived competence, and positive affect are critical to determining whether an experience is leisure or not leisure.

Perceived freedom refers to an individual's ability to choose the activity or experience in that the individual is free from other obligations as well as has the freedom to act without control from others. Perceived freedom also involves the absence of external constraints to participation.

The second requirement of leisure as state of mind, intrinsic motivation, means that the person is moved from within to participate. The person is not influenced by external factors (e.g., people or reward) and the experience results in personal feelings of satisfaction, enjoyment, and gratification.

Perceived competence is also critical to leisure defined as state of mind. Perceived competence refers to the skills people believe they possess and whether their skill levels are in line with the degree of challenge inherent in an experience. Perceived competence relates strongly to satisfaction, and for successful participation to occur, the skill-to-challenge ratio must be appropriate.

Positive affect, the final key component of leisure as state of mind, refers to a person's sense of choice, or the feeling people have when they have some control over the process that is tied to the experience. Positive affect refers to enjoyment, and this enjoyment comes from a sense of choice.

What may be a leisure experience for one person may not be for another; whether an experience is leisure depends on many factors. Enjoyment, motivation, and choice are three of the most important of these factors. Therefore, when different individuals engage in the same activity, their state of mind can differ drastically.

## Definition of Play

Unlike leisure, play has a more singular definition. Play is imaginative, intrinsically motivated, nonserious, freely chosen, and actively engaging. While most people see play as the domain of children, adults also play, although often their play is more entwined with rules and regulations, which calls into question how playful their play really is. On the other hand, children's play is typified by spontaneity, joyfulness, and inhibition and is done not as a means to an end but for its inherent pleasure.

## Definition of Recreation

There is some consensus on the definition of recreation. Recreation is an activity that people engage in during their free time, that people enjoy, and that people recognize as having socially redeeming values. Unlike leisure, recreation has a connotation of being morally acceptable not just to the individual but also to society as a whole, and thus we program for those activities within that context. While recreation activities can take many forms, they must contribute to society in a way that society deems acceptable. This means that activities deemed socially acceptable for recreation can change over time.

Examples of recreational activities are endless and include sports, music, games, travel, reading, arts and crafts, and dance. The specific activity performed is less important than the reason for performing the activity, which is the outcome. For most the overarching desired outcome is recreation or restoration. Participants hope that their recreation pursuits can help them to balance their lives and refresh themselves from their work as well as other mandated activities such as housecleaning, child rearing, and so on.

People also see recreation as a social instrument because of its contribution to society. That is, professionals have long used recreation programs and services to produce socially desirable outcomes, such as the wise use of free time, physical fitness, and positive youth development. The organized development of recreation programs to meet a variety of physical, psychological, and social needs has led to recreation playing a role as a social instrument for well-being and, in some cases, change. This role has been the impetus for the development of many recreation providers from municipalities to nonprofits such as the YMCA, YWCA, Boy Scouts of America, Girl Scouts of the USA, and the Boys and Girls Clubs of America. There are also for-profit agencies, such as fitness centers and spas, designed to provide positive outcomes.

# Theoretical Foundations

The leisure services field is replete with the concepts of play, leisure, and recreation. Without a strong understanding of the terminology, it is often unclear as to how we as providers go about ensuring that our participants have those experiences.

**Table 1.2**  Theories of Leisure

| Theory | Description |
|---|---|
| Spillover | Leisure reflects the type of work individuals do in their paid jobs. |
| Compensatory | People engage in activities that make up for what they do not get from their jobs. |
| Flow | Leisure is a state of mind. People enter a leisure state when the challenge of an activity is a good match for their skill level. They have an experience that puts them into a state of flow, which is typified by total immersion in the activity and a sense that nothing else exists outside of that activity. |
| Serious leisure | Serious leisure pursuits are those that people engage in at a level higher than they do for casual leisure, which is characterized by pleasure but does not require special skills or knowledge. Serious leisure is a commitment to an amateur, hobby, or volunteer activity that is intense and similar to the development of a career in that it comes with special skill, knowledge, and experience that participants can gain. |
| Classic leisure | Leisure is the contemplation of the good life and the acquisition of knowledge through writing, reading, and other scholarly pursuits. |
| Nash's pyramid | Nash's pyramid outlines how people use their free time with regard to what a society values as acceptable or unacceptable leisure activities. The lowest form of leisure as free time is identified as acts performed against society. Creative participation is the highest use of free time. |
| Sociological leisure | This theory outlines freedom and meaning as they relate to leisure and the context in which leisure occurs. That is, the meaningfulness of a leisure experience must be contextualized within social frameworks such as community, family, and friends. In addition, the degree of freedom a person has in the leisure experience or activity influences meaningfulness. |

## Theories of Leisure

Beyond the definitions of leisure, there are also numerous theories on the reasons why people engage in leisure and on the characteristics of leisure pursuits. Participants may choose to engage in leisure and recreation for a multitude of reasons that include everything from the characteristics and enjoyment (or lack thereof) of their paid work to their desire to be challenged by leisure pursuits. The following sections offer a brief glimpse into popular theories on why people engage in leisure. Table 1.2 summarizes these theories.

### Spillover Theory

The spillover theory explains that leisure might reflect the type of work that people do in their paid jobs. For instance, an editor at a publishing house may also enjoy reading for leisure. In fact, some people may choose jobs that allow them to indulge in their leisure activities. These people find that the tasks they perform for their job are enjoyable and provide the type of beneficial outcomes that leisure provides. For this reason, they choose to continue to participate in these activities after their paid work is over.

### Compensatory Theory

This theory is the opposite of the spillover theory in that it recognizes that many people engage in activities that make up for what they do not get from their jobs. For instance, a person who works in a cubicle all day may pursue active leisure experiences outdoors such as hiking. For these individuals, leisure fills the holes in their lives that their work tasks do not fill.

### Flow Theory

Csikszentmihalyi's (1990) flow theory is a psychological theory that reflects the idea of leisure as a state of mind. The theory suggests that people enter into a leisure state when the challenge of an activity is a good match for their skill level. They have an experience that puts them into a state of flow, which is typified by total immersion in the activity and a sense that nothing else exists outside of that activity (they lose track of time, lose self-consciousness, and so on).

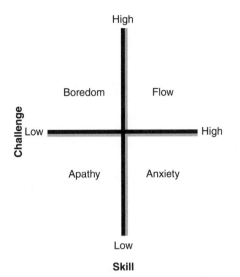

**Figure 1.1**  An optimal leisure experience requires a balance between challenge and skill, particularly high challenge and high skill.

Adapted from C. Csikszentmihalyi, 1997, *Finding flow: The psychology of engagement* (Cambridge, MA: Basic Books).

Figure 1.1 illustrates how challenge and skill need to be matched in order for an individual to enter into a state of flow. That is, if a person with a high level of skill engages in a recreational pursuit that involves a high level of challenge, that person is likely to enter a state of flow. However, if the challenge is high and the skill is low, a person enters a state of anxiety, whereas pairing high skill with low challenge results in boredom and pairing low skill with low challenge leads to apathy.

## Serious Leisure Theory

Serious leisure pursuits are those that people engage in at a level higher than they do for casual leisure, which is characterized by pleasure but does not require special skills or knowledge. Serious leisure is a commitment to an amateur, hobby, or volunteer activity that is intense and typically long lasting. Individuals who engage in serious leisure possess or experience six qualities related to their serious leisure pursuit: the need to persevere; finding a career in the endeavor; significant personal effort based on special knowledge, training, or skill; durable benefits such as self-actualization, self-enrichment, social interaction, or renewal; strong identification with their chosen pursuits; and a special social world that emerges over time (Stebbins 1999, 51).

## Classic Leisure Theory

A more philosophical approach to leisure is the classic leisure theory that Aristotle as well as Plato and others of the classical Greek era held to be true. Under the classic leisure theory, leisure is the contemplation of the good life and the acquisition of knowledge through writing, reading, and other scholarly pursuits.

## Nash's Pyramid Theory

John Nash's pyramid of leisure (figure 1.2) outlines how people use their free time with regard to what a society values as acceptable or unacceptable leisure activities. The lowest form of leisure as free time is found at the bottom of the pyramid and is identified as acts performed against society. An example of this category is a person who spray paints a building with graffiti. Although the graffiti artist may identify his actions as leisure, this activity has caused monetary damage to someone else's property. Nash identified creative participation as the highest use of free time. An example of this type of leisure activity is creating a clay vase in a pottery class. The individual is creating something new that is also acceptable within the context of societal norms.

## Sociological Leisure Theory

This theory, developed by John Kelly (1972), is based on freedom and meaning as they relate to leisure and the context in which leisure occurs. That is, the meaningfulness of a leisure experience must be contextualized within social frameworks such as community, family, and friends. In addition, the degree of freedom a person has in the leisure experience or activity influences meaningfulness; the freedom is very often tied directly into the social frameworks that surround the activity. Freedom can be either high or low, and meaning can range from intrinsic (i.e., internal) to social as it is related to family, community, relationships with others, and so on.

Kelly's theory includes four sociological states of leisure (see figure 1.3): unconditional, compensatory or recuperative, relational, and role determined. Unconditional leisure is relatively unconstrained by family and other social roles and is chosen intrinsically. Compensatory or recuperative leisure is chosen for what the activity provides the individual in contrast to work constraints—the leisure provides something that work does not. A person chooses a form of

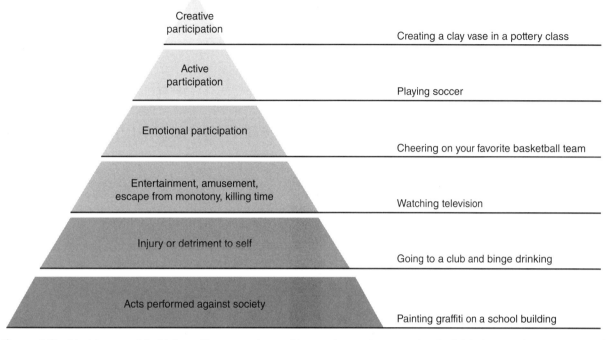

**Figure 1.2** Nash's pyramid of leisure illustrates the positive and negative ways that individuals may choose to spend their free time.

Reprinted from *Philosophy of Recreation and Leisure*, J.B. Nash, Copyright 1953.

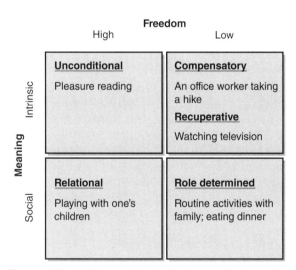

**Figure 1.3** Kelly's sociological theory of leisure illustrates that people will often choose their leisure activities based on the social contexts of their lives.

KELLY, LEISURE, 1st Edition, © 1982, p. 166. Reprinted by permission of Pearson Education, Inc., Upper Saddle River, NJ.

recuperative leisure in light of work constraints but chooses the activities primarily for rest and relaxation rather than stimulation. Relational leisure is chosen with little perception of role constraints but with positive values of building

relationships. Finally, in role-determined leisure the individual is very aware of relationships when choosing the activity, and the activity is chosen in response to role expectations within a social context such as family.

## Theories of Play

When most people hear the word *play*, they conjure up visions of children running around playgrounds or enjoying a game of hide and seek. Regardless of the activity, people tend to think of the actors as children. There are a multitude of definitions for play, such as nonserious activity done for fun, to occupy oneself, or to rejoice. There is no consensus on the definition of play or on the theoretical foundation for why play occurs. There is also the belief that play is not just for children. The following are a few examples of the theories describing why people play. Table 1.3 summarizes the theories of play.

### Surplus Energy Theory

This theory suggests that once the basic needs (sleeping, eating, safety, and so on) are met, people often have extra energy left for activity that has little to no purpose but is considered

**Table 1.3**   Theories of Play

| Theory | Description |
|---|---|
| Surplus energy | Once the basic needs are met (sleeping, eating, safety, and so on) people often have extra energy for activity that has little to no purpose but is considered enjoyable. |
| Recreation | Play is necessary for when exhaustion sets in; play can be used to recover (or re-create oneself) from overuse of energy. |
| Conflict enculturation | Play is an opportunity to experience and learn new behaviors in a safe environment. |
| Developmental tool | Play is a developmental tool and therefore reflects the developmental level of the participant. |
| Optimal arousal | Play can provide the stimulus that individuals seek in order to reduce boredom. |
| Instinct practice | Play has a role in children's development because it provides an environment for practicing the skills needed later in life. |

enjoyable. Children running around aimlessly, expending physical energy, is an example of this type of play.

### Recreation Theory

The theory of play as recreation sees play as necessary for dealing with exhaustion; play can be used to recover (or re-create oneself) from overuse of energy. Play has a restorative property that allows an individual to return to a normal state of energy.

### Conflict Enculturation Theory

This theory views play as an opportunity to experience and learn new behaviors in a safe environment. Through play, a child can learn

skills such as cooperation, competition, and fair play without experiencing serious consequences if these concepts are misunderstood. Play allows children to learn social and other skills without a great deal of emotional risk.

### Developmental Tool Theory

In this theory play is a developmental tool and thus reflects the developmental level of the participant. For instance, the play that a 9-year-old engages in differs from that of a 3-year-old.

### Optimal Arousal Theory

The optimal arousal theory suggests that play can provide the stimulus that individuals seek in order to reduce boredom. This stimulus can provide novelty and complexity that may challenge an individual or at least provide an experience that holds the individual's attention. Note that optimal stimulus does not mean maximum stimulus; once above a certain level stimulus can produce anxiety.

### Instinct Practice Theory

The instinct practice theory imagines play as helping children to develop because it provides an environment for practicing the skills needed later in life, such as cooperation, leadership, and communication. In some instances, play may actually serve as a context for fulfilling future adult roles such as that of a parent or a professional (e.g., playing teacher).

Play is central to a child's physical, cognitive, and socio-emotional development.

## Conclusion

The history of the leisure services field continues to inform the mission and vision that today's leisure services agencies develop in their quest to meet the leisure and recreation needs of individuals as well as communities. Throughout history our leisure philosophies as well as our theories have attempted to explain why people engage in leisure, recreation, and play. This knowledge continues to grow and adapt to a changing world. It moves us forward in a way that allows the field of leisure services to meet the challenges of both today and tomorrow as it engages participants in activities and experiences that shape their lives in meaningful ways.

## Review Questions

1. Describe how the role of leisure has changed over time.
2. How do the five philosophical approaches to leisure differ from one another?
3. Which philosophical approach to leisure do you subscribe to and why?
4. List the six theories of play. Describe each of the theories.
5. Describe the seven theories related to why people engage in leisure.
6. Differentiate among the definitions of leisure as time, activity, or state of mind. Which best describes your definition of leisure? Why?
7. Select four theories of recreation. Describe each of them.

 **Visit the online resource at www.HumanKinetics.com/TheParkAndRecreationProfessionalsHandbook for keywords, activities and assignments, and more.**

# Programming

chapter 2

## OUTCOMES

- Understand the program planning process.

- Illustrate the value of partnerships in programming.

- Identify key elements of a program plan.

- Understand the three phases of direct leadership.

Programming is the cornerstone of the leisure profession. Sport coordinators schedule leagues and tournaments, cultural arts supervisors plan art exhibits, and resort activities directors develop trips and daily activities for guests. Although these are three very different jobs in the leisure services field, the common thread is planning programs. Programs are structured leisure opportunities offered by recreation services providers. Programs can be special events such as Milwaukee's Summerfest music festival or be an ongoing activity such as a beginning pottery class or a soccer league.

Since programming is the crux of what recreation professionals do, this chapter focuses on the program planning process. Within this process you will explore programming formats and areas and learn the different steps taken to deliver the desired activities to the community.

## Program Planning Process

Planning programs requires managers to be creative yet thoroughly organized. Being creative allows managers to meet the needs of the community and attract participants by offering programs, events, and activities that are interesting to their constituents. Following a systematic programming process allows managers to bring together a plethora of steps that need to be completed to provide a high-quality, organized program to the constituents. The program planning process (see figure 2.1) includes four steps:

1. Assessing the community and its needs
2. Designing and planning the program
3. Implementing the program
4. Evaluating the program

### Assessing the Community and Its Needs

A common mistake made by programmers in the field today is ignoring the needs of the community. Too many programmers think they know what

their community needs and then are surprised when their programs have low registrations that result in cancellations. The best way to avoid this scenario is to gain a thorough understanding of the community and its trends and to implement techniques to assess the community's needs.

### Understanding the Community and Its Trends

Understanding the community requires knowledge of its composition, existing conditions, and trends. A common starting point for gaining this knowledge is assessing demographics. **Demographics** are descriptors of a population, such as age, race, income, and geography. Demographic information is readily available through the U.S. Census Bureau, local chamber of commerce, or city planning department. See table 2.1 for a demographic profile of Kokomo, Indiana. The demographic profile influences the programs that may be of interest to the community. For example, demographics can indicate the age breakdown in a community so that a program manager can offer the appropriate number of age-related programs. If a large portion of the community is low income, then the manager can implement more free or low-cost programs. The demographic profile can also show the demographics of specific neighborhoods. Since neighborhoods tend to consist of similar households, programs can be planned for these specific sections of the community. However, a demographic profile is only a small piece of the information needed to meet the program needs of the community.

Another important aspect of understanding the community is an existing conditions analysis (Russell and Jamieson 2008). This analysis identifies the programs, facilities, and other recreation resources available to the community. Examining what programs and facilities are offered by agencies such as the local parks and recreation department, the YMCA, and commercial businesses keeps an agency from duplicating services while identifying gaps in service provision. Duplicating services that another agency provides is a waste

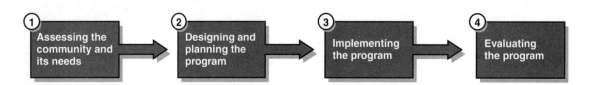

**Figure 2.1**    Program planning is a four-step process.

**Table 2.1**  Sample Demographics of Kokomo, Indiana

| Kokomo population | Number (46,113) | Percent (100.00) |
|---|---|---|
| Male | 21,793 | 47.26 |
| Female | 24,320 | 52.74 |
| Under 5 years | 3,616 | 7.84 |
| 5 to 9 years | 3,162 | 6.86 |
| 18 years and over, female | 18,726 | 40.61 |
| Asian | 525 | 1.14 |
| Total housing units | 22,292 | 100.00 |

Source: http://kokomo.areaconnect.com/statistics.htm (via the U.S. Census Bureau)

of time and money unless there are community members whose needs are not being met by the current services. In addition to identifying what others are doing, the existing conditions analysis opens up opportunities for partnerships in which two or more agencies work together to provide programs. Partnerships are discussed later in the chapter. Finally, finding gaps in service provision can identify a niche that an agency can fill for the community.

The needs of a community can change quickly due to trends and fads. Trends are tendencies that become popular in society over a long duration while fads are things that are popular for a shorter period of time. While it is easy to dismiss trends and fads as something that will pass quickly, they can often lead to very popular programs. For example, fitness programming is based on trends and fads. The following are a few ways to track trends:

- Conduct surveys. The American College of Sports Medicine (ACSM) conducts surveys of health and fitness services and providers, including commercial gyms, fitness retailers, medical and other clinical environments, and recreation and community program environments, in order to determine trends in the population. From this the ACSM develops recommendations for addressing these trends (American College of Sports Medicine 2007).

- Talk with professionals across the country to see what trends they are experiencing.

- Read local and national newspapers.

- Talk with the community to see how friends and family are spending their leisure time.

- Read professional magazines in your area and associated areas.

- Research Web sites and books from futurists such as Faith Popcorn.

Staying on top of trends is a challenge because they change. Using multiple methods to track trends keeps a programmer up to date and offering cutting-edge programs.

### Identifying Needs

A discussion on programming cannot occur without a mention of needs. A need is "something that drives individuals to act in a certain way . . . and is born out of a physical, psychological, emotional, spiritual or social deficiency an individual is currently experiencing" (Jordan, DeGraaf, and DeGraaf 2005, 81). Much has been written about the differences between a need and a desire and which of these two should be focused on by parks and recreation services. The field predominantly uses the term *need* based on the definition presented here. Assessing the recreation needs of a community requires a planned approach to gather the pertinent information. A detailed description on how to assess needs can be found in chapter 4.

## Designing and Planning the Program

Designing and planning the program is the fun part of programming. In this step you get to use the information gathered in the previous step to determine the program goals and objectives, select the program area and format, develop the program schedule, and write the program plan.

### Setting Goals and Objectives

Program goals and objectives should be tied to the agency vision and mission. A **goal** is a clear statement of what the program is intended to achieve. A program can have goals related to how the program operates as well as goals for what the participants achieve or experience. For example, a Boys and Girls Club of America might have the following goals:

- Provide a day camp with fitness as a central component
- Improve the after-school tutoring program
- Decrease the cancellation rate of sport programs for girls

Because goals are so broad in their intention, they need objectives to make them achievable. **Objectives** are specific statements directed at achieving a goal. They are the "measurement points of the goal" (Russell and Jamieson 2008, 118). Objectives tie in directly to the goals and are a way of understanding how the goal will be achieved. Objectives are much more difficult to write and follow a specific format, such as the ABCD format (Jordan 2007):

**Audience**—The audience members are the people who complete the behavior within the objective. The audience can be the participants, the staff members, the coaches, the leaders, or others.

Example: *The camp director*

**Behavior**—The behavior is the action that is to be completed by the audience. Only one behavior (rather than multiple behaviors) should be identified for each objective (Jordan, DeGraaf, and DeGraaf 2005). Multiple behaviors can make an objective difficult to measure if one behavior is achieved and the other is not.

Example: The camp director *will implement a fitness activity*

**Condition**—The condition further describes the behavior and often adds additional information about that behavior.

Example: The camp director will implement a fitness activity *with 20 minutes of games that require physical activity*

**Degree**—The degree is a central measurement piece of the objective. It describes how well or to what extent the objective is achieved.

Example: The camp director will implement a fitness activity with 20 minutes of games that require physical activity *in which all campers are constantly involved in the activity*

Well-written goals and objectives provide a framework for the purpose of the program and the reasons why the program is being developed. Objectives fall within three domains: cognitive, behavioral, and affective (Bloom 1956; Anderson and Krathwohl 2001). Cognitive objectives deal with thinking and often focus on what a person will learn. For example, a cognitive objective for golf lessons might be the following:

The participants in the golf clinic will learn the rules of golf by the end of the second session.

Behavioral objectives deal with actions taken and skills learned, such as learning to hit a pitched ball or improving cardiorespiratory fitness. The following is an example for a stained glass class:

By the end of the stained glass program, the participants will complete a 12- × 12-inch project with instructor guidance.

Programs such as pottery classes will have measurable objectives written to follow the ABCD format.

Affective objectives address feelings, emotions, and social elements. Affective objectives, arguably the most difficult objectives to measure within recreation programs, can focus on things such as positive sporting behavior or social interaction. The following is an example for a youth softball program:

> Youths registered for the unified softball program through Special Olympics will demonstrate positive sporting behavior during all practices and games.

Once the goals and objectives are determined, the programmer has a better focus on what the program design should be in order to achieve the goals and objectives.

### Selecting Program Areas and Formats

Once goals and objectives are established, the next step in planning and designing the program is to determine the activity area and program format. The activity area is the type of activity that will be planned. Russell and Jamieson (2008) list 14 different areas, but many more could be added to that list. The 14 areas are sports, aquatics, adventure, dance, drama, fine arts, crafts, music, hobbies, outdoors and nature, intellectual or literary pursuits, travel, social recreation, and volunteer services. A programmer may choose any one area or a combination of areas as dictated by the needs assessment. The programmer's job can also dictate the activity area. For example, an athletic supervisor focuses on sports as the chosen area. The cultural arts coordinator can choose dance, drama, or a combination of nature crafts. The creativity of programming can be expressed in the selection of the program area.

Once the program area is selected, a program format is chosen. Program formats (see figure 2.2) are the structure a program takes. There are five formats to consider. First, a competition format consists of leagues, tournaments, meets, or situations in which participants compete against themselves or others or are judged based on their performance. Competitive activities can include swim meets, dance competitions, or a field hockey league.

The drop-in or open facility format encompasses unstructured and self-directed programs. In this format, a facility or an area is open for people to come by to participate in an informal atmosphere. A common drop-in activity is open gym. For example, the Wellesley (Massachusetts) Recreation Department has open-gym hours set aside for a number of groups, including elementary

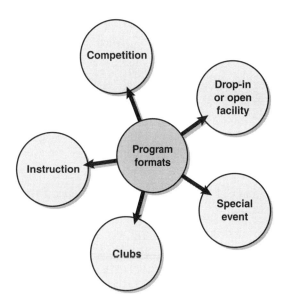

**Figure 2.2** Program formats are the structure a program takes. Different formats can enhance program delivery.

children, coed volleyball players, and women's basketball teams (Wellesley Recreation 2009).

A third program format is a special event. A special event is a "planned occurrence designed to entertain, inform, or provide enjoyment and/or inspiration to audiences" (Jackson 1997, xii). Special events are held infrequently and occur outside the realm of programming provided by the sponsoring agency (Getz 1991). Special events can be themed; examples are the Guacamole Festival in Lincoln Heights (California) or the famed Spam Jam in Austin (Minnesota). They can center on sports; consider the Super Bowl or the Boston Marathon. Furthermore, special events such as the Taste of Chicago or Macy's Thanksgiving Day Parade can be used to stimulate tourism by attracting visitors from outside of the community.

The next program format is clubs. Clubs are groups with a common interest such as a hobby or some other activity. Clubs bring together people to participate in the activity and often have a social aspect to them. Generally clubs are managed by a core set of members and rely on a sponsoring agency such as a local parks and recreation department to provide a meeting space or administrative needs. The Pleasant Hill (California) Recreation and Park District, for example, has clubs for dog owners, quilters, and magicians, among others (Pleasant Hill Recreation and Park District 2009).

The last common program format is instructional programs. Classes, clinics, workshops, and seminars are forms of instructional programming

**Table 2.2**  Sample Program Formats

| Program and format | Softball | Photography | Classic cars |
|---|---|---|---|
| Competition | Softball tournament | Photography competition | Rod and custom car shows with judging |
| Drop-in | Pickup game | Darkroom open hours | Informal classic car buff gathering in the park |
| Special event | Old-fashioned baseball game | Juried art show | Classic car show and swap meet |
| Club | 55+ softball club | Photography club | Vintage Corvette club |
| Instructional | Camps and clinics | Class on black and white photography | Seminar on classic car upholstery |

in which participants are taught by a skilled instructor and either learn new skills or enhance existing skills in a specific area. The arts use the instructional format to teach watercolor, stained glass, or drawing techniques.

Programs can be offered in more than one format. They may appeal to different people depending on how they are offered. Table 2.2 provides examples of how programs can be offered in many different formats.

Knowing the community constituents and their needs helps guide programmers in determining what formats to use in programming. Programmers learn quickly that certain formats are better suited to their community.

### Developing the Program Schedule

Scheduling programs and activities is an important aspect of program design and planning. Scheduling can help a program thrive or can lead to its cancellation. As with the other aspects of programming, the key to good scheduling is simply to meet the needs of the customers.

The first issue in scheduling is deciding when the program will be offered. Agencies have a number of different systems in place for scheduling. They may have seasonal programs that are offered in only one or two seasons, such as a golf program in the northern parts of the United States and in Canada. Another example is indoor tennis, which has limited appeal in the summer if outdoor courts are readily available. Agencies not affected by the seasons may establish monthly or weekly schedules for programs. For example, fitness facilities can establish their monthly or weekly program schedule for the classes offered during that month or week (see figure 2.3).

The day of the week and the time of a program are dictated by the potential users. Knowing the composition of the community tells the programmer what days might be more desirable than others and what times people are most likely to participate in a program. Consider a teen program that is scheduled on a Tuesday morning during the school year. This may be a good day and time if the program is specifically targeted to homeschooled children. If that is not the target audience, however, then a serious error in scheduling has occurred. The Asheville (North Carolina) Parks, Recreation and Cultural Arts Department scheduled an all-day biking program on the Virginia Creeper Trail on a Wednesday as part of its Home School Adventures for children ages 9 to 17 (City of Asheville, North Carolina 2010). The Asheville programmers know their target market and plan programs that match their target group's desires.

If multiple facilities exist, selecting one to use for the program should be dictated by the customers as well as the amenities within the facility. Knowing geographically where customers live dictates which facility to choose. The closer people live to the facility, the more likely they are to participate in a program. Facility selection can also be determined by the amenities and equipment in the facility. A fitness spinning class needs stationary spinning bikes, and obviously a facility without these bikes is not a good place to hold a spinning class. Room size can dictate program scheduling in that a class of 50 participants must be located in a room that can hold that many people and at a facility that has available parking for 50. Conversely, a class of 5 people wastes valuable gym space if it is scheduled in a gym and replaces a program that attracts 75 people in that same gymnasium.

Scheduling can become quite challenging for facility programmers who have to prioritize programs in limited spaces. Following the rule

Series 1 sessions begin Monday, May 11th.
Series 2 sessions begin Monday, June 22nd.

### MONDAY

| Session | Time | Location | Leader |
| --- | --- | --- | --- |
| Power yoga | 4:30-5:30 p.m. | HP 171 | Ann |
| Pilates I | 5:45-6:45 p.m. | HP 171 | Ann |

### TUESDAY

| Session | Time | Location | Leader |
| --- | --- | --- | --- |
| Power yoga | 12:15-1:15 p.m. | MS3 | Stephanie |
| Yoga I | 5:30-6:30 p.m. | MS3 | Devin |

### WEDNESDAY

| Session | Time | Location | Leader |
| --- | --- | --- | --- |
| Pilates I | 5:45-6:45 p.m. | HP 171 | Mary Lou |
| Pilates ball | 7:00-8:00 p.m. | HP 171 | Mary Lou |

### THURSDAY

| Session | Time | Location | Leader |
| --- | --- | --- | --- |
| Yoga I | 5:30-6:30 p.m. | HP 171 | Stephanie |
| Power yoga | 6:45-7:45 p.m. | HP 171 | Stephanie |

MS=Multisport gym at SRSC. HP 171—Health, physical education, and recreation room 171.

**Figure 2.3** Indiana University Recreational Sports has seasonal schedules for its fitness programs.

Reprinted, by permission, from Indiana University Recreational Sports. Available: http://www.iurecsports.org

that the agency should do the greatest good for the greatest number of people will always mean that a class with 5 people will not be offered. However, that class may be quite valuable and fill a need for an underserved segment of the population. The facility manager has the responsibility to meet the needs of the community while adhering to the mission of the agency. To do all of this often requires creative programming and scheduling.

Russell and Jamieson (2008) give the following guidelines for assigning facilities:

- Assign facilities equitably so that there is a balance of programs that reflect the community composition. Having 70% of all programs in a general recreation facility be sports related is not often considered equitable.

- Assign facilities efficiently so that programs make the best use of space and are offered when desired by the users.

- Coordinate with outside agencies to maximize facility use. For example, a local church may use a recreation facility on a Sunday morning when the facility is normally closed. Furthermore, a public agency can make soccer fields available to the YMCA after agency practice and game demands are met.

In addition to these facility scheduling suggestions, avoid planning incompatible programs in close proximity to each other. For example, swim lessons and lap swim may be better for the users if they are not held in the same pool at the same time. Loud programs should not be placed next to programs such as yoga or meditation classes.

Often programmers have the responsibility to plan many programs each season or month. They have the challenge of determining when to offer what classes and how to bundle or package their services. Bundling or packaging is a means of scheduling programs at the same time to accommodate a family's schedule. For instance, Carmel Clay Parks and Recreation (2010) in Indiana offers more than 40 fitness classes per week, with the classes starting every half hour. At the same time there are a multitude of preschool and youth classes that children can take while their parents are in a fitness class.

Although bundling programs in a facility is quite common, scheduling programs that attract

Program scheduling is challenged by the need to balance types of programs, needs of the community, and efficient use of space, among other things.

the same target market at the same time can detract from one of the programs. An agency should not place all of its fitness classes at 5:00 p.m. on Monday, Wednesday, and Friday. The classes need to be staggered by time and day so they can attract people who want to take multiple classes.

A last scheduling issue is planning around important events and religious holidays or beliefs. If a community has a dominant religion or one that affects a number of participants, programmers can plan special activities, plan around major holidays, and modify activities accordingly. For example, the Massachusetts Institute of Technology (MIT) reserves pool time once a week for women only. This was done after women who are Muslim and Orthodox Jewish requested time to swim without worrying about being immodest in front of men (Sacirbey 2009).

Program scheduling can be quite challenging, especially if there are a large number of programs and facilities to deal with. There are software packages available to assist programmers with scheduling, but even so a thorough working knowledge of scheduling is an important skill to have.

### Writing the Program Plan

The multitude of programs any supervisor is responsible for in a season makes it difficult to keep all of the details on each program straight without writing these details down. A program plan serves as the template for creating the program. The categories for a program plan can change from agency to agency or even from one supervisor to the next. A typical program plan consists of the following:

- **Program title and description:** This section gives the title of the program, lists the sponsoring agencies, and describes the program, explaining what the program is and where and when it will take place (Rossman and Schlatter 2008).
- **Goals and objectives:** This section lists the goals and states measurable, well-written objectives describing what the program is designed to accomplish.
- **Operation details:** This is the most detailed section of the plan. It gives the specifics on the activities or events and their setup; the facility needs and setup; the equipment and supplies needed; the marketing; the program budget and pricing; the registration process; the staff and volunteers needed; the cancellation plan; the safety and risk management plan; the inclusion plan; and the evaluation process (Rossman and Schlatter 2008; Russell and Jamieson 2008).

The length of a program plan varies depending on the complexity of the program or event. A program plan for a major special event is much more detailed than the plan for a movie night at the pool.

The first two sections of the program plan have already been discussed. The operational details will be outlined in the following section because those elements are part of the implementation phase of programming.

## Implementing the Program

Program implementation is the result of all the program designing and planning. It is at this stage that participants get to enjoy what an agency is offering. Some of the things discussed in this section on implementation could arguably be discussed under the section on planning. Sometimes it is a fine line and a seamless transition between the planning phase and the implementation phase of a program. The implementation phase involves staffing and supervision, leadership and instruction, budgeting, marketing, registration and reservations, payment methods, risk management, monitoring, and program conclusion and follow-up.

### Staffing and Supervision

Hiring staff members and recruiting volunteers are key components to program implementation. Staffing requires recruiting, selecting, compensating, training, supervising, and evaluating staff members. This entire process is beyond the scope of this chapter and is covered in chapter 9.

The type of program or event dictates the type and number of staff members and volunteers needed. Programs require two levels of staff members: supervisory and direct leadership. A program that is held in a facility often can have a facility supervisor who oversees the programming in the entire facility. This person may or may not have supervisory jurisdiction of the programs in the facility. Some facilities have facility supervisors who manage and schedule facility programs that are created and supervised by the program staff. The program staff members then manage the instructors or coaches in the program. These coaches are considered direct leaders. Direct leaders are the people most likely to teach the class, oversee open gym time, work with clubs, or manage the competitive league each night.

Staff members can be full-time, part-time, or contractual employees. Supervisory employees are often full-time employees who work 40 or more hours per week. Part-time staff members work less and do not have the benefits (e.g., paid vacation, health insurance) that full-time employees have. Contractual employees have their duties, responsibilities, and pay outlined in a contract. Staff members who act as direct leaders tend to be either part-time or contractual personnel. For instance, the site supervisor for a softball league can be part time and paid by the hour. A person who teaches a dance class can be hired on contract and be paid a set number of dollars for each student enrolled in the class. Contractual instructors can also be paid a flat rate or a percentage of revenue earned on the program. With a contract the agency keeps a percent or flat rate of the program registration fee and the instructor also receives a percent or flat rate of the fee.

Regardless of whether staff members are full time, part time, or contractual, there are three issues to consider when staffing programs. First, the ratio of staff members to participants must be adequate. Agencies or the industry can set these ratios. For example, the American Camp Association (ACA) sets these standards for their accredited camps (see table 2.3).

A second issue with staffing is that staff members must be qualified for the job. This means they must possess the skills necessary to lead a class or program; have adequate experience for the

**Table 2.3** American Camp Association Standards for Ratio of Staff Members to Campers

| Camper age (in years) | Type of camp | Staff members to campers |
| --- | --- | --- |
| 4-5 | Overnight camp | 1:5 |
| 4-5 | Day camp | 1:6 |
| 6-8 | Overnight camp | 1:6 |
| 6-8 | Day camp | 1:8 |
| 9-14 | Overnight camp | 1:8 |
| 9-14 | Day camp | 1:10 |
| 15-18 | Overnight camp | 1:10 |
| 15-18 | Day camp | 1:12 |

From American Camp Association's Accreditation Process Guide 2006 edition.

program; or obtain the proper certifications such as first aid, CPR, or water safety. An agency employing staff members who do not have the qualifications necessary for their position is vulnerable to lawsuits if something goes wrong in the program.

The last staffing issue involves using volunteers. Volunteers give their time and talents to parks and recreation agencies on a regular basis. Many agencies come to depend on volunteers to help their programs financially. Volunteers are often integral parts of a special event but also serve in instructional, competitive, drop-in, and club programs as well. Volunteers should be treated like employees in that they should be given a job description and be trained for the position. Some programs dictate a paid staff person as well as volunteers. This situation increases the number of people available to run a quality program while also helping the bottom line. The YMCA of Central Kentucky (2009) estimates that in 2008 their volunteers gave a market value of $275,380. Volunteers are discussed later in the chapter.

## Leadership and Instruction

Leadership and instruction are a programming aspect requiring special attention and planning. They encompass *how* the program will be delivered. The plans for how an instructor implements a program are called *activity, lesson, curriculum,* or *instruction plans.* For our purposes, we will use the term *instruction plans.* Instruction plans are developed so that the instructor has a road map to follow when delivering the program. An instruction plan ensures that a program is implemented in the proper sequence so skills are built in a logical manner. Sequencing requires an activity analysis, or a breakdown of skills into essential elements, so participants learn each aspect of the total skill (Hurd et al. 2007).

The contents of an instruction plan can vary among agencies and programmers. A sample template is located in chapter 3 (figure 3.2 on p. 53). A typical instruction plan is designed around the three phases of direct leadership: preparation, priming the group, and delivery (Jordan 2007; see table 2.4). Preparation is the planning aspect of the program and is often the most time-consuming phase. Preparation details group composition, program goals and objectives, and equipment setup. The next phase, priming the group, occurs at the beginning of the program and addresses the motivational and technical aspects of getting the group ready to participate. Lastly is the delivery phase, which is when the actual program participation occurs—the group begins learning skills, enjoying the special event, or playing golf. The priming and delivery phases are instrumental in successful delivery of the program.

The instruction plan outlines all of these elements so that the instructor knows what to do during the program before beginning delivery. While some instructors feel they have the ability to wing it when leading a program, few are successful. The result is a program that appears unorganized or haphazard. Furthermore, instruction plans give consistency when there are multiple instructors for a program or instructors change from season to season.

Part of developing the instruction plan is selecting activities that meet the goals and objectives established for the program. Selecting appropriate activities requires an activity analysis of the component parts of each activity. Activity analysis "assumes that each activity, as an inherent requirement of participating, compels participants to perform or respond in predictable ways that utilize unique and specific behavioral outcomes" (Hurd et al. 2007, 86). An activity analysis requires

**Table 2.4**  Three Phases of Direct Leadership

| Direct leadership phase | Plan contents |
|---|---|
| Preparation | Preparation details group composition, including age, gender, number of participants, physical and mental abilities, and experience (beginners versus advanced participants); goals and objectives; equipment needs; and equipment setup. |
| Priming the group | Priming the group includes attention getters, dividing the group into smaller groups, and establishing ground rules. An orientation to the program can also be given. An orientation can include the plans for the day, an overview of what the participants will be doing, safety issues and rules, policies, participant expectations, staff expectations, and goals for the program. |
| Delivery | Delivery encompasses the actual activities or skills, activity transitions, program closure, and a contingency plan if needed. |

activities to be examined from the perspectives of four behavioral domains (Hurd et al. 2007):

1. **Physical:** What physical abilities and skills are needed for participation, such as strength, speed, endurance, and eye–hand coordination?

2. **Social:** What social interaction occurs among participants and between participants and instructors?

3. **Cognitive:** What thought processes or bits of knowledge are needed to participate? What kind of mental ability, ability to understand rules, or ability to concentrate is needed?

4. **Affective:** What are the emotions, such as joy, fear, fun, or pride, required for the program?

Activity analysis assesses the degree to which the program meets goals and objectives. This is particularly true with programs for people with disabilities. In therapeutic recreation settings the activity components are analyzed to determine whether the program is appropriate for a participant and to address any potential modifications that can enhance the experience for the individual.

## Budgeting

Most programs require the programmer to develop a budget. The budget is established before the start of the **fiscal year** and dictates the planning and design of the program. The budget accounts for revenues, or moneys coming into the agency, from sources such as program registrations and sponsorships. Program expenditures, or money going out of the agency to pay bills and personnel, are also accounted for in the budget. The budget dictates the price of the program and many of the decisions made about the program. The budget controls things such as the number of staff people hired, the equipment purchased, and the advertising done.

During program implementation the budget is monitored and adjustments are made depending on program demand. If demand is lower than expected, then revenue projections are not met and expenditures must be decreased. Conversely, if the agency exceeds revenue projections, the program either increases profits or requires additional expenditures such as more staff members or supplies. Pricing and budgeting are discussed in depth in chapter 8.

## Marketing

Marketing is an ongoing process for the agency and its individual programs. Marketing is the "purposeful planning and execution of the pricing, place, and promotions of ideas, goods, and services to create an exchange of time or resources that result in the satisfaction of individual needs and organizational objectives" (Hurd, Barcelona, and Meldrum 2008, 167). Thus programmers must create programs that meet the needs of consumers so that people value the programs enough to participate. Programs have to be selected carefully so that people view them as something worth spending time and money on. If the agency does not have a marketing department, then the programmer must assume the marketing tasks.

## Registration and Reservations

Registration and reservations are a part of most leisure services delivery systems. Rossman and Schlatter (2008) suggest that a registration and reservation system is needed for four different situations. These situations are demonstrated here with the following examples from Massanutten

Hours of program planning go into special events such as Piastonalia in Opole, Poland. This 5-day event is part of spring break at Opole University of Technology.

Resort in McGaheysville, Virginia (Massanutten Resort 2009):

1. Participants pay a fee for a program or service. For example, golfers wanting to play the Mountain Greens Golf Course must pay and register to do so.

2. The number of participants in a program is limited due to space or equipment limitations. For example, the Massanutten Adventures Vineyards Tour is limited by the number of seats on the bus and requires preregistration.

3. The program is expensive to provide. For example, the Virginia Winemakers' Dinner is $60 per person and features a five-course meal and wine pairings for each course. The cost, popularity, and room size require preregistration.

4. Special qualifying procedures are required for participation in the program. For example, programs such as the river expeditions, area excursions, and rock climbing require that the participants stay at the Massanutten Resort. Registration is a means of controlling this requirement.

Registrations and reservations are not just for programs. They can also be taken for hotel rooms, cruises, picnic shelter reservations, or ball field reservations. All three sectors utilize some system to register participants and users.

Registration can be taken via six different methods: central location, program location, mail in, phone in, fax in, and Web based. Most agencies use a combination of some or all of these methods.

- **Central location registration:** Agencies that have multiple facilities and locations may have a central location (single location) for registering. Having only one location requires well-trained staff members who can process registrations efficiently. This method ensures that cash is accepted at only one location and increases the control over large amounts of money. However, the registration location may be inconvenient to some users and does not allow participants to see actual locations of programs run in a different facility. Also, the hours the central facility is open for registering may prohibit working people from registering (Rossman and Schlatter 2008).

- **Program location registration:** With this registration method, registration is accepted at the facility where the program is held. This is convenient for participants who choose programs at facilities close to home. Participants can also register at many facilities rather than just one. Furthermore, it allows participants to see the actual location of the program and possibly talk with staff members at the facility. The major disadvantages of this registration method are the decentralization of cash collection, an increased need for cash control procedures, an increased need to train staff on registration procedures, and limited open hours.

- **Mail-in registration:** Mail-in registration requires participants to complete a form and return it with payment to the agency. Once received, staff members process the registration and mail a receipt and confirmation of registration or a refund if the program is full. This registration method is quick and convenient for participants because they can register from home even after the agency closes for the evening. Flexibility is also key for the agency, as staff members can process mail-in registrations when they have time available versus having to immediately register a walk-in customer. The downside of mail-in registration occurs when a program is full and payment must be returned to the customer or when the registration form is incomplete or incorrectly filled out and the customer must be contacted.

- **Phone-in registration:** To register by this method, participants call the agency and register over the phone. A staff member takes the registration information and credit card number for payment. This method of registration is convenient for the user as long as the agency is open. It also centralizes cash collection. Phone-in registration is often used with another type of registration process. However, there are some agencies, such as Ticketmaster, that rely heavily on phone-in and more recently Internet payments. A drawback is the limited type of payment that can be accepted on the phone.

- **Fax-in registration:** Fax-in registration has decreased in use as other technologies have become more prevalent. Customers registering by this method fax the completed registration form and their credit card number to the agency. The fax-in method has all of the same advantages and disadvantages of mail-in registration with the added issue that many people do not have fax machines in their homes. Many home computers have fax capabilities, but it may be simpler for participants to register via the Web rather than send a fax through the computer.

- **Web-based registration:** Online registration allows participants to complete their registration process, pay, and receive confirmation 24 hours a day. Most of the popular registration software allows for online registration so that those registering are automatically placed in the class without any further processing by staff. This aspect is a time and money saver for the agency. The disadvantage is that not all participants have computer access or Internet capabilities.

Because each of these registration methods has its disadvantages, most agencies employ a combination of methods. For example, the Westerville (Ohio) Parks and Recreation Department (2009) provides central location registration, Internet registration, and mail-in registration. River Expeditions (2010) books its rafting trips via the phone and Internet.

Regardless of the method of registration used, a registration form is needed. Registration forms vary by agency, and their format is dictated by any number of issues including the registration system, the order in which information must be entered into the system, and the waiver and release requirements mandated by the agency attorney. Typical registration forms include the following pieces of information: participant information (e.g., name, address, phone), emergency contact information, program information, payment information, request for accommodations for disabilities, and waiver and release information.

### Payment Methods

Agency policies dictate payment methods. Cash, checks, debit cards, credit cards, automatic withdrawal, and installments may be options; each has its advantages and disadvantages. The following is a brief overview of payment methods.

- **Cash:** At one time the most popular form of payment, cash is also the simplest form. However, cash requires handling proce-

dures to keep it accounted for at all times. Cash makes theft a real issue.

- **Checks:** Checks can be used for walk-in or mail-in registrations, but some checks can be returned for nonsufficient funds (NSF). NSF checks usually have a penalty fee associated with them and require the agency to work with the bank to get them covered. An agency can use a company that verifies whether checks are good (e.g., VeriCheck) to decrease this problem.

- **Debit and credit cards:** These cards are being used as a method of payment more and more often and are replacing the use of checks. Debit cards are essentially electronic checks that remove money quickly from the back account. These cards can also be prepaid, meaning that money is available up to the amount placed on the card. Credit cards, on the other hand, accumulate balances that must be paid partially or fully each month. When making credit card transactions, businesses must pay a small percentage (e.g., 2 percent) of each purchase to the bank that issued the card. This transaction fee is rarely passed onto the customer directly, but it is covered through the increased cost of products and services (Pritchard 2009).

- **Automatic withdrawal:** Automatic withdrawal is used in places such as fitness facilities, after-school programs, or karate or dance studios. For example, the Leaps & Bounds Children's Fitness Centre accepts membership and class fees through automatic withdrawal.

- **Installments:** The last payment option is paying through installments. Programs requiring a high fee sometimes offer installments. For example, the Edwards YMCA Camp and Conference Center (Edwards YMCA 2009) in East Troy (Wisconsin) allows members registering for the winter camp to pay a $100 deposit with the balance due on a designated date. The company Fan Trips Travel offers trips for fans of books and movies such as the Harry Potter books and Pirates of the Caribbean movies. Some of these trips can cost more than $1,000, so Fan Trips Travel (2010) allows travelers to make monthly payments or pay a deposit with the balance due 90 days before the trip.

## Risk Management

Because we live in a litigious society, programmers need a thorough understanding of risk management. Risk management is the process of identifying and minimizing elements that could cause injury or damage to people or property. Hronek and Spengler (2007) outline a four-step process to minimize risk: (1) identification, (2) evaluation, (3) treatment, and (4) implementation.

1. **Identification:** Identification requires staff members to identify hazardous areas. Hazards include things such as unsafe playground surfaces, poorly lit parking lots at facilities, or exposed electrical lines at a special event.

2. **Evaluation:** Once hazards are identified they must be evaluated based on their frequency and severity. The more frequently an incident occurs and the more severe an incident is, the higher the priority it is to be corrected.

3. **Treatment:** Once the hazard has been identified and evaluated, staff members must determine how to handle it. There are four options for treating a hazard (Hurd, Barcelona, and Meldrum 2008). First, an agency can avoid the problem by stopping the activity. Second, the agency can reduce the frequency or severity of the damage, perhaps by providing safety equipment for softball players, filling a hole in the outfield, or changing the rules of a game. A third option is to transfer liability to another person or organization. This is usually done through a contract. Lastly, the agency can retain the risk. With this strategy the agency knows there is a risk for the activity but chooses to continue the activity as it is. Consider the risk associated with some outdoor recreation activities. Snowboarding, regardless of the safety equipment, still has risks associated with it. Avoiding high-risk activities such as snowboarding may be acceptable to some people, but it is not to avid snowboarders.

4. **Implementation:** Once the treatment plan is determined, it is implemented. Upon implementation, the situation is reevaluated to ensure that the proper treatment was implemented.

Risk management is a complicated aspect of recreation programming. Whole courses are dedicated to it. The best process for programmers is to develop a risk management plan for the program. A risk management plan outlines necessary reports and records, facility inspection processes,

Public, nonprofit, and commercial sector agencies such as Old Town Trolley Tours will have a risk management plan detailing how to deal with the risks associated with programs, events, and facilities.

participant safety briefings, staff supervision, emergency procedures, and applicable safety policies and procedures (Kraus and Curtis 2000).

### Monitoring

Ongoing events and programs require monitoring. For example, supervisors monitor their budgets to ensure that revenues and expenditures are met. In addition, they monitor program supplies and equipment, registration numbers, and staff members, among other things. A one-day special event also requires monitoring by the event planner, who might monitor by checking the needs of vendors, ensuring that volunteers are placed correctly and have required resources, keeping an eye on weather conditions, and watching crowd control.

Even though all the planning that goes into a program should ensure a quality experience for participants, monitoring is the activity that ensures that the program runs smoothly. It is also during monitoring that unexpected situations occur and must be addressed by the program manager. For instance, accidents and incidents can happen during programs and events. The manager must deal with them by following agency policy and then completing accident and incident reports.

### Program Conclusion and Follow-Up

A program or event is complete once it ends for the participants. However, staff members often have conclusion or follow-up tasks to finish after program completion. These tasks might include the following:

- Cleaning up the location and putting away equipment
- Writing thank-you notes to people involved in the program both internally and externally, including staff members who worked the event, sponsors, and volunteers
- Putting away or reordering equipment
- Paying hired workers and other outstanding bills

The time and energy put into a program can be extensive. While this makes it easy to ignore or halfheartedly complete the follow-up tasks, it is important to acknowledge the people involved in the program and to clean up so that the next program can take place.

### Evaluating the Program

The final step in the program planning process is evaluation. Evaluation is the systematic judg-

ment about the worth and influence of a program (Henderson and Bialeschki 2002). The key to this definition is that evaluation is a systematic process. Agencies determine what things are evaluated, when evaluation is done, and what process is followed. The evaluation should not be an afterthought or feel haphazard because it is a means to program improvement. A program is evaluated during both the planning and implementation phases so that program planners know what to do differently next time in terms of both planning and implementing the program. While this is a solid means of improving programs, getting the opinions of participants gives a different perspective and allows the programmer to see the program through the eyes of the users. The process outlined in detail in chapter 4 is a good place to start when evaluating a program.

## Coordination With Other Agencies

Being a good programmer requires thinking beyond the programming process. As agencies are continuously seeking to meet the needs of the community in the most efficient and effective way possible, they have to maximize their resources. To do this, programmers have to consider several key programming issues. One of those key issues is coordinating with other agencies.

During the discussion on the program planning process, a system was outlined to develop a program. Most of the process described was internal to the agency. However, a growing trend in the leisure services profession is coordination with other agencies. This coordination can take on many names, including *cooperative venture* or *agreement, joint agreement, alliance, collaboration,* and *interagency cooperation.* However, the most popular term in the industry is *partnership.* A leisure services agency has unlimited demands for services and a limited budget. A popular means of stretching the budget and better meeting the needs of the organization is to develop a partnership. A **partnership** is "a relationship between two or more parties for the purposes of addressing a common challenge" (Hurd, Barcelona, and Meldrum 2008, 131). Partnerships allow programmers to "draw on more constituencies and interests" (Congdon 2008, 75).

It is easy to confuse partnerships with sponsorships. Partnerships are more involved with program delivery. They provide assistance with programming, staff expertise, or facilities. Sponsorships are relationships with other organizations that provide funds or other resources in return for specific deliverables that are used for commercial advantage. Sponsors seek to enhance their business image through benefits such as publicity. Partners are more likely to gain recognition from the delivery of the program rather than promised advertising. Sponsorships are detailed in chapter 8.

Partnerships can be between agencies from the same sector, such as two nonprofit agencies. They can also be intersectoral, meaning that the agencies working together come from different sectors. Partnerships are formed to enhance services, and agencies pool their resources to make a program stronger. For example, the City of Marietta's (Ohio) Men's 18 and Over Basketball League is held at the Washington County Juvenile Center because the recreation department does not have enough gym space for the league and the juvenile center does not use its gym in the evenings nor has enough staff to offer the program. The partnership makes for a solid basketball program that neither agency could offer on its own. Services are also enhanced when one partner agency has an area of expertise that the other does not. For example, the Virginia Winemakers' Dinner at the Massanutten Resort is a partnership involving the resort, a local chef, and an area winery. The resort alone could not do this program because it lacks a high-caliber chef and the ability to provide and properly pair wines. Thus, the resort relies on the expertise of its partners.

Although partnerships may seem like a positive addition to any program, there are always situations in which partnerships do not work. It may be that one agency wants more control or power than the other, an agency does not deliver all the resources promised, the program does not adhere to the mission of one of the agencies, or turf wars erupt in which one agency is trying to protect and maintain what it considers to be its own.

Boccaro and Barcelona (2003) provide the following suggestions on how to develop effective partnerships:

- Create different types of partnerships. Not all agencies can provide the same resources. Build partnerships that take advantage of agency strengths.
- View partnerships as a mutually beneficial relationship and consider what each agency can offer the other one.

- Clearly identify the roles and responsibilities of each partner, stating who will do what and who will provide what.
- Make partnerships formal by putting them in writing. Outline what each partner brings to the program and what responsibilities each accepts.

Partnerships can open up a whole new aspect to programming. Programmers who are willing to look beyond traditional program offerings can give constituents a vast array of services that better meet their needs while at the same time making the most out of the available resources.

# Programming for People With Disabilities

Programmers need to be aware that some of their program participants may have disabilities that affect the delivery of programs. The Americans with Disabilities Act (ADA), passed in 1990, gives people with disabilities the right to (1) participate in programs specifically designed for them, (2) participate in programs with people who do not have disabilities, or (3) do both (Manschot and Kerrins 2009). Some agencies have therapeutic recreation (TR) divisions with certified therapeutic recreation specialists (CTRS) that provide services where people with disabilities can participate in programs only for people with disabilities. Other agencies have a TR specialist who helps with all aspects of inclusion. Inclusion services enable any participant to enjoy a program while experiencing the fewest restrictions possible. This may mean that an activity or a piece of equipment is adapted to accommodate the individual or that a buddy is provided to assist the participant. Each individual is unique and has different needs. Consulting a TR specialist can help an agency to determine what services to provide to make the program truly inclusive, safe, and enjoyable for each individual.

## Physical Accessibility

The physical accessibility of parks and facilities describes how people with disabilities can approach, enter, and use them without facing barriers (Anderson and Brown Kress 2003). Curb cuts on sidewalks, ramps over or in addition to stairs, raised markings on elevator buttons and signs, flashing alarm lights, wider doors, lower

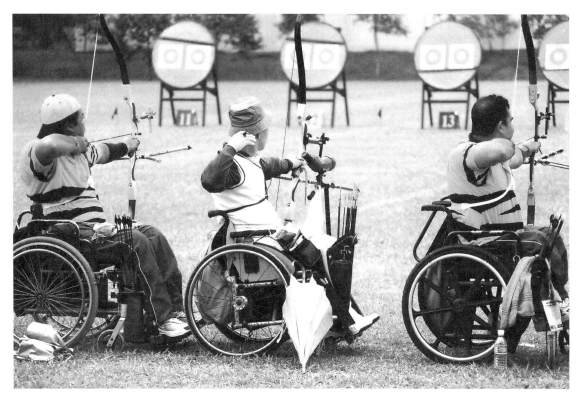

Programs and facilities should be designed with universal accessibility as a top priority.

countertops, turnstile bypasses, accessible door hardware, grab bars in restrooms, properly positioned sinks and soap dispensers, and lower doorway entry thresholds are just a few examples of making a facility more accessible to people with disabilities (LaRue and Rogers 2005).

There are a number of sources of accessibility standards that enable an agency to reach its ultimate goal of being universally accessible. Universal accessibility takes the ADA one step further and is "a design approach that ensures maximum inclusion and participation for everyone. It is based on the belief that people who have disabilities should have the same access to buildings and facilities that other citizens enjoy" (Anderson and Brown Kress 2003, 18). In addition to the ADA Accessibility Guidelines, the standards developed by the Architectural and Transportation Barriers Compliance Board (also known as the Access Board) serve as the main source of facility accessibility standards (Dattilo 2002).

## Program Accessibility

Program accessibility means that people with disabilities have the ability to participate in recreation programs through support or accom-

modation. A six-step process should be followed to ensure inclusion for people with disabilities (adapted from Anderson and Brown Kress 2003).

### Step 1: Program Promotion

All promotional materials should include nondiscriminatory or welcoming statements for people with disabilities. For example, the Columbus (Indiana) Parks and Recreation Department makes the following statement:

➤ The Parks and Recreation Department intends that all meetings, programs and facilities be accessible to all members of the community, including those with special needs. If anyone requires special accommodations to attend or participate in a department activity, he or she may call the administrative office at least 48 hours prior to the special need. (Columbus Parks and Recreation Department 2010)

### Step 2: Registration and Needs Assessment

Registration forms should ask if accommodations are needed. If so, the participant should provide the information and a designated staff member should follow up on the needs. The participant's strengths and issues should be assessed to determine the participant's needs, abilities, and desires.

### Step 3: Accommodation and Support

Based on the information gathered from the participant, a plan should be developed to provide the needed accommodations. Dattilo (2002) suggests that adaptations can be made to the following program elements:

- **Size:** The size of equipment and supplies can be increased or decreased based on the participant's needs. For example, if game equipment is too small to grasp, it can be enlarged.
- **Speed:** If gross motor skills are diminished, the speed of an activity may need to be slowed. For example, a ball with less air moves more slowly.
- **Weight:** If a piece of equipment is too heavy for the participant to handle, the equipment can be adapted by changing to a lighter piece or a similar piece. For example, a softball can be replaced with a tennis ball or Wiffle ball.
- **Stabilization:** If balance or stability is an issue, equipment can be anchored to ensure it will not tip over and injure the participant.
- **Safety:** All adaptations must maintain the safety of the program. The program area may need to be changed to increase the safety of participants. This might include using safe chemicals and supplies such as paints, removing unnecessary furniture, and removing sharp edges.

In addition to adapting activities and equipment it is sometimes necessary to provide staff members or volunteers to aid the participant. This helper might be an assistant assigned to the participant or a peer in the class who gives assistance.

Planning for people with disabilities also includes developing goals and objectives for the participants and strategies through which to achieve those goals and objectives. In TR settings, these plans are often referred to as *treatment plans, rehabilitation plans,* and *care plans,* among others.

### Step 4: Staff Training and Program Implementation

Staff members and volunteers should be trained to work with people with disabilities and should understand the purpose and process of inclusion. You cannot assume that all staff members will be comfortable and knowledgeable in working with people with disabilities. Training on the multitude of disabilities that might be encountered enhances the experience of the staff members and participants. Once the accommodations and support staff members or volunteers are in place and properly trained, the program is ready for implementation.

### Step 5: Documentation

Many participants with disabilities have an individual program plan. This plan is developed with the participant, family member or guardian when appropriate, CTRS staff member, or other inclusion specialist. With the individual program plan there is a need to document the participant's progress during the program. Documentation assesses the individual's progress toward achieving the goals and objectives established for the program.

### Step 6: Evaluation

At the end of the program, an evaluation is used to assess the quality of the program itself. Program evaluation is done regardless of whether a person with a disability is in the program. The evaluation process was detailed earlier in the discussion on the program planning process. In addition to the program evaluation, documentation gathered during the program (see the previous step) is used to evaluate how effectively the program helped the participant achieve the program goals and objectives. The evaluation can result in a full achievement of goals and objectives, a referral to another program to accomplish these same goals or new ones, or a referral to another agency to better meet the needs of the participant.

## Special Event Accessibility

Inclusion services can be implemented in advance when the agency knows which disabilities to accommodate. However, special events and programs not requiring advanced registration can make inclusion and access a bit more difficult. In

## Ball State University Sample Accessibility Checklist

### Accessible Entrances

- Is there an entrance that does not require the use of stairs?
- Are there appropriate signs directing attendees to accessible entrances and bathroom facilities?
- Is the path at least 36 inches wide?
- Are curb cuts located in parking lot and drop-off areas?
- Are there accessible parking spaces near the accessible entrance?

### Meeting Rooms

- If the location for your event or program has multiple floors, is there an accessible elevator to the meeting room?
- Is an accessible path of travel available to the meeting room?
- Is the meeting room accessible for speakers and presenters? Can participants navigate easily in the space?

### Event Publicity and Invitations

- Do your publicity pieces and invitations contain information regarding reasonable accommodations?

### Accommodation Requests From Participants

- Has a participant, either an audience member or a speaker, requested an accessible meeting space?
- Has a staff member been assigned to ensure that accommodation arrangements are handled appropriately?
- Has a participant requested an assisted listening system?
- Has a participant requested a sign language interpreter?
- If a video is part of the program, are the videos equipped with captions for participants with hearing impairments?

**Figure 2.4** This sample accessibility checklist demonstrates areas to address when planning an event. The full checklist includes solutions for making the event more accessible.

Reprinted, by permission, from Ball State University. Available: http://cms.bsu.edu/About/AdministrativeOffices/DSD/PoliciesProcedures/EventsChecklist.aspx

this case, programmers must anticipate what they may encounter and accommodate people the best they can. Ball State University has developed an accessibility checklist for people who are planning events (figure 2.4).

## Creative Programming

A rewarding and fun side of programming is developing creative programs for constituents. While many agencies have standard programs that they offer each season because of demand, they also take the opportunity to add new and innovative programs to address trends in the profession.

Creative programming allows staff members to think outside of the box and offer something different to the community. Ideas for new programs come from a variety of sources: NRPA Congress sessions such as 99 Second Programs or Call of the Wild; the Edith Upchurch Innovative Programming Forum; local, regional, or national newspapers; other agencies; and trends popping up in the media.

## Volunteers

Public and nonprofit agencies often utilize a large corps of volunteers for their programs

## Volunteer Trends

While researching the role of volunteering for the individual, the Corporation for National and Community Service found several key volunteer trends (Reingold and Nesbit 2006):

- Volunteering is at a 30-year high.

- The growth in volunteering has been driven by three age groups: older teenagers (16-19 years), midlife adults (45-64 years), and older adults (65 years and older).

- Teenagers continue to be interested in episodic volunteering, such as for special events, special projects, or one-time programs.

- Volunteering by older adults has been on an upward trajectory through the last three decades, going from 14.3 percent in 1974 to 23.5 percent in 2005. Older adults are the group most likely to serve 100 or more hours a year.

- In 1989, 40.1 percent of volunteers served 100 or more hours in a year, compared with 34.9 percent serving 100 or more hours today.

and events. These volunteers can take on any number of responsibilities, including building a playground, landscaping, giving facility tours, teaching a class, aiding in the passing of a referendum, or performing maintenance or carpentry projects. Tapping into volunteer power decreases agency expenditures, increases expertise levels in programs, allows people to give back to the community, and adds to the health and well-being of the volunteers.

Programmers are at a critical point in terms of volunteers. The baby boomers (born between 1946 and 1964) are beginning to retire and have discretionary time that they want to fill with meaningful experiences. They have a plethora of skills that they can bring to agencies and are willing to do just that. According to the U.S. Census Bureau (2009), there are more than 22.4 million people aged 65 and older in the United States. This number is rising, as the youngest baby boomers will not turn 65 until 2029. These staggering numbers do not take into account the youths, teenagers, and adults other than baby boomers who volunteer.

Agencies expound the benefits that volunteers provide the agency; however, the Corporation for National and Community Service Office of Research and Policy Development has examined the role of volunteering on the individual and has found that volunteering has a positive effect on social psychological factors; increases health, happiness, life satisfaction, and self-esteem; and lowers depression (Grimm, Spring, and Dietz 2007). By providing these benefits, volunteering isn't just a means of providing programs and services to a community but is also a program in and of itself.

## Conclusion

Programming is the cornerstone of the leisure services industry. As detailed throughout this chapter, it is a four-step systematic process:

1. Assessing the community and its needs
2. Designing and planning the program
3. Implementing the program
4. Evaluating the program

Programming allows us to merge our creative sides with our highly organized and detailed sides. Being a good programmer allows us to tap into both of these qualities. As programmers, we assess needs and then develop a wide variety of programs to meet these needs. Understanding all aspects of the process and gaining planning skills will lend to a positive program experience for our constituents.

## Review Questions

1. Explain each of the four steps in the program planning process.

2. How can demographic data affect program planning decisions?

3. Differentiate between goals and objectives.

4. List the elements that should be included in a program plan.

5. What are the three phases of direct leadership? Explain what each phase entails.

6. Describe the program registration methods and their advantages and disadvantages. When should program registration be used?

7. Explain the four-step process used to minimize risk in a recreation program.

8. Define partnerships and why they are created. Explain the five types of partnerships.

9. Describe the six-step process used to provide programs for people with disabilities.

**Visit the online resource at www.HumanKinetics.com/TheParkAndRecreationProfessionalsHandbook for sample documents, keywords, activities and assignments, and more.**

# Motor Development and Recreation

chapter 3

## OUTCOMES

- Understand the concept of developmentally appropriate practices in recreation.

- Apply the model of motor development to recreation activities.

- Create an activity plan using age-appropriate activities and leadership techniques.

Parks and recreation professionals have the responsibility of planning activities for all ages and abilities. These activities may be part of a special event, a specific program, a sport league, an after-school program, or a day camp, just to name a few. As people age they develop physically, socially, and cognitively, and programs must reflect these changes by ensuring their activities are age appropriate. While the changes that occur during childhood are obvious and easy to envision, people experience nearly as many changes once they become adults and move to older adulthood. This chapter focuses on development from early childhood through older adulthood, because these are the age groups we as leisure services professionals tend to interact with the most. This chapter provides brief highlights of motor skills found within a given age group; however, you are encouraged to pursue additional readings for a complete understanding of the development of movement skills across the life span.

## Physical Activity Throughout Life

According to the Centers for Disease Control and Prevention (CDC), a seismic shift in the rate of obesity among Americans has occurred since 1985:

➤ In 2008, only one state, Colorado, had a prevalence of obesity less than 20%. Thirty-two states had prevalence equal to or greater than 25%; six of these states (Alabama, Mississippi, Oklahoma, South Carolina, Tennessee and West Virginia) had a prevalence of obesity equal to or greater than 30%. (CDC 2009)

The alarming health concerns related to obesity have caused many organizations to consider how they might develop programs to improve the health status of our nation. In a national survey of city managers, "89% indicated that the primary governmental agency responsible for helping address the obesity problem is parks and recreation" (Bocarro and Wells 2009, 2). The NRPA identified two initiatives for changing the sedentary generation (National Recreation and Park Association 2009), and both are associated with movement and its role in promoting physical activity. Play was the first initiative identified. Most people identify play as a *children's* activity; however, many of today's children do not know

how to play unless doing so involves teammates or a computer or video game.

The NRPA has launched a variety of initiatives to bolster the value of play to ensure that the public adopts lifelong habits that contribute to healthy lifestyles. According to the NRPA, "play is the cornerstone to achieving personal and community health. Play not only resonates with all people, stimulating creativity and inspiration, it also strengthens intergenerational ties, solidifies a direct connection to nature, and promotes physical activity" (National Recreation and Park Association 2009).

The second initiative, health and livability, centers on promoting "healthy, active lifestyles for all Americans, regardless of age" (National Recreation and Park Association 2009). In addition to the NRPA's initiatives, five major strategies emerged from the first Summit on the Value of Play, which was held in 2009 at Clemson University:

1. Strategically grow the Coalition for Play by targeting others from related professions and organizations in areas of needed emphasis.
2. Mobilize children and young adults as key players in developing a play movement.
3. Identify the costs to society and individuals that result from lack of play.
4. Inspire families to change their perceptions and behaviors regarding the essential value of play.
5. Change liability laws to be friendlier to play.

Parks and recreation programs can contribute to improving the health of Americans by promoting physical activity. Bocarro and Wells (2009, 2) state the following:

➤ Parks and recreation professionals are in a position to provide physical activity opportunities to a variety of ages and abilities. The potential for using park and recreation amenities and programs to help people become physically active, and thus healthier, are great.

In order for people of all ages to participate in recreational pursuits, especially pursuits dealing with physical activity and play, recreation professionals must consider the ages of clients when planning meaningful experiences. In order to do this, recreation professionals must have a basic understanding of development and developmentally appropriate practices, because learning occurs in many forms and in many locations and not just in schools.

# Developmentally Appropriate Practices in Recreation

The term **developmentally appropriate practices** was originally used in early childhood education but applies to any field in which learning is involved. While many community recreation programs include adults, numerous programs focus on preschoolers, school-age children, and adolescents. Thus, a focus on younger participants is not out of the question. In a newly revised position statement, the National Association for the Education of Young Children (NAEYC) stated that "developmentally appropriate practice requires both meeting children where they are and enabling them to reach goals that are both challenging and achievable" (National Association for the Education of Young Children 2009). Regarding movement activities, the physical education profession defines developmentally appropriate movement tasks as "activities designed with the student's cognitive, psychomotor, and affective levels in mind" (Kovar et al. 2007, 580).

In the field of recreation, developmentally appropriate practices refers to planning experiences for participants based on two important variables: (1) the participants' *current ability* and (2) the *appropriateness* of tasks for the age of the group participating. For example, when working with a group of 25 seven-year-olds, it would not be developmentally appropriate for the leader to plan a full-court basketball game with regulation-height baskets and the traditional five-versus-five player configuration. Seven-year-olds do not, nor should be expected to, have the same motor and cognitive capacities that teens and adults have. They do not have the physical capabilities to dribble the ball and keep it under control for a lengthy distance, the upper-body strength to complete passes, or the coordination and strength to shoot at a basket that is 10 feet high. Finally, young children do not have the cognitive capacity to use various defensive or offensive strategies.

## Need for Developmentally Appropriate Practices in Recreation

Many opportunities in recreation relate to the three learning domains that each of us use when taking on new experiences. The three domains are psychomotor, cognitive, and affective. Psychomotor abilities are the physical skills and movement abilities of the individual. Cognitive tasks involve

Play is a valuable element in the lives of both children and adults and leads to lifelong physical activity.

using intellectual knowledge as it relates to the movement skill being learned. Lastly, the affective focus encompasses the attitudes, values, social skills, and interactions common in all recreation pursuits. This chapter focuses on movement skills and their relation to recreation. However, the cognitive and affective components of learning are made stronger when tied to the movement skill being learned, whether a 5-year-old or an 85-year-old is the person doing the learning.

Recreation through movement, such as participating in individual and team activities, hiking, kayaking, and playing games, requires basic skills specific to each activity used for recreation. When using developmentally appropriate practices in planning recreation experiences, the professional should consider the age of the participant and acknowledge individual differences among participants. In order for participants to have meaningful experiences, leaders need a basic understanding of what to expect from a given age group.

Within the profession of **kinesiology** exists a subdiscipline known as **motor development**, which focuses solely on how people acquire motor skills, beginning in utero (in the womb) and ending with death, and how those skills change over time. Motor development as defined by Gallahue and Ozmun (2006, 5) is "a continuous change in motor behavior throughout the lifecycle, brought about by interaction among the requirements of the movement task, the biology of the individual, and the conditions of the environment."

The development of movement skill occurs within approximate time frames that serve as a guide for parents, recreation professionals, and teachers. During childhood, girls and boys learn **fundamental motor skills.** These fundamental skills can be divided into locomotor, manipulative, and stabilizing skills:

- Locomotor skills move the body from one point to another and include running, hopping, skipping, jumping, leaping, sliding, and galloping.
- Manipulative skills include catching, throwing, tossing, rolling, striking, kicking, and dribbling and require the individual to impart force to or receive force from an object. Movement skills in which we *impart* force to an object include striking, kicking, and throwing. Examples of movement tasks requiring us to *receive* force from an object include catching, trapping,

receiving any shot in tennis, and receiving a forearm pass in volleyball.
- Stabilizing or stability skills are present in everything we do and relate to maintaining balance while in motion (dynamic balance) and while stationary (static balance). Stabilizing movements include twisting, dodging, and any type of balancing task.

These fundamental skills provide the springboard from which all other movements used in recreational activities are based. Think of your favorite physical activity. If you dissect that activity you will find that it comprises several fundamental motor skills. For example, let's look at basketball. The locomotor skills involved in basketball include running, jumping, and sliding, which in this case is a sideward motion. Manipulative skills include passing and receiving the ball, which are modified versions of throwing and catching; shooting; and rebounding. Stability comes into play in many ways, including guarding, dodging, and setting picks.

It is imperative that all participants, regardless of age, have ample opportunities to practice movement skills in safe recreational environments that foster the positive development of self-esteem. In order to provide these opportunities, professionals should have an understanding of what each age group is capable of doing. To assist in this, a theoretical model explaining the acquisition of movement skills is reviewed in the next section.

## Model of Motor Development

There are many models explaining human development, some of which you may recognize. For example, Sigmund Freud had the psychoanalytic theory, while Jean Piaget had the developmental milestone theory. However, few models focus on how individuals obtain motor skills depending on their environment, heredity, and specific movement tasks. The theoretical framework guiding this chapter is based on the lifework of David L. Gallahue, professor and dean emeritus at Indiana University at Bloomington, and looks at movement skill acquisition "as a descriptive means for better understanding and conceptualizing the product of development" (Ozmun and Gallahue 2005, 344). In the context of Gallahue's work, focus is placed on the motor, or movement, domain.

### Motor Domain

**Gallahue's hourglass model of motor development,** also known as the *hourglass model,* adheres to a phase-stage theoretical framework, which is a framework that aligns with the need for developmentally appropriate practices in recreation. We have all heard the phrase, "it's just a phase he's going through" or "it's just a stage she's going through." Gallahue's model suggests that there is truth to these statements. In the case of developing the motor skills needed to participate in recreation activities, phase-stage theorists believe that there are "universal age periods characterized by typical behaviors that occur in phases or stages and last for arbitrary lengths of time" (Gallahue and Ozmun 2006, 509). By understanding this particular model of motor development, recreation professionals have the ability to plan age-appropriate and successful movement experiences for all clients.

The hourglass model (figure 3.1) reflects development from the beginning of life, in utero, to the end of life, or death. Everything a person does involves some aspect of movement—from getting out of bed in the morning to rock climbing, downhill skiing, dancing, and everything in between. In the hourglass model, Gallahue uses four phases of development. These phases are aligned with representative stages and serve as approximate guidelines to skill development. Motor development is highly individualized and is age related but not age dependent. This means that while the movement guidelines help inform parents, teachers, recreation professionals, and pediatricians, they are not etched in stone. For instance, while the average age at which a child begins to walk is 12 months, you may find out from your parents that you began walking at 13 months and your sister began walking at 10 months. Many different variables can help create the difference between you and your sister—for example, some children are more motivated than others to start walking. However, having a baseline understanding of the phases of motor development allows the recreation leader to design motor activities based on what is developmentally appropriate for participants.

### Reflexive Movement Phase

The first phase of the hourglass model is the reflexive movement phase, which covers the age span from in utero to the end of the first year of life. It is easy to think that recreation professionals rarely work with these age groups, but some

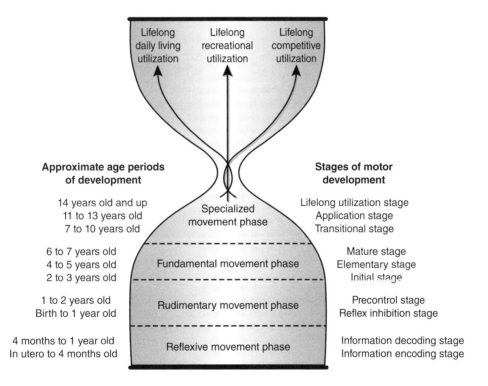

**Figure 3.1** Gallahue's hourglass model of motor development.

public and nonprofit agencies in particular offer programs for newborns and their parents. Even if you do not work with this very young age group, you should realize that these reflexive (involuntary) responses are the imprint for future voluntary movements.

As the name indicates, the movements found in the reflexive movement phase are reflexive, meaning the fetus or infant has no control of movement. As it turns out, the movement experiences of a young child are based on more than just experiences. Reflexive movements tell doctors and parents how a fetus is doing. First-time moms and dads are ecstatic when they feel the baby kick in the womb for the first time. That kicking motion is a reflex, meaning that some stimulus caused the baby to respond by kicking its leg. Reflex responses also assist doctors in assessing the neurological health of the newborn baby.

There are two types of reflexes: primitive (reflexes that the baby uses for survival) and postural (reflexes that lead to voluntary movements). An example of a primitive reflex is the sucking reflex. If the baby's lips are stimulated, they respond by completing a sucking motion. This is a survival reflex in that the infant needs it in order to eat. Postural reflexes, such as the stepping reflex, are precursors to the first voluntary movements. For example, when two-month-old babies are held upright "with their feet touching a surface, the pressure on the feet stimulates the legs to perform a walking motion" (Payne and Isaacs 2008, 238). Of course the baby is not able to walk—the walking motion is just a necessary reflex used to move onto bigger and better tasks. Children born with a disability may or may not move through this reflexive phase according to the age guidelines. A delay in one phase of development can lead to subsequent delays in the other phases of development.

The reflexive movement phase of motor development has two stages: (1) information encoding and (2) information decoding. The information encoding stage occurs in utero through the first four months of life and has the fetus or infant taking in information that will help with obtaining nourishment and finding "protection through movement" (Gallahue and Ozmun 2006, 50). The information decoding stage begins around the fourth month of life and allows the infant to "process" the information received (Gallahue and Ozmun 2006, 50). While these reflexes are found in infants before and after they are born, some early reflexes last a lifetime. Two that may be familiar to you are the patellar tendon reflex, in which a tap on the kneecap results in a reflexive knee jerk, and the withdrawal reflex, in which an accidental touch with a hot pan causes you to jerk your hand away from the heat.

### Rudimentary Movement Phase

The rudimentary movement phase of development begins at birth and ends approximately at age two. You might have noticed that this phase overlaps with the reflexive movement phase; keep in mind that all the phases of motor development are interrelated. The rudimentary movement phase depends on the ending of the reflexive movement phase, as one phase builds off the other (Gallahue and Ozmun 2006, 140). The movements found during this period are the first forms of voluntary movement a human being makes. There are three main categories of movements during this phase: stability, locomotor, and manipulative movements. Stability movements in the rudimentary phase include gaining and maintaining control of the head, neck, and torso, while locomotor movements include creeping and crawling (Payne and Isaacs 2008, 264-265). Manipulative movements in the rudimentary phase are exemplified by reaching, grasping, and releasing objects. Though these sound like very simple movements, they are imperative to the future movement abilities of each individual, because they help the young child to learn about the environment, to play, and to explore the surroundings.

Within this second phase of motor skill development the child moves through two stages: the reflex inhibition stage and the precontrol stage. The reflex inhibition stage starts around the age of birth and occurs through the first year. Just as the name *reflex inhibition* implies, it is during this stage that an infant begins to move away from reflexive movements. As the brain develops, movements become more voluntary but still lack smooth coordination. This makes sense since the movements are at the rudimentary level of development, and Merriam-Webster (2001, 1020) defines *rudimentary* as "consisting in first principles and very imperfectly developed." During the precontrol stage, children exhibit better control and accuracy in their movements. This is best exemplified by their ability to feed themselves and hold a bottle or cup.

The following are examples of developmentally appropriate programs for children in the reflexive and rudimentary movement phases. Sample descriptions are provided for each program:

## Swimming Programs

Organizations such as the American Red Cross (ARC) and YMCA have developmental aquatic programs for children and adults. Infant and toddler aquatic programs are very popular; approximately 5 to 10 million infants and preschoolers participate in formal aquatic instruction programs. However, children are not developmentally ready to learn how to swim until approximately 5 years of age (Committee on Sports Medicine and Fitness and Committee on Injury and Poison Prevention 2000, 868). Because of this, the ARC swim program focuses on water acclimation for children 6 months to 5 years and on learning to swim for children 6 years and up.

The following ARC aquatic classes are offered at the Jewish Community Center of Greater Baltimore (2010):

- **Parent infant swim:** For children aged 6 months to 2 years. Parents and infants acclimate to water through kicking, reaching, and blowing bubbles.
- **Parent child swim:** For children aged 2 to 5 years who have had two or more previous sessions of water adjustment lessons. Parents and children develop water confidence together through basic water exploration and primary swimming skills.

- **Wiggle 'n' giggle:** This parent-and-me program helps tots develop basic movement skills that will allow them to enjoy a range of fun physical activities. Target age range is 12 to 18 months (Ottawa Parks and Recreation 2009).

- **Music for tots:** Develop your child's talent with music for tots. This class introduces several types of sound and music while your child moves in interactive play. Parents are required to attend this class with their child. Target age range is 1 to 3 years (Milwaukee Recreation 2009).

### Fundamental Movement Phase

The third phase of the Gallahue model is one that recreation professionals, physical education teachers, and youth sport coaches definitely come into contact with: the fundamental movement phase. Think of children in this phase in the same way you look at children learning their ABCs and basic mathematical functions such as addition, subtraction, and multiplication. When children are taught how to move, initially through quality physical education experiences at the elementary school level, they are provided with the foundational skills needed to be lifelong movers. Just as parents, teachers, activity leaders, and after-school instructors are responsible for practicing basic cognitive skills with children, they are also responsible for providing meaningful learning opportunities through movement. While foundational movement skills are learned in physical education, the same skills should be practiced and developed outside of the classroom—perhaps in the backyard, at the local YMCA, at the local Boys and Girls Club, or through the city parks and recreation department.

This phase of movement development occurs between ages 2 and 7. During this time children must have opportunities to experience many forms of movement through play, cooperative activities, and basic games with minimal rules and limited equipment (Gallahue and Cleland 2003). A common mistake made among the general public is the belief that fundamental movements can be learned naturally, or that children can learn these movements on their own. This is the furthest thing from the truth. Gallahue and Cleland (2003, 52) state that "failure to develop and refine fundamental and specialized movement skills during the crucial preschool and elementary school years often leads children to frustration and failure during adolescence and adulthood." Stability, locomotor, and manipulative skills are categories of fundamental movements. While these categories of movements are named the same as the movement categories found in the rudimentary movement phases, the types of movements experienced in the two phases are very different. As mentioned earlier, stability movements always relate to gaining and maintaining balance and are included in every type of movement completed on a daily basis, from getting out of bed to taking out the trash to making any type of movement related to physical and recreational activities.

Locomotor skills developed in the fundamental movement phase include skills that allow the body to move about an area. These movements include walking, running, hopping, skipping, jumping (vertical and horizontal), galloping, sliding, and leaping. Think of all the childhood games and sports that include these locomotor skills, such as parachute games, musical statue games, and jump rope games.

Manipulative skills learned and applied in this phase of the hourglass model are activities in which an individual applies force to an object, such as when throwing a ball or hitting a ball off of a tee, or receives force from an object, such as when catching a beanbag or trapping a ball in soccer. The skills found within this category of movement include rolling a ball, underhand tossing, throwing, catching, kicking, striking, dribbling, and trapping.

If you were to list the physical activities you participated in as a child and adult, you would find that all include fundamental movement skills. As we move through adolescence and adulthood, we begin to refine our fundamental skills and to com-

bine them into the more complex movements and strategies commonly found in youth sports and in team and individual activities. The stages of development that make up the fundamental movement phase again serve as a guideline in identifying the potential abilities of the child, given the environment, the task, and the individual.

**Stages of Development**  The first stage in the fundamental movement phase is the initial stage, which occurs between ages 2 and 3. As the name indicates, it is during this stage that children make their first attempts at fundamental movements. At this point they are missing many pieces of the movement puzzle and lack coordination. For example, consider the manipulative skill of overhand throwing. At the initial stage of throwing, a throw does not look like the typical throw from first to second base in a competitive softball game. Rather, for a 2- or 3-year-old much of the action comes from the elbow, the throwing motion resembles a pushing motion, the child's fingers are spread at the release, the follow-through (the movement after the release of the object being thrown) is forward and downward, and the feet are stationary (Gallahue and Ozmun 2006; Ulrich 2000). It does not look like a well-developed overhand throw, and we should not expect it to look that way.

Around the ages of 4 and 5 years, a child begins to exhibit greater coordination and bodily control while completing movements, though some pieces of the specific task remain missing. The classic statement "you throw like a girl," albeit a stereotyped and sexist comment, conveys a specific image and reflects what we would see at this particular stage of development, which is the elementary stage. The child steps with the foot that is on the same side as the throwing hand and completes little follow-through across the body. Regardless of the fundamental movement skill, "many adults fail to move beyond this stage" (Gallahue and Ozmun 2006, 52), meaning that many adults function at the level of a 4- or 5-year-old in relation to their fundamental movement abilities.

The final stage in the fundamental movement phase is the mature stage. All things being equal (e.g., the child, instruction, practice, and so on), children have the ability to reach the mature stage of performance by the time they are 7 years old. A child who is at the mature stage of a given skill exhibits "coordinated, efficient and controlled

During the fundamental movement phase, children must have ample opportunity to experiment with all types of movements.

movements (Gallahue and Ozmun 2006, 52). It is at the mature stage that a child demonstrates what we all know as a correct overhand throw: the throwing arm moves downward to begin the windup, the hips and shoulders rotate, the foot opposite of the throwing arm steps forward, and there is diagonal follow-through across the body. Again, many adults never reach this mature stage of fundamental motor skill development due to a lack of quality instruction, opportunities for practice, and feedback on their performance.

The skill of overhand throwing, which was just used to demonstrate the different stages of the fundamental movement phase, is a skill used in many games and recreational and sport-related activities, including softball, football, baseball, and so on. Similarly, many elements of the overhand throw are found in movements in related activities, such as the serves in tennis and volleyball. Thus, this simple childlike skill is a prerequisite to many activities enjoyed across the life span and in recreational settings.

**Major Learning Factors** Regardless of whether children are developing stability, locomotor, or manipulative skills, they must receive three major learning factors from their recreation leader. These are (1) quality instruction, (2) age-appropriate language, and (3) multiple opportunities for practice.

The first learning factor is quality instruction, which should include a physical demonstration, repeated multiple times, by the adult. Most people are visual learners, so it is important that they get to see what it is they must do. When teaching a movement, demonstrate it several times and be sure to have the group you are leading seated nearby so that they can see you. Then have one of the participants come up and demonstrate the movement. It is important that the group members you are working with observe one of their own demonstrating the task at hand.

In addition to providing a proper physical demonstration, it is very important that you use age-appropriate language when explaining the task. Using age-appropriate language means using terminology the specific age group understands. It is very common for people leading an activity to use terminology that is unfamiliar to a beginner. For example, many young children may not know what the term *dominant foot* means when they hear, "I want you to kick the ball with your dominant foot." However, if you ask them to use their *favorite foot,* they quickly get your point.

The use of age-appropriate terminology also ties into your ability to provide feedback to the learner on a recently completed performance. Feedback lets learners know what they are doing well and what needs work. If learners are just permitted to practice without receiving any feedback, how do they know if they are performing the task correctly? Beginners can make the same mistake over and over unless the recreation leader lets them know what they need to change. When providing feedback it is best to remember that sooner is better than later. Another good rule of thumb is that the younger the learner, the more immediate the feedback. When teaching high schoolers, for example, you might wait to share feedback because you are on the opposite side of the field. High schoolers have the cognitive ability to understand your comments 5 to 10 minutes later, while a younger participant does not.

A final learning factor that recreation leaders must provide is many opportunities for practice. Whether you are working with the youngest or oldest of clients, multiple opportunities to practice the task are required. Practicing a skill just once or just doing a five-minute practice session is a classic example of developmentally inappropriate practice.

Keep in mind that most of what occurs in the fundamental movement phase takes place during childhood. Technically, a child between ages 3 and 5 is in early childhood. Recreational opportunities that incorporate gross motor play and use the large muscles of the body need to be experienced in formal (with a recreation leader) and informal (self-directed) settings. Movement tasks that encourage exploration and creativity, incorporate fundamental movements, and foster positive interactions should be the focus for this age group (Gallahue and Ozmun 2006, 177). The role of play cannot and should not be overlooked. Children learn *through* play. Play is their work. Physical play, or play that involves the fundamental motor skills, relates to much of what is experienced in recreation settings. Unfortunately, many children in today's society are growing up without being able to enjoy the outdoors or participate in activities that do not require a team of players or a computer. While there is certainly a time and place for competitive extracurricular opportunities and for opportunities involving technology, they should not occur at the expense of childhood.

The City of Kettering (Ohio) Parks, Recreation and Cultural Arts (2009) offers programs for all ages, especially those in the fundamental movement phase. The sidebar on page 48 describes an example of a developmentally appropriate peewee basketball program. When reading the description

## Peewee Basketball

What a great way to get that first taste of organized basketball! Boys and girls will receive instruction on individual skills such as shooting, dribbling, and passing as well as instruction on basic team play. This six-week developmental class will enhance each participant's coordination and conditioning as well as introduce the team concept and the fundamentals of organized sport. Let our professional staff members prepare your child for organized basketball in a fun, rewarding, nonthreatening environment utilizing age-appropriate equipment (miniature basketballs and youth basketballs and 6- to 8-foot rims). The target age range for this class is 5 to 7 years.

of the program, notice how the program is adapted and structured for the target age group. The program uses special equipment and focuses on basic basketball skills rather than strategies and skills beyond the abilities of the child participants.

### Specialized Movement Phase

The fourth and final phase of Gallahue's hourglass model is the specialized movement phase, which covers a very large age range, including later childhood (6-10 years of age), adolescence (10-20 years), and adulthood (20 years and older). During this phase individuals take previously learned movement skills and apply them in more complex and challenging settings, such as community recreational programs, after-school programs, and youth sport leagues.

Once again, let's examine the fundamental motor skill of overhand throwing. Upon gaining throwing proficiency during the fundamental movement phase, a child may have the opportunity to apply this skill in game and sport settings. The throwing motion is used in numerous sport-like activities, such as fishing, softball, football, and tennis, to name a few. Games or sports may also incorporate throwing strategies, such as force outs in softball. These types of skills and strategies would be expected in the specialized movement phase of development.

**Transitional Stage**   The specialized movement phase has three stages, the first of which, the transitional stage, begins anywhere from age 7 to 10. During this stage of the specialized movement phase, children make their first attempts at refining various mature movement patterns and exploring combinations of movements. Recreation leaders, physical education teachers, and coaches should begin helping children in this stage to become more accurate in their skill development. However, as Gallahue notes, children should not be forced to specialize in a given activity (Gallahue and Ozmun 2006, 53).

Unfortunately, too many children today specialize in a given sport, participating in year-round related events and ultimately damaging their developing bodies, possibly causing lifelong injuries. Technically, children at this age are in later childhood. Children in this category are ready to take on more responsibility given by their recreation leader.

**Application Stage**   The second stage in the specialized movement phase is the application stage. Between age 11 and age 13, children have the ability to develop higher levels of proficiency, and practice is of the utmost importance (Gallahue and Ozmun 2006, 315). While practice does not make perfect, when combined with quality leadership it can improve the particular skill in question.

Given the age range of adolescents in the application stage of the specialized movement phase, youth sport programs are a common place for children to apply their movement skills. The American Academy of Pediatrics estimates that approximately 20 to 45 million children between age 6 and age 18 participate in some type of youth sport activity (Brenner 2007, 1242). These activities include school-related athletics and community-based sport teams. In addition, Siedentop (2004, 113) notes that "community recreation departments sponsor programs that account for 36% of the (youth sport) participants." However, not all youth sport opportunities are organized. For example, pickup games at local parks and newer opportunities such as skateboarding at skateboarding parks account for a large number of participants who do not fall under the category of organized youth sport activities (Siedentop 2004).

Youth sport opportunities are not new, as these programs have been around since the 1950s, beginning with the baby boomers as the first participants. In Siedentop (2004, 114), Duquin states that youth sport programs were designed to nurture healthy physical, psychological and emotional growth and development in children when they are fun and enjoyable, provide a reasonably safe means for developing activity skills, exercise a spirit of discovery, adventure and creativity, provoke a commitment to lifelong involvement in activity, inspire a sense of community.

However, today's youth sport experiences may or may not provide the opportunities originally intended. Wells and Arthur-Banning (2008, 190) found that youth sport participation provides children with opportunities to improve their "moral behavior and attitudes," but there are also findings that suggest that youth sport participation results in the opposite, including negative behaviors such as aggression (Wells and Arthur-Banning 2008, 190). One only needs to read the headlines of today's newspapers to find that violence at youth sport competitions is on the rise. Unfortunately, many adults are the role models who are displaying this negative behavior.

In addition to adopting inappropriate behavior, youth sport participants are in danger of experiencing debilitating injuries due to sport seasons that never end. Gone are the days when softball begins in February and ends in July, as today most student–athletes are tied into one sport year round. This monotony adds to the wear and tear on their developing bodies. Lyle Micheli, a world-renowned orthopedic surgeon specializing in youth sports, noted that an estimated 3 million children end up in emergency rooms each year due to sport-related injuries (Micheli, Glassman, and Klein 2000, 821). Originally, youth sport programs were designed to be seasonal so that children could participate in different activities and not specialize in one sport. For example, basketball began in November and ended in March and softball followed from March to June. Today, however, it is highly unusual for youth sport participants not to be involved in year-round activities tied into their one sport. The lengthening of a sport season well beyond the end of the school year, the existence of travel teams, the pursuit of athletic scholarships (although very few in number), poorly trained coaches, year-round training schedules, and dedication to a single-sport focus (Bach and Schilling 2008) provide ripe conditions for catastrophic injuries.

The injuries experienced by children who have not yet completed their growth cycle include overuse injuries, which result from "microtraumatic damage to a bone, muscle, or

Single-sport, year-round training schedules and poorly trained coaches are increasingly contributing to injuries in young athletes once found only in adults.

tendon that has been subjected to repetitive stress without sufficient time to heal or undergo the natural reparative process"(Brenner 2007, 1243). Children are not able (and should not be expected to be able) to handle numerous practices, sport camps, and training workouts (Bach and Shilling 2008, 27).

Growth plate injuries can damage the growth of the child. Growth plates are located at the ends of a bone and are the weakest part of the skeleton (MayoClinic.com 2009). Statistics reveal that competitive sports such as football, basketball, softball, track and field, and gymnastics account for one-third of all growth plate injuries. Recreational activities such as biking, sledding, skiing, and skateboarding account for one-fifth of all growth plate fractures (National Institute of Arthritis and Musculoskeletal and Skin Disease 2007). The bottom line is that the growing bones of a child cannot handle the same stress as the fully grown bones of an adult (Brenner 2007, 1243). In addition to overuse and growth plate injuries, children also can experience tears in their rotator cuff, tendinitis, and burnout.

**Lifelong Utilization Stage**    The lifelong utilization stage is the final stage in the specialized movement phase of development. It begins around age 14 and lasts throughout adulthood. While teenagers may engage in youth sport activities throughout their high school years, whether through interscholastic activities or community recreation leagues, the high school years are a very small portion of the time spent in the lifelong utilization stage. This stage covers the longest span of life. As people age, life factors become intertwined with their recreation pursuits. Life factors include employment, socioeconomic status, family and work responsibilities, and health issues, and they affect one's decision to participate in recreation opportunities. In other words, adult responsibilities affect recreational choices. Thus as professionals we must convey to younger and older adults the need for physical activity through recreation and leisure opportunities.

Most adults move away from team sports once they join the workforce. It is imperative that more age-appropriate options—ones that move beyond team sport offerings—be developed. Activities such as hiking, kayaking, and yoga are wonderful recreation opportunities for the adult population.

American adults, just like American youth, are not as physically active as they need to be. Given the health concerns of the American population, physical activity for adults is more important than ever. Table 3.1 demonstrates the decline in physical activity that occurred between 2000 and 2005 (Barnes 2007) and reveals that as a nation, Americans are becoming more sedentary. Such statistics give cause for alarm, especially if adults are the role models that children and adolescents emulate.

Along with many other agencies (schools, universities and colleges, health organizations), recreation agencies can help to increase the activity levels of their constituents, keeping in mind that as people age, their needs and interests change.

While much of the development preceding adulthood is progressive, the converse is true once adulthood is reached. As people get older, consideration must be given to the physical changes that accompany age and the injuries and health issues associated with aging. However, many of these issues can be alleviated by remaining physically active.

According to the *2008 Physical Activity Guidelines for Americans* (U.S. Department of Health and Human Services 2008), adults should get at least 150 minutes of moderate-intensity aerobic activity (walking briskly, performing water aerobics, bicycling, ballroom dancing, and so on) each week. In addition, they should perform muscle-strengthening activities that increase bone strength and muscular fitness two or more days a week. Older adults (65 years and older) should continue to participate in physical activity as their health allows. As always, appropriate progressions, equipment, and activities that align with the client's current fitness level and health goals must be considered.

The lifelong utilization stage of the specialized movement phase is an example of how everything should come together. Consider running, which is a fundamental motor skill that is used in a variety of childhood activities. Later it is also used in the specialized movement phase and is a major component of most sport-related activities (e.g., softball, basketball, tennis). Finally, during the specialized movement phase, running is an activity that people of all ages choose to participate in through turkey trots, 5Ks, and half and full marathons. For example, in 2005 Ginette Bedard completed a marathon with a time of 3:46:18. She was within six minutes of qualifying for the Boston Marathon in the 18- to 34-year-old division. However, Ginette was actually 72 years young when she posted this remarkable time (Haywood and Getchell 2009, 140). The sidebar on page 51 contains examples of programs that specifically target older adults.

**Table 3.1**    Physical Activity in the United States of Women and Men 18 to 65 Years of Age

| Activity | 2000 | 2005 |
| --- | --- | --- |
| Sitting | 36.8% | 39.9% |
| Walking | 49.8% | 48.1% |
| No participation in leisure-time physical activity | 38.5% | 40.0% |
| Regular participation in leisure-time physical activity | 31.2% | 29.7% |

By remaining physically active, older adults can alleviate some of the health and injury issues associated with aging.

## Programs for Older Adults

### Senior Softball

The town of Jupiter (Florida; Town of Jupiter Parks and Recreation 2004) runs a senior softball league for players 55 years and older. Minor adaptations for this league include the following:

- There are two bases at first base and at home plate so as to eliminate any contact between players.
- No sliding is allowed for runners going into bases, but a runner may slide back when attempting to return to a base.
- Only players who cannot run from the batter's box are allowed a designated runner from behind home plate. Players who need designated runners must be determined before the game. The designated runner is the last batter to make an out or the last batter who can run.

Local softball leagues like this one are common across North America. In addition, there are several associations such as Senior Softball USA and the International Senior Softball Association that hold state, national, and international tournaments for more than 1.5 million players a year (Senior Softball USA 2010).

### National Senior Games

The Summer National Senior Games are held during odd years. Participants 60 years and older must qualify at their state level to be eligible for the national level. Medal competition is held in archery, badminton, basketball, bowling, cycling, golf, horseshoes, race walking, racquetball, road racing, shuffleboard, softball, swimming, table tennis, tennis, track and field, triathlon, and volleyball. Demonstration sports include equestrian events, fencing, lawn bowling, rowing, sailing, soccer, and water polo. To make competition fair, the following age divisions apply to both men and women for all individual, doubles, and relay competitions: 60 to 64, 65 to 69, 70 to 74, 75 to 79, 80 to 84, 85 to 89, 90 to 94, 95 to 99, and 100 and older (National Senior Games Association 2009).

This chapter's discussion on the hourglass model of development is an abbreviated conversation. Entire classes exist on motor development, and only a brief amount of information has been shared in this chapter. As mentioned earlier, each of us progresses through our motor development on a highly individualized time frame. Motor development is age related but not age dependent. This means that the age ranges provided for each phase and stage of development (e.g., ages 2 to 7 for the fundamental movement phase) are meant only as guidelines. An individual's movements are based not only on age but also on the environment in which the person lives, the specific task to be completed, and heredity. The abbreviated information presented in this chapter is intended to introduce the recreation professional to the capabilities of a given age group and to the movement tasks that an age group may or may not be able to complete successfully.

## Applying Developmentally Appropriate Practices in Real-World Settings

When planning activities, the recreation leader needs to know what underlying movement abilities are needed as prerequisites to successful participation. It is not enough to just plan a tee-ball league for 6-year-olds, as success depends on what each 6-year-old brings to the field. Children who have had some instruction in physical education, ample practice opportunities outside of school, and continued instruction from the recreation leader more than likely will have a developmentally appropriate interaction. However, children who have not had basic instruction in tee-ball movement skills (e.g., throwing, catching, striking, and running) will have a different experience. Too often people treat young children like adults by designing and leading games for children the same way they would do so for adults. As indicated throughout this chapter, there are age guidelines describing the motor abilities of young children that should be observed. Very few children will become the next Annika Sörenstam, Peyton Manning, or Dot Richardson; the rest need dedicated leaders to help them enjoy their recreation pursuits.

When leading activities or coaching a sport, it is imperative to have an activity plan. An activity plan outlines what the leaders will do throughout the time they are with participants. The templates used by professionals vary; figure 3.2 is an example that is derived from Jordan (2007) and

follows her three phases of direct leadership—preparation, priming the group, and delivery. The preparation phase focuses on setting the stage to run activities. It requires knowledge of the group composition, the equipment needed, the goals and objectives, the risk management plan, and the necessary setup. Priming the group is getting the participants ready to begin the activity and dividing the participants into groups if needed. Lastly, delivery occurs as the activity plan is implemented. These three phases are covered in more depth in chapter 2.

This chapter discusses developmentally appropriate practices for different age groups. In order to gain a better understanding of how this applies to the recreation field and to planning activities, consider the activity plan template in figure 3.2 and the tips discussed in the following sections. Activity planning requires much thought about what will occur in the gym, on the playground, or on the playing field. Very few leaders are skilled enough to lead a group effectively by providing developmentally appropriate activities and leadership techniques without having a plan in front of them. The following sections provide tips for creating a solid activity plan that meets the needs of the participants.

### Preparation Information

The preparation information at the top of the activity plan provides details on the group you will be leading. This information helps you to better prepare activities for the group. Here are some tips to consider:

- Know the number of people in the group so you can estimate how many activities to plan. Small groups complete activities faster than large groups do.
- When working with large groups, provide more structure. Large groups need more structure than smaller groups require.
- Provide more structure for younger children. Younger groups need more structure than older groups need due to differences in cognitive development. Younger children are unable to process information the same way that older groups of children can.
- When working with children, never have a group that ranges in age from 5 to 10 years. The motor skill variation within this age range is enormous. If you have a group with such an age range, consider playing several games at once: one for 5- and 6-year-olds, one for 7- and 8-year-olds, and one for 9- and 10-year-olds.

## Preparation Information

Leaders: _____ Date: _____

Number of participants: _____ Ages of participants: _____

Theme of the day: _____

Equipment needed (include numbers of each):

| | | |
|---|---|---|
| _____ | _____ | _____ |
| _____ | _____ | _____ |
| _____ | _____ | _____ |

## Goals and Objectives

Describe or diagram the preactivity arrangement, including equipment placement:

| Time: | Attention getter and division of groups: | Leader: |
|---|---|---|
| Time: | Transition and division of groups: | Leader: |
| Time: | Activity 1: | Leader: |
| Time: | Transition and division of groups: | Leader: |
| Time: | Activity 2: | Leader: |
| Time: | Transition and division of groups: | Leader: |
| Time: | Activity 3: | Leader: |
| Time: | Transition and division of groups: | Leader: |
| Time: | Activity 4. | Leader: |
| | Closure: | |

**Figure 3.2** The activity plan is a way for leaders to ensure they are instituting developmentally appropriate practices and have a structure for delivering programs and activities to participants.

From A.R. Hurd and D.M. Anderson, 2011, *The park and recreation professional's handbook* (Champaign, IL: Human Kinetics).

- Allow the age range to dictate the way instructions to activities are given and the complexity of those instructions. The older the group, the more complex the instructions can be.
- Select developmentally appropriate equipment to help children be more successful. For example, use smaller soccer balls and smaller fields for younger players. Lower the basketball hoops and use baseball tees to enhance the quality of the experience by increasing the chances of success.

## Goals and Objectives

Establish goals and objectives that are realistically achievable for the age group with which you are working. Goals and objectives should be written according to the format discussed in chapter 2. The objectives should address audience, behavior, condition, and degree.

## Equipment Arrangement

Think about the composition of the group when placing equipment around the room. How likely are the participants to pick up and play with the equipment? Consider the participants' coordination and the likelihood of the group members stepping on equipment even if it is off to the side of the gym.

## Division of Groups

Larger groups often need to be broken into smaller ones to participate in many activities. In addition to planning how to divide participants into groups, you should know how you will get the attention of the participants.

First, identify the game or sport to be played. Next, divide participants into groups. Avoid selecting captains or choosing teams because they work against less-skilled players. Dividing by gender or standing on a line and counting off is also discouraged because doing so can create competitiveness and cause children to shuffle on the line to ensure they get to be on their friend's team. These methods are disadvantageous to less-skilled players. Being the last one chosen or the player no one wants is not conducive to building self-esteem.

## Transitions

The transitional aspect of the activity plan moves participants from one activity to the next and sets up the next activity to be played. How will you explain the tasks to your group? The way instructions should be given is part of activity planning.

- Consider whether the participants can see from where they are located. The leader should be the one looking into the sun.
- If the group is younger and quite active, holding their attention long enough to give instructions can be a challenge. Consider where the group is placed during this time. Lining participants against the wall, making them sit in a semicircle, moving to the corner of the room, or having the participants stand on a carpet square or hot spot can enhance their ability to focus.

## Planning Transitions on a Kayaking Trip

When considering how to plan transitions, consider this example of a one-day kayaking experience for community residents. The leader learns that the majority of the group members have never kayaked before. How might the leader respond?

- A good leader would demonstrate how to get in and out of the kayak, how to hold the paddles, how to steer the kayak, and, most importantly, how to travel safely when out on the water.
- A poorer leader would meet the participants, obtain their waiver information, secure their equipment requests, and then dismiss them until the class meets the next day for the kayaking experience.
- An even poorer leader would permit the group members, even those with no previous experience, to get into the water with their boats and take off on their own.

Before conducting swimming lessons, the recreation leader should make an activity plan for using equipment, dividing the class into small groups, following a progression of movement activities, and other factors.

- Give instructions and then distribute equipment. Giving children equipment such as a pool noodle or a scooter before explaining the activity results in chaos because interest is diverted to the equipment rather than to the leader. Do not get caught thinking that this applies to children only. Adults can be quite guilty themselves of being distracted by equipment.
- Plan transitions to minimize downtime. Downtime results in boredom, and boredom can lead to behavior management issues.

## Activity Selection

Activity selection is the fun and creative aspect of recreation leadership. Selecting the right activities increases the chance of success for both the participants and you.

- When selecting activities consider what movement skills the participants need in order to be successful and whether or not they have these skills.
- Consider what you will teach the participants and the progression you will follow. When planning movement activities, you should develop progressions regardless of the activity. A progression is a series of movement experiences that move from simple to complex.
- Consider what basic skills you need as the leader. Can you physically demonstrate what you want your participants to do? Physical demonstrations, especially for younger participants, are a necessity.
- Consider whether what you are asking participants to complete is developmentally appropriate. Are participants physically and cognitively able to understand what you are asking them to do? For instance, explaining player-to-player defense when leading a group of 5-year-olds in a basketball game is developmentally inappropriate. Five-year-olds do not have the physical skills to remain with their opponent or the cognitive abilities to understand this strategy.
- Consider how you can modify the activity so that all participants are involved and active. Just because a game or activity has rules does not mean you cannot modify the rules so that everyone can participate. Again, eliminate the elimination. In order for participants to improve their motor abilities, they need to practice. If you

remove participants from the game or activity because they cannot play the game the way it is being played, they will never improve.

- Consider the effects of the game on the participant. A game such as dodgeball requires participants to throw balls at other participants. This type of activity is inappropriate for children. Adults can make the decision to participate, but children are not able to make that choice.

- Select activities that are appropriate for the number of players. Playing a game of Wiffle ball with 30 people ensures that some players will stand around and not participate.

- Do not be afraid to modify activities as they are being played so that they match the skill of the group. To increase or decrease the challenge of an activity, you can make the playing space smaller or larger, change the size or amount of equipment used, increase the duration of play, institute repetitions to build skill, or change the rules to better the activity.

## Closure

Plan the closure so that the participants quit while they are still having fun. This leaves them with a positive attitude toward the activity.

## Conclusion

Through special events, programs, and sport leagues, the recreation professional is responsible for planning and implementing activities that are developmentally appropriate for participants. By incorporating a developmentally appropriate philosophy, professionals provide participants with the opportunity for success, a lifelong affiliation with parks and recreation programs, and a commitment to being physically active for a lifetime. The model for motor development outlined in this chapter explains how people change physically as they age. These stages of physical development affect programs in terms of planning appropriate activities and establishing sequencing patterns that provide the correct level of challenge and skill development to make the activity a positive leisure experience.

## Review Questions

1. What does motor development have to do with recreation?
2. Define developmentally appropriate practice. Why is knowledge of it necessary in leisure services?
3. Define the three learning domains people experience in leisure and other new activities.
4. Define and give an example of each of the three categories of fundamental motor skills.
5. Describe the four phases of Gallahue's model of motor development.
6. Give an overview of the health status (e.g., obesity rates) of Americans today.
7. What are the contents of an activity plan?

Visit the online resource at www.HumanKinetics.com/TheParkAndRecreationProfessionalsHandbook for sample documents, keywords, activities and assignments, and more.

# chapter 4

# Evaluation and Assessment

## OUTCOMES

- Understand the eight steps of evaluation.

- Understand the purpose of needs assessments and how they can be utilized in a leisure services agency.

- Describe different methods of data collection for evaluations and needs assessments.

- Define qualitative and quantitative data and provide examples of each.

- Describe different types of evaluation models that can be used for recreation programs and facilities.

- Understand the process for developing an evaluation report, including the types of information that should be included.

Research, often referred to as *assessment* and *evaluation* within the recreation field, is at the heart of ensuring that an agency meets the recreation needs of its community as well as advances the role that recreation can play in addressing problems within society. Whereas an assessment, particularly a needs assessment, may be more future oriented with respect to the needs of the community, an **evaluation** tends to focus on both newly designed and older programs and how well they produce the desired outcomes. This chapter outlines the various tasks involved with conducting research, including evaluations and needs assessments, and focuses particularly on types of data, data collection, and evaluation models.

# Evaluation Steps

Blankenship (2010) outlined eight steps to conducting research: identify the problem; review the related literature; clarify (focus) the problem; define relevant terms and concepts; define the population from which data will be collected; develop an instrumentation plan, commonly known as the *methodology;* collect the data; and, finally, analyze the data. The terms *research* and *evaluation* are largely one and the same, and thus the processes listed here are important to both, though some of the steps in an evaluation may be more truncated (e.g., a federally funded research project might have pages and pages dedicated to theory and literature review compared with a program evaluation report).

The eight steps Blankenship outlined are described in more detail in the following sections. Figure 4.1 provides a visual representation of the steps.

## Step 1: Identify the Problem

The researcher or evaluator must determine the problem that needs to be addressed. For example, a programmer for youth recreation programs may be concerned with rising rates of childhood obesity—in this case, childhood obesity is the problem.

## Step 2: Review the Literature

A thorough review of the literature helps the researcher better understand the topic under investigation. For example, a review of the literature related to childhood obesity can help the programmer gain a better understanding of how to develop programs that more effectively address obesity issues for the agency's after-school programs. Research findings can outline effective programs from the past that the programmer may be able to implement through program adaptations. The literature also provides information on how to best evaluate the effects of those adaptations.

## Step 3: Clarify the Problem

In step 3 the researcher focuses the problem so that it is more feasible to measure. For instance, childhood obesity on the national level is far too large a problem for the youth recreation programmer to tackle. However, setting up an after-school activity to get children to be more active is doable. Therefore, the programmer may decide to test whether children who participate in a 20-minute jump rope program three times a week after school improve their health. The clarified problem is also known as a *purpose statement:* The purpose of this program is to determine whether a 20-minute jump rope program three times a week will improve a child's health.

## Step 4: Define Terms and Concepts

It is typical to see the terms and concepts relevant to a research project clearly spelled out in research journal articles or reports. However, this step is also important to the youth recreation programmer who presents findings only to other staff members or supervisors. The researcher needs to complete this step before writing any type of report *after* the research or evaluation has been finished, and the program developer or evaluator should complete this step before the program starts so that everyone involved with the program and evaluation is on the same page. One example of a concept that needs defining is the "20-minute jump rope program." The programmer must clearly explain this concept so that everyone involved knows what constitutes 20 minutes—is it an active 20 minutes or does that 20 minutes involve some resting? Without this type of clarification, the findings are not as useful because the data are not necessarily valid.

## Step 5: Define the Population

The population is the group from which the researcher collects the data. Typically the evaluator investigates a subsample of the population, not the entire population. For example, a researcher who wants to know if an after-school jump rope program can help all school-age children will likely not study all school-age children in the program if the agency has a large program with numerous after-school sites; the researcher will most likely choose a smaller sample within the program until there is a clearer picture of the program's effectiveness. However, defining the larger population allows the researcher to remain focused on the group for whom the results may be applicable. In addition, if the researcher has a clear sense of who his population is, he can choose a sample that is representative of the population, thus increasing the odds that generalizing the results beyond the smaller sample is appropriate. Defining the population also makes the project more manageable as it limits the groups of people to whom the project is applicable, thereby limiting the number of demographic variables that the researcher needs to take into consideration.

## Step 6: Develop an Instrumentation Plan

The instrumentation plan, or methodology, is the road map for every step the researcher must take to carry out the project. The plan outlines a representative sample of the population; describes what data the researcher will collect, including when and how the data will be collected; and explains how the data will be analyzed. Therefore, in our jump rope program example, the sample may be the children participating at one of five sites where the after-school program is being offered. The survey data may be collected before and after the program in anticipation of a paired statistical analysis being conducted to determine if there are significant differences on health-related items that may be attributed to the program.

## Step 7: Collect the Data

Data collection takes place after the instrumentation plan is developed. The researcher may collect data through a variety of methods, including surveys, interviews, and observations. The instrumentation plan outlines when and how data collection will occur. In our jump rope program example, the programmer may issue pre- and post-program surveys asking students about relevant health measures and also hold focus groups with the participants to ask them about their participation and health.

## Step 8: Analyze the Data

After collecting the data, the researcher analyzes the data in order to answer the problem identified in step 3 (e.g., does participation in a 20-minute

jump rope program three times a week have a positive effect on children's overall health?). Data analysis of all the collected data allows the researcher to answer the question created for the program. If the researcher has rigorously followed the eight evaluation steps and used an appropriate implementation plan, the programmer may be able to apply the findings to the other four after-school jump rope programs.

## Additional Considerations

As mentioned, leisure services professionals commonly refer to *research* as *evaluation* because the primary problem is usually to determine whether a program, facility, or service is meeting participants' needs or producing intended outcomes. An evaluation connotes appraisal more than investigation. Again, the eight evaluation steps outlined by Blankenship are highly relevant to both research and evaluation, but appraisal of programs, services, and facilities is the primary purpose of most measurement in

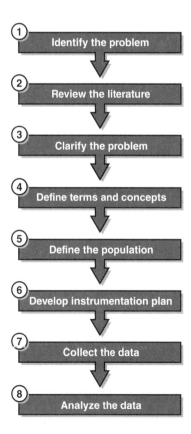

**Figure 4.1** The eight-step evaluation process provides guidelines for completing a useful evaluation of a program.

Based on Blankenship 2010.

Focus groups and public meetings are both effective ways to gain community members' input.

the recreation field. Additional factors must be considered when evaluating programs, services, and facilities.

### Formative and Summative

It is important to identify whether evaluations will be formative or summative or both; the answer to this can be included in the implementation plan. A **formative evaluation** provides evaluative feedback on a program while it is ongoing, and so the programmer can use the information from a formative evaluation to improve a program before it concludes. Thus formative evaluations allow programs to be adapted midstream and allow an agency to improve a program before the end rather than having to wait until the end. Nothing is worse than finding out what went well or poorly when it is too late to make reasonable changes and having to wait to make changes until the next time the program is offered.

A **summative evaluation** summarizes how a program performed. For instance, did the program meet its goals and objectives? The summative evaluation is conducted at the end of a program and focuses on what the program produced and what expectations the program met. This type of evaluation is concerned with questions that a programmer often cannot answer until the program has concluded. Often it is not a choice of using one evaluation or the other, as both have their place in most programs. The evaluation questions that

the evaluator asks in each will, however, likely be different, and the audience may differ as well.

### Reliable and Valid

Regardless of the purpose of the evaluation, all forms of assessment require **reliability** and **validity.** Data are reliable when the technique used to collect the data yields the same information repeatedly; reliability describes the consistency of the data. Certainly, asking people information about which they have some knowledge is one way to help ensure reliability. Validity refers to whether the data measure what they purport to be measuring, whether the data are a true measurement of a concept, attitude, or preference and a true representation of reality. An agency that makes decisions based on invalid or unreliable data may find itself with new programs or facilities that people do not want.

Data that are reliable are not necessarily valid—if a measurement is inaccurate, it can produce consistent results that are not necessarily correct. If data are valid, however, by definition they are also reliable. When a researcher takes the proper steps in data collection, the agency can be more confident that the data collected are valid and reliable. Without this confidence, an agency is hard pressed to make programming and development decisions with any degree of certainty that the decisions represent the community's needs or the participants' opinions.

# Models of Evaluation

There are a number of evaluation models that an agency may use. Again, the purpose of the evaluation should be of utmost consideration when choosing how to conduct an evaluation. That is, when choosing the evaluation model, the evaluator must always tie the model to the overall problem of the evaluation. For example, an importance–performance evaluation allows program personnel to identify gaps in services that are important to participants and is the ideal model if the purpose of the evaluation is to determine whether a program meets participants' expectations. While a satisfaction survey provides data on how happy participants are with a program or facility, it often does not collect data on what is most important to the participants or why. Certainly satisfaction data are important, but if the agency desires to know what areas are most important to its patrons, it needs to take the data collection a step further.

The following are descriptions of various evaluation models. In addition, the purpose of each is outlined so that researchers and evaluators can better determine the best match for the purposes of a given assessment.

## Importance–Performance Evaluation

Importance–performance analysis is used to measure the worth of an agency's performance with respect to program and facility attributes. These attributes may include friendliness of staff, knowledge of staff, equipment, cleanliness, and other variables of interest. Measurement of worth is based on participants' perceptions of how important each attribute is as well as perceptions of how well the agency provides each attribute. The importance score and performance score for each attribute are then compared and placed on a matrix divided into four categories labeled "Concentrate here," where importance is high and performance is low; "Keep up the good work," where importance and performance are both high; "Possible overkill," where importance is low but performance is high; and "Low priority," where both importance and performance are low. The midpoint that divides the matrix into the four sectors is typically the location where the midpoints of the measurement scales used to determine importance and performance cross. For example, if the evaluator uses a five-point scale ranging from "Strongly agree" to "Strongly disagree," then 3 is the midpoint of that scale. In some instances it is more helpful to use the

mean scores of the two data sets rather than the midpoints of the scales, as data can often be overinflated, meaning that participants tend to be more positive than negative. Thus if the midpoints of the scales are used to create the midpoint of the matrix, much of the data end up falling into the "Keep up the good work" quadrant, and the agency receives little direction for improvement when often improvement is warranted, as nothing is ever perfect (Rossman and Schlatter 2008).

Figure 4.2 provides an example of an importance–performance matrix created from data collected for an evaluation of a youth soccer program. Items are rated on a seven-point scale. As you can see, the agency seems to be doing an outstanding job with its equipment and fields. It is also doing a good job with concessions; however, given the importance of concessions to the participants, it is perhaps spending too much time and effort on this aspect of the program. On the other hand, both coaching and officiating fell into the "Concentrate here" quadrant, suggesting that these are areas for improvement. As with all types of evaluation, the variables being measured must be ones about which the participants can make a knowledgeable judgment.

## Satisfaction-Based Evaluation

The purpose of the satisfaction-based evaluation is to measure the different potential outcomes of leisure engagement. The potential outcomes are tied to 10 identified domains of satisfaction,

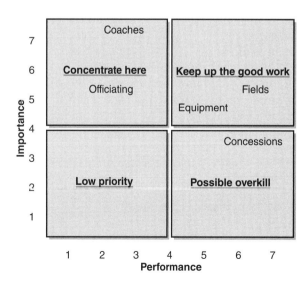

**Figure 4.2** An importance–performance evaluation for a youth soccer league can provide programmers feedback on where they need to focus their attention to improve the program.

including achievement, physical fitness, social enjoyment, family escape, environment, risk, family togetherness, relaxation, fun, and autonomy (Rossman 1983; Rossman and Schlatter 2008, 387). While not all of the domains are relevant to every type of recreation experience, for those domains that are relevant the satisfaction-based evaluation provides an idea of whether the program helped the participants engage in a satisfying leisure experience. Research indicates that participant satisfaction with a program is tied to the provision of a leisure experience, and therefore measurement of the satisfaction domain can help programmers know whether their participants are experiencing leisure engagement. For example, an item that measures achievement might ask participants how satisfied they were by opportunities to learn new things or develop new skills, while an item measuring relaxation might assess satisfaction for the opportunity to relax or de-stress. Figure 4.3 lists items that can be used to measure a variety of domains of satisfaction with a recreation program.

## Service Hour Evaluation

Service hour evaluation is primarily concerned with output—how many people are being served and to what extent. For example, an after-school program that serves 40 children for 2 hours a day has a daily service hour measurement of 80. The meaning and implications of this number are tied to the context and goals of the program. This measurement examines not only how many people are participating but also how much time they are spending participating. Thus the service hour evaluation provides a measurement of the amount of service that the agency provides the community. One purpose of the service hour measurement is to determine ways in which to improve organizational management: Does the input-to-output ratio show efficiency in programming, and if it does, does it do so in the course of providing quality programming?

For a service hour measurement to give a more complete picture of how well the agency is serving the public, the evaluator must look at the outputs for specific variables such as participant age, program area, program format, participant gender, geographic location, activity, operating division, ethnic background of participants, program fee, and special populations. Through these data the agency gains a very concrete and quantitative picture of how widely the community is utilizing its services and how much service it is providing.

## Goals and Objectives (Process) Evaluation

A goals and objectives evaluation, or process evaluation, compares the plan of a program with the actual operation or outcome of the program. Was the program run in such a way that it met its goals and outcomes? Were the processes that were designed to facilitate the successful realization of the outlined goals and objectives actually carried through? If they were not carried through, then it should not be surprising if the goals and objectives fell short.

According to Rossman and Schlatter (2008), the goals and objectives evaluation examines the program design (inputs and resources, animation process, and desired goals and outcomes) together with the program operation (actual inputs and resources, actual animation process, and observed outcomes) to determine if there is congruence. Inputs and resources are items such as staffing, supplies, budget support, and facilities. The animation process is how the programmer puts the program components into motion. For example, if the program is a round-robin tournament, how is it structured and how should it take place? Once the tournament began, did all teams play each other, or did something prevent that from occurring? Desired outcomes encompass planned expectations for the program and are what participants should experience as a result of participating in a program. In some instances a desired outcome may be as simple as "Have fun," while other outcomes may be more detailed, such as "Increase cardiorespiratory fitness."

In order for an agency to use the goals and objectives evaluation model, the programmer must write clear goals and objectives for the evaluated program, as those are what the agency ultimately uses to determine whether the program is effective. If there are discrepancies between the program goals and objectives and the program outcomes, the agency can examine two primary areas to determine what produced the discrepancies: program inputs or unrealistic program expectations. Chapter 2 provides a detailed description on writing quality goals and objectives.

## Triangulation

Much of the time, one form of evaluation cannot tell the entire story of the success of a program. **Triangulation** involves combining different types of evaluation in order to attain data from different

# Evaluation of Satisfaction

Below you will find elements that may or may not lead to satisfaction in the program in which you participated. Please circle the number that best represents your level of satisfaction with each item listed.

| | Very Satisfying | Satisfying | Not Satisfying | | Not Applicable |
|---|---|---|---|---|---|
| **Achievement** | | | | | |
| New things learned in the program | 5 | 4 | 3 | 2 | 1 | 0 |
| New skills developed | 5 | 4 | 3 | 2 | 1 | 0 |
| Accomplishments resulting from the program | 5 | 4 | 3 | 2 | 1 | 0 |
| **Physical Fitness** | | | | | |
| Physical activity involved in the program | 5 | 4 | 3 | 2 | 1 | 0 |
| Health benefits of the program | 5 | 4 | 3 | 2 | 1 | 0 |
| **Social Enjoyment** | | | | | |
| Meeting new people | 5 | 4 | 3 | 2 | 1 | 0 |
| Participating with friends | 5 | 4 | 3 | 2 | 1 | 0 |
| **Family Escape** | | | | | |
| Opportunity to get away from family | 5 | 4 | 3 | 2 | 1 | 0 |
| Opportunity to spend time with family | 5 | 4 | 3 | 2 | 1 | 0 |
| **Environment** | | | | | |
| Location of the facility | 5 | 4 | 3 | 2 | 1 | 0 |
| Aesthetics of the location | 5 | 4 | 3 | 2 | 1 | 0 |
| **Risk** | | | | | |
| The level of risk involved | 5 | 4 | 3 | 2 | 1 | 0 |
| The physical challenge of the program | 5 | 4 | 3 | 2 | 1 | 0 |
| **Family Togetherness** | | | | | |
| Opportunity to participate as a family | 5 | 4 | 3 | 2 | 1 | 0 |
| **Relaxation** | | | | | |
| Opportunity to relax | 5 | 4 | 3 | 2 | 1 | 0 |
| Opportunity to de-stress | 5 | 4 | 3 | 2 | 1 | 0 |
| Opportunity to escape from work or school | 5 | 4 | 3 | 2 | 1 | 0 |
| **Fun** | | | | | |
| Opportunity to experience enjoyment | 5 | 4 | 3 | 2 | 1 | 0 |
| Have fun | 5 | 4 | 3 | 2 | 1 | 0 |
| **Autonomy** | | | | | |
| Freedom to control the situation | 5 | 4 | 3 | 2 | 1 | 0 |
| Choose my own level of participation or involvement | 5 | 4 | 3 | 2 | 1 | 0 |
| Be on my own | 5 | 4 | 3 | 2 | 1 | 0 |

**Figure 4.3** A satisfaction-based evaluation provides feedback on satisfaction levels of participants related to numerous leisure domains.

From A.R. Hurd and D.M. Anderson, 2011, *The park and recreation professional's handbook* (Champaign, IL: Human Kinetics).

perspectives. For example, it might utilizing a focus group and interview, a survey, and a suggestion box. It may also mean using an importance–performance survey along with a process evaluation. Triangulation allows an agency to gain a much clearer understanding of program success, because it involves collecting data in different formats from different perspectives. In addition, a program supervisor can use the triangulated data to test conclusions drawn from the data by looking for verification and discrepancy among the different data sets. These different perspectives help ensure that the decision made regarding the future of a program—whether the decision is to drop, modify, or continue with the program—is that much more valid.

## Needs Assessments

Needs assessments are a specific type of evaluation designed to gain input and ideas from the public as well as get public reactions to issues affecting the community. The assessor can use any of the data collection methods already outlined for this purpose. A needs assessment can have multiple purposes, including determination of satisfaction of quantity, quality, and management of parks, programs, and facilities. Other purposes include determining usage rates, determining acceptable rates of funding (taxes, fees, and so on), identifying a community's interest in future programming and facilities, determining how effective the agency is at communication, identifying how well registration procedures work, gathering community demographic information, identifying reasons for nonuse, and identifying needs for new programs and facilities.

For example, the YMCA gathers input from its members and the community when deciding to build a new facility, expand a current facility, or develop new programs. Specifically, the Armed Services YMCA of San Diego (ASYMCASD) received a grant to conduct a needs assessment. To gather the information for the assessment, the ASYMCASD and consultants inventoried the offerings of the ASYMCASD, met with focus groups of the target population, developed a survey, and interviewed 27 leaders of the community from health care, housing, military, family, and child support groups. The ASYMCASD's purpose for the assessment was to evaluate the effectiveness of teen and family programs and to determine concerns that current or future programs could address (Merrick and Steffens 2008).

A needs assessment can often be mistaken for a wants assessment. It is important to keep in mind the expectations that the needs assessment may cultivate. Community members may assume that if they indicate on the assessment that they want a service or program, then the agency will provide that service or program. Therefore, it is important to make sure that unrealistic expectations are not an outcome of the needs assessment.

# Types of Data

An evaluator can collect two types of data for an evaluation: qualitative and quantitative. At the most basic distinction, qualitative data are narrative, or words, while quantitative data are numerical, or numbers. Both types of data can be collected in different formats, and both have their strengths and weaknesses. It is often in the best interest of an agency to collect both types. The purpose and related questions of an assessment should dictate what types of data are collected. In addition, the perceptions of relevant stakeholders on the validity of hard numbers versus soft words may influence the acceptability of different types of data.

## Qualitative Data

**Qualitative data** are nonnumerical and are typically expressed in narratives or descriptions. Qualitative data can lend richer meaning to evaluative data, as they are much better than a numerical rating at telling the story of someone's experience. An evaluator can collect qualitative data to understand the meanings that people attach to things or to understand the reasoning behind their thoughts and opinions (Henderson 2006). Qualitative data can get at the why question because, unlike most survey data, which tend to be quantitative, it allows for questions that follow up on participant ideas. Face-to-face qualitative data collection procedures such as interviews and focus groups also allow the evaluator to ensure that participants are interpreting questions correctly because the participant can ask for clarification on questions (whether written or spoken). Thus the evaluator can ensure greater accuracy, or validity, in data collection. The interpretation of questions in quantitative data collection techniques such as mailed or online surveys, on the other hand, typically relies solely on the reader; there is no opportunity for a person sitting at home to ask for clarification. This may lead to data that are less valid if questions are misunderstood.

A drawback of qualitative data is that board members, others in higher management, and even the public may be hesitant to accept non-numerical data as valid indicators of an agency's performance. For many people, numbers speak volumes. They view quantitative data, correctly or incorrectly, as providing a completely objective viewpoint of a situation, not allowing for systematic errors that may arise when evaluators interpret data incorrectly because they are using something other than a computer for analysis (such as a human, which is the case with qualitative data). Incorrect interpretation on the part of the evaluator is referred to as *evaluator bias* (Babbie 2009). People also have the somewhat misguided belief that numbers don't lie—yet an evaluator using quantitative data still controls which data to respond to, and systematic errors in interpretation as well as data collection can also lead to evaluator bias. In addition, in certain instances an evaluator can present qualitative data numerically and thus has the opportunity to obtain the richness of qualitative data while also presenting hard numerical data. For example, the evaluator may ask focus group participants if they would be willing to support a bond referendum to build a new facility and then to explain why or why not. The quantitative data would be the number of participants who say *yes* versus *no,* while the qualitative data would be the explanations why or why not.

Another thing to keep in mind when collecting qualitative data is that qualitative data allow the evaluator to collect nonverbal data, as typically data collection is face to face. On the other hand, coordinating this type of data collection (e.g., interviews, focus groups) can be very time consuming, because the evaluator must work around people's busy schedules. Figure 4.4 provides an example of survey questions that Portland (Maine) asks when evaluating Camp Play All Day. Questions 1 through 5 produce quantitative data, while the final question provides qualitative feedback.

Certainly, misinterpretation of data is possible with qualitative data analysis. The person collecting and analyzing the data should be skilled in working with qualitative data. Analyzing qualitative data takes a different skill set, and often more time, than working with numbers requires. Another challenge of qualitative data is that generalizing results to larger groups is trickier than it might be with quantitative data. While there are statistical parameters that allow an evaluator to generalize quantitative data to larger groups with

Surveys can be used to collect data for a number of evaluation models.

predetermined accuracy according to population size and sample size, there is no statistical analysis that provides that same type of accuracy for generalizing qualitative data. However, if data are collected from participants who provide a representative sample of the community, some generalization is appropriate, especially if it is supported by quantitative (triangulated) data and is collected as part of a well-designed evaluation project (Henderson 2006).

## Quantitative Data

**Quantitative data,** or numerical data, have their own advantages and disadvantages, some of which have already been alluded to in the discussion on qualitative data. As mentioned, certain people are more comfortable with conclusions based on numbers—they view quantitative data as being more scientific and easier to sell to the public. Numerical data indeed can be more generalizable and can be easier to report and interpret. Quantitative data are more generalizable if an evaluator draws an appropriately sized random sample from the population. A random sample is one where the probability of each individual selected to be included in the sample is equal. This kind of sample is more likely to be representative of the larger population because it reduces the potential for bias in sampling. If an evaluator draws a representative random sample, statistical analysis can be used to make generalizations onto the larger population with a predetermined level of accuracy. The sample survey in figure 4.4 is one that a programmer might use to produce

### City of Portland Department of Recreation Summer Day Camp Evaluation

Please take a moment to fill out this evaluation form by circling the number that best describes your level of satisfaction for each of the listed issues. Please return the completed survey to the Portland Recreation Department, 134 Congress Street, Suite 2, Portland, Maine 04101. Thank you!

### Camp Name: Camp Play All Day, Summer 2009

|  | Unsatisfactory |  |  |  |  |  | Satisfactory |  |  |  |
|---|---|---|---|---|---|---|---|---|---|---|
| 1. Overall quality of the program: | 1 | 2 | 3 | 4 | 5 | 6 | 7 | 8 | 9 | 10 |
| 2. Camp counselors: | 1 | 2 | 3 | 4 | 5 | 6 | 7 | 8 | 9 | 10 |
| 3. Camp leaders: | 1 | 2 | 3 | 4 | 5 | 6 | 7 | 8 | 9 | 10 |
| 4. On-site activities: | 1 | 2 | 3 | 4 | 5 | 6 | 7 | 8 | 9 | 10 |
| 5. Field trips: | 1 | 2 | 3 | 4 | 5 | 6 | 7 | 8 | 9 | 10 |

We value your opinions! Do you have suggestions for next year? Do you have specific comments about this year? We'd like to know them:

_____

_____

_____

_____

_____

_____

_____

_____

_____

_____

_____

_____

_____

_____

_____

_____

_____

Name: _____    Phone number: _____

**Figure 4.4** This example summer day camp evaluation from the City of Portland illustrates how both quantitative and qualitative data can be collected through the use of a survey.

From City of Portland, Maine, Department of Recreation.

quantitative data by applying the Likert scale to satisfaction questions.

However, as mentioned earlier, quantitative data often leave unanswered questions. For example, when used as the sole method of data collection, such as with surveys, quantitative data collection typically does not allow for clarification of questions, particularly when questions are mailed or distributed online. In addition, quantitative data collected via surveys, which is typical, are biased with respect to who completes the instrument—for example, data collected within populations with high rates of illiteracy certainly miss out on a segment of the population. Surveys mailed to lower-income families who feel that they won't be listened to and do not complete the survey also miss out on a population segment. Potential respondents may also perceive a survey as impersonal and thus easier to ignore or to refuse to complete.

# Data Collection

Regardless of the purpose, conducting an evaluation as well as an effective needs assessment can be a challenge. Good data are key to usable assessments. In determining how data should be collected, there are a number of things to consider, including budget, staffing, purpose, audience, stakeholders, and evaluation model. There are several ways to collect data; the way in which the evaluator implements these methods dictates the validity and reliability of the data.

## Data Collection Methods

Data collection techniques are varied and often incorporate both qualitative and quantitative data. As mentioned earlier, the specific techniques chosen depend on a number of factors relevant to the assessment or evaluation, particularly the overall purpose or problem that the evaluation is addressing. Other considerations include population age, population reading level, location of data collection (e.g., a focus group may not be feasible or desirable at a street fair), and cost. Regardless of the collection technique chosen, the evaluator must give the choice a great deal of thought in order to ensure that usable data are collected. If an agency does not have a well-formed purpose in mind for the data, then the data may end up serving no purpose despite the expense entailed in the data collection. For example, if it is not clear that the purpose of the data collection is to ascertain

the public's willingness to pay for programs, the evaluator may inadvertently exclude questions related to pricing from the data collection. From citizen advisory committees to online surveys, there are a multitude of data collection techniques that an evaluator can use with great success when applying them correctly.

## Citizen Advisory Committees

One way to collect data is through citizen advisory committees, although input is limited to a select part of the population. Citizen advisory committees include community members who are interested in giving feedback to the leisure services agency with respect to programming, parks, and related topic areas. Ideally the committee members are representative of the community's population. As you might imagine, self-selection into the data collection process can have the drawback of inducing bias. For this reason an agency would likely want additional forms of data collection, particularly on topics that have broad public implications.

## Public Meetings and Focus Groups

Two additional ways to collect data are public meetings and focus groups. During a public meeting, the agency presents its plans to attendees and solicits comments from those present. Thus when holding a public meeting, the agency already has a pretty good idea of actions that it plans to take. Focus groups are a similar method for collecting data. In some instances an agency invites specific community members to join the group because they have a strong interest in a particular topic, represent a portion of the community, or have an expertise that is critical to the data collection process. In other instances the focus group is more like a public meeting and there is an open call for participants so that everyone in the community feels they have the opportunity to voice their opinions. Typically the focus group meeting is an open-ended series of questions related to community needs rather than a presentation of plans followed by input.

Focus groups generally are limited in size to 8 to 15 participants. Because focus groups involve greater sharing of information in response to the facilitator's questions, having a smaller number of participants makes the process more manageable. A note taker is also necessary in order to retain a thorough record of the conversation that takes place during the focus group meeting. A public meeting typically is not limited in size. Again,

An effective public meeting will often use a moderator to ensure equitable participation among attendees.

it is held to provide information to participants, who are then given a limited amount of time for sharing their comments.

The nominal group technique is used to increase participation when an agency wants to utilize more-structured focus groups. The technique gives everyone a voice during the process and can help reduce the propensity for a small but vocal group of individuals to dominate the conversation. There are six steps to this technique:

1. Select participants
2. Have individuals brainstorm ideas in response to a topic
3. Go around the table and have everyone list their ideas
4. Have individuals rank the top five priorities from the larger list
5. Tabulate the overall ranks
6. Discuss the ideas within the context of the rankings

At the conclusion, the agency should have a short list of priorities with respect to the purpose of the focus group (Siegenthaler and Riley 2002). For example, an agency may use the nominal group technique to determine the public's need for new youth programming. Participants invited into the focus group may include youths, parents, athletic association representatives, and school

representatives. Their answers to an overall question regarding youth programming as provided by the parks and recreation give the agency public input as to what its priority should be for new program development.

## Interviews and Key Informants

Interviews are another way to collect qualitative data. Unlike focus groups, interviews use a one-on-one format. Some agencies collect quantitative data during an interview; in this case they are simply collecting survey data by having interviewers ask questions verbally rather than by having the participant complete a written or online survey. Qualitative-oriented interviewing often includes more open-ended questions that are seeking in-depth discussion of the topic (Henderson 2006). Interviews typically are limited to individuals with a specialized knowledge or with a position where it is important that their answers are given heavier consideration. These interviewees are also known as *key informants*. Examples of potential interviewees might be city council members, agency staff members, and other administrators (Siegenthaler and Riley 2002).

## Surveys

Surveys are by far one of the most popular forms of data collection. This is particularly true for program evaluation, although surveys are certainly used a great deal in conducting needs assessments. An agency needs to determine the purpose of the evaluation in order to best develop a survey. While many surveys are merely a descriptive measurement of a program, service, or facility, others utilize well-developed, valid, and reliable measurement tools that allow the evaluator to collect data that more deeply measure the effect programs have on participants. Instruments that allow an evaluator to go beyond descriptive data collection include preference scales, rating scales, and instruments tied to program outcomes such as self-esteem, efficacy, and identity development.

Using surveys to pre- and posttest program participants can be especially fruitful if the agency is trying to gauge the effects a program has on a desired outcome. Surveys are popular because they are relatively easy to put together (depending on what type of data are to be gathered) and they do not require as much people power, particularly when they are Web based. Today agencies have the option of collecting survey data via paper copies or via low-cost, commercially available Web-based products such as SurveyMonkey or Zoomerang (see sidebar below).

However, because it may be difficult to reach certain community members, such as those living in lower-income areas, through electronic surveys, many agencies continue to provide a paper-based option in order to reduce bias in data collection. While agencies may prefer to have surveys mailed to residents, the necessity for follow-up mailings combined with postage-paid envelopes can quickly turn this method into a costly one. A lower-cost alternative may be to have locations throughout the community where surveys are distributed and collected. However, this process may also introduce bias, as it may eliminate people who are not active throughout the community and who would not complete a survey unless it was mailed to them. However, the cost savings can outweigh this drawback even more if the agency is careful to be geographically diverse when making the survey available, not limiting pickup and drop-off points to agency facilities but also including alternative locations such as the public library or the post office as permitted.

While the survey content should tie into the purpose of the evaluation or needs assessment, there are some general sections that most surveys include, particularly a section for collecting demographic data. It is useful, when compiling the final data, to have a picture of who responded

## So Easy a Monkey Could Do It?

For most agencies, gone are the days when surveys came in a single form—the standard paper-and-pencil survey. Back in those days often hundreds of surveys would go out and only a few completed ones would trickle back in. The related costs were staggering, and after factoring in printing costs, paper costs, and, most importantly, postage costs, the return on investment often came up short. Enter today's world of the online survey. Whether we have used them, we all have seen them. Once in awhile we might complete a customer satisfaction survey or a marketing survey in the hopes of winning a prize, whether it be a coupon or cold, hard cash. Given the variety of low-cost and sometimes free online surveys available today, an agency can save a great deal of money when evaluating its programs and services and conducting needs assessments.

SurveyMonkey and Zoomerang are two online companies that offer basic services free of charge. In addition, an agency or business can pay to gain access to higher levels of service, such as question filtering, different types of survey questions, response options, and custom charting and analysis.

The Alamance County Recreation and Parks Department in Burlington, North Carolina, utilizes Zoomerang for a number of different evaluative purposes, including a Recreation Master Plan Survey, a Fishing Rodeo Program Evaluation, a Youth Athletic Postseason Evaluation, a Shelter Reservation Evaluation, and an in-house Employee Satisfaction Survey. The agency has found Zoomerang to be easy to use and implement. In addition, the ease of being able to analyze the data without having to enter it into another program is a benefit and time saver that the agency appreciates. The agency's biggest challenge when using Zoomerang is making sure surveys also reach participants or citizens who do not have Internet access, and thus paper survey availability is still important.

and how their answers differed depending on their demographics. For instance, respondents under the age of 30 may feel very differently about youth programming compared with respondents over the age of 50, whose children are likely grown. Demographic data may include gender, age, household income, presence of children in the household, race, years lived in the community, geographic location of the household, and other variables that may be of interest for the purpose of the survey. Other forms of data collection such as focus groups and interviews may also utilize a short written survey to collect demographic data on participants.

Figure 4.5 provides an example of the demographic portion of a needs assessment survey taken in Greer, South Carolina. The researcher used the first few questions to identify community citizens. Because Greer's city lines are very irregular and there are pockets within the city lines that are not city property, the researcher determined, through consultation with the parks and recreation department, that the most accurate predictor of residency was the possession of a city garbage container.

Certainly less demographic data need to be collected for program evaluations, as the programmer should already have a good sense of who is participating in the program (unlike the researcher conducting a community-wide needs assessment). If certain questions have no real relevance to the purpose of the evaluation, the evaluator should not ask them in order to reduce the time commitment of completing the evaluation and reduce suspicion about demographic questions that seem to be asked for no apparent reason. For example, if household income is irrelevant to the study, then do not ask about it. While some evaluators feel that putting demographic questions at the beginning helps respondents ease into the survey process, others place them at the end so that respondents are not automatically suspicious about the data collection.

An agency may use the remainder of the survey to confirm suspected trends in the community; prioritize parks and recreation services; measure attitudes toward issues such as program fees, facility development, and current programs; and gather data on other related issues. Some surveys are short, such as those that are program specific, while others are quite long, such as those used for a community needs assessment. Surveys can collect quantitative data in the form of scale items as well as qualitative data through open-ended questions. Regardless of the purpose of the study, the ques-

tions must be relevant to the task at hand or the respondents will feel that the survey is at best a waste of time and at worst an invasion of privacy.

## Delphi Technique

An agency may use the Delphi technique to collect evaluation and needs assessment data that are necessary to determine priorities, set goals, or determine future directions. The Delphi technique can be classified as a specific type of survey methodology. Often an agency uses the technique with experts in the field, and the survey is conducted either by mail or electronically so that the agency may reach a wide variety of individuals. It is a worthwhile technique to consider when bringing experts together face to face is logistically difficult or impossible. The general process involves asking expert panelists to voice their opinions on a topic and then to examine the opinions of the other panelists and finally to reevaluate their original opinions in light of the new information (Siegenthaler and Riley 2002).

While the Delphi technique can vary logistically, it has four common steps:

1. Select appropriate experts.
2. Create and distribute the first questionnaire.
3. Create and distribute the second questionnaire.
4. Create and distribute the third questionnaire.

The purpose of the project dictates the list of experts. For instance, an agency working to develop new programs to help combat a growing gang problem may select programmers with success at handling this type of challenge, youth development experts, and law enforcement officials. While the list may include other experts as well, these individuals could undoubtedly provide insight into this type of challenge.

Once the agency chooses its list of experts, it can begin the questionnaire process. Likely, the first questionnaire will ask very open-ended questions related to gangs, youth violence, and recreation programming. These questions will provide breadth and depth in data collection during step 2 before ideas are whittled down during steps 3 and 4. For example, the first questionnaire may ask only one question: "What issues need to be addressed in order for parks and recreation agencies to help provide alternatives to gang life for youths in the community?"

# Demographic Section of a Survey

1. **What is your zip code?**
   - ❑ 29650
   - ❑ 29651
   - ❑ Other
   - ❑ 29652
   - ❑ 29687

   If you chose "Other," please enter your zip code: _____

2. **Do you have a rollout residential garbage container collected by the City of Greer?**
   - ❑ Yes
   - ❑ No

3. **Are you a resident of the City of Greer?**
   - ❑ Yes
   - ❑ No

4. **What is your age (in years)?**
   - ❑ Under 18
   - ❑ 26-35
   - ❑ 46-55
   - ❑ 66-75
   - ❑ 18-25
   - ❑ 36-45
   - ❑ 56-65
   - ❑ 76 or older

5. **Are you male or female?**
   - ❑ Male
   - ❑ Female

6. **How many years have you lived in the City of Greer?**
   - ❑ Less than 1
   - ❑ 3-5
   - ❑ 11-20
   - ❑ 1-2
   - ❑ 6-10
   - ❑ More than 20

7. **Do you have dependent children living at home?**
   - ❑ Yes
   - ❑ No

   If you answered "Yes," please enter the number of dependent children you have living at home in each of the following categories:

   Preschool age (under 5 years) _____

   Elementary school age (5-10 years) _____

   Middle school age (11-13 years) _____

   High school age (14-19 years) _____

8. **What is your ethnic background?**
   - ❑ Native American/Alaskan Native
   - ❑ Hispanic
   - ❑ Black/Non-Hispanic
   - ❑ White/Non-Hispanic
   - ❑ Asian/Pacific Islander
   - ❑ Other

9. **What is the joint annual income of your family?**
   - ❑ Under $25,000
   - ❑ $75,000-$99,999
   - ❑ $25,000-$49,999
   - ❑ $100,000 or more
   - ❑ $50,000-$74,999

**Figure 4.5** These demographic questions were asked to gain a clear picture of respondents to a needs assessment survey in Greer, South Carolina.

Used with permission by City of Greer, SC.

In step 3 the expert panel is presented with a second questionnaire that lists the ideas generated from the first questionnaire and asked to rate each item from "Very important" to "Not important at all" on a Likert scale of 1 to 5. From these results the facilitator chooses a numeric cutoff point based on the mean scores. Everything above the cutoff point is included in the final questionnaire. On this third and final questionnaire, the experts rank the items in order to determine the most important issues to address. The cutoff point is flexible, although the recommendation is to retain no more than 20 items for the third questionnaire. Upon completion of the third questionnaire, the agency should have a good idea of where to start addressing the gang problems influencing the agency's community (Siegenthaler and Riley 2002).

The overall goal of the Delphi technique is to attain consensus. Thus it is possible for the steps involved to expand beyond four before consensus is reached.

## Observation

Although not used as often as the other data collection techniques, observation of participants is another method agencies can use to collect data (Henderson 2006). Observation does not require any effort by participants but may require some interpretation by the observer, and thus training is a critical component of this data collection method to ensure that the data are valid and reliable. An evaluator simply wanting to know how many participants use a piece of playground equipment could stand and count how many children used the equipment—this is one example of observation data. However, if the observer also tried to guess the approximate age of the children, then a greater degree of error would enter the process.

Data collection and interpretation may be even more involved, as it is when an evaluator observes verbal and nonverbal communication patterns to determine participant satisfaction with a program. Often observational data collection involves using a well-designed checklist in order to reduce error and increase reliability in the collection process. With a well-designed checklist, the data collection process can remain reliable even if the observer changes, as the checklist makes it easier to focus on what is to be observed. The cost of the observation method is limited to paying for the time and travel of the people conducting the observation; while time and travel may prove to be costly, there are no additional expenses and there are instances in which the data produced can be very beneficial. For example, it might be more helpful to observe how children use a piece of equipment rather than to ask the children or their parents to describe how they use it, as observation reduces recall error and avoids involving the participant.

## Existing Records

An additional, completely noninvasive form of data collection is to use existing records. This involves gathering data from materials that already exist, such as program registration forms, attendance sheets, or usage records. For this type of data collection, accurate records must be kept over time so that they provide valid and reliable data upon which to make decisions. For example, a facility director trying to determine whether to purchase more sport equipment for open gyms may examine usage rates of the basketball courts and the rate at which equipment is checked out to determine if more equipment is needed. Again, the cost of this type of data collection is in the time of the evaluator.

## Mixed Methods Approach

Although there are multiple assessment tools, each has its own drawbacks that can result in a non-representative sample of data. For example, when data are collected from a small but vocal group of

Observation can be an effective data collection method with children playing on a playground.

citizens whose opinions do not represent those of the community, the agency may give these data more weight than warranted when making its decisions. In other words, the squeaky wheel gets the grease. Issues such as nonresponse rates, illiteracy, lack of Internet availability, time constraints, and feelings of "Why bother? No one will listen!" can severely affect the validity of data, whether the data are collected from a survey, a focus group, or a public meeting. A mixed methods approach can help an agency obtain a more representative sampling of data because one method's strengths can counterbalance another's weaknesses.

A mixed methods approach utilizes more than one data collection method in order to overcome the shortfalls associated with relying on only one type of method. For instance, a community may choose to post an Internet survey to reduce the costs associated with a mail survey, have paper surveys available at community centers for people without Internet access, hold interviews with a select group of stakeholders, and hold focus groups open to the general public. It would be hard to argue in this case that the community members did not have a variety of options available to them to express their opinions. In addition, the more community members take advantage of the process, the more valid the results (Carter and Beaulieu 1992).

## Other Considerations

There are additional considerations to make when choosing which evaluation model to use, what type of data to collect, and how to collect data. These considerations include budgets, staffing, and the stakeholders associated with the assessment. For example, printed and mailed surveys cost a great deal more than Web-based surveys. In addition, they take more people power, as data have to be entered manually from printed surveys whereas Web-based surveys typically dump data into a spreadsheet for analysis. Staffing considerations include not only the time spent to prepare for data collection but also the skill set staff members must have in order to collect data as well as analyze and interpret data.

While some analyses such as computing frequencies or mean scores are relatively straightforward, other analyses, both quantitative and qualitative, can be more difficult. Spreadsheet packages such as Excel allow staff members to analyze quantitative data, but there is skill involved in both the analysis as well as the interpretation. The same is true for analyzing qualitative data,

which can be quite time consuming. If there are no staff members who can complete the data analysis, then the agency may need to hire an outside consultant.

Often staff members are comfortable with conducting program evaluations but are less comfortable with performing larger assessments such as community-wide needs assessments. Therefore, the purpose of the assessment plays a role in determining both the budget and the staff requirements.

Stakeholders indirectly influence the budget and staffing because they influence the purpose of the assessment. It is important to identify both the internal and external stakeholders. Internal stakeholders can include program staff, management, and park board members. External stakeholders may include community members, participants, and parents. The final reporting is tailored to the reader, and thus it may differ depending on who the stakeholder happens to be. Therefore multifaceted, multiple versions of the final report may be necessary.

## Data Analysis

As outlined at the start of this chapter, the final step in the research or evaluation process is data analysis. This step also tends to be the one that scares most professionals. However, without analysis, the data collected are meaningless—without analysis it is impossible to address the research purpose or problem. Analysis allows the evaluator to make sense of the data and to answer the evaluation questions.

Most evaluators can handle basic data analysis, including descriptive statistics such as frequencies (simple counts) and mean (average) scores. For many programs this level of analysis may be sufficient. However, if the purpose of the evaluation requires more expansive analysis than the evaluator is comfortable conducting, outside consultants such as university faculty members or graduate students may be able to assist with the process. Sometimes these services are offered as a free service for small projects; other times there may be a charge. An evaluation may serve as a good, real-world project for a research methods class at the local university. Regardless of how the analysis is completed, the evaluator needs to do what it takes to make sure the analysis is accurate. Otherwise the final results will be biased, a problem introduced earlier in the discussion on quantitative and qualitative data.

Certainly, as mentioned earlier, there are differences in analyzing quantitative and qualitative data; the analysis of quantitative data may often be more straightforward. An evaluator can perform a quantitative analysis by using standard computer programs such as Excel or a simple calculator. Qualitative analysis is less clear cut in that the analysis does not involve simple calculations unless the evaluator is reporting frequencies of how often someone reported something. Analysis of qualitative data typically involves looking for themes, or patterns of similar responses, and this task can be time consuming. On the other hand, it can also produce clearer, richer answers to evaluation questions. The two types of data together often help the evaluator be more accurate in answering the questions produced by the problem statement.

Consider the earlier example of a youth recreation programmer developing an after-school jump rope program to combat childhood obesity. In this example the programmer may collect basic statistics on the children's weight and then use a five-point scale to ask the participants about the program. An example item might be, "As a result of the jump rope program, I find myself exercising even more at home," with answers ranging from "Strongly agree" at five points to "Strongly disagree" at one point. The resulting scores give the programmer an average score on each item. In addition, the programmer may sit down in a focus group with some of the participants and ask them qualitative questions that enhance the quantitative analysis. For example, the programmer might ask, "Why do you exercise more after participating in the jump rope program?" The evaluator could then analyze the qualitative answers by looking for general themes in the responses. Combining qualitative data with numerical data gives the programmer a much better idea of how the program worked than collecting only one type of data could give.

# Evaluation Reports

An evaluation report is an important tool. In it, an agency systematically organizes the collected data in order to produce a document that can guide program, park, and facility development. While an agency may personalize the document to suit its purposes and to suit the stakeholders who are reading the report, evaluation reports come with relatively standard sections. Knowing what should be included in the final report can help an agency ensure that it has collected the appropriate data during its assessment. This leaves less room for holes in the final report and minimizes additional work in collecting data retrospectively. Figure 4.6 shows the standard components of an evaluation report.

## Standard Components of an Evaluation Report

1. Title page
2. Names of authors and affiliations
3. Outline of evaluation's intended audience
4. Executive summary of findings
5. Table of contents
6. List of tables, figures, and photographs
7. Body of report
   a. Purpose of evaluation (to contextualize results)
   b. Specific evaluation questions
   c. Description of program
   d. Evaluator's background and expertise
   e. Regulations inherent to programs evaluated (if applicable)
   f. Evaluation methods
   g. Findings
   h. Conclusions and recommendations
   i. Supplementary material

**Figure 4.6**   Evaluation reports typically have standard components that allow the reader to gain a clear sense of the effectiveness of a program.

The depth provided for each of these standard components may differ depending on the audience of the evaluation. However, one of the most important aspects to include in the report is the purpose statement outlined in step 3 of the evaluation process. This purpose statement contextualizes the results for the reader and should be followed by the specific evaluation questions, which also help the reader better understand the findings and the implications of the findings. Without knowing the purpose statement, the reader will have difficulty utilizing the findings effectively.

The program description is also important. Without this description the reader will be uncertain of how everything fits together and of the relevance of both the findings and the conclusions of the report. It is also useful to explain, before listing the findings, the background of the evaluators so that the report can be read with an eye turned toward the objectivity of the evaluators (are the evaluators internal or external?) and the expertise of the evaluators in developing and implementing the evaluation methodology. In addition, if there are any regulations inherent to the evaluated program, the report should mention them as well in order to provide context for evaluation findings. For example, if a community aquatics facility is being evaluated, the report should outline regulations concerning aquatics facilities (such as public health guidelines) that may affect the evaluation findings. To help illustrate the components that should be included, figure 4.7 shows a typical table of contents for a final evaluation report.

## Example Table of Contents for a Program Evaluation Report

### Table of Contents

**Figure 4.7** An evaluation report should provide relevant stakeholders with background information and findings from a program assessment.

The methods used to conduct the evaluation must also be outlined so that the reader can understand how data were collected as well as judge whether the methods were appropriate in light of the context. Methods may include conducting a pre- and postprogram survey of participants to measure how a variable of interest changed because of the program or may include a focus group held to gain a richer understanding of the experience participants had in a class. Either way, the plan needs to clearly outline the methods used. Whether the data are quantitative or qualitative, the report needs to present the findings in a way that the reader can easily understand; often this entails using a combination of narrative and tables. Finally, the body of the report should include conclusions and recommendations so that the reader can see the full picture of the data analysis and what the data mean within the context of particular programs. This type of information provides insight into how to use the results to refine programs or develop new programs.

One of the final pieces of the report is the appendixes. The appendixes should include supplementary materials that detail more greatly the information provided in the narrative of the report. Supplementary materials might include instruments used for data gathering; program materials such as marketing tools, schedules, and budgets; and agency materials that may provide insight into the report, such as the agency's mission and vision statements. The report should end with a list of any references utilized within the report (Rossman and Schlatter 2008).

## Developing Programs From Assessment

One of the primary outcomes of a well-conducted assessment is the ability to use the resulting data to develop new programs or revise existing programs. Assessment data can help an agency set priorities with respect to relevant issues such as participant demand, budgeting, facility availability, and staffing. As mentioned earlier, specific techniques such as the Delphi technique and the nominal group technique can help an agency use citizen or expert input in order to determine priorities on specific topics or for the agency as a whole.

Evaluation results can also help programmers develop and refine goals and objectives tied to specific programs. Well-designed programs have clear goals and objectives that assist the programmer in judging the success of a program. For example, a goal for a youth basketball league may be to increase the passing skills of participants, and a related objective might be that 90 percent of all participants are able to complete 9 out of 10 chest passes to a partner by the end of the first week. The goal and objective allow the programmer to determine if the program is indeed helping the participants improve their basketball skills, which is an overarching goal of the program. Evaluation would measure the participants' passing skills and assist the programmer in modifying the program if the goal and objective were rarely met. For instance, if an evaluation indicated that at the end of week one only 20 percent of participants could meet the objective, then the programmer would likely adjust the instruction as needed.

A programmer often ties goals and objectives to anticipated program outputs and outcomes. This type of programming, and the related assessment, is referred to as *outcome-based programming* and is today's industry standard. Outputs are the direct products of the program and are usually measured in terms of the work accomplished, such as the number of individuals served or the number of hours of programming. While these measurements are useful and often of the highest importance to some stakeholders, outcomes can give the agency a much greater picture of the effect that the program has on participants. Outcomes are the benefits or changes an individual experiences after participating in the program. While influenced by outputs, outcomes suggest that a person has changed and improved as a result of participation in the program.

Outcome-based programming, which is informed through research and evaluation, requires a programmer to identify goals and objectives for a program in the form of outputs and outcomes and to use research and theory to tie program development to those outputs and outcomes. It is no longer acceptable to offer recreation programming and services and hope that positive outcomes will result. Funders, community members, customers, and others demand programs that are designed to ensure certain outcomes are realized as long as the programs are implemented correctly and in line with current practices informed by previous research.

Therefore, program development must be process oriented and focus on program implementation that has a good chance of producing the desired outcomes. For example, a programmer may desire to increase the academic performance of youths involved in an after-school program, but if the programmer does not take into consideration research that indicates how this might be facilitated, there is as good a chance that it will not happen as there is that it will happen.

A logic model can go a long way in illustrating to the programmer and evaluator what levels of measurement are needed to determine if the program is successfully producing its designed goals and objectives. The logic model not only provides a clear plan for program implementation but also allows a programmer to see what aspects of the program should be evaluated; this is outcome evaluation.

Figure 4.8 illustrates a logic model for an after-school program. The first column lists inputs, which are the resources necessary to conduct the program, including money and facilities, as well as the constraints on the program, including relevant laws and regulations. The second column lists activities the staff must develop in order to make sure the stated outputs and outcomes of the program can be achieved. The third column outlines the outputs, or the direct products of the program, including the number of children served, the mentoring relationships formed, and all the other results of the activities. Finally, the fourth column shows the outcomes, which are the effects the program has on participants—the changes that occur because of successfully implemented activities. Without a logical connection between what happens and what should happen based on previous research and theory, the model breaks down. That is, if there is nothing to suggest that creating mentoring relationships for youths leads to any of the listed outcomes, then the program needs to go back to the drawing board so it can be redesigned to produce the desired outcomes.

Strong programming takes into account past evaluation results and research in program development in order to do everything possible to ensure that a program produces positive outcomes. This use of evaluation data can help a programmer see consistent improvement in outcome measurements over time.

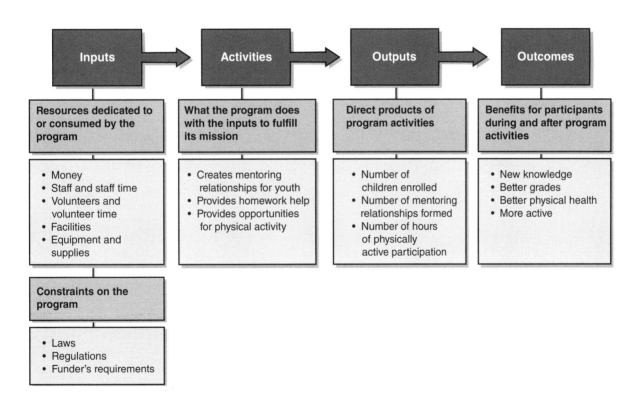

**Figure 4.8** A well-developed logic model can be an effective tool for developing a program and evaluation plan for an after-school program.

## Conclusion

Despite its importance, professionals often overlook evaluation for multiple reasons. Some fear conducting an evaluation because they are not sure where to start the process. Others simply lack the time to complete the evaluation process. Whatever the cause—or in some cases the excuse—for their omission, evaluations are a critical component of successful program, service, and facility design and development. Whether employees work for a hotel, a local YMCA, or a city parks and recreation department, they need to have a general understanding of the different purposes of evaluation as well as the different ways to use evaluation tools and results in order to best serve their customers.

### Review Questions

1. What are the eight steps of evaluation? Describe what occurs within each step.
2. List three reasons why an agency may want to conduct a needs assessment.
3. Describe the different methods of data collection for evaluations and needs assessments.
4. Define and provide examples of quantitative and qualitative data.
5. Describe different types of evaluation models that can be used for recreation programs and facilities. Give an example of when to use each type.
6. List the components of an evaluation report.

Visit the online resource at www.HumanKinetics.com/TheParkAndRecreationProfessionalsHandbook for sample documents, keywords, activities and assignments, and more.

# Planning

# chapter 5

**OUTCOMES**

- Differentiate between strategic planning and master planning.
- Understand the strategic and master planning processes.
- Outline the business planning process.
- Comprehend the role of stake-holders in the planning process.

Planning in leisure services has become commonplace. Leisure services professionals plan programs, events, staffing schedules, and meetings, among other things. This chapter moves beyond this type of planning to agency-level planning. At the agency level there are many different plans that must be developed, including strategic plans, master plans, business plans, and marketing plans. The reasons for completing these large-scale plans come down to four results: efficiency, effectiveness, preparation, and accountability.

First, planning drives the efficient use of **resources.** Plans outline the resources needed and the resources the agency already has as well as the best way to use the resources to meet the needs of the community. The outcome of most plans in leisure services is to focus an agency's often limited resources on the agency's highest priorities. The second reason for planning is that doing so requires an agency to define its values, vision, and mission and to design products and services around these foundational aspects. Planning ensures that staff and board members are in agreement as to what the agency should do, when it should be done, and how it should be done. All of this leads to agency effectiveness and a greater ability to achieve goals and objectives. Third, planning prepares the agency to deal with change. Whether it comes in the form of evolving trends in the field, an economic crisis, the loss of a facility, or a staff turnover, change is inevitable and an organization that plans is better able to respond to this change. Lastly, and arguably most impor-

tantly for public and nonprofit agencies, planning provides accountability to the public. When an agency is questioned about its service provision, it can rely on a planning document to show the community what it is doing and why. Planning provides direction on where the agency is headed in the future and how it will use its resources.

This chapter focuses on strategic planning, master planning, and business planning. In addition, a capital improvement plan (chapter 8) emerges from the master plan and a marketing plan (chapter 11) results from the completion of the business plan.

## Strategic Plans

A strategic plan shapes and guides an agency's strategies, directions, decisions, and allocation of resources. In most agencies the strategic plan is the overarching plan designed to guide the agency. It takes an incredible amount of time and effort to produce a quality plan, but when done correctly the strategic plan can be the guiding force for years to come. Most strategic plans cover approximately five years. Because of the resources needed to develop a strategic plan, it could be argued that the plan should span a longer time period. However, a changing field such as leisure services is served better by a shorter time period.

Before starting a strategic plan, it is imperative to determine who will be involved in the planning. The planning committee that best serves the

Plans for agencies, facilities, and major events are designed to increase an agency's efficiency, effectiveness, and ability to deal with change and to demonstrate accountability to the public.

**Table 5.1** Pros and Cons of Hiring a Strategic Planning Consultant

| Pros | Cons |
|---|---|
| Consultants have less bias than staff members have. | Consultant cost can be prohibitive. |
| Consultants have strategic planning experience and expertise. | Consultant can use a cookie-cutter approach by pushing the agency to implement essentially the same plan the consultant's other clients have used. |
| Consultants increase the credibility of the plan. | Staff members have a better command of the community and its resources than a consultant. |
| Consultants have access to and knowledge of data sources that enhance the quality of the plan. | Consultants make it easy to infuse bias. |
| Consultants can supplement staff time. | |

needs of the agency and the community is the one that has a mix of representation on it. A governing body should not have the sole responsibility of developing the plan because then the plan becomes the board's plan and not an agency-wide plan. On the other hand, if only the staff members have the responsibility for planning, it becomes easy for the board and community to say that the plan is self-serving for the staff. In addition, without community input a valuable perspective is lost. Because of these issues, representation on the planning committee is a critical decision and one of the most difficult aspects of strategic planning.

Here are a few things to consider when developing the planning committee:

- What is the best size for getting the work done efficiently?
- Are all areas within the agency represented?
- Are multiple staff levels represented?
- Are multiple age groups represented?
- How will nonplanning committee voices be heard?
- What is the role of the board members on the planning committee?
- What is the role of the community in the planning process?

A representative planning committee enhances buy in from board and staff members. Neither group can feel it was left out and then unfairly expected to embrace and implement the plan. It takes the support and effort of the entire staff to implement the plan, and buy in is a necessity.

In addition to establishing a planning committee, it must be decided whether to hire a consultant to facilitate the planning process. While many agencies do hire a consultant to facilitate the strategic planning process, there are both positive and negative aspects to doing so (see table 5.1). An agency should consider both sides before determining whether to hire a consultant.

Hiring a consultant is often done by preparing a request for proposal (RFP). The RFP outlines the services needed by the agency, and interested firms then submit their proposals for meeting the agency's needs. The RFP typically ranges from 6 to 12 pages, depending on the work, and contains the following items (Haines 2001):

- Title page with the agency name, project name, and contact information
- Overview of the project
- Overview of the community's history
- Scope of services
- Logistics and requirements for the submission package
- Deadline for submissions
- Deliverables required from the consultants
- Evaluation process for selecting a consultant
- Equal opportunity clause
- Noncollusion affidavit
- Statement of liability
- List of references
- Appendixes with maps, drawings, and lists of necessary projects and studies

Once the deadline for submitting proposals passes, the proposals are reviewed and two or three of the best proposals are passed onto the next round of review, during which the consultants are interviewed and their references are checked. Finally a consultant is selected, the contract is negotiated, and work commences on the established timeline.

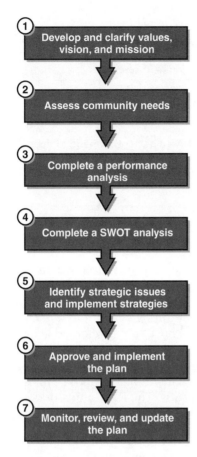

1. Develop and clarify values, vision, and mission
2. Assess community needs
3. Complete a performance analysis
4. Complete a SWOT analysis
5. Identify strategic issues and implement strategies
6. Approve and implement the plan
7. Monitor, review, and update the plan

**Figure 5.1** The seven-phase strategic planning model can be adapted to meet the needs of the agency.

A number of planning models are used in leisure services. Most of them have many of the same components. The planning model presented here (see figure 5.1) is a combination of many models in the field and can be adapted to fit the needs of an agency. While the model looks like a step-by-step process, a number of these steps can go on simultaneously during the early stages of the planning process. As such, the planning model described here is in phases rather than steps. The following sections describe each phase of the planning process. Keep in mind that this chapter serves as a guide to strategic planning and is not detailed enough to guide a novice through the process. The purpose is to familiarize leisure services professionals with the different aspects of planning that they may encounter.

## Phase 1: Develop and Clarify Values, Vision, and Mission

The values, vision, and mission of an organization are cohesive elements that serve as the foundation of what the agency is and what it does. Their development starts at the bottom so that everything in the agency is values driven: The vision adheres to the values, and the mission carries out the values and vision for the organization. The first phase of the strategic planning process sets the course for the rest of the plan. At this point an understanding and framework of what the agency believes in, where it wants to go, and what it wants to do to get there are established. All of the strategic issues that form the bulk of the plan are directly influenced by the values, vision, and mission of the agency.

### Values

In the strategic planning process, agencies must first examine their existing values or determine what their values will be. **Values** are the standards and beliefs that guide the behaviors of the organizational members. The values encourage and discourage certain behaviors within the organization and clarify what the organization stands for and what it believes to be important. Individuals who do not believe in the values of an organization should probably not work there. Values are developed through three perspectives: member values, leader values, and societal values (McLean, Bannon, and Gray 1999).

Member values come from the staff members. Employees are drawn to a company because their own values match those of the company. When this match exists, the staff reinforces a common set of values.

Leader values come from top managers such as chief executive officers, owners, or board members. Top managers have great influence in infusing values throughout the organization. Like staff members, leaders are drawn to companies or create companies that match their own values. For example, REI is an outdoor equipment store that values authenticity, quality, service, respect, integrity, and balance. The company leaders expect these values to be embraced and displayed by their staff, and they state that "REI's values are reflected in everything we do—from our focus on customers to our commitment to environmental stewardship. Our values serve as a foundation for how we conduct business, how we serve members and how we treat each other" (REI 2009).

Societal values come from the community and society in which people live. Societal values influence an organization by dictating what is acceptable and unacceptable behavior. Some programs are acceptable in one community and not in another because of the influence of societal values. For example, there is a company named

## Brainstorming Technique

Brainstorming is a process used to generate a lot of ideas on a specific topic. There are three basic rules to brainstorming:

1. Come up with as many ideas as possible.
2. Do not judge any ideas as they are presented to the group no matter how ridiculous they seem on the surface.
3. Use the ideas of others to spark your own creativity.

Brainstorming is an informal, fun means to solve problems, develop new programs, or challenge the status quo in an agency.

From Mind to Body that offers exotic dance and pole fitness as a means to learn dance and increase fitness (From Mind to Body 2009). This company is located in New York, Las Vegas, and San Francisco. Societal values in these cities tend to be far more liberal than they are in other cities. If these same classes were offered in highly religious, conservative communities, the citizens there would most likely express their disagreement with the program based on their societal values.

Since values come from three different perspectives, establishing a values statement for an agency can be challenging. Values—even those within the workplace—are quite personal to all of us. For strategic planning purposes, staff members should go through exercises to discern organizational values. They can use brainstorming or nominal group techniques (chapter 4) to generate a list of potential values and then narrow that list to the most important values describing the agency. From this list of core values, a values statement results. Here is an example of a values statement from Campus Recreation at Colorado State University (2009):

➤ • Our *integrity* lies in trusting each other to maintain high standards in all we do.

• Our *community* is united through a common vision and shared experiences while respecting and supporting one another.

• We *develop* individuals through education and teachable moments while guiding the sustainable growth of others and ourselves.

For values to work within the organization, several things must occur (Heathfield 2009):

• The values must be modeled in the actions of all staff and board members.

• The values should establish agency priorities and decision making.

• The agency's goals and objectives must reflect the organization's values.

• The agency should hire people whose values are consistent with those of the agency.

• All of the agency staff members must embrace and demonstrate their commitment to the values in their work.

### Vision

Kouzes and Posner (2007, 105) define vision as "an ideal and unique image of the future for the common good." Forward-thinking organizations develop a **vision statement** that defines what they want to be like in the future. Vision statements attempt to look forward five years or more and are derived from organizational values. Since the vision statement is future oriented, it should not simply describe what the organization looks like currently—it should describe what the organization can achieve. The company needs not only a vision statement but also a **shared vision**—an ideal that the entire organization believes in. Having the CEO as the only visionary does not motivate staff to work to achieve the vision. Developing a vision is a company-wide process that increases employee motivation, attracts like-minded employees, and makes the company better able to withstand challenges (Kouzes and Posner 2007).

For example, the vision statement for the Therapeutic Recreation Division of the Arlington Virginia Parks, Recreation and Cultural Resources (2009) is "to create a community environment that promotes healthy leisure lifestyles for individuals who are at an increased level of risk or have special needs." Another good example is the vision statement of the Allegheny

College Department of Athletics and Recreation (2010):

> The vision for the Department of Athletics and Recreation is to create an innovative, challenging and supportive learning environment, where individuals can pursue personal growth in areas of sports, wellness, outdoor programming, and recreational activities; where 80% of student-athletes graduate in four years and where participants act as role models in sportsmanship and conduct. Further, the vision is to become known as a leader among Division III programs offering broad based, equitable, Title IX compliant student-centered programming.

## Mission

The organization's mission is steeped in the organization's values and vision. The **mission statement** is a clear and concise statement of purpose. It purports the reason for the agency's existence. A good mission statement explains who the customers are, what services are provided, and how services are provided (McLean, Bannon, and Gray 1999). Mission statements are often posted in facilities or listed in brochures so that they are available to the public. For example, the mission statement for Navy Morale, Welfare, Recreation (2009) is

> to contribute to the retention, readiness and mental, physical, and emotional well being of active duty, reserve and retired personnel and to the welfare of their families by providing a varied program of recreational, social and community support activities.

Another example of a mission statement comes from Planet Hollywood (2009):

> Planet Hollywood International, Inc. is a guest-driven company committed to providing our guests with an exciting inside look at Hollywood, combined with exceptional food, outstanding merchandise and uncompromising service in every one of our restaurants. We recognize that our success is achieved by hiring, retaining and developing quality associates.

## Phase 2: Assess Community Needs

Needs assessment for program planning is discussed in chapter 2. Needs assessment for strategic planning follows the same process but most often is conducted on a larger scale. Needs assessments for strategic plans utilize community surveys, community meetings, focus groups, and individual interviews.

Doing a needs assessment has several advantages. First, it allows the agency to gather input from the community on a wide variety of topics. A single needs assessment can provide data on parks, facilities, and programs and their use. It can provide information on what the community sees as a new direction for the agency, what the agency does well, and what the agency does not do so well. An end result is a good picture of the priorities of the community. Second, a needs assessment can garner input from a variety of groups beyond users, including underrepresented groups and nonusers. It is users who are most likely to give feedback throughout the year; it is the other groups who need to be given an opportunity to share their opinions through a needs assessment. Third and last, the needs assessment can prompt change. It is easy to continue providing leisure services the same way they have always been provided. If people are not complaining, programs are full, and parks are used, then business can continue as usual. A needs assessment can prompt change by pointing to a missing service, an unfilled niche, or an unknown problem in the community.

It is always possible that some staff members will not like the idea of doing a full needs assessment of the community. Often this is due to a negative preconceived attitude about needs assessments. A common statement is, "We know what our community wants." This is true only if the agency is diligent in using the various needs assessment techniques. Without these techniques, it is difficult to have a solid grasp on the needs of the community. A second misconception is that a needs assessment is a waste of money that could be better spent on programs and parks. Needs assessments can be expensive, but they do not have to be. Assessing the strengths and weaknesses of each method of data collection can help the agency decide what method is best given the available resources. A final concern regarding needs assessments (if a survey technique is used) is that the statistics are too difficult to understand or that they exaggerate the truth. If an agency hires an outside firm to conduct the needs assessment, the firm will provide an executive summary of the results. This summary presents the data in a way that is quite understandable. If the data are not understandable, the agency can ask the consultant to rewrite the executive summary. A large amount of data can lead to many different statistical analyses. A reputable consulting firm will present all of the data and not just those data that reinforce what the agency wants to hear.

The needs assessment process varies based on the community and the agency. For example, Lloydminster (Alberta) uses an online needs assessment to determine use patterns for its parks and programs, use patterns for other leisure services providers, and benefits derived from this city department. This is an ongoing assessment and not one implemented for strategic planning purposes.

When the Essex (Vermont) Parks and Recreation Department updated its most recent strategic plan covering 2004 to 2010, it used several different techniques to assess the needs of the community, including the following (Recreation and Leisure Services Consultants 2004):

- Interviews with residents and municipal employees of the community
- A focus group meeting to which 20 key community leaders were invited to attend
- A community recreation survey
- A draft report reviewed by the original focus group and the Essex Selectboard and made available to the public for comments before finalization

It is not uncommon to follow the process used in Essex and to gather information from more than one source. Doing so allows the agency to target different groups of people, get multiple perspectives, and therefore strengthen the data collected.

## Phase 3: Complete a Performance Analysis

A performance analysis reflects whether the agency is doing things right and whether the agency is doing the right things. It is a review of programs, services, and facilities; the result is a **services portfolio**. A performance analysis requires an internal review of programs as well as an external comparison of programs.

An internal investigation of programs analyzes adherence to values, vision, and mission; resources available; marketing; and overall program value. This analysis can uncover stronger programs versus weaker programs, highlight programs that the agency should be offering based on its mission, and find programs that require more

A needs assessment might lead to a new program, such as a kayaking class, that provides a missing service to the community.

resources than the agency should be dedicating. A caution in using an analysis such as this is that staff members can become quite territorial or unnecessarily attached to their programs, and this can inflate ratings. Discussing this issue with staff members or pairing staff members from different areas to review programs can remove some of the inherent bias. Figure 5.2 shows a sample form for analyzing programs.

Once the internal analysis of programs and facilities is complete, it is necessary to compare the agency's programs to those of other service providers. This comparison is needed because there can be too much competition in the community, and this competition can stretch valuable resources. Some competition can be a good thing, because it can result in higher-quality services. However, too much competition can result in a loss of revenues. A popular tool used to conduct this sort of performance analysis is the MacMillan matrix developed by Ian MacMillan of the Wharton School of the University of Pennsylvania.

The MacMillan matrix (figure 5.3) was developed for nonprofit agencies to help them compare their programs with those of other local providers. The matrix is based on the assumption that duplication of services can reduce resources within all agencies to the point where the agencies are spread too thin and are too weak to provide quality services. The goal of the matrix is to help agencies focus their resources on the programs that are best suited to them and their competitive advantage. In essence, the matrix focuses program delivery on a few high-quality programs rather than many mediocre programs. It also requires the agency to investigate how it can work cooperatively with other agencies to provide services and to decide which agency is best able to provide certain services (California Adult Literacy Professional Development Project 2010).

## Internal Program Analysis

| Program or service characteristic | SCORE | | | |
|---|---|---|---|---|
| | 4 Excellent | 3 Good | 2 Fair | 1 Poor |
| 1. Program or service adheres to the values, vision, and mission of the organization. | | | | |
| 2. Agency has land or facilities to support the program or service. | | | | |
| 3. Program or service is unique to the community (is not duplicated within the community). | | | | |
| 4. Agency has adequate staff members to operate the program or service. | | | | |
| 5. Agency has adequate financial resources to operate the program or service. | | | | |
| 6. Agency has the equipment and technological resources to provide the program or service. | | | | |
| 7. Agency has the ability to market the program or service. | | | | |
| 8. Overall program or service quality is . . . | | | | |

Total score  _____

Average score  _____

### Program and Service Information

_____ Number of sessions offered per year

_____ Number of people served per year

_____ Cancellation rate over past 3 years

_____ Wait list (yes, no, or sometimes)

_____ Minimum enrollment

_____ Maximum enrollment

Comments: _____

_____

_____

_____

**Figure 5.2**  This sample program analysis requires an extensive review of programs from multiple perspectives.

The matrix has four analysis areas: fit, program attractiveness, alternative coverage, and competitive position:

- *Fit* is the degree to which the program fits the mission of the agency and utilizes the skills the agency has.
- *Program attractiveness* describes the program appeal; a highly attractive program has a high market demand, has stable funding, and is a good use of resources.
- *Alternative coverage* is the extent to which other agencies are offering the same service;

low alternative coverage means that there are few, if any, competitors offering the program.

- *Competitive position* is the potential the agency has over another agency to deliver the service; criteria for a strong competitive position (Partnership for After School Education 2009) include the following:

  o Good location and logistical delivery system

  o Extensive client and community support and loyalty

| | | High program attractiveness | | Low program attractiveness | |
|---|---|---|---|---|---|
| | | Alternative coverage is high | Alternative coverage is low | Alternative coverage is high | Alternative coverage is low |
| Good fit with mission | Strong competitive position | 1. Compete aggressively | 2. Grow aggressively | 5. Support the best competitor | 6. Soul of the agency |
| | Weak competitive position | 3. Divest aggressively | 4. Build, strengthen, or get out | 7. Divest systematically | 8. Work collaboratively |
| Poor fit with mission | | 9. Divest aggressively | | 10. Divest systematically | |

**Figure 5.3**    The MacMillan matrix is an intensive means of analyzing resources and competition and how well an agency is positioned to offer a service.

Adapted from California Department of Education. Available: http://www.calpro-online.org/o_guides/sft_res_og/4.asp#theorganizations

- ○ Superior image of quality service delivery
- ○ Large market share of the clients served
- ○ Growing market share compared with competitors
- ○ Most cost-effective delivery of service

After a program is analyzed according to these four criteria, it is placed on the matrix in 1 of 10 boxes:

1. Compete aggressively: Programs in this box have a lot of competition in the community, but the agency has a strong competitive position. These programs should be held onto even though there is someone else in the community who can offer them.

2. Grow aggressively: There is not much competition in the community and a strong competitive position is held. These are programs that the agency does well and not very many others offer. It is safe to examine how these programs can grow.

3. Divest aggressively: A lot of agencies are providing these programs and your agency does not have a strong presence in the market. It is best to stop offering these programs.

4. Build, strengthen, or get out: Since there are not a lot of competitors, there is room in the market to offer these programs. However, at this point the agency is not well positioned to do so. The agency needs to improve program offerings or discontinue offering the program.

5. Support the best competitor: Since the program attractiveness is low and there are an abundance of competitors, it is best to support the agency best suited to provide the program.

6. Soul of the agency: The services make a unique contribution to the community, and the agency is well suited to provide them. In public and nonprofit agencies these programs can be heavily subsidized. While an agency cannot survive with a lot of soul programs, it can create alternative funding sources or cross subsidize them with other programs.

7. Divest systematically: Since these programs have low attractiveness and a lot of competition and the agency is in a weak competitive position, the agency should withdraw from providing the service.

8. Work collaboratively: These programs may be served best in a collaborative effort in which two or more agencies work together to provide the programs.

9. Divest aggressively: As with the programs falling into box 3, the agency should get out of these programs immediately, as other agencies are better at providing these programs.

10. Divest systematically: As with the programs falling into box 7, the agency should end these programs, but it should end them in a more systematic way, with a planned discontinuation.

Once the internal program analysis and the MacMillan matrix are completed and programs are placed, a services portfolio is created. This portfolio is a plan in and of itself because it outlines the information regarding programs to keep, strengthen, partner, or stop.

Since this section of the strategic plan calls for an overall performance analysis, a performance analysis for the facilities may be needed as well. The same process can be followed internally with facility-specific criteria such as capital improvement needs, ongoing maintenance needs, cost of operation, facility use rates, and uniqueness of the facility to the community. A performance analysis for the facilities can also be done by following the resource analysis outlined in phase 2 of the master planning process.

## Phase 4: Complete a SWOT Analysis

The next step in the strategic planning process is to do an environmental scan to analyze the agency's overall situation. This requires a strengths, weaknesses, opportunities, and threats analysis, also known as a *SWOT analysis* (figure 5.4).

Strengths are the internal capabilities, attributes, and resources that help the agency to reach its objectives and create a competitive advantage. Agency strengths can include high-quality, efficient facilities; cost-conscious, creative staff

members; and solid community image. Weaknesses are internal limitations that impede the agency from reaching its objectives or creating a competitive advantage. Weaknesses can include reliance on property tax revenue, aging facilities, and local competition and duplication of services. Analysis of both strengths and weaknesses focuses on internal operations. It examines the agency's marketing, business, financial, manufacturing (or program development), and organizational competencies (Kotler, Bowen, and Makens 2010). Strengths and weaknesses may come from the following (Gray and McEvoy 2005):

- Products and services
- Personnel development, including training and education of the staff
- Management of the organization
- Financial resources
- Information and communication such as reports, records, and access to information
- Customer needs and the knowledge the agency has about its customers

The remaining elements of the SWOT analysis—opportunities and threats—are external to the agency and are the influences of things outside the organization. Gray and McEvoy (2005) describe external influences as the following:

- Demographics of the customers and community
- Economic trends and issues
- Demand trends for products and services
- Technological trends
- Government and public policy trends
- Macroenvironmental trends such as ethical and legal issues, population changes, and the obesity epidemic
- Competitors

Opportunities are external factors that the company may be able to take advantage of in order to grow, increase profits, and enhance effectiveness. Opportunities may include the development of new technology, completion of a new facility, or increasing image of the community as a tourism destination. The final piece of the SWOT analysis is threats. Threats are changes in the external environment that have the potential to impede the agency's performance. Threats

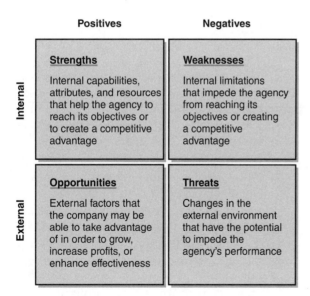

|  | **Positives** | **Negatives** |
|---|---|---|
| **Internal** | **Strengths**<br>Internal capabilities, attributes, and resources that help the agency to reach its objectives or to create a competitive advantage | **Weaknesses**<br>Internal limitations that impede the agency from reaching its objectives or creating a competitive advantage |
| **External** | **Opportunities**<br>External factors that the company may be able to take advantage of in order to grow, increase profits, or enhance effectiveness | **Threats**<br>Changes in the external environment that have the potential to impede the agency's performance |

**Figure 5.4** The SWOT analysis enables agencies to examine their strengths and weaknesses to determine how to use them to take advantage of opportunities and deal with threats.

sometimes require their own analysis, called a *PEST analysis,* which examines the political, economic, social–cultural, and technological forces that affect an agency (see figure 5.5). Threats to an agency can include emerging competition, rising costs of doing business, and poor economic climate.

The results of the SWOT analysis are unique to each agency. There may be some common driving forces among similar agencies within similar communities, but most factors are unique to each agency (see figure 5.6).

The SWOT analysis provides a picture of the environment within which the agency operates. It also helps the agency develop the strategies that are discussed in the next phase of the planning process. To do this, the SWOT analysis needs to be taken one step further. The planning group should examine the opportunities and strengths of the organization to determine what strengths

**Political**
- Tax laws and policies
- Labor laws
- Government regulations
- Environmental regulations
- Government intervention

**Economic**
- Economic growth and stability
- Inflation
- Exchange rates
- Minimum wage changes
- Interest rates
- Unemployment rates

**Social–cultural**
- Population growth changes
- Social issues
- Population health and education
- Employment patterns
- Community lifestyle

**Technological**
- Technology advancements
- Technology changes
- Automation
- Research and development

**Figure 5.5** The PEST analysis is an extension of the SWOT analysis and requires a much more in-depth review of the external environment.

**Present strengths**

Brand awareness
Climate
Culture and history
Destination allure and appeal
High visitor satisfaction
Natural resources
People and aloha spirit
Quality and variety of accommodations
Safe but exotic
Variety of activities and attractions
Geographic isolation

**Present weaknesses**

Geographic isolation
Inadequate public and private infrastructure
Insufficient visitor–resident interaction
Lack of "new" experiences
Lack of accurate pre- and post-arrival information
Lack of stakeholder consensus
Lag in business tourism
Visitor expectations and misperceptions
Volatility of the inter-island transportation services
Volatility of the national and international airline industry
Maintenance of public facilities
Limited awareness and limited access to new experiences
Lack of professional (certified) guides

**Future opportunities**

Business tourism development
Cruise industry development
Cultural tourism development
Customize marketing programs by geographic market areas
Development of new markets
Ferry development
Improve stewardship of natural resources
Improve public and private infrastructure
Increase stakeholder involvement in tourism
Preservation and perpetuation of host culture
Sports tourism development

**Future threats**

Aging public and private infrastructure
Anti-tourism sentiment
Crime and drug use
Disruptive world events
Inadequate state funding
Increased global competition
Increased Homeland Security measures
Insufficient airlift
Internal strife and complacency
Loss of identity differentiation
Cost of Hawai'i experience
Cost and availability of airline fuel

**Figure 5.6** This example SWOT analysis from the Hawai'i Tourism Authority (2005) was completed as part of a strategic planning process.

Adapted, by permission, from Hawai'i Tourism Authority. Available: http://www.hawaiitourismauthority.org/pdf/tsp2005_2015_final.pdf

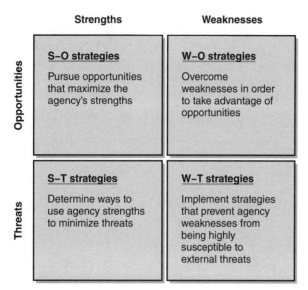

**Figure 5.7**  The SWOT matrix depicts how the agency should take advantage of strengths and opportunities and react to weaknesses and threats.

the agency can utilize to take advantage of the opportunities that present themselves. The SWOT matrix (figure 5.7), sometimes called the *TOWS matrix*, illustrates what agencies should do once they complete the SWOT analysis (MindTools 2009).

The value of the SWOT analysis cannot be overemphasized. This analysis is the means to understand the environment in which the agency operates and how that environment is affecting the agency's day-to-day and future operations.

## Phase 5: Identify Strategic Issues and Implement Strategies

Up to this point in the planning process the agency has been actively gathering both internal and external information. It is this information that drives the next phase of the strategic planning process. Many consider this phase to be the nuts and bolts of planning because it outlines what needs to be done by identifying strategic issues and then developing strategies to address the issues. There are several different labels for the issues and strategies. It is not uncommon to hear the terms *initiatives*, *tactics*, *goals*, *objectives*, and *actions*, among others.

To illustrate this phase of the planning process, it is best to use examples from the field. The first example is the Michigan Department of Natural Resources Parks and Recreation Division strategic plan (Michigan DNR Parks and Recreation Division 2009). This plan covers 2009 to 2019 and took two-and-a-half years to complete (figure 5.8).

## Michigan Department of Natural Resources Parks and Recreation Division Strategic Plan

Goal 1 Take the best possible care of Michigan's natural and cultural resources in our state parks and boating facilities:

1.1 Develop a land strategy to protect natural and cultural resources, provide new recreation opportunities, and consolidate holdings:

1.1.1 Prevent loss of recreation lands to other interests (e.g., easements, rights-of-way, and so on):

1.1.1.1 Develop and maintain inventory and maps of all easements, leases, rights-of-way, and so on with contact information for holders of those rights.

1.1.1.2 As part of the management planning process, dedicate lands that are appropriate for protection under the natural areas statute.

1.1.2 Clearly identify and mark boundaries:

1.1.2.1 Utilizing available resources and tools (survey preferred), establish boundary to clearly delineate ownership.

1.1.2.2 Properly post and maintain boundary signs.

1.1.2.3 Complete annual boundary review.

1.1.3 Identify, prioritize, and mitigate trespass and boundary issues:

1.1.3.1 Identify potential problems.

1.1.3.2 Follow established department trespass guidelines.

**Figure 5.8**  The Michigan Department of Natural Resources Parks and Recreation Division strategic plan identifies goals (1), objectives (1.1), actions (1.1.1), and tactics (1.1.1.1).

Adapted, by permission, from Michigan DNR Parks and Recreation, 2009, *Sustaining 90 years of excellence: 2009-2019 strategic plan.* Available: http://www.michigan.gov/documents/dnr/COMPLETE_DOCUMENT_Signed_279037_7.pdf

The plan details goals, objectives, actions, and tactics, but it does not define a timeline for the completion of these. The Michigan Department of Natural Resources creates an annual work plan each fiscal year that does the following (Michigan DNR Parks and Recreation Division 2009, 69):

1. Identifies what goal, objective, action, and task will be addressed by the proposed action

2. Specifies who is responsible (position or person) for the action

3. Describes the resources needed (e.g., funding, personnel, and so on) to accomplish the action

4. Describes how the action will be accomplished

5. Defines a target date of completion

Different agencies approach this phase of strategic planning differently, but the end result is a detailed guide to direct the agency to achieve its vision and mission while embracing its values. A strategic plan covers many years and cannot possibly be achieved in one or two years if it is done as thoroughly as needed. It is imperative to have an action plan before completing this phase of the strategic plan. An action plan ensures that the agency is accountable for achieving the strategies identified and prevents the document from simply gathering dust rather than being used to its full potential.

The second example of strategic issues comes from the Hawai'i Tourism Authority (figure 5.9). This plan covers 2005 to 2015 and has eight strategic initiatives: access, communication and outreach, Hawaiian culture, marketing, natural resources, research and planning, tourism product development, and workforce development. The measures of success are the levels of achievement of the goal and objectives. A separate document is needed to detail when the objectives and measures of success are to be achieved.

The Hawai'i Tourism Authority has a separate table (table 5.2) that shows the lead for each goal (the group with primary responsibility for accomplishing the goal), the other agencies who will help with the goal, and the way in which successful achievement of the goal will be measured. This plan omits a timeline for accomplishing the objectives within the goal.

Hopefully during the entire process of establishing strategic issues and strategies, the agency's values, vision, mission, needs assessments, performance analysis, and SWOT analysis are regularly reviewed and used. They are the foundation for developing a strong strategic plan that will move the agency in the right direction. Ignoring the resources that required many hours of time and effort is not a good planning technique and can be detrimental to the end result.

## Phase 6: Approve and Implement the Plan

The last two phases of the strategic planning process work together cogently. Once the previous phases are complete, the plan is approved by the governing body of the agency. This governing body could be the board of directors, agency commissioners, the city council, or shareholders. The approval process should be quite simple because the governing body has contributed to the plan development.

## Hawai'i Tourism Authority Sample Goal and Corresponding Objectives

Goal: Maintain and improve transportation access, infrastructure, and services to facilitate travel to, from, and within Hawaii.

### Objectives

- Ensure adequate lift to Hawaii.
- Improve interisland transportation services.
- Improve airports and supporting systems.
- Improve harbors and supporting systems.
- Improve roads, highways, and ground transportation systems.
- Ensure safe passage for residents and visitors.
- Expedite visa processing.
- Encourage coordination, collaboration, and improved ground transportation services.

**Figure 5.9** These goals and objectives are from the access strategic initiative within the Hawai'i Tourism Authority strategic plan.

From Hawai'i Tourism Authority, 2005, *Hawaii tourism strategic plan 2005-2015*. Available: http://www.hawaiitourismauthority.org/pdf/tsp2005_2015_final.pdf

**Table 5.2** Hawai'i Tourism Authority Goal Plan

| | |
|---|---|
| Lead | **Government:** Department of Transportation, Department of Land and Natural Resources, county planning and transportation-related departments<br>**Private sector:** Transportation companies (e.g., airlines, tour bus and taxi companies, rental car agencies, cruise lines, ferry services)<br>**Community:** Hawaii Car and Truck Renting and Leasing Association; Hawaii Transportation Association |
| Supporting groups | Office of the Governor, Homeland Security Departments of Customs and Border Protection and Transportation Security Administration, legislature and county councils, Hawai'i Tourism Authority, Public Utilities Commission, Federal Aviation Administration, Federal Department of Transportation, other government agencies, other harbor and airport users, residents and visitors |
| Measures of success | Specific to issues related to access, the following measurements provide an indication of success:<br><br>• Increased number of scheduled flights to and within Hawaii during shoulder seasons<br>• Updated and coordinated state and county master plans for airports, harbors, and highways<br>• Faster check-in, customs and immigration, and security processing times at airports and harbors<br>• Decreased congestion in airports and harbors<br>• Decreased traffic congestion on roadways<br>• Increased visitor satisfaction with airports and ground transportation<br>• Fewer visitor complaints about airports and ground transportation |

Reprinted, by permission, from Hawai'i Tourism Authority, 2005, *Hawaii tourism strategic plan 2005-2015*. Available: http://www.hawaiitourismauthority.org/pdf/tsp2005_2015_final.pdf

The implementation process puts the strategies into action. The strategies and issues developed in the previous phase cover a timeline of five years or longer. Because this timeline is quite broad, a more streamlined implementation process is instituted. Some plans establish deadlines for the strategies and others create annual action plans such as the Michigan Department of Natural Resources Parks and Recreation Division strategic plan. Regardless of the approach, the strategies that should be completed each year are discussed and the responsibility for completing the strategies is delineated.

## Phase 7: Monitor, Review, and Update the Plan

Strategic planning does not stop with the development and approval of the plan. Using it to its fullest potential requires it to be monitored, reviewed, and updated on a regular basis. Monitoring the plan requires staff members to review their annual action plans to ensure they are on track to complete their responsibilities within the given time frame. Following through on assigned responsibilities can be a part of an employee's performance review or the program area's goals and objectives. The main issue with monitoring is ensuring that the plan is carried out as designed.

Although a great deal of work is put into developing a strategic plan, it will undoubtedly require review and updating. To do this, an annual review process can be implemented. During the annual review, strategic issues and strategies are discussed and their strengths and weaknesses are reviewed, and then a decision is made to keep the strategic issue and strategy, replace them with a new or revised element, or remove them (Bryson and Alston 2005).

The Michigan Department of Natural Resources Parks and Recreation Division has a monitoring and review process defined within its strategic plan (Michigan DNR Parks and Recreation Division 2009):

➤ On a fiscal year basis, the Strategic Plan will be assessed for:

1. The prior year just completed, assess performance in completing the last year's actions.

2. Identifying Objectives, Actions and specific Tasks to complete in the coming year.

3. Identifying any new Goals, Objectives, Actions or Tasks to incorporate into the plan or existing ones to remove or modify.

4. Use the above as a basis for an 'Annual Report' to be prepared for the Department, NRC, CCMSP and MSWC, and put on the web for public information.

After reading through the seven phases of strategic planning, it is easy to see that the process is extensive and time consuming. However, the end result is worth the effort if the plan is implemented properly. The plan serves as a guiding force to help the agency achieve its vision and mission and meet its goals and objectives. In addition, it is a demonstrated effort to meet the needs of the community and run the organization efficiently and effectively.

# Master Plans

Master plans address land, facilities, bike and pedestrian paths, and natural resources. They can be part of the strategic plan or they can stand alone. Strategic plans focus on the entire agency, whereas master plans have a much narrower focus. Even so, developing a master plan uses much of the same process. Master plans tend to cover a longer term than strategic plans cover and outline the next 5 to 15 years (Mull, Beggs, and Renneisen 2009). Master plans are required for some grant programs such as the Land and Water Conservation Fund that provides federal matching grants for outdoor recreation facilities and sites.

The master planning process is often carried out by a consultant or a staff member who is well versed in park planning and natural resources management. The process (see figure 5.10) requires input from a multitude of stakeholders, including staff, community, and board members as well as others affected by parks and natural resources. The unique features of the master plan are detailed in the following sections.

## Phase 1: Assess Community Needs

If an agency is creating a strategic plan at the same time as the master plan, then one needs assess-

**Figure 5.10** Master planning is a five-phase process that resembles the process for developing a strategic plan.

ment will suffice. If not, the needs of the community should be assessed to determine use patterns, opinions about the positives and negatives of parks and natural resources, ideas for potential growth, and knowledge of conservation policies within the agency. The same needs assessment process can be used for both plans.

## Phase 2: Conduct a Resource Analysis

Doing a resource analysis (also called an *infrastructure analysis*) is arguably the most time-intensive step in the planning process. Whereas the strategic plan calls for a program analysis and a SWOT analysis, the master plan requires a resource analysis. This part of the planning process can differ from agency to agency, depending on what resources an agency has. The following are a few assessments that help an agency with its resource analysis.

### Parks and Facilities Inventory

Parks and facilities that are inventoried include undeveloped land, school parks and facilities, regional parks, neighborhood parks, pocket parks, and linear parks. It is not enough to simply count these parks—the inventory should also include information such as size, extent of development, recreation amenities, location within the community, size of the neighborhood the park or facility serves, parking availability, pedestrian connectivity, water features, riparian corridors, accessibility, and sport access. Reports are developed that describe the acres of land per thousand residents, miles of bike path per thousand, and number of people per ball diamond, among others. Table 5.3 shows an existing conditions analysis from the McCall (Idaho) Parks and Recreation master plan.

A key result of the parks and facilities inventory is an idea of the future development of these areas. In the 1980s the NRPA provided recreation, parks, and open spaces guidelines (Lancaster 1983) on how many acres or areas were needed per 1,000 people in the population. However, the NRPA has since recommended that communities develop their own standards based on the needs of their

**Table 5.3**   Existing Parks and Recreation Land Base and Facilities

| Name of park/facility | Size | Recreation facilities available | Type of park |
|---|---|---|---|
| **LOCAL PARKS MAINTAINED BY THE CITY** | | | |
| Veterans' Memorial/ Community Park | 0.20 acres | Benches, landscaping, Veterans' Memorial, historic jail interpretive site | Mini-park/pocket park |
| Art Roberts Park | 0.50 acres | Docks, grassy area, picnic benches, beach access (small sandy beach) | Mini-park/pocket park |
| Pine Street Park | 0.50 acres | None—not yet developed; play structure and parking needed | Mini-park/pocket park |
| Wild Horse Neighborhood Park | 0.76 acres | None—not yet developed; play structure planned | Neighborhood park |
| Davis Beach Park | 1.20 acres | Beach access, swimming; boat mooring and docks are privately held but public for pedestrian use; portable restrooms in season | Neighborhood park |
| Rotary Park | 1.65 acres | Grassy area, picnic tables, swimming beach, and parking lot | Neighborhood park |
| Brown Park (formerly Mill Park) | 1.76 acres | Swimming beach, playground, restrooms, fish pen docks (proposed to be relocated/rebuilt this fall, already permitted and funded) | Neighborhood park |
| Legacy Park | 3.20 acres | Volleyball court, restrooms, picnic tables, pathways, swimming beach, public boat launch | Neighborhood park (with some special uses and community functions) |
| Fairway Park | 5.00 acres | Softball fields, portable restrooms; play structure planned | Neighborhood and special use park/ sports fields |
| River Front Park | 40.00 acres | Current uses include passive hiking/ walking; development is planned to include paths, nature viewing, sports fields, river-oriented uses, an amphitheater, and other types of uses | Community park |
| **Total parks and open space area** | **54.77 acres** | | |

| Name of park/facility | Size | Recreation facilities available | Type of park |
|---|---|---|---|
| OTHER FACILITIES OPERATED AND MAINTAINED BY THE CITY | | | |
| Municipal Golf Course | 166 acres | 27-hole golf course, club house | Special use |
| Multiuse paths and bike paths | 5 miles | Signed pathways, paved and unpaved trails | Paths and trails |
| Central Idaho Historical Museum/Grounds | 4.00 acres (approx.) | Historical museum building and other historical buildings, interpretation, trees and landscaped grounds | Special use; not counted in acreage above because the site does not function as an official city park |
| Broken Ridge Park | 6.69 acres | None—not yet developed; may be able to develop for passive use such as nature trails, and possibly a small tot lot; further study needed | Natural area preserve: may be able to develop some passive recreation and neighborhood park-type uses; further study needed; not included in acreage because use as park is tentative |
| Skateboard Park | NA | Skate bowl, ramps, half pipe, quarter pipes, rails, fun box, benches, viewing area, restrooms (under development) | Special use |
| FACILITIES OPERATED AND MAINTAINED BY PRIVATE ENTITIES | | | |
| Heartland Gymnastic Center | NA | Full-facility, gymnastic equipment (e.g., trampoline, spring floor) | Special use |
| Manchester Ice and Event Center | NA | Year-round indoor ice skating rink and programs | Special use |

Adapted, by permission, from The Otak Team, 2005, *City of McCall parks and recreation master plan*, pg. 8. Available: http://www.mccall.id.us/government/committees/Parks_Rec_Advisory/Parks_Rec_Master_Plan.pdf

residents. Some communities still use the NRPA standards, while others compare themselves with similar communities in the state and country. The Northville (Michigan) Parks and Recreation Department used the NRPA standards in its 2007 to 2011 master plan (2007; see table 5.4).

The information gathered in the parks and facilities inventory as well as the natural resources inventory (see the next section) is usually illustrated on a site plan. A site plan is a depiction of what currently exists on a site or what is proposed to be built on the site. These plans resemble a map that is drawn to scale. Site plans are updated regularly so they remain true to the reality of the site.

## Natural Resources Inventory

The natural resources inventory focuses on undeveloped land and other resources in the natural environment. This inventory includes things such as endangered species protection zones, flood zones, forest covering (e.g., hardwood, deciduous), grasslands, ground water pollution, soil ratings, wetland plants and wildlife, streams and other bodies of water, and threats to natural resources.

## Maintenance Assessment

Maintenance processes and needs are analyzed within the maintenance assessment that is included in the parks and facilities inventory. Facilities are examined both internally and externally for structural, electrical, and mechanical conditions. Landscape maintenance on things such as irrigation systems and mowing equipment, **hardscape maintenance** on things such as sidewalks and pavilions, and playground inspections are performed. In addition, costs for preventative maintenance and long-term maintenance needs are estimated, and the annual maintenance operating budget is reviewed. This assessment can

**Table 5.4**   Sample From the Northville (Michigan) Parks and Recreation Master Plan

| Park classifications | NRPA guideline: minimum acres[1] | Recommended acreage in Northville | Public Northville park | Public regional park | Public school park[3] | Northville total | Surplus (deficiency) |
|---|---|---|---|---|---|---|---|
| Mini or neighbor-hood parks | 1.25-2.50 | 41-82 | 8.4 | 0.0 | 106.2 | 114.6 | 32.6+ |
| Community parks | 5-8 | 164-263 | 201.7 | 0.0 | 92.4 | 294.1 | 31.1+ |
| **Subtotal** | — | **205-345** | **210.1** | **0.0** | **198.6** | **408.7** | **63.7+** |
| Regional parks | 5-10 | 164-328 | 0.0 | 926.2 | 0.0 | 926.2 | 598.2+ |
| **Total** | — | **369-673** | **210.1** | **926.2** | **198.6** | **1,334.9** | **661.9+** |

[1]Per 1,000 residents

[2]Based on the August 1, 2006, SEMCOG population estimate of 32,830

[3]All school parks were considered neighborhood parks except Northville High School, Northville High 8 Mile Athletic Complex, and Hillside Middle School, which were classified as community parks

Reprinted, by permission, from Northville Parks and Recreation Department, 2007, *Northville Community Parks and Recreation Master Plan 2007-2011*. Available: http://www.northvilleparksandrec.org/RecMasterPlan/MasterPlan2007-2011.pdf

also include a staff analysis to determine number of staff members, staffing patterns, hours worked, and seasonality of staff.

### Policy Analysis

The last element in the parks and facilities inventory concerns the policies that are in place to guide maintenance; land development; land acquisition; use of natural resources; and management practices to protect, preserve, and enhance natural resources. For example, Portland (Oregon) has bicycle policies that guide the way the city develops and manages bikeways. Here is an example of one such policy (City of Portland 1998, 16):

➤ **Policy 6.12 Bicycle Transportation**
Make the bicycle an integral part of daily life in Portland, particularly for trips of less than five miles, by implementing a bikeway network, providing end-of-trip facilities, improving bicycle/transit integration, encouraging bicycle use, and making bicycling safer. Objectives:

• A. Complete a network of bikeways that serves bicyclists' needs, especially for travel to employment centers, commercial districts, transit stations, institutions, and recreational destinations.

• B. Provide bikeway facilities that are appropriate to the street classifications, traffic volume, and speed on all right-of-ways.

• C. Maintain and improve the quality, operation, and integrity of bikeway network facilities.

## Phase 3: Develop Strategic Issues and Strategies

Phase 2 involves compiling a vast amount of information about the current state of parks, facilities, and natural resources. These data drive the development of the strategic issues and strategies. This process is the same as that described for strategic planning. See figure 5.11 for a sample from a plan that covers issues and strategies.

## Phase 4: Develop a Capital Improvement Plan

The **capital improvement plan (CIP)** is a projection of capital projects over the life of the master plan. The CIP is a cost analysis of the implementation of the master plan's strategies and issues if the improvements are considered capital expenditures. The CIP not only lists but also prioritizes capital projects. As capital money becomes available, projects are completed.

## Dublin (Ohio) Division of Parks and Open Space and Division of Recreation Services Master Plan Sample

Policy 7: Develop prairies and meadows while protecting endangered, threatened, potentially threatened, and vulnerable species.

Issue: There are very few prairies and meadows within the city limits.

### Strategies

- Develop a policy encouraging the planting of prairies and letting turf areas revert to meadows.

- Educate the public about the benefits of no-mow areas and prairies.

- Perform floristic assessments every 5 to 7 years in preidentified areas (woodlots, grasslands, prairies, meadows, ecotones) to help identify species richness and determine whether parkland is losing some of its endangered, threatened, and potentially threatened plants.

**Figure 5.11**   This sample from the City of Dublin (Ohio) Division of Parks and Open Space and Division of Recreation Services (2008) master plan depicts issues and strategies Dublin faces.

This phase may also address other funding sources for both capital and operating expenditures. Suggested sources for funding include mandatory dedication of land by developers, land dedication fees, bonds, tax increases, user fees, and grants such as Land and Water Conservation Fund and transportation enhancement grants.

## Phase 5: Approve, Implement, Monitor, Review, and Update

Like any plan, the master plan must be approved by the governing body, whether this body comprises a board of directors, trustees, or shareholders. The implementation is outlined with an action plan, and the master plan is regularly monitored, reviewed, and updated, just as a strategic plan is.

You can see there are several similarities between a master plan and a strategic plan. The main difference is the area of planning. Parks, facilities, and natural resources require a different analysis than programs and services require. Yet both analyses have the same result: strategies and issues to improve the agency and an action plan to accomplish this improvement.

## Business Plans

Although the term *business plan* conjures up visions of the commercial sector, the nonprofit and public sectors also use business plans because of their increased drive to become entrepreneurial

in their programs and services. A business plan details a "business's vision and objectives as well as the strategies and tactics that will be employed to achieve them" (Friend and Zehle 2009, 1). Business plans are a blueprint for the successful operation of a new venture, whether it is a new resort, a new ice rink, or a new boat rental service within an existing facility. Business plans also provide the data that guide business decisions and attract investors (Pfister and Tierney 2009). Investors are unlikely to invest in a company when they know nothing about the company or they lack solid information on the company's likelihood of success. Commercial agencies use business plans to appeal to investors. However, public and nonprofit agencies appeal to board members rather than investors. The purpose of the plan is to appeal to the board to allow the investment of current agency resources into the businesslike opportunity.

There are numerous resources on business planning, including books, Web sites, templates, and consultants, to steer you through this process. The business planning process differs from that of master plans and strategic plans. Business plans are very much content driven whereas strategic plans and master plans are process driven. Both the strategic and master plans collect a vast amount of information that is used for future directions, but the business plan mainly comprises information about the potential business and a description of what the business will look like. It does not necessarily enlist an action plan for the next few years.

## Capital Improvement Funding

Columbia (Missouri) Parks and Recreation Department (2010) has a capital improvement plan. The following are examples of how these projects are funded:

- Ballot: Funds authorized by public vote via a ballot issue.
- Capital improvements sales tax: Funds generated from the 1/4 cent sales tax in the state.
- Sales tax improvement: Sales tax issue voted on in 2005.
- CDBG (Community Development Block Grant): A federal entitlement grant program (annual) administered by the U.S. Department of Housing and Urban Development; 100-percent grant that requires no matching local funds.

A capital improvement plan details expenditures such as the construction and renovation of campus recreational facilities.

The typical business plan consists of the following:

- Executive summary
- Business description
- Products and services description
- Competitive analysis
- Marketing plan
- Operations and management plan
- Development plan
- Financial statements

## Executive Summary

Executive summaries are found in many plans, including strategic, master, and business plans.

They summarize the content of the plan in a clear and concise way. In the case of a business plan that is trying to secure financial investors, the executive summary either entices potential investors to continue reading and possibly invest in the business or turns off potential investors. Here are a few strategies for writing a good executive summary:

- Write the executive summary last, as it should summarize the entire plan.
- Discuss the main points of the plan and give enough information so that the plan is understandable.
- Avoid technical jargon; cover the technical aspects within the plan itself.
- Organize the content in the summary so that it follows the order of the sections

within the plan. If marketing comes before the financials in the plan, it should precede the financials in the executive summary as well.

- Keep the executive summary to one or two single-spaced pages in length.

The most important thing is that the executive summary is well constructed and enhances the business plan. It is worth taking extra time to follow these key points when constructing the executive summary, because this section could be the only part of the plan read.

## Business Description

The business description introduces the purpose and logistics of the business, including the name and location of the business and the contact information of the owners or managers. This section also outlines the ownership and legal structure of the business venture, gives the company history, and provides an industry overview.

The ownership and legal structure are straightforward for public and nonprofit agencies but require more detail for a commercial entity, as a commercial business can be structured as a sole proprietorship, partnership, C corporation, subchapter S corporation, or limited liability partnership or company:

- **Sole proprietorship:** The business is owned by one person who has unlimited liability for that business. Unlimited liability means that the owner is financially responsible for the business; the owner's personal finances and business finances are not separate.
- **Partnership:** The business is owned by two or more people who share the financial liability of the business.
- **C corporation:** The business is owned by shareholders. The business is seen as a fictional, legal person in that it can own land, have contracts signed on its behalf, and sue and be sued.
- **S corporation:** The business is formed like a C corporation, but the S corporation distributes all of its profits to the shareholders and does not retain them for the company itself.
- **Limited liability partnership or company:** The business is formed and structured like a partnership, but the owners have limited liability for debt.

It is also recommended to include other legal considerations in this section of the business description, including any licensing and distribution agreement, **trademark, copyright,** and **patent** obtained or applied for (Abrams 2005). The discussion of the company history covers where the company has been and where it is now. Businesses can be in several different stages of development (Abrams 2005):

- **Seed company:** The basic business concept has been developed, but the business has not been launched and no sales have been made.
- **Start-up:** The business is in the early stages of operation and has just begun to sell products or provide services.
- **Expanding:** The business is experiencing rapid growth and wants to increase its product offerings.
- **Stable:** The business is currently in operation and has had consistent sales with a modest growth.
- **Retrenchment:** Because of little or no growth in sales, the business needs to make changes to its product line or organizational structure to attempt to boost sales.

The last piece of the business description is the industry overview. This is essentially an environmental analysis that identifies the changing and influential factors in the environment. This information is often gathered from a PEST analysis (which was described earlier in the discussion on strategic planning).

## Products and Services Description

A detailed description of the products and services demonstrates to the potential investors what the business is selling. A product that is going to be successful will fill a gap in the market. The product description should emphasize the qualities and benefits of the product that will fill a niche within the market. It should also demonstrate the research done on the willingness of people to pay for the product or service, name the potential suppliers, and describe the availability of the product if it is a tangible item. If the service is intangible, a discussion on the available equipment or supplies needed should be included.

## Competitive Analysis

Competition exists for any business and can be direct or indirect. Direct competition is an agency that provides the same or similar products that your business provides. Indirect competition is a business that meets the same customer needs that your business meets but with a different product, such as a bowling alley versus a miniature golf course. Both types of competitors should be considered, with a bit more emphasis placed on direct competition. The competitive analysis should focus on major competitors, competitive advantages and disadvantages, market share, and barriers to entry into the market.

First the major competitors are scrutinized. Their products, prices, features, and services are studied and compared with those of your business to demonstrate how your business competes with each of them. This information leads to a better understanding of your competitive advantages and disadvantages. This is an analysis of the strengths and weaknesses of the business proposition. The third part of the competitive analysis, market share, demonstrates how much of the total sales of the product goes to each of the competitors in the market:

$$\text{Market share} = \text{the agency's sales} / \text{total market sales}$$

Information regarding an agency's sales is often available in annual reports, but the total market sales number can be a bit more difficult to obtain. Market research firms can help gather these data.

The last section of the competitive analysis examines the barriers to entry into the market. Some businesses face barriers that prohibit them from entering or reduce the chance for success once they have entered. These barriers include patents and trademarks needed, high start-up costs due to equipment or manufacturing requirements, substantial or difficult-to-locate staff expertise, and licensing and regulation restrictions (Abrams 2005).

## Marketing Plan

Because there are competition and choices for products and services, marketing is an instrumental contributor to business success or failure. A marketing plan includes the following:

- Executive summary and introduction
- Situational analysis

- Customer analysis
- Marketing goals and strategies
- Implementation, monitoring, and evaluation

Chapter 11 provides a step-by-step process for completing a marketing plan, and a further description of each item can be found in that chapter.

## Operations and Management Plan

To ensure potential investors that the business will run efficiently, an operations plan is included within the business plan. The operations plan has three key pieces: organizational structure, production and quality control, and location and facilities. The organizational structure is the staffing portion of the plan. An organizational chart shows the span of control for managers, the staff levels within the organization, the salaries of staff members, and the necessary qualifications for key positions. In many cases resumes are included for those who will have the primary responsibility of managing the organization. Since staffing is the bulk of a budget in many leisure services agencies, this section of the plan provides a snapshot of ongoing annual expenditures.

The next part of the operations plan, production and quality control, represents much of the start-up costs of a new venture. These start-up costs cover equipment and technology needs for manufacturing products and services as well as for operating the business. They may include computers, networking, registration software, or point-of-sale systems. For the manufacturing of products, there are quality control and inventory management issues that must be explained in the plan. If the product is actually a service, quality control is still an issue, but the business will have different means of ensuring that a superior service is delivered to the customer.

The last component of the operations plan focuses on location and facilities. Everyone has heard the phrase *location, location, location*. A location may be chosen because of its cost, proximity to the target market, access to transportation, desirable building and amenities, or ability to meet production requirements. The reason a particular location is chosen should be stated clearly in the operations plan so as to show that thought was put into the decision and to reiterate that location is a key to success.

The operations plan can easily become quite detailed. Keep in mind that it is an overview of the business operations and not the operations manual. It gives readers a solid idea of what the start-up funds will be used for as well as how the staffing plan will dictate a large portion of the operating budget.

## Development Plan

The development plan is arguably the most difficult section of the business plan to write. It projects what the business will look like in 1, 5, or 10 years in the future. It starts with a vision for what the business seeks to become. It projects things such as the number of employees, the profit margin, the market share, the plans for expansion, and the goals for the next year.

In addition to creating a positive vision for the future, the development plan should assess the risks the business might face in the future. These risks should cover six key areas (Abrams 2005):

1. Competition: New competitors can enter the market or current competitors can become more aggressive; either situation drives down the costs of products as well as the profit margin.

2. Market risk: The economy can turn and the needs of the target market can change.

3. Operational risk: Suppliers might downsize or dissolve, while manufacturing equipment or technology may change.

4. Financial risk: Resources such as staff, equipment, utilities, and manufacturing may rise in cost.

5. Execution risk: The business may not grow as quickly as predicted or may grow too quickly and become difficult to manage.

6. Economic risk: The overall economy may change.

The risks that could affect the business and the means to address these risks complete the development plan.

Even small sole proprietorships should consider developing a business plan. The plan can provide insight into the operation of the business and increase its chance for success.

## Financial Statements

The last section of the business plan is probably the most important one for potential investors and could be the section they read first. Unless an owner or a top manager has a background in finances, this section can be quite daunting to write. In some situations it is best to hire an accountant to help prepare the needed financial statements.

If investors are being sought, it is in this section of the business plan that the needs of the business are explained. This section lists how much money is needed and how the money will be used. Key financial statements demonstrating these needs are included, such as an income statement, a cash flow projection, and a balance sheet (these are all covered in chapter 8). In addition to these, a solid business plan includes sales projections for one to five years, a marketing budget (which is most likely completed during the marketing planning process), an operational budget, a break-even analysis, and a capital expenditures budget.

Developing a business plan can be an overwhelming task, much of it coming from the financial statements alone. However, a well-devised plan increases the likelihood of attracting investors if investors are needed. A solid business plan is also a map for success. It ensures that managers do not go into a situation blindly and that they have thoroughly thought through the entire process of establishing a business.

## Conclusion

This chapter provides an overview of three prominent plans used in the leisure services field: the strategic, master, and business plan. Each has its own elements, and yet all three plans share many similarities. The goal for each is to manage an agency as efficiently and effectively as possible, meet the needs of the consumer, and institute sound management principles and practices. All three plans can be developed internally or written by an external consultant. Sound management practices rely on good planning to guide the future and lead to decisions that are in the best interest of the staff, agency, and constituents. Furthermore, planning makes an agency less vulnerable to sudden changes in the environment, because it makes an agency more stable and able to adapt. As such, planning should be a part of everything an agency does and should not end once a plan is adopted.

## Review Questions

1. Differentiate between strategic planning and master planning. What are the steps involved in each?
2. Why is a business plan written? Explain the steps in the business planning process.
3. What is the role of stakeholders in the planning process?
4. Explain how an agency might do a services analysis.
5. What is a resource analysis in master planning?
6. Define the CIP.

**Visit the online resource at www.HumanKinetics.com/TheParkAndRecreationProfessionalsHandbook for sample documents, keywords, activities and assignments, and more.**

# Maintenance

chapter 6

**OUTCOMES**

- Describe grounds maintenance, building maintenance, and equipment maintenance.

- Categorize maintenance activities and scheduled or unscheduled maintenance.

- Understand the importance of standards, records, and work orders.

- Comprehend the unique maintenance requirements of parks, playgrounds, and aquatic areas.

Recreation facilities provide people with spaces where they can participate in leisure activities and have a positive experience. An expectation of facility users is that recreation facilities provide a safe environment where they can participate with minimal disruption. In order to create these types of experiences, recreation facilities must be well maintained. A well-maintained facility is aesthetically pleasing, provides safe equipment, and has amenities that are in good working order. Maintenance is important to all aspects of a facility and may vary based on the type, location, and purpose of the facility or space within the facility. Facility maintenance refers to the functions associated with keeping facilities and equipment in proper, safe, and usable condition (Mull, Beggs, and Renneisen 2009).

## Maintenance Categories

Maintenance is important to the operation of equipment and facilities because it keeps things in good working condition. As mentioned, maintenance varies based on the type, location, and purpose of a facility or space. Typically, there are three categories of maintenance: grounds maintenance, building maintenance, and equipment maintenance (Mull, Bayless, and Jamieson 2005).

### Grounds Maintenance

**Grounds maintenance** is the maintenance of outdoor spaces. These spaces might be an outdoor facility such as a playground or park. Outdoor spaces may also be exterior areas to indoor facilities, such as the landscaping outside a health club or recreation center. Exterior areas to indoor facilities may also include walkways or parking lots.

Regardless of the type of outdoor space, grounds maintenance is important in creating the first impression people experience when approaching or entering a facility (Hughes 1997). In fact, many people form an opinion of a facility based on this initial impression. This is especially true for people who do not use the facility but see it as they pass by. If the facility does not look good to them, then they are likely to have a bad impression of it. However, if the outdoor space creates a positive impression, it may attract people into the facility.

In addition to creating an environment that is aesthetically pleasing, grounds maintenance creates outdoor spaces that are safe. For instance, a walkway that is not properly maintained may

gather gravel or debris and become slippery. A park bridge that is not maintained may create a dangerous situation and the potential for injury among park users. Parks and playground maintenance is discussed in greater detail later in this chapter.

Grounds maintenance incorporates all the tasks associated with keeping outdoor areas attractive, functional, and safe. It includes removing trash; planting plants, trees, and grass; trimming shrubs and bushes; controlling pests; pruning trees; controlling weeds; mowing; removing leaves; removing snow; grooming athletic fields; maintaining playground surfaces; watering and fertilizing plants; checking playground equipment; repairing parking areas; and controlling water runoff (Mull, Beggs, and Renneisen 2009).

### Building Maintenance

Maintenance of indoor facilities and spaces such as offices, weight rooms, classrooms, lounges, reception areas, courts, hallways, stairwells, and restrooms is referred to as **building maintenance.** The same principles of grounds maintenance also apply to building maintenance. There is a need to keep indoor spaces clean, functional, and safe. People entering a building such as a health club form an opinion of the club by how clean and aesthetically pleasing they find the reception area. They continue to develop their impression of the facility as they move from the reception area to the locker room, weight room, aerobics area, and so on. No areas within a facility can be ignored, because it takes only one unclean or poorly maintained area to create a negative impression.

Cleanliness is important not only for aesthetic purposes but also for keeping equipment and spaces sanitary. This is one of the safety elements associated with maintenance. As with outdoor spaces, maintenance is important for keeping indoor spaces safe. A gym floor that becomes dirty may be slippery and cause injury. A tear in the carpet may cause someone to trip, or a loose handrail in a stairway can send a person tumbling down the stairs. These are all examples of building maintenance issues. Specific maintenance tasks may include vacuuming, mopping, and sweeping; removing trash; replacing lightbulbs; and checking and repairing items such as windows, doors, plumbing, carpet, and handrails.

Building maintenance also includes maintaining facility systems such as heating and cooling, plumbing, and electrical systems. While maintenance staff should be familiar with utility monitoring and repair, many agencies contact outside contractors to handle this type of maintenance, because it may require specific skills and certifications that are not necessarily required of maintenance staff (Daly 1995).

## Equipment Maintenance

**Equipment maintenance** refers to the maintenance of items that participants and employees utilize during facility operations. Participants may encounter a wide array of objects, such as exercise bikes, weight machines, treadmills, slides, swings, stage props, microphones, basketball hoops, and diving boards. Obviously, the type of equipment encountered greatly depends on the type and purpose of a facility. Equipment may include items that are used in outdoor or indoor facilities. Objects that employees encounter may include a sound system, computer system, vehicle, copier, lawn mower, vacuum, or leaf blower, just to name a few. Typically, employee equipment is the equipment employees use to provide a better experience for participants.

While equipment should look clean, the more important maintenance issue is the safety and functionality of the equipment. Regular maintenance to ensure safety and functionality is especially important when a piece of equipment gets a lot of use. For instance, a treadmill in a busy health club may be in use for 18 to 20 hours a day. That leaves very little time to clean it and check its components for safe operation. It's important to establish and adhere to a schedule for checking equipment.

# Types of Maintenance

So far, we have discussed the different roles that maintenance plays in relation to aesthetics, safety, and functionality. In order to uphold each of these roles, maintenance must be further classified by type. There are two types of maintenance: scheduled and unscheduled.

## Scheduled Maintenance

**Scheduled maintenance** refers to maintenance activities that are planned in advance and are part of a maintenance schedule. Developing this schedule and establishing a maintenance checklist (figure 6.1) assure that tasks are completed. The maintenance checklist is simply an itemized list

Equipment, including that used for field maintenance, undergoes scheduled maintenance to ensure it is ready to use for indoor and outdoor maintenance tasks.

of specific maintenance tasks that must be completed. Once employees complete an item on the checklist, they initial or check off that item.

The scheduling of maintenance activities must be done in such a way that it minimizes the effects maintenance has on facility users. Typically, scheduled maintenance tasks are completed after hours or at times when usage is low. It is very common for maintenance staff to work during late evening hours to complete scheduled maintenance jobs. There are three subclassifications of scheduled maintenance: routine, preventative, and cyclical.

### Routine Maintenance

**Routine maintenance** includes daily and weekly activities that preserve or improve the appearance of a facility or piece of equipment (Hurd et al. 2007). Common types of routine maintenance include the following:

- Cleaning
- Vacuuming
- Mowing
- Mopping
- Removing trash
- Finishing floors
- Painting
- Changing light bulbs

These types of activities primarily serve an aesthetic purpose in keeping the facility clean

## Facility Maintenance Inventory Form

| | Facility items | | Condition | Location of problem | Comments |
|---|---|---|---|---|---|
| General | Sport activity areas | Pool #1 | | | |
| | | Pool #2 | | | |
| | | Basketball court #1 | | | |
| | | Basketball court #2 | | | |
| | | Racquetball court #1 | | | |
| | | Racquetball court #2 | | | |
| | | Exercise or weight room | | | |
| | Office areas | Office #1 | | | |
| | | Office #2 | | | |
| | | Office #3 | | | |
| | | Break or meeting room | | | |
| | | Reception or lobby area | | | |
| | Locker and storage areas | Women's locker room | | | |
| | | Men's locker room | | | |
| | | Storage area #1 | | | |
| | | Storage area #2 | | | |
| | Safety | Fire alarm system | | | |
| | | Security system | | | |
| | | Sprinkler system | | | |
| | | Back-up generators | | | |
| Structural | Interior | Ceiling | | | |
| | | Floor | | | |
| | | Walls | | | |
| | | Windows | | | |
| | | Doors | | | |
| | Exterior | Roof | | | |
| | | Gutter and downspouts | | | |
| | | Wall treatment | | | |
| | | Windows | | | |
| | | Doors | | | |

**Figure 6.1** This sample daily maintenance checklist guides scheduled maintenance to ensure tasks are completed on a systematic basis.

From A.R. Hurd and D.M. Anderson, 2011, *The park and recreation professional's handbook* (Champaign, IL: Human Kinetics). Reprinted, by permission, from R. Mull, B. Beggs, and M. Renneisen, 2009, *Recreation facility management*, 4th ed. (Champaign, IL: Human Kinetics), 182.

| | Facility items | | Condition | Location of problem | Comments |
|---|---|---|---|---|---|
| Utilities | Water and sewer | Water lines | | | |
| | | Sewer lines | | | |
| | | Water heaters | | | |
| | | Water treatment systems | | | |
| | | Sink and shower fixtures | | | |
| | | Toilets | | | |
| | | Drinking fountains | | | |
| | Electric and gas | Electric lines | | | |
| | | Gas lines | | | |
| | | HVAC systems | | | |
| | | Electrical fixtures | | | |
| Grounds | Vegetation | Trees and shrubs | | | |
| | | Grass | | | |
| | Parking and walkways | Parking lot #1 (asphalt) | | | |
| | | Parking lot #2 (gravel) | | | |
| | | Sidewalk #1 | | | |
| | | Sidewalk #2 | | | |
| | | Mulch path | | | |

Conditions: S = Satisfactory condition, H = Hazardous condition, R = Routine maintenance needed, M = Large-scale maintenance needed (more than $500), m = Small-scale maintenance needed (less than $500)

**Figure 6.1**    *(continued)*

From A.R. Hurd and D.M. Anderson, 2011, *The park and recreation professional's handbook* (Champaign, IL: Human Kinetics). Reprinted, by permission, from R. Mull, B. Beggs, and M. Renneisen, 2009, *Recreation facility management*, 4th ed. (Champaign, IL: Human Kinetics), 182.

and attractive. Cleanliness can also help prevent illness from being spread and thus is also important in user safety.

### Preventative Maintenance

**Preventative maintenance** is used to protect areas and equipment from wearing out or breaking down and to extend the lives of spaces and equipment (Mull, Bayless, and Jamieson 2005). Preventative maintenance includes employee assessments of facilities and equipment. It can be as simple as changing the oil in a vehicle or refinishing the surface on a hardwood basketball floor. Preventative maintenance tasks are scheduled but are not performed as regularly as routine maintenance tasks are. The type of preventative

maintenance task determines its scheduling. For example, the schedule for changing the oil in a vehicle depends on how frequently the vehicle is driven. Refinishing a hardwood floor might be something that an agency schedules every other year.

Preventative maintenance also involves equipment inspection, which is used to make sure equipment is working properly and is in good condition. An inspection is a scheduled event that is conducted to monitor the condition of equipment. A piece of playground equipment may be inspected once a month to make sure swing chains are in good condition or bolts are tightly secured. This preventative maintenance promotes user safety and extends the life of a piece of equipment. Most preventative maintenance is done to assure user safety and functionality, but in some instances, such as refinishing a hardwood floor or repaving a parking lot, it is done for aesthetic value.

### Cyclical Maintenance

**Cyclical maintenance** encompasses scheduled maintenance activities that typically have numerous processes involved in completing the full cycle of the activity (Mull, Beggs, and Renneisen 2009). Many cyclical maintenance activities take place outdoors and are regulated by the seasons. A common cyclical maintenance process involves maintaining green spaces in parks. The process typically involves preparing the soil, seeding, fertilizing, watering, mowing, and aerating. These practices are repeated in a cycle.

## Unscheduled Maintenance

**Unscheduled maintenance** describes the maintenance activities that are not regularly scheduled. This may include small-scale activities such as repairing a broken swing on a playground or replacing a light in a gymnasium. Larger activities, such as installing a new filter system in a pool, can also be unscheduled maintenance. These types of maintenance activities can be classified as either unforeseen maintenance or maintenance projects.

### Unforeseen Maintenance

This is the most common type of unscheduled maintenance and can be considered to be reactive maintenance. It is the response to an area or a piece of equipment that has failed and requires repairs. In some instances, an immediate response is not essential. If a basketball net tears or breaks, for example, it is still usable. However, if the rim on the basketball goal is torn down, then activities on that basketball court may come to a halt, and a more urgent response may be needed. A similar situation might occur if a treadmill malfunctions. If a facility has many treadmills, this maintenance may be delayed until there are fewer users in the facility. However, if there is only one treadmill, then a quicker response may be required. If a situation occurs where a piece of equipment breaks down, it should be addressed immediately and signage should be posted in order to prevent participants from trying to use the broken equipment.

There are also instances in which **unforeseen maintenance** requires immediate attention and response time is of greater urgency. When a toilet overflows, for example, immediate action should be taken. Sometimes unforeseen maintenance may require an emergency response such as when lighting malfunctions during evening hours or there are electrical or mechanical malfunctions in a facility. For situations like these, an emergency

Keeping facilities, grounds, and equipment well maintained will encourage customer use and participation.

preparedness plan should be in place to determine what procedures should be followed. Emergency preparedness plans are discussed in greater detail in chapter 7.

### Maintenance Projects

**Maintenance projects** are larger-scale maintenance activities that involve major repairs or renovations in a facility. They are not regularly scheduled maintenance activities, but they do require planning. They may include projects such as replacing indoor turf, installing a new air conditioning system in a health club, or replacing the flooring in an aerobics room. Typically when these projects take place, the area worked on is blocked off from the public and users are notified in advance.

Often maintenance projects go beyond the scope of the maintenance resources within a recreation agency. It is common for agencies to hire external contractors to complete these projects (Hurd et al. 2007). Even when responsibility has been contracted out, the recreation agency must monitor the work to ensure that it meets the agency requirements.

## Maintenance Systems

The discussion on the various categories of maintenance cannot be completed without considering maintenance systems. Maintenance systems give agencies procedures to follow in providing maintenance. In other words, these systems provide the agency with a protocol for determining how to handle maintenance situations. Maintenance systems require an understanding of standards, records, work orders, and maintenance staff.

## Standards

**Standards** are established for a variety of maintenance situations. They may be in place so an agency can determine the amount of work necessary to make an area aesthetically appealing and safe or so an agency can determine how often areas should be cleaned. For example, standards addressing the frequency of vacuuming spaces or mopping floors could be established for an indoor facility. Standards for maintenance of outdoor spaces might include guidelines for maintaining lighting, plants, turf, and irrigation.

Maintenance also involves dealing with chemicals that could affect public and employee safety. Because of this, there are standards in place for handling chemicals. Guidelines established by the Occupational Safety and Health Administra-

tion (OSHA) within the U.S. Department of Labor and the CDC should be followed when agencies are handling chemicals or hazardous waste. In addition, each organization has guidelines that an agency must follow when using and storing hazardous chemicals. These organizations provide information about how to store, utilize, and dispose of specific chemicals. They also include standards for responding to emergency situations in which individuals are exposed to chemicals. Considerations in handling chemicals typically include temperature, ventilation, mixing, and identification. Storage and handling information is required for all hazardous chemicals in the workplace, and that information is available through labels on chemical storage containers or through the material safety data sheet (MSDS). The MSDS also provides information about the manufacturing company, chemical composition, and health hazards as well as procedures for dealing with first aid, fire, leakage, disposal, and environmental issues. Chemical manufacturers are required to provide an MSDS for all chemicals they sell. MSDS information is also available through the CDC. Standards for handling chemical and hazardous waste are also available through www.osha.gov/pls/oshaweb/owadisp.show_document?p_table=STANDARDS&p_id=10099 and www.cdc.gov/niosh/topics/chemical-safety.

## Records

Keeping records of maintenance work serves an agency in a variety of ways. **Records** include documentation of routine maintenance, preventative maintenance, inspections, cyclical maintenance, unforeseen maintenance, maintenance projects, and maintenance manuals. Records allow an agency to monitor the amount of resources required to maintain facilities and equipment. They also assist the agency in budgeting and scheduling. In addition, keeping records of the work done helps keep a facility clean and aesthetically pleasing. However, of greater importance is the role that records play in keeping facilities and equipment safe. Records are also important for risk management, as they allow agencies to present documentation of maintenance completed, repair work, and scheduled maintenance. Records are also important in providing users with a safe experience.

In addition, records are used to monitor equipment use. Items such as treadmills, copiers, and vehicles have systems within them that allow for easy monitoring of use. Keeping records of use is important in understanding the life of a product and when maintenance should be performed.

## Work Orders

Scheduled maintenance consists of activities that are routine and are a part of the daily, weekly, monthly, or annual schedule. Because these activities are scheduled and routine, they do not require any special action for them to take place. Unscheduled maintenance is not routine and therefore requires an action system to evaluate the maintenance issue, determine the steps of action, prioritize the steps, and assign staff to complete the steps. This formal action system is organized through the use of work orders.

A **work order,** also known as a *maintenance request form* (figure 6.2), is a formal document that begins with the identification and evaluation of an unforeseen maintenance problem (Mull, Bayless, and Jamieson 2005). Once the problem has been identified and evaluated, steps of action for fixing the problem must be determined. In determining these steps of action a manager must consider safety, usage patterns, costs, resources needed, and length of time needed to complete the project. These steps of action are documented on the work order and then prioritized against other maintenance projects. The work order is then assigned to a maintenance staff person to complete. Work orders are often initiated with a number or code so that they are easy to track and include information about the manager requesting the work order. Once a work order has been completed and signed off, it is filed according to its assigned number or code.

## Maintenance Staff

The maintenance staff consists of the employees who are responsible for completing scheduled and unscheduled maintenance activities. The size and skill set of the staff depend on the size of the agency and the number, size, and types of its facilities. The size of the maintenance staff is also affected by the management philosophy of the agency. Some agencies try to handle all maintenance issues in-house and employ many maintenance staff members who have the skill sets necessary to handle all the scheduled and unscheduled maintenance problems. Other agencies prefer to outsource maintenance problems to other organizations (Daly 1995). Again, this decision may be dictated by the agency's size and facility issues.

Agencies that perform maintenance in-house often use specific maintenance units that specialize in a particular area. One unit may be dedicated to maintaining grounds and outdoor spaces, while another may focus on indoor spaces or dedicated spaces such as aquatic areas. Units allow the maintenance staff members to become more familiar with the specific tasks and equipment associated with their particular area. All maintenance staff members should be trained in how to operate equipment safely and efficiently.

In some situations, regular maintenance staff members may not be able to handle the problem, and agencies may employ maintenance personnel with specialized skills such as plumbers, electricians, or mechanics. These skilled employees may be from specialized maintenance staff that consists of full-time employees for the agency, or they may be outside contractors.

For any given job, hiring outside contractors typically costs more than using in-house employees, but employing full-time maintenance staff with specialized skills is also expensive. By contracting out, the agency can save money over time, because even though the initial cost for the job is higher, the agency avoids paying full-time

## 🍁 Maintenance and Energy: Tips for Efficiency

- Turn lights off when a room is not being utilized.
- Repair dripping water faucets and leaks.
- Make sure exterior doors are closed.
- Turn the thermostat up during the warmer months and down during the cooler months.
- Turn off computers and appliances when they are not in use.
- Unplug chargers and appliances when they are not in use, because most of them use energy when they are plugged in regardless of whether they are in use.
- Reuse paper and recycle.
- Put a facility plan in place so that all employees and users can help save energy.

## Maintenance Request Form

Facility and location _____ Date _____

Requested by _____ Date needed _____

Specific and complete nature of work requested_____

_____

_____

_____

_____

_____

_____

Date request received _____

Assigned to _____

Date completed _____

Priority check _____

Comments _____

_____

_____

_____

_____

_____

_____

_____

_____

Labor: _____ Hours: _____ Hourly rate: _____

Materials needed: _____

_____

_____

_____

_____

_____

**Figure 6.2** Agencies use maintenance request forms to track what jobs need to be done, who completes them, and other details needed for record keeping.

From A.R. Hurd and D.M. Anderson, 2011, *The park and recreation professional's handbook* (Champaign, IL: Human Kinetics). Reprinted, by permission, from R. Mull, B. Beggs, and M. Renneisen, 2009, *Recreation facility management*, 4th ed. (Champaign, IL: Human Kinetics), 184.

salaries and benefits to specialized maintenance personnel. The downside to contracting out is that it may take longer to complete the task, and the agency has less control over the job.

## Maintaining Recreational Spaces

Much of the discussion in this chapter focuses on general building and grounds maintenance. However, there are a few specific areas that require special consideration. Three common recreational spaces that have unique maintenance requirements are parks, playgrounds, and aquatic areas.

### Parks

Parks are a part of every community. They can be operated at any level of government or can be privately owned. Regardless of who operates a park,

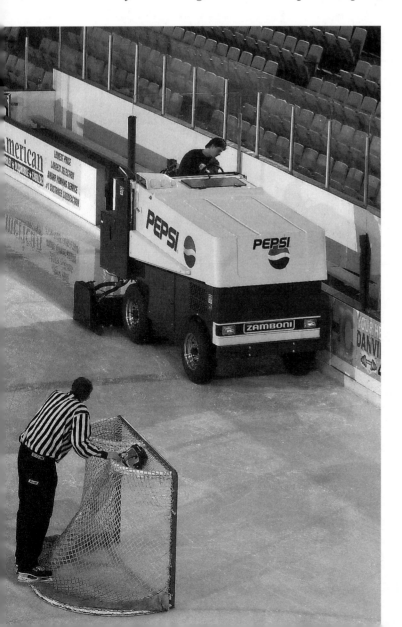

there are special considerations for maintenance. There are many types of vegetation in parks that require special knowledge from the maintenance staff members so they can administer proper care (Molnar and Rutledge 1992). In addition to the many types of grasses, trees, and plants that must be cared for in a park, there are other amenities that require maintenance attention, such as trails. Maintaining trails is important to the safety of users and the longevity of the trails (Ciancutti 2005). In addition to keeping trails clean and accessible, it is important to make sure that trails drain properly. Because trails are usually natural turf and grasses, they can erode during heavy rains or during periods of heavy usage. Thus maintenance staff must move dirt and soil on a regular basis to preserve the desired trail slopes.

Many parks also provide restrooms, shelters, and playground areas that require maintenance. Restrooms and shelters typically generate lots of trash and unforeseen messes that must be dealt with. It is common practice to hose off outdoor restrooms and shelters on a daily basis, especially during periods of high usage. Shelters may also require monitoring; the maintenance staff should routinely check the condition of picnic tables or the shelter structure itself. Structures made of wood deteriorate in the outdoors if they are not properly cared for and protected. In addition, roofing materials must be checked and maintained. Restrooms and shelters in park areas should be constructed with durable materials so they can handle daily cleaning and wear and tear (Potter 2005).

### Playgrounds

Playgrounds are often an important part of parks. However, playgrounds may also be found at community centers, child care facilities, and schools. It is also becoming common to see playgrounds around restaurants, hotels, and resorts catering to family experiences. Regardless of its location, a playground must be well maintained for the safety of users, which are primarily children.

Playground maintenance focuses on the play structures themselves and the surface beneath the play equipment. Most pieces of playground equipment have bolts or screws that need to be inspected and tightened on a regular basis. In

Because they are unique, ice rinks also can require specialized maintenance and a specific skill set to maintain them.

addition, the material a structure is made out of may also dictate maintenance. Equipment made from wood requires attention to prolong the life of the structure and to make sure that there are no protruding pieces that may cause splinters or even greater harm to users. Structures made from plastic also have a limited life expectancy and should be examined regularly to make sure they remain free of cracks and warping. Play structures made from metal typically last the longest, but they should also be examined to make sure there is no damage such as rust (Thompson, Hudson, and Olsen 2007). Playground maintenance should include inspections for missing handholds, loose rungs, deteriorated wood, uncapped ends of pipes, sagging guardrails, rusted swings, deteriorated pipes, loose bolts, worn surfacing, and split fiberglass (Christiansen and Vogelsong 1996). The optimal inspection frequency for a given play structure depends on its usage and type. Most pieces of play equipment have inspection and maintenance guidelines provided by the manufacturer. Figure 6.3 shows a sample daily playground inspection checklist.

The surface beneath a play structure may be even more important to maintain than the play structure itself. This area is called the *use zone* or *safety zone*. This area should be free of other equipment and structures and should include a specialized surface designed to prevent injury should a child fall from the play structure. Different types of surfaces provide different levels of safety. The level of safety a surface provides is called *fall protection* and depends on how absorbent the surface is or how much give there is in the surface. Different playground surfaces provide different qualities for fall protection. Many playgrounds utilize loose-fill materials for surfacing.

Loose-fill surfaces include sand, pea gravel, wood chips, shredded rubber, and synthetic wood fibers (Thompson, Hudson, and Olsen 2007). The Consumer Product Safety Commission (CPSC) has established guidelines for how deep these surfaces should be in order to be safe. By maintaining these depths, the use zone has greater absorbency qualities. The issue in maintaining these spaces is trying to preserve the required depths. As a loose-fill surface is moved around, it becomes displaced and its fall protection changes. Thus containment of the loose-fill material and replacement of displaced surfacing are of great importance. A good example of a surface maintenance issue is the area directly beneath a playground swing. If that area is filled with wood chips, the wood chips get

kicked around and displaced as children swing and drag their feet. Another area that is commonly displaced is the area at the end of a slide. When children slide into the surface, they kick, displace, or even take home some of the material with them. Just think about how many times you returned home from a playground with a sandy surface and you had to dump sand out of your shoes or pockets. These are all very common examples of displacing a loose-fill surface. Maintenance staff members must examine play areas to make sure that any loose-fill material is maintained at its proper depth. This kind of surface maintenance is typically achieved by sweeping, raking, or just adding more material to the area.

Some playgrounds consist of unitary surfaces, which are rubberized surfaces that are fixed to the ground. These surfaces can consist of one large rubberized tile or multiple tiles that are interlocked to prevent displacement. Unitary surfaces are more expensive than loose-fill surfaces are, and they are more complicated and expensive to install. Installation typically involves leveling a surface, pouring a concrete subsurface, and adhering the rubberized surface to the subsurface. Although unitary surfaces are more expensive, they do not require as much maintenance attention, because they do not displace and they are very durable. Maintenance for these surfaces typically consists of hosing them off and checking that the adhesive is secure.

Safety standards for playgrounds are updated regularly by the American Society for Testing and Materials (ASTM) and the CPSC. These standards are published and are available to any recreation agency. However, it can be difficult for an agency to monitor and maintain these standards in its play areas. The Certified Playground Safety Inspector (CPSI) program is a training program administered by the National Playground Safety Institute through the NRPA. The CPSI program provides training to agencies and individuals in maintaining safe playgrounds and incorporates the standards of the ASTM and CPSC. Individuals who complete the CPSI training are certified to inspect playgrounds for safety hazards.

## Aquatic Areas

Aquatic spaces can be as simple as a recreational pool or as complex as an aquatic center with many amenities such as lazy rivers, slides, aquatic playgrounds, wave pools, lap pools, and waterfalls. Aquatic spaces can also be located

# Daily Playground Inspection Checklist

Name of playground _____

Date of inspection _____ Inspected by _____

| Playground equipment | Yes | No | N/A | Comments |
|---|---|---|---|---|
| Is equipment properly anchored? | | | | |
| Are all bolts in place and secure? | | | | |
| Are there any open S hooks? | | | | |
| Are all nails flush against wood? | | | | |
| Is there any splintering on wood? | | | | |
| Are there any sharp points or edges on equipment? | | | | |
| Is any equipment damaged or missing? | | | | |
| Is equipment in good overall condition? | | | | |
| Other comments about playground equipment: | | | | |

| Grounds | Yes | No | N/A | Comments |
|---|---|---|---|---|
| Are there any obstructions that may limit safety or accessibility? | | | | |
| Is there any trash on the grounds? | | | | |
| Are the grounds clean and free of vandalism? | | | | |
| Are there any safety hazards such as broken glass or nails on the grounds? | | | | |
| Is there any animal feces in the area? | | | | |
| Are there any signs of unwanted animals in the area? | | | | |
| Is the grass well maintained? | | | | |
| Other comments about grounds: | | | | |

| Playground surfaces | Yes | No | N/A | Comments |
|---|---|---|---|---|
| Have loose-fill surfaces been raked and leveled in displaced and compacted areas? | | | | |
| Do loose-fill surfaces have adequate depth? | | | | |
| Have unitary surfaces been damaged? | | | | |
| Does the surface extend 6 feet beyond the play structure? | | | | |
| For swings, does the surface extend twice the height of the structure in back and front? | | | | |
| For slides, does the surface extend the height of the slide plus 4 feet at the end of the chute? | | | | |
| Are there any weeds growing in the surface? | | | | |
| Is there any glass or dangerous materials in the surface? | | | | |
| Are surface borders secure and in place? | | | | |
| Are surface borders in good condition? | | | | |
| Other comments about playground surfaces: | | | | |

Notes _____

**Figure 6.3** Agencies use a daily playground inspection checklist to ensure playgrounds are safe for use by children.

From A.R. Hurd and D.M. Anderson, 2011, *The park and recreation professional's handbook* (Champaign, IL: Human Kinetics).

Agencies will most likely have a policy that dictates how often playgrounds are inspected and the process used to inspect them.

indoors or outdoors. As with other spaces, maintenance is important to the aesthetics of an aquatic area. Regardless of whether aquatic areas are located indoors or outdoors, they share some common maintenance concerns. Like parks, aquatic areas may contain additional spaces that require routine maintenance, such as locker rooms, restrooms, concessions, and deck areas. Of greater importance in an aquatic area is safety. Ensuring safety through proper maintenance involves access control, inspection of equipment and pool areas, operation of mechanical systems, and sanitation.

### Access Control

**Access control** systems are those that allow or limit entry to a facility or an amenity within a facility. State codes require that aquatic areas have an access control system in place. For outdoor aquatic areas, this often means fencing and controlled access areas where there is supervised

entry (Gabrielsen 1987). For safety and security purposes, it is vital that fencing, locks, and access control points be inspected and maintained to minimize the possibility of unsupervised access to an aquatic space.

### Inspection of Equipment and Pool Areas

Aquatic spaces often include different amenities and equipment for people to use during their leisure experience. These items must be in good working order and safe to use. Aquatic play structures, slides, and diving boards all have materials that should be inspected for wear and bolts or screws that need to be checked regularly. In addition, the surface in the pool area should be inspected on a regular basis to make sure it has not been damaged. Pool surfaces may consist of tiles that can come loose or can lose their safety or water resilient qualities due to abuse or overuse. Concrete surfaces should be checked for cracks and also maintained through proper sealing procedures. Some aquatic spaces are constructed with a synthetic unitary surface that absorbs water and provides some fall protection. Proper maintenance of these surfaces includes inspecting for rips or tears.

### Operation of Mechanical Systems

Aquatic spaces utilize mechanical systems to filter and sanitize the water. These mechanical systems typically include a pump, filter system, and water sanitation system (Walsh 1993). The pump is used to circulate the water from the usage areas to the filter and sanitation systems. The filter system then removes loose materials from the water before it is pumped to the sanitation system. The sanitation system uses chemicals to treat the water and sanitize it before it is pumped back out to the aquatic usage areas. The process of filtering all the water in a standard pool typically takes 4 to 6 hours (Shalley and Barzdukas 1997).

The filtering process takes place multiple times a day, and if the pump should malfunction, the aquatic space would become unsafe and would be forced to shut down. It is very common for aquatic areas to have a maintenance person specifically trained to maintain the mechanical systems and to handle nonroutine maintenance problems. Properly scheduled maintenance helps to minimize nonroutine problems. The most common form of routine maintenance for aquatic mechanical systems is backwashes. During a backwash, the pump and system are run in reverse to loosen and remove any materials that may have built up in the filter.

Proper maintenance also involves handling the chemicals used to sanitize the water. The most frequently used chemical in sanitation is chlorine, but some aquatic systems use bromine. A maintenance staff member should know how to properly add chemicals to the system and how to store the chemicals properly in order to ensure the safety of staff members and patrons. As mentioned earlier, the guidelines to follow for chemical storage should be listed on the chemical containers. They are also available through OSHA and the CDC.

### Sanitation

If not properly sanitized, aquatic areas can be a breeding ground for bacteria and parasites. Locker rooms, restrooms, showers, and deck areas must be sanitized in order to protect users. These spaces typically are constructed of materials that allow them to be sanitized on a daily basis. A mixture of water and bleach is used to sanitize these areas. Then they are hosed down to complete the process.

## Conclusion

Maintenance plays an important part in creating a positive appearance and image for a facility. However, its greater purpose is to keep the facility safe for participants and employees to enjoy. Establishing scheduled maintenance procedures can minimize or eliminate many maintenance problems. A quick response to unscheduled maintenance issues is also vital to creating a positive and safe leisure experience for users. Managers should not overlook maintenance and the important role it plays in leisure services.

---

## Review Questions

1. What are the three categories of maintenance? Briefly explain each.
2. What is the difference between scheduled maintenance and unscheduled maintenance? Give an example of each.
3. Compare and contrast routine, preventative, and cyclical maintenance.
4. Explain the role that standards, records, and work orders play in maintenance.
5. How does the material that playground equipment is made from affect its maintenance?
6. How do loose-fill surfaces and unitary surfaces differ in their maintenance requirements?
7. What are the different maintenance concerns in an aquatic area?

---

 Visit the online resource at www.HumanKinetics.com/TheParkAndRecreationProfessionalsHandbook for sample documents, keywords, activities and assignments, and more.

chapter 7

# Facility Management

**OUTCOMES**

- Understand facility opening and closing procedures.

- Differentiate between facility scheduling and facility coordination.

- Describe classifications for different types of equipment.

- Recognize factors that can affect safety and security.

- Comprehend the unique supervision characteristics of parking areas, shelters, locker rooms, reception areas, day cares, and commodity outlets.

Recreation facilities provide places for people to participate in leisure activities. They are instrumental in facilitating quality leisure experiences. From a recreation practitioner perspective, facilities are essential to delivering a service. Because of the benefits facilities bring to both users and practitioners, a high level of importance is placed on managing facilities.

Managing facilities includes developing policies that provide recreation staff members with guidelines for operating the facility and various spaces within the facility and for handling situations that may occur during facility use. These policies typically prescribe procedures for opening and closing, scheduling and coordination, equipment and supply management, safety and security, emergency preparedness, and supervision of spaces within a facility.

# Opening and Closing Procedures

**Opening and closing procedures** can refer to daily procedures or to seasonal procedures. Both of these procedures utilize checklists to assure that all steps are followed the same way every time an employee opens or closes a facility. These checklists should be reviewed during employee training.

## Daily Procedures

Procedures for the daily opening and closing of a facility are called *daily procedures.* Daily procedures should be specific for each facility; however, there are general steps to opening and closing that most agencies follow.

### Opening Procedures

Opening procedures ensure that a facility is ready to be used by participants at the designated opening time. There are various checklist items that an employee may be required to follow in opening a facility; figure 7.1 provides an example opening checklist.

The first task for most employees is unlocking and accessing the facility. In some instances, employees may need to enter the proper codes to disarm any alarms activated for security purposes. Once the employee has accessed the facility, opening procedures typically include setting the lighting and temperature controls (Hurd et al. 2007). In some instances, these settings may be automated and the employee must simply check the settings to make sure they are correct. Next the employee examines different areas in the facility to make sure they are unlocked, clean, and safe. It is during this time that the employee looks for anything unusual, such as evidence of a break-in or facility damage. If it is evident that something is wrong, the employee follows the actions established by the agency for addressing these issues. Once the general inspection of the facility is complete, the employee makes sure that any spaces in the facility requiring a specific setup are ready.

### Closing Procedures

Closing procedures focus on properly shutting down and securing a facility (Hurd et al. 2007). One of the first steps in closing is to make sure that all participants leave the facility. Once the facility has been vacated, the closing employee cleans and inspects the equipment and spaces in the facility

## Facility Opening Checklist

1. When opening for the day, arrive at the recreation center no less than 15 minutes before opening to the public.

2. Complete the following items before allowing public access:

   a. Turn on all necessary lights and set up proper equipment for the scheduled programs.

   b. Inspect all program areas for potential safety hazards and cleanliness.

   c. Inspect bathrooms and replace necessary toiletries on days when custodian is not scheduled to work.

   d. Review daily schedule and check your employee mailbox.

3. Prepare and post daily activities on the entry easel.

4. Make last-minute preparations to meeting rooms as necessary.

5. Open the building for public access promptly at opening time.

**Figure 7.1**    The opening procedures checklist is precisely followed each time the facility is opened.

to make sure they are safe, clean, and in working order for the next day. Often maintenance tasks are completed at this time so that facility users are not affected during hours of operation. While closing, the employee makes sure that windows and doors are closed and locked. Once the facility has been inspected, the employee adjusts the lighting and temperature to their designated settings and sets the security alarms.

## Seasonal Procedures

Seasonal procedures are used to open and close a facility that is open only during certain times of the year. In this instance, employees must open a facility that has been shut down for a lengthy period and close a facility with the idea that it will not be open for awhile. Examples of facilities requiring seasonal procedures include outdoor pools, ski areas, and beachfronts. Seasonal procedures may also include opening and closing amenities such as restrooms and shelters in facilities such as parks that remain open year round.

Seasonal opening procedures prepare a facility to be used by participants. The specific checklist to be followed depends on the type of facility being opened. In general, seasonal opening procedures focus on turning on mechanical systems and assuring that a facility is in good operating condition (Hurd et al. 2007). Seasonal closing procedures are directed toward preserving the vital systems of a facility until it is opened for the following season (Hurd et al. 2007). This can involve many different practices, such as shutting off water pipes, treating surfaces, draining chemicals, and storing equipment. Again, the specific checklist to be followed depends on the type of facility being closed.

# Scheduling and Coordination

Two important responsibilities for facility management are scheduling and coordination. These procedures prepare a facility for use by ensuring that people, space, and equipment are integrated efficiently.

## Scheduling

**Scheduling** is the assignment of time, place, and people for facility use (Mull, Beggs, and Renneisen 2009). The procedures that an agency uses for scheduling are dictated by facility size, purpose, and programming. If a facility is large, there may be many different spaces to schedule

Opening a shelter for the season often requires bringing in picnic tables and doing routine maintenance such as cleaning and painting.

within. If a facility is multipurpose, there may be many different types of activities to schedule. In many instances, users may be able to reserve facility space for personal or professional activities. There are also facilities where most of the scheduling revolves around programs run by the agency. Regardless of the facility size, purpose, or programming, there are general issues to consider in scheduling. The most important issue is the establishment and use of a master schedule.

The master schedule provides a central point for recording all facility reservations. Using a master schedule greatly minimizes the probability of scheduling conflicts and provides recreation staff members with a central location where they can get schedule information. In some instances, the master schedule is a logbook where reservations are hand recorded. However, due to the emergence of recreation software, most master schedules are maintained electronically.

## Scheduling Software

There are many different types of recreation scheduling software. In addition to scheduling, this software can be used to manage registrations, membership, and events. Software packages can also be used to track equipment, create identification cards, market programs and events, and control facility access.

Regardless of the system used, the scheduling procedures should be formalized.

Scheduling procedures provide directives to follow in reserving space within a facility. Having formalized scheduling procedures minimizes the possibility for error and allows for agency control of spaces (Mull, Beggs, and Renneisen 2009). Scheduling procedures typically include guidelines for prioritizing the use of space. In most instances programs offered by the agency have first priority. Once agency activities have been scheduled, an agency may allow outside individuals or groups to reserve space in the facility. This is done through permits or facility use agreements.

Permits and facility use agreements allow users to request a space as well as provide the agency with information about the user. Permits and facility use agreements require the potential users to provide the date, time, and location they are seeking to reserve. The documents also provide user contact information and information about the type of activity taking place. Information regarding any fees to be paid or deposits to be made is also included in these documents. The permits and facility use agreements should outline the policies of the agency and address ramifications if these policies are violated (Fried 2005). For instance, if a group reserves a room in a facility and damages equipment during its activity, the guidelines for how the damage is handled should be already included in the policies on the permit and facility use agreement.

Permits are more common in spaces that do not require any special setup or supervision. Permits are common in reserving park shelters, pavilions, and campsites. A facility use agreement (figure 7.2) is more common for reserving indoor spaces, but it may also be used for outdoor facilities. The facility use agreement is typically more detailed than the permit and includes information regarding equipment needs, food service, setup and takedown, personnel requirements, and safety and security concerns (Mull, Beggs, and Renneisen 2009). The agreement serves as a tool to clarify the details and responsibilities of an event

so that both the user and the agency understand their responsibilities and the ramifications of not fulfilling those responsibilities.

## Coordination

Coordination procedures are often implemented concurrently with schedule procedures. Scheduling and coordination are connected in that efficient scheduling cannot occur without coordination. **Coordination** is the planning and organizing of all the details associated with a program or event. As mentioned previously, permits and facility use agreements document this type of information. Coordination is actually putting those actions into place to make sure that equipment, staff, and setup are adequate for an activity. Coordination addresses setup and takedown issues, equipment needs, electrical needs, area load and layout, supervision, security requirements, access control, charges, and food service (Mull, Beggs, and Renneisen 2009).

Coordination also involves assigning space that is appropriate for an event. As previously discussed, activities programmed by the agency have first priority in the master schedule. In facilities where multiple activities may occur at the same time, such as community centers or health clubs, great care needs to be exercised to make sure these activities do not conflict with one another. For instance, scheduling a teen activity in a space directly next to a senior citizen program could be disruptive to both groups. Another example is a youth birthday party scheduled close to a yoga class. In this case the noise from the party could disrupt the yoga class.

Another consideration in addition to avoiding disruption is avoiding scheduling programs that attract the same users at the same time. When two preschool activities are scheduled at the same time, the attendance to both activities may suffer. Scheduling the two activities at different times of the day or on different days of the week allows participants to sign up for both programs instead of choosing one or the other. The timing of events

## Sample Parks and Recreation Department Pool Rental Agreement

Group or organization name: _____     Date of use: _____

Number in group: _____     Arrival time: _____

Name: _____     Departure time: _____

Address: _____     Home phone: _____

City, state, zip: _____     Work phone: _____

### Guidelines

- Lifeguards will be provided.
- Adult supervision is required.
- All pool rules must be followed.

### Rental Fees

The rental fee is $200.00 for two hours with up to 50 guests. A $100.00 deposit is required. If no damage is present as a result of the rental, the deposit will be applied to the rental fee. Otherwise, the deposit will be forfeited and the full rental fee will be due.

### Inclement Weather Provision

A rental will be considered complete once one hour of the rental has lapsed without inclement weather. If inclement weather occurs within the first hour of the rental, a makeup date will be established or the deposit and rental fees will be refunded.

### Agreement

I certify that all information provided on this form is accurate and I assume full responsibility for the proper care and utilization of the Parks and Recreation Department Pool. I and my organization agree to hold the Parks and Recreation Department harmless from any loss, injury, or claim of liability arising from use of the pool. I agree to follow the posted rules and to leave the facility undamaged. I understand that any cancellations must be made one week before the reserved date or my deposit will be forfeited.

Signed: _____     Date: _____

**Figure 7.2** A typical facility use agreement is more detailed than a permit because it outlines the responsibilities of the agency and the user.

Reprinted, by permission, from R. Mull, B. Beggs, and M. Renneisen, 2009, *Recreation facility management,* 4th ed. (Champaign, IL: Human Kinetics), 171.

is also important for agency programs. This is a big reason why hosting agencies have first priority in scheduling. Programs should be scheduled at times that make them the most accessible to potential users.

Activity type may also dictate the size and location of the space needed. This is true for agency-sponsored programs and for reservations from users. If someone wants to reserve a space for a wedding reception, for example, there may be only one space in a facility that can accommodate the number of people attending. Activities that require physical activity and movement are more likely to require more space. Some activities may require access to cooking areas or cold food storage and therefore need to be in specific

spaces that provide those amenities. These are all elements of coordination.

## Managing Equipment

Vital to the management of any facility is the management of equipment. **Equipment** can be defined as anything in a facility that contributes to administrative and program operations (Mull, Bayless, and Jamieson 2005). Equipment is considered to be permanent, expendable, or fixed.

**Permanent equipment** is not affixed to the facility but is necessary in order for the facility to operate. Although this equipment is labeled as *permanent*, it does have a life span, which typically is two or more years. Permanent equipment costs more than $500 and includes items such as vehicles, scoreboards, and volleyball standards. Permanent equipment can be moved and, barring cost, is not difficult to replace.

**Expendable equipment**, which is frequently referred to as *supplies,* usually costs less than $500 and has a life expectancy of less than two years. Expendable equipment is purchased on a regular basis and is used in day-to-day administrative operations and in running programs. For instance, the supplies purchased for participants to use in a craft class can be classified as expendable equipment. In a sport setting, field-marking chalk and baseballs can be classified as expendable equipment. The expectation for expendable equipment is that it will be consumed during use or will wear out over time.

**Fixed equipment** is attached permanently to a facility and is usually installed during construction. Fixed equipment is prevalent in all facilities and may include mechanical systems such as heating, ventilation, and air conditioning (HVAC), sound systems, alarms, showers, and sinks. Fixed equipment may also include items essential to program delivery, such as play structures, fences, goalposts, basketball goals, and soccer goals.

## Equipment Classifications

Equipment can also be classified in a more specialized manner. It can be categorized as efficiency system equipment, structural equipment, administrative equipment, delivery equipment, or maintenance equipment (Mull, Beggs, and Renneisen 2009).

Efficiency systems are the electrical and mechanical systems that support the overall use of the facility. **Efficiency system equipment** includes HVAC, irrigation, security, and lighting systems. Efficiency systems usually are installed during construction and are classified as fixed equipment.

**Structural equipment** is also installed during construction and is classified as fixed equipment. In addition, it is usually included in the construction cost. It is not movable, and it includes items such as doors, windows, railings, and permanent seating.

All recreation facilities have **administrative equipment** that supports the administrative and executive operation of the facility. Administrative equipment includes computers, copiers, cash registers, printers, furniture, and telephones. Administrative equipment can also include supplies used in administrative delivery, such as paper, pens, pencils, and paper clips.

**Delivery equipment** is used to run programs or to allow users to participate in the primary activities of the facility. Delivery equipment can include permanent equipment such as golf carts, weight equipment, or fitness machines. It can also include program supplies such as basketballs, crayons, and jump ropes.

**Maintenance equipment** is used to keep facilities and equipment in proper working condition. It includes items such as lawn mowers, floor cleaning equipment, and custodial equipment. It can also include supplies such as cleaning chemicals, fertilizer, toilet paper, soap, and trash bags.

## Equipment Use

All equipment plays a role in enhancing leisure services and creating better experiences for facility users. Because of this, it is important that equipment is utilized properly. Some recreation facility equipment is easy to use and requires little instruction or preparation before use. However, some equipment is more difficult to use and creates greater responsibility for management.

Responsibility for equipment starts as soon as a piece of equipment is received. Once a piece of equipment has been received, it should be documented. The process of recording the receipt and ownership of equipment is the beginning of the **inventory process** (Olson 1997). Inventory systems can be handwritten or electronic and are used to keep record of when equipment arrives, how much equipment arrives, and what condition equipment is in when it arrives (Cohen 1997). The inventory system identifies the equipment by assigning each piece an identification number or a code.

Once equipment has been inventoried and coded, it is either distributed or stored. Sometimes equipment requires special arrangements for storage and protection until use. All security measures, including proper lighting, locks, and inventory controls, should be taken under consideration when equipment is stored (Fried 2005). Also, since the storage environment can affect equipment, temperature and humidity should be considered. Special requirements for storing equipment should be provided by the manufacturer. If a piece of equipment is stored, then its storage should be documented in the inventory system. When a piece of equipment is distributed for use, whether immediately or after a period of storage, that action should also be documented.

Once equipment has been distributed, it must be used responsibly by employees and participants. Responsible use means following the instructions for use that either the manufacturer recommends or the agency has set forth. In some instances, employees and participants may be required to complete equipment orientation or training before use. This may be the case before using strength equipment, climbing equipment, or specialized maintenance equipment such as chain saws. Some pieces of equipment may require certifications. For example, certifications are required for driving specialized vehicles or for operating a piece of equipment where hazardous chemicals are being used.

Responsible use also includes taking care of equipment through inspections and preventative maintenance. Equipment should be inspected and its condition should be recorded in the inventory system. If the equipment shows signs of damage or wear, arrangements should be made for repairs or replacement.

## Equipment Check-Out Systems

In many instances, facilities provide equipment for participants to use. Sometimes the equipment is out for users to utilize freely. This is very common in weight rooms and fitness rooms. Some aquatic spaces also leave flotation devices out for users to pick up and use when they want.

There are also situations in which participants can check out equipment to use in the facility. This may include checking out specialized equipment that is necessary for a recreation activity, such as tennis rackets, basketballs, and horseshoes. Users may also check out items for the locker room, such as locks or towels. Agencies that allow users to check out equipment should have a system in place to monitor the condition of the equipment, track who is using the equipment, and document when equipment is returned. Like the agency inventory system, this system can be handwritten or electronic and should be supervised by agency employees. Typically, there is an equipment desk staffed by agency employees where users can check out equipment. Users are required to provide identification or some type of deposit. Employees document the piece of equipment being checked out and record information about the person checking it out. When the user returns the equipment, the employee inspects it for damage before returning the identification or money. The agency should have policies in place that explain procedures for handling equipment that is returned damaged. As with other equipment maintained by the agency, if the equipment is damaged, arrangements should be made to repair or replace it.

# Safety and Security

Managing a facility includes a responsibility to both users and employees to take measures ensuring that a facility is safe and secure. If potential users feel that a facility is not safe or secure, they may not utilize that facility. On the other hand, if they do use that facility, their participation experience may be less than positive if their safety and security are threatened.

## Safety

Creating a safe facility environment involves minimizing risk as much as possible. Like programs, facilities should implement risk management practices. The guidelines outlined in chapter 2 for risk management in programming—identification, evaluation, treatment, and implementation (Hronek and Spengler 2007)—also apply to facility management. Risk management practices in a facility can be affected by a variety of factors. In creating a safe environment, a facility manager should consider issues related to activities, user behavior, environmental conditions, and equipment.

In recreation activities, there are a number of issues that can affect safety. Participant age should be considered, especially if children are users. Similar to age is the experience level of users. When facility users are new to an activity or a piece of equipment, their safety may be

A thorough check-out system ensures that equipment is returned undamaged and remains safe for the next user.

compromised. For instance, if a novice swimmer jumps into the deep end of a pool, then a safety situation has occurred. Another factor that should be considered is the degree of risk inherent in an activity due to its physical nature. Activities that involve greater risk should have more supervision (LaRue 2004).

People who use a facility can also affect safety (Byrnes 2009). Users can become disruptive when they participate in activities in a facility. Individuals have different reasons for using a facility and different attitudes about participation. When competition is part of an activity, there is a greater risk of verbal or physical confrontations. Confrontations can also occur when facility users conflict in their use. For example, users who are visiting a park to relax and read a book may be interrupted by a user listening to music or a group of users making noise.

A facility manager has the responsibility to protect users and employees from environmental conditions such as inclement and severe weather that might affect safety. Natural weather hazards such as lightning, heavy winds, rain, tornadoes, or snow might compromise safety. A facility manager may have to cancel an activity or close a facility in these situations in order to protect users and employees. An activity taking place in extreme temperatures also creates a situation that requires monitoring and appropriate precautions.

Environmental conditions can also be affected by mechanical systems in a facility. Indoor temperatures should be regulated and monitored through HVAC systems. In addition, mechanical systems using chemicals can affect the environment. Chemicals used in sanitation or in maintaining aquatic areas, ice rinks, turf, or surfaces can be harmful if they are not properly administered and stored (Mull, Beggs, and Renneisen 2009).

Equipment should be inspected regularly to ensure it is in good working order. Inspection procedures should include using checklists and observing the condition of equipment on a regular schedule (Fried 2005). Inspections can be performed daily, weekly, monthly, or annually depending on the type of equipment and the frequency of use. Equipment inspection is considered part of the maintenance procedures that all facilities should have in place. This information is discussed in detail in chapter 6.

## Security

Security is a part of safety. It comprises the specific systems put into place to protect users and employees. The three primary forms of facility

Major facilities such as stadiums will have a tightly controlled access area for both safety and ticket purchase control.

security are lighting, surveillance, and access control.

Lighting is a simple way to keep a facility secure. Lighting in areas inside and outside facilities can deter intruders and vandals (Phillips 1996). Lighting may give the impression that employees are in a facility, so some facilities keep the lights on after hours of operation. In addition, lighting indoor and outdoor facilities can make it easier for security staff or cameras to patrol an area.

A surveillance system allows management to monitor space, equipment, and people (Mull, Beggs, and Renneisen 2009). Surveillance systems may include security cameras, security staff members, or a combination of both.

Security cameras serve as a deterrent and as a way to monitor a facility. Just the presence of a security camera may prevent harmful or destructive behavior. In some instances, cameras are placed in discreet locations so they cannot be noticed. This may be done to prevent individuals from damaging the cameras and from being aware that they are being observed. Surveillance cameras may be continuous or motion activated. Typically, the information they record is stored on video or computer systems. A surveillance system may feed video to a control center or security desk where staff members monitor the displays of the facility. In some instances, the video feeds are not constantly monitored, but the recorded video is stored and can be reviewed should an incident occur.

Security staff members serve the same purpose that the cameras serve. They can deter negative behavior and monitor the facility. Security is part of the job for most facility employees, but it is not their primary responsibility. Some facilities may employ security staff members whose sole purpose is observing and guarding the facility. These employees are valuable because the visibility that results from their uniforms and sometimes a marked security vehicle can deter unwelcome behaviors. Security staff may patrol a facility on foot or may use bicycles or motor vehicles to patrol a large area such as a park. Security staff may also work in tandem with security cameras by monitoring the video feeds at a security desk or control center.

Access control helps maintain security by allowing managers to control who can enter an area or facility (Seidler 2006). Different forms of access control are used depending on the type of space. For instance, a very common form of access control for outdoor spaces is fencing. Other common outdoor access controls are natural barriers such as shrubs and bushes. These access control systems may be used to deny access or to funnel people toward a central access point. Another common access control tool is to use sidewalks and paths to direct people toward central access points.

Once an individual reaches the central access point, access control is applied further. For some outdoor spaces, such as a national park, a staff person may check identification or collect fees at an entry point. The entry point can also be used to limit the number of people entering a facility. For indoor facilities, doors are used as access points. In some instances, users entering through a door encounter an identification system designed to control access. Users may be required to produce a membership card or identification card to access interior spaces. Identification may be verified by facility staff or by a computerized system that recognizes specific identification cards (Patton 1997).

Once access to an interior space has been granted, access control is still utilized. The facility design, doors, and signage direct people to certain areas of a facility. Signage is an important tool for access control. It not only provides directional information but also provides information about access to an area. Doors have locks, which are the most common form of access control. Locks are used to control access to areas designated for employees only.

# Emergency Preparedness

**Emergency preparedness** is a necessity for all facilities. It refers to procedures that are implemented when emergency situations arise. These procedures can be called *emergency preparedness plans* or *emergency action plans.* Emergency responses vary greatly and must be effective and efficient to minimize the damage to facilities, equipment, users, and employees. The most important part of emergency preparedness is ensuring that facility staff members are adequately trained to supervise emergency responses. Staff members should be able to assess a situation and understand what actions should be taken. They should then be trained in how to implement those actions. For instance, if an emergency requires a facility to be evacuated, staff members should be able to implement evacuation procedures. When a person is injured, a staff person should know who to contact and what other steps to take. The actions that an employee takes can be very specific to an agency and a facility and may also vary depending on the type of emergency. The most common types of emergencies are related to weather, fire, plants and animals, and human behavior.

## Weather

Inclement weather is the most common emergency for outdoor facilities. However, inclement weather can also threaten the safety of indoor facilities. Heavy rains, high winds, snowstorms, tornadoes, hurricanes, earthquakes, landslides, floods, and avalanches can all create emergency situations. There may also be cases when extreme temperatures create an emergency situation. Regardless of the emergency weather condition, systems should be in place to protect users and employees from inclement weather. The most important elements to an emergency weather procedure are warning and communication. Facility managers should monitor weather conditions and, should emergency action need to be taken, activate a warning system that may include announcements, sirens, and flashing lights. Once employees and users are aware that a weather emergency is occurring, then directions explaining what they should do must be communicated. This may be done through a public address system, signage, or broadcast media (Hurd et al. 2007). Users may be asked to cease participating in an activity, evacuate an area, or take cover, depending on the type of weather emergency.

## Fire

Fires can be caused by a number of sources in a facility. Fires and smoke from fires can be extremely dangerous to users and employees. Ideally, preventative measures such as staff training in the use of fire extinguishers and sprinkler systems have been implemented to help control fire situations. However, some fires are too large or move too quickly to control. If this is the case, common emergency procedures include activating smoke or fire alarms, calling 911, and evacuating the building (Mull, Beggs, and Renneisen 2009). Communication to staff members and users is important; alarms, flashing lights, and public address systems are common forms of communication. Facilities are also required to post signage with emergency evacuation procedures.

## Plants and Animals

Emergency situations involving plants and animals predominantly occur outdoors. These emergency situations can be greatly reduced by using signage to communicate potential threats to users. For instance, if a dangerous plant is prevalent in an outdoor recreation area, providing signage or brochures with that information minimizes the threat. Also, animal threats in an area or precautions that users can take to keep animals away should be communicated. For example, a sign telling users not to feed the animals or a brochure with information about places to avoid because of dangerous animals is a helpful tool. In the event that a plant or animal endangers a user or employee, guidelines for proper response should also be communicated through staff training, brochures, and signage. Typically the first step is to call 911 and seek medical assistance.

## Human Behavior

Human behavior may also create emergency situations (Potter 2005). The behavior can be that of a facility user or an employee. Emergency response may be required when a person comes to a facility and antagonizes others or causes physical violence (Mull, Bayless, and Jamieson 2005). Reasons for bad behavior range from simply having a bad disposition to using alcohol and drugs. Handling these types of emergencies often involves calling security personnel.

People can become a large-scale threat when group behavior is involved. Crowds can be dangerous because they can result in negative and irrational behaviors that are supported by the crowd members. Plans should be in place to handle unruly individuals who might incite negative crowd behavior (Cotton and Wolohan 2003). Should a crowd crisis occur and there is a situation in which people can become hurt or trampled, security personnel should be notified to take over the situation. The goal is to disperse the crowd in an orderly manner.

Even larger-scale human threats are terrorist threats. In some cases, a facility may be informed of a bomb or another dangerous device in a facility. In this type of situation, immediate evacuation should occur followed by a call to 911. Terrorist actions can also come without warning and can happen anywhere (Pitts 2007). Since in these situations no warning can be issued, facilities must be proactive to try and prevent these events. The U.S. Department of Homeland Security regularly updates the status of threats and has guidelines for dealing with threats (Mull, Beggs, and Renneisen 2009). Some facilities may be able to limit terrorist threats through the use of security personnel or access control. If a terrorist threat does occur, the facility should be evacuated immediately and emergency personnel should be contacted.

Emergency situations involving human behavior can also result from employee behavior. For instance, chemical use in a facility can be potentially dangerous to employees and users if the chemicals are not handled properly. A chemical spill or misuse may require the evacuation of a facility and the help of emergency personnel. If people come into contact with a dangerous chemical, the common emergency response is to remove clothing and flush the exposed skin with water (Mull, Beggs, and Renneisen 2009). Chemical containers usually provide guidelines for how to deal with unintended exposure and how to clean up spills. If they do not, the chemical manufacturer should be contacted.

# Supervising Spaces

Within a facility there may be multiple spaces that require supervision. Different spaces and facilities have unique characteristics as well as common issues to consider when supervising. Regardless of type, spaces should be supervised by cameras or staff members or both. Some spaces may require constant supervision while others can be supervised intermittently. Supervision should include routine inspections to ensure equipment is working properly and spaces are clean and safe for users.

Facility spaces that have unique supervision characteristics include parking areas, shelters, locker rooms, reception areas, day cares, and commodity outlets. The following sections discuss these areas in detail.

## Parking Areas

Parking is a necessity for indoor and outdoor facilities. It is utilized by employees and facility users. Different facilities incorporate different types of parking options for staff and employees. A surface parking lot is the most common type of parking option. Other parking options include metered parking, parking garages, perimeter parking that utilizes shuttle services, and gated parking. Direct supervision of parking may occur in gated areas or areas that use security cameras. Security is important in supervising parking areas and can be accomplished in a variety of ways. Lighting is the most common form of security (Popke 2009). Lighting in parking areas not only deters negative behavior but also helps users to feel safe when walking to their vehicles (Zamengo 1995). Other security measures include using gates for access control, using surveillance cameras, employing

a parking lot attendant, providing call boxes, or having security personnel patrol the area.

Maintenance is also an important part of parking supervision. A parking lot is often the first thing people encounter when they visit a facility. In order to create a positive impression, parking areas must be kept clean. Maintenance of parking areas should also include inspection of parking surfaces, parking lines, signage, meters, and gates to make sure they are in good working order.

## Shelters

Shelters located in outdoor spaces require a different type of supervision. Typically staff members and cameras are not utilized to monitor these spaces on a frequent schedule. The focus of supervision is on maintenance. Shelters are used by different groups each day and sometimes by different groups on the same day. It is essential that equipment such as picnic tables, grills, and trash cans are checked daily and that shelters are hosed down daily so that they can be ready for use the next day.

Supervision of shelters may also require staff members to make sure there are no conflicts with groups that may have reserved a shelter for an event. It is common for agencies to issue permits for shelter use (figure 7.3). Should there be a conflict in use, the involved parties should be able to contact security or agency staff members to resolve any problems.

## Shelter Permit

Group or organization name: _____     Date of use: _____

Number in group: _____     Arrival time: _____

Name:_____     Departure time:_____

Address:_____     Home phone:_____

City, state, zip:_____     Work phone: _____

I certify that all information provided on this form is accurate to the best of my knowledge. I will assume all responsibility for the proper care and utilization of the public park area or facilities listed on this form.

Signed:_____     Date: _____

### Rental Fees Required

Resident $50.00

Nonresident $75.00

### Refundable Deposit

A $100.00 deposit is required and will be refunded following the proper utilization of park facilities. Your deposit (check or cash) will be returned to you within 1 week after your reservation.

**Figure 7.3**   To avoid a scheduling conflict between user groups, require shelter permits. Permits also allow staff to track usage patterns and generate revenue if a rental fee is charged.

Locker rooms are especially challenging to supervise because users store valuables, shower, and change clothes there. Also, they are sometimes used by unsupervised children.

## Locker Rooms

Locker rooms create multiple concerns for supervision. The primary purpose of these spaces is to provide an area where users can change clothes, shower, and securely store personal items.

A significant element to locker room supervision is hygiene. At a minimum, all wet surfaces must be cleaned and disinfected daily (Peterson and Tharrett 1997). This can be difficult to accomplish when users are in the locker room at all times of the day. Maintenance staff members must pick up, clean, and inspect amenities in locker room spaces multiple times in a day. Common locker room amenities include showers, restrooms, grooming stations, and saunas.

Security concerns are also a top priority in locker rooms since users store personal belongings there while using the facility. Personal belongings are usually stored in lockers. Users often provide their own locks, but some facilities allow users to check out locks (Cohen 1997). Some spaces may even sell locker usage and provide users with a key to an assigned locker.

Supervision for locker rooms must also account for times when children are in locker rooms without adult supervision. This may be the case if a parent and child of different gender need to use the locker room. These situations can be difficult to supervise; often facilities post locker room rules near or in the locker rooms to explain procedures. Facilities also provide family changing areas that can accommodate all members of a family, regardless of gender.

## Reception Areas

The reception area gives users a first impression of a facility. A disorganized and unattractive reception area can cause users to draw negative conclusions about a facility. Because of this, supervision should include keeping the area clean and free from clutter. Efficiency at a reception desk can also create a first impression. Efficiency is usually reflected in the staff members working the front desk and their knowledge of the facility and agency. It is vital that employees working in a reception area are well trained and able to answer common questions from users. While being able to answer user questions is an element of customer service that is essential for all employees, it is especially important for those working in a reception area. Employees should be friendly and helpful and dressed appropriately. Typical personnel working in reception areas are receptionists, attendants, security personnel, ushers, and ticket takers.

Reception areas may also serve as an access control point. Typical access control devices include gates, turnstiles, counter areas, and card-reading equipment. Supervision of the operation of these systems is essential in a reception area. Reception areas may also serve as an area for fee collection. Because of this, security should be an aspect of supervising these areas. In addition, checks and balances of fee collection should also be a component of supervision. This comes in the form of inventory control and receipts from purchases, among other things.

## Day Cares

Day care is becoming very common for indoor facilities, especially facilities that provide adult programming. Day care can be viewed as an hourly babysitting service or as a full-time child care service. The policies of day care and the ages of the children allowed in day care should be made available to users and posted in the day care or reception areas. The focus of day care operators may be on the health, education, and recreation of the children under their care. However, for facility managers, the focus is on security and hygiene. Local and state guidelines for day care services should be followed closely.

Parents leave their children in day care with the understanding that the children will be safe. Control systems should provide established procedures for dropping off and picking up children. It is also necessary to maintain constant supervision of children in day care; this is accomplished by having an adequate number of staff members working, by properly training staff members, and by restricting the mobility of the children to the day care area. Having restrooms and water fountains in day care spaces greatly reduces the need to take children outside the area. Thus the maintenance of these amenities is of great importance. Maintenance is also important in preserving the hygiene of a day care area. Equipment and spaces should be cleaned and disinfected daily to reduce the spread of germs and disease.

## Commodity Outlets

**Commodity outlets** are spaces in a facility where users can purchase items such as equipment, apparel, food, and gifts. Commodity outlets can be excellent sources of revenue for a facility (Sawyer 2005) and can take the form of gift shops, pro shops, concession stands and snack bars, and retail outlets. Financial transactions occur in these spaces, so security measures are an important element of their supervision. The use of personnel and cameras to monitor these spaces is very common. In addition, procedures for handling money and receipts should be established and followed closely. Staff members working in commodity outlets should be trained in these procedures before being allowed to work in these spaces.

Security staff members and cameras can be used to monitor user behavior in commodity outlets and to prevent theft of merchandise. In addition, inventory procedures should be implemented to keep track of merchandise. Inventory should also be tracked so that merchandise is available to sell (Fried 2005). For instance, before a large event, a manager should examine the anticipated concession demands and then make sure that the concession inventory is adequate to meet the needs of the event.

The appearance of a commodity outlet is important to its success, especially when food is the commodity. Keeping these areas clean and sanitized attracts more users and also creates a safer area (Sawyer 2005). Supervision of areas where food is sold includes making sure that the commodity outlet adheres to the standards and codes of OSHA, public health agencies, state liquor agencies, and local ordinances.

## Conclusion

Facility management requires putting procedures in place for opening and closing a facility, scheduling and coordination, managing equipment and supplies, ensuring safety and security, being prepared for an emergency, and supervising spaces within a facility. These procedures allow for the effective and efficient operation and supervision of a recreation facility.

## Review Questions

1. How are seasonal opening and closing procedures different from daily opening and closing procedures for a facility?
2. What factors affect facility scheduling?
3. What activities should be taken into consideration in facility coordination?
4. Compare and contrast permanent, expendable, and fixed equipment.
5. Give examples of equipment that can be classified in each of the following categories: efficiency system equipment, structural equipment, administrative equipment, delivery equipment, and maintenance equipment.
6. How do activities, user behaviors, environmental conditions, and equipment affect facility safety?
7. What are the three primary forms of facility security? Briefly explain how each contributes to facility security.
8. What are the most common types of emergencies affecting facilities?
9. What are the unique supervision characteristics of parking areas, shelters, locker rooms, reception areas, day cares, and commodity outlets?

 **Visit the online resource at www.HumanKinetics.com/TheParkAndRecreationProfessionalsHandbook for sample documents, keywords, activities and assignments, and more.**

# chapter 8

# Budgets and Finance

131

## OUTCOMES

- Describe sources of funding for leisure services agencies.

- Outline the merits of partnerships for leisure services agencies.

- Differentiate among the five types of public–private partnerships.

- Illustrate various pricing strategies for recreation programs and facilities.

- Analyze five types of commonly used budgeting procedures.

- Articulate the procedures involved in soliciting and awarding bid contracts for purchases and outsourcing.

- Explain various financial monitoring procedures used to track the fiscal health of an agency.

Management of the financial aspects of parks and recreation operations is becoming more and more critical as resources become more and more scarce. Regardless of management level, all employees have some financial responsibility—if not for financial management, then for fiscal soundness. Budgeting, setting fees, purchasing, fund-raising, and hiring are but a few of the multitude of actions affecting an agency's bottom line.

# Budgets

At some point in their career, almost all professionals working in parks and recreation must deal with budgets. The involvement may range from following a budget assigned to a program to developing the overall budget for an entire department or agency. Programs and facilities cost money to run, and professionals need to have a good understanding of their agency's finances from revenues to expenditures.

## Operating Budgets

An **operating budget** outlines the day-to-day expenses of the agency and includes items such as salaries, supplies, and utilities. Operating budgets can vary widely as program registrations and other fees come in and revenue fluctuates, supplies wear out more quickly than anticipated, and utility rates change. The administrator needs to keep this in mind during budget development each year.

## Capital Budgets

A **capital budget** covers larger expenses that do not recur on an annual basis. In some instances capital budgets address one-time costs such as new facility construction. Common capital budget items are facility developments or improvements, motor vehicle purchases, and land purchases. The capital budget can also fluctuate, although it usually does not fluctuate as much as the operating budget fluctuates, because it is not exposed to the same variability of fees and charges. The capital budget tends to remain more stable unless costs unexpectedly go up, particularly during construction projects.

# Revenue Sources

There are a multitude of revenue sources from which leisure services agencies draw. While in the early days of parks and recreation, public

agencies were able to rely solely on support through tax funding, today that is no longer feasible, because those coffers have grown smaller. Today, multiple sources of revenue through taxes, fees and charges, gifts, grants, partnerships, and sponsorships make programming, access to open space, and facility development possible. For commercial agencies as well as nonprofit organizations, tax revenues were never a revenue stream. Commercial and nonprofit agencies depend on self-generated revenue such as fees and charges and also may benefit from partnerships and sponsorships, grants, and other forms of revenue. Whatever the funding source, accurate prediction of revenues as well as expenses assists in designing a realistic budget.

## Taxes

As government-supported agencies, public parks and recreation agencies have the ability to collect a portion of local taxes in order to support their operating and capital budgets. There are three types of taxes that parks and recreation agencies rely on to provide base-level funding: property tax, sales tax, and, in some cases, hospitality tax.

### Property Tax

Property tax serves as the relatively stable foundation of a public agency's budget and is one of the most significant forms of revenue for government-based agencies. It provides the funding base from which a parks and recreation agency starts its budgeting process in that it makes up what is considered the general fund of the agency. Property tax collections are based on the appraised value of a property, which depends on development, zoning status, and other factors, and thus collections fluctuate considerably from community to community. The entire compilation of property taxes available within a community is known as the *tax base*. Because the tax base influences the amount of guaranteed revenue that a public agency has at its disposal, the tax base also influences the type and level of borrowing that an agency can do in order to develop capital projects. To protect the taxpayers, there are government regulations that limit the economic vulnerability of public agencies by ensuring that their borrowing is fiscally responsible; these caps help prevent irresponsible spending that could lead an agency into financial ruin through borrowing too much money.

Agencies that are part of a municipal government receive, as part of their allocated budget from the municipality, a portion of the property taxes to help support their services. Because priorities differ among communities and property taxes are also used to support services such as the police, fire, and sewer departments, the proportion of tax revenue received by parks and recreation agencies can vary greatly among communities. For an agency in a special district, however, the community has consented that a specific portion of its property taxes goes directly to parks and recreation services, because the agency is not part of the municipality's governmental structure but is an independent, tax-supported, nonprofit agency in its own right (Brayley and McLean 1999; Crompton 1999).

### Sales Tax

A community can also use sales tax to support parks and recreation services and facilities. Sales tax is typically the second largest source of revenue for municipalities (Crompton 1999). Sales tax is charged on tangible items, not services, although it is greatly reduced for unprepared foods and prescription drugs. Sales tax percentages vary by state and municipality and to some extent depend on what the citizens will tolerate.

### Hospitality Tax

In some communities a hospitality tax is earmarked to support activities and facilities that directly increase tourism within the community. For example, an agency that hosts large softball tournaments may receive hospitality tax dollars to support the facility, because those tournaments draw in large numbers of outside participants who can have a significant economic effect on the community. Typically a hospitality tax is charged to people who stay in hotels and eat in local restaurants, and part of that money goes to supporting agencies that help attract people to the hotels and restaurants. The hospitality tax may also be referred to as a *hotel–motel, bed,* or *accommodations tax* if it is limited to an extra charge on accommodations.

   This more specific type of "hospitality tax," the accommodations tax, is also used to support local convention and visitors bureaus (CVBs), of which 85 percent receive this type of funding, as well as convention centers. In fact, over half of all convention centers are also managed by a government entity (Destination Marketing Association International 2009). Because CVBs are designed to bring paying visitors into a community and thus support the local economy, it is logical for them to

Many agencies, including public parks and recreation departments as well as convention and visitors bureaus, rely on hospitality taxes from visitors for funding.

receive operating funds from the local government via allocation of these specialized taxes.

## Fees and Charges

Fees and charges also constitute a large, albeit fluctuating, percentage of agency budgets. The more that governmental allocation of funding dwindles, the more that agencies use fees and charges to make up this difference. There is also a philosophical approach to charging fees, because fees put the burden of payment on those who benefit directly from the services. While some amenities such as community parks are an inherent benefit to the entire community and thus are appropriate for governmental funding, other amenities such as an adult softball league or a ballet class are more focused on individual benefits rather than a community goal and thus are highly subsidized through fees and charges. (A **subsidized program** is one that obtains funding from a source other than program fees because its expenditures exceed the revenue it otherwise generates.) There are numerous kinds of fees and charges that agencies can utilize depending on the types of services and programs that they offer. Employees should provide input on what to charge for each type of program or service related to their area of responsibility.

### Program Fees

The most common fee is the program fee. An individual pays a program fee to take part in a structured program provided by the agency, such as youth sport leagues, classes, field trips, or other activities. How the fees for these programs are determined is discussed later in this chapter.

### Entrance Fees

Entrance fees are paid by individuals wishing to enter a facility. The types of facilities that may charge entrance fees include aquatic facilities, fitness centers, and sport complexes where games or tournaments are taking place.

### Membership Fees

Agencies can use membership fees to help control access or to generate a baseline of funding by offering members a discounted price on programs. For instance, many agencies charge membership fees that grant access to amenities such as swimming pools, gymnasiums, and fitness facilities.

### Rental Fees

Rental fees allow individuals to reserve access to facilities or equipment. For instance, a group interested in running a softball tournament or holding a swimming party can pay a rental fee to reserve the softball fields or the pool at a specific time and date. Rental fees can also be charged for equipment such as balls, nets, and bats to provide individuals the opportunity to recreate outside of a formal program without having to purchase the equipment.

### Service Fees

An agency may charge fees for services it provides to the community that do not fall under other categories. An example is a fee an adult softball team pays for an employee to turn on the lights while the team rents a field at night for practice.

### License and Permit Fees

License and permit fees give a person permission to engage in a specific activity. These activities may include hunting, fishing, and camping.

### Admission Fees

Admission fees are relatively self-explanatory. They allow the user to enter facilities when an exhibit or a performance is taking place so that the user can observe the activity.

## Capital Project Funding

While fees and charges and tax revenues are used not only for operating budgets but also for capital budgets, there are two specific categories of capital funding that are used when the agency needs access to substantial amounts of money. These are full faith and credit funding and nonguaranteed debt (Crompton 1999).

## Full Faith and Credit Funding

Full faith and credit funding is debt that is taken on by a public sector agency and that is backed by the tax base of the agency. Therefore, sources of full faith and credit funding, such as **general obligation bonds,** certificates of obligation, and contractual obligations, are a safer investment in that the agency has promised to use part of its tax base to make the loan payments and the agency has a consistent cash flow it can use to make the payments. Because tax dollars are used to secure the funding, voter approval is required for general obligation bonds and can be requested for certificates of obligation and contractual obligations. These types of funding are not available to commercial or private nonprofit organizations.

A general obligation bond is a form of long-term debt funding for which the leisure services agency must obtain voter approval. The agency pays an interest rate to the lender (which is an individual, an organization, or a group), which is the profit that the bondholders earn off of their bond purchase. Because a general obligation bond is a full faith and credit obligation, it can be obtained at a lower interest rate.

Although also backed by the tax base, certificates of obligation and contractual obligations do not require voter approval. However, the public may request a public referendum on their use. Certificates of obligation can be used only for real property acquisition or improvements. There is more flexibility in how contractual obligations are used. These loans tend to be for capital purchases that are smaller than those using general obligation bonds.

For example, the San Antonio (Texas) Parks and Recreation Department partnered with the University of the Incarnate Word on the Denman Estate Park Improvement Project to develop 20 acres into a jointly used park and adjacent retreat center for the university. More than $2.5 million in park bonds were used to purchase the land, while a certificate of obligation worth $688,000 was used to fund the improvements to the land. The project includes a half-mile walking trail, parking, fencing, and lighting. The city and the university entered into a joint use agreement in which the university maintains the property and uses the buildings as a retreat center.

## Nonguaranteed Debt

Nonguaranteed debt is not backed by the security of the tax base. In the case of revenue bonds, it depends on the new facility (or whatever was funded through the money) to make enough revenue to pay off the loan. While the full faith and credit mechanisms come with a lower interest rate for the agency, most also require voter approval. In some instances the time it would take to gain voter approval would eliminate an opportunity and nonguaranteed debt would be a more attractive funding option. In addition, full faith and credit funding limits the extent to which an agency can borrow, because the agency can secure loans only against a certain percentage of the tax base. This restriction does not apply to nonguaranteed debt. While nonguaranteed debt is not backed by the tax base, because loan defaults put an agency's credit rating at risk (and thus lead to higher interest rates)

as well as jeopardize an agency's reputation, agencies often keep a debt reserve of funds available to meet payments if original sources come up short.

Examples of nonguaranteed debt are revenue bonds, tax increment bonds, and certificates of participation. Revenue bonds are funding mechanisms paid off with revenue earned from the project that they funded. Tax increment financing focuses on improvements to a public area that increase property values in surrounding areas. The bonds are paid off with the difference between the increased tax value of the improved surrounding property and the previous value. This is because without the improvements, there would be no increase in property values. Certificates of participation can get a little more complicated. These certificates involve using an intermediary (such as a special interest group) to borrow the money for a project so that the agency can avoid the legal and political impediments to directly borrowing the money. The agency commits to pay off the debt over time, with the end result of the agency owning the facility or land once all debt payments are made (Crompton 1999). Table 8.1 compares the different mechanisms available to public parks and recreation agencies for capital project funding.

**Table 8.1** Mechanisms for Capital Project Funding

| | Referendum required | Use |
|---|---|---|
| General obligation bonds | Yes | Variety of capital projects, no real limits on type of project |
| Certificates of obligation | No, but can be requested | Real property acquisition or improvement |
| Contractual obligations | No, but can be requested | Property acquisition, renovations, equipment purchases (less restrictive than certificates of obligation) |
| Revenue bonds | No | Capital projects that the agency deems should be supported by users of the new facility and thus be paid by revenue generation, not taxes |
| Tax increment financing (bonds) | No | Projects in areas in need of urban redevelopment that lead to increased property values (bonds are paid off through the increase in tax collections resulting from higher property values) |
| Certificates of participation | No | Indirect property or facility acquisition (agency gets access to the land or facility through a third party and then pays the third party in order to cover the debt, owning the property once the debt has been retired) |

## Building the SilverRock Resort

La Quinta (California) has been largely successful with tax increment financing through the establishment of California redevelopment agencies. These agencies make improvements to blighted parts of the city or to undeveloped land within the city where the city makes improvements to encourage economic development. Due to a desire to not displace residents living in low-cost housing in these areas, 20 percent of the low-cost housing is set aside during the redevelopment. A specific example of the use of tax increment financing is the SilverRock Resort, a very high-end golf course that was built on farmland to create interest among hoteliers to buy adjacent land for hotel development and increase local revenue through the transient occupancy tax.

## Capital Funding for Commercial and Private Nonprofit Agencies

There are numerous ways that a private nonprofit agency or a commercial business can develop capital for projects. Private nonprofit agencies such as the YMCA, Boys and Girls Club, and Boy Scouts often develop capital campaigns to raise money through donations. Because these agencies are nonprofit, they can offer individuals a tax incentive for donating money. Like bond referendums, capital campaigns are not done on an annual basis but are developed when the agency determines that it has capital needs that can be met only with substantial amounts of money. While big donors are usual targets for the campaign, small donors are also necessary contributors to the larger fund. Projects range from new facilities to facility renovations to land purchases.

Commercial businesses, being for-profit entities, cannot offer individuals any type of tax incentive for providing capital as an investment. Individuals who put their money into a commercial business do not just donate the money—they expect some type of return on investment. While independently wealthy entrepreneurs may choose to be the sole investor in their own business, most individuals or groups look for outside funding, either through nonequity or equity investments. **Equity investments** occur when people invest in a company not expecting to get their money paid back as they would with a loan but instead expecting to gain a percentage of ownership and hopefully a percentage of earned profits. **Nonequity investments** must be paid back over time, and the investor does not own any part of the company unless the loan goes into default. Lines of credit, installment loans, and home equity loans are all nonequity investments. Other forms of nonequity investments are credit cards; trade credit, which is credit extended by suppliers, usually interest free and for a set amount of time; and equipment leasing, which is useful when the equipment purchase costs are too high as the company starts out. The drawback of equipment leasing is that while the company is paying for it on a monthly basis, the company has no equity in it and gets nothing back when getting rid of it. However, the benefit is that equipment that is outdated quickly is easy to rotate out for newer equipment.

## Alternative Funding

Budgets are tight, and agencies have been forced to look beyond the traditional funding sources just discussed and to become more creative in their acquisition of revenue. Alternative funding sources sought out by agencies include grants, partnerships, sponsorships, and gifts.

### Grants

More and more agencies are turning to grants as a way to fund programs and facilities. Unlike funding mechanisms that involve borrowing money, grants do not have to be paid back. While competition for grant funding can be tight, grants offer an alternative way to supplement existing funds or bring in new funds for projects that meet the goals of the granting agencies. Grants are often sought from private foundations such as the W.K. Kellogg Foundation or the Women's Sports Foundation, from local businesses, or from governmental agencies. For instance, the Greenville (South Carolina) Department of Parks and Recreation received grant funding of $5,000 for community garden projects from its local Pepsi bottler, while the Rock Hill (South Carolina) Parks, Recreation and Tourism received grant funding of $27,000 from the U.S. Department of Housing and Urban Development for an after-school program.

## Partnerships

Partnerships also provide opportunities to expand services or facilities. While partnerships may not bring in dollars, they may provide an agency with alternative forms of capital that can bring a project or program to fruition. Unlike sponsorships, partnerships are designed so that both parties, who share a mutual desire for the accomplishment of a goal, reap the rewards of the successful partnership but also take on the risks associated with the partnership. While a partnership can be entered into with other nonprofits or government agencies, there is often great monetary benefit to entering into a partnership with a commercial business. There are a number of reasons why partnerships may be attractive to the parks and recreation agency as well as to the commercial partners.

**Public Sector Benefits** As part of the public sector, parks and recreation agencies may be able to offer some of the following benefits. The public sector, or the government arm of the partnership, often has access to open space or land banks that the commercial sector can gain access to at a lesser cost. The public sector also has access to low-cost capital, and this can be an attractive benefit to the commercial sector in a partnership. That is, the public agency can borrow money at a lower interest rate through municipal bonds. This may behoove the commercial sector if it is interested in developing a new facility and the public sector invests in the development using money that, at a lower interest rate, makes the development less expensive overall (Crompton 1999).

Tax incentives are a third benefit that the public sector can bring to the partnership. If a community is interested in bringing in a new commercial business that will serve the needs of community members, it may offer the commercial business a tax incentive such as reduced property taxes for a limited time in order to entice the business to move (Crompton 1999).

One additional benefit the government can offer is its control over permit and zoning processes. Whenever building takes place there are multiple

## 🍁 Grant Seeking

Grant seeking is not an easy process, and more and more agencies are hiring staff members with experience in grant writing so they can win grants to subsidize their revenue streams. Brayley and McLean (1999) outline a six-step process for seeking grants:

1. Identify an idea for the grant. What program would you like to develop or support that would be a good match for a grant opportunity?

2. Find an appropriate grant opportunity and make contact with the grant maker. Once you find a match for the program, identify the grant coordinator, find out if you are on the right track with your idea, and ask relevant questions that will help in the preparation of the grant application. Personal contact can go a long way when a funder receives an application and is already familiar with the idea as well as the applicant.

3. Prepare the grant proposal, being sure to include all requested information and signatures. Often the grant proposal will include a detailed program outline as well as a budget.

4. Submit the grant proposal, making sure to meet any posted deadlines. Do not leave the application to the last minute, as surprises will often delay completion of the final application.

5. Wait for the funding agency to respond. This response can take a number of forms, such as a request for additional information, a flat-out denial, or an award of the grant. If the application is not funded but the funding agency provides good feedback, it may be possible to revise the application and resubmit it to the original granting agency or to one with similar grant opportunities.

6. If the grant is received, administer it; if the grant is rejected, seek a new source for grant funding. Remember that multiple submissions may be necessary before success is had. In the case of a grant award, ensure that there is strict oversight of how the money is spent and how the program is presented in order to follow the guidelines set by the granting agency and to avoid jeopardizing future grant opportunities with the same agency.

permit and zoning procedures that need to be handled, and all move through the local government (and sometimes the state government). If the government is in a partnership with the commercial entity that is constructing the building, it can help this process move much more smoothly (and quickly), saving the company both time and money (Crompton 1999).

**Commercial Sector Benefits**   The government side of the partnership is not the only side that brings benefits to the table. The commercial sector also has things it can offer to the government to make

the partnership more attractive. While the government can borrow money more cheaply, the commercial sector can raise money more quickly. Because commercial businesses do not share the same limitations in raising or borrowing money that government entities face, the government may want to partner with a commercial entity when it desires to improve its services but is hindered by a lack of funding (Crompton 1999).

A second advantage held by the commercial sector is specialized management expertise. In some instances a partnership involves managing a facility that the parks and recreation agency

## An Urban Parks Institute Success Story: Sacramento, California

Sacramento has turned a problematic central city park into a vibrant town square with careful event planning and management of concessions. While the city covers the park's basic maintenance costs, a public–private partnership concentrates on creating worthwhile programs and activities in the park and running the concessions at a profit. This allows the partners to put their earnings back into park enhancements and services.

In the early 1980s, Sacramento began a downtown revitalization effort. A new library and galleria, as well as an office tower, were planned for the area surrounding Plaza Park, an underused downtown park the size of one square block.

The first step was taken by the Sacramento Housing and Redevelopment Agency, which committed $213,000 for park redesign and event planning. A farmers' market, new programs, and special events were begun. Users began to trickle back into Plaza Park. Then a plan was developed and a process undertaken to understand how the park itself could be improved.

Encouraged by the new activity, the general managing partner of a new office building adjacent to the park contributed an additional $250,000 for park improvements, including lighting redesign and the establishment of food services and community outreach programs. With the new funds, the management team of the office building, the Sacramento Housing and Redevelopment Agency, and the city itself renovated an existing restroom facility in the park, turning it into a cafe. The city then turned over the management of the park to the Downtown Sacramento Partnership, a nonprofit corporation. The job of the Downtown Sacramento Partnership was to create and manage park programs and activities, including the concessions.

Revenues and lease payments from the cafe went directly to the Downtown Sacramento Partnership (and the city received a percentage of the gross sales receipts if they reached a certain amount), where the money was used for basic enhancements and to bring events into Plaza Park. The cafe generated about $12,000 per year for the Partnership. The Partnership also began a Friday night concert series in the park highlighting Sacramento musicians. Despite the high costs of putting on a concert, the program made money, mostly due to the ability of the Partnership to sell beer and wine at the concerts. The concert series, now in its seventh year, has brought in as much as $40,000 a year and has attracted thousands of residents to the park every week.

Additionally, the Downtown Sacramento Partnership brought hot food vendors and bakeries into the burgeoning weekly farmers' market. The group received fees from these new vendors but did not require the farmers to pay beyond their city-negotiated license agreement. This concession has made about $13,000 per year for the Partnership.

The Downtown Sacramento Partnership also kept the adjacent commercial district clean and patrolled and provided retail recruitment and marketing services through an assessment on local businesses that amounted to slightly less than $2 million per year. However, none of this money went into park programs. Concessions (beer and wine at the weekly concert series) were the single largest source of revenue in Plaza Park for the Downtown Sacramento Partnership outside of the assessment.

does not have the expertise to manage. Forming a partnership with a commercial agency that has the needed expertise makes the management process more time and cost efficient, particularly if the commercial agency has a solid reputation in the specialized area of service (Crompton 1999).

Reduced labor costs can also be realized when partnering with the commercial sector. Public agencies are often required to provide more fringe benefits than the commercial sector must provide; the reduction of this overhead and the hiring of part-time labor by the commercial entity can reduce labor costs associated with services. Therefore, having a public facility such as a golf course managed by a private company reduces the costs associated with operations and thus allows for greater revenue and lower fees. It is also possible for a public agency to reduce its liability risks by partnering with a commercial business. For instance, agencies often hire private contractors to serve as instructors for classes, in which case the liability is transferred to the instructor (Crompton 1999).

**Types of Partnerships** Crompton (1999) identified different types of partnerships that the public sector may enter into with the private sector. The first type involves using existing commercial facilities to supplement what the parks and recreation agency offers. Potential opportunities for this type of partnership include the use of recreational facilities, the development of urban parks on lease until a developer is ready to use the land, the use of private land in order to give citizens access to more open space for outdoor recreation, or the use of local utility lands and related easements in order to expand open space for recreation opportunities. A public agency may also take over a failing commercial facility in order to ensure that the community does not lose a valued resource that the public agency may be able to do a better (and cheaper) job of offering.

The second type of partnership, joint development with the commercial sector, focuses on working hand in hand with a private entity in order to increase recreation opportunities in a community. Agreements can outline multiparty partnerships or leaseback arrangements and can involve multiple exploitation of resources such as landfills or expansion of existing facilities.

The third type of partnership is commercial sector pump priming. In this partnership the private sector partner offers the public sector agency an incentive to make an investment in a facility that will benefit both parties. For example,

Some recreation facilities require specialized management expertise that can best be provided by a commercial sector enterprise.

a private developer may donate land to the public sector to turn into a park knowing that this addition will likely make the new neighborhood more attractive and increase the selling price of the homes. The public agency gains an additional facility and the private developer makes more money. For another example of commercial sector pump priming, see the sidebar on page 138.

### Sponsorships

Unlike partnerships, sponsorships involve an agreement between parties that may or may not have a mutually defined goal in place. The sponsor, in providing something to the agency, is hands off when it comes to the event or program it is sponsoring. For instance, a local bottling company sponsoring a day-in-the-park activity may provide soft drinks at a reduced cost or provide monetary support in exchange for being recognized as a sponsor. However, the bottling company would not have anything to do with planning or running the event. The sponsor's motive is to be seen as a supporter of a community event and to gain good will and a reputation that will translate into more business. The sponsor takes on none of the risks of running the event, as the sponsor's goal is purely financial.

The goals of sponsorships are different than the goals of partnerships. There are a number of goals that the sponsor may have. At just stated, usually the overarching goal is a fiscal one in that the sponsor hopes its involvement will result in more business; sponsorship is basically a marketing tool. Before a leisure services agency accepts a sponsorship agreement, it must consider whether the agreement is good for the agency. First, what are the goals of both the sponsor and the agency? While marketing is the primary goal for the sponsor, is it compatible with the mission of the agency or the event? Does the product that the company is known for complement the image of the agency or program? A second consideration is what the marketing will entail. That is, how will the sponsor's name be out there? Will the sponsorship give the sponsor some type of naming rights? Will it mean signage? What is the agreement for the marketing

plan, and how does that plan fit into the feel of the event, program, or facility?

If the answers to these questions are satisfactory to both parties, they enter into a sponsorship agreement. The agreement outlines the length of the sponsorship, the items or services the sponsor is providing in return for publicity (e.g., money, in-kind contributions, staffing, food, product, and so on), the guidelines for publicity, and the language concerned with liability. Figure 8.1 shows an example of a sponsorship agreement that is used by the Winterville (North Carolina) youth sport program. This agreement outlines the guidelines for sponsoring a youth sport team.

It is beneficial for agencies to follow a four-step model for developing a sponsorship proposal. At the top of the sponsor heap, or the top level, is the title sponsor, as can be seen with the Chik-fil-A Bowl or the Bank of America Chicago Marathon. This sponsor typically retains the right of first refusal on other sponsors (after all, Chick-fil-A probably does not want Kentucky Fried Chicken as a cosponsor) and provides the event or agency with a great deal of money to put its name on a program, park, or facility.

The second level is the presenting sponsor. The presenting sponsor typically provides a funding level that is 25 to 50 percent of that provided by

Sponsorships often provide a much needed source of funding for a wide variety of recreation programs and facilities.

# Sponsorship Agreement for Winterville Youth Sports

## Winterville Parks and Recreation Sponsorship Agreement

This agreement between the Winterville Parks and Recreation Department and _____ (hereinafter referred to as *Sponsor*) is for the _____ season.

Sponsorship of a team in a Winterville Parks and Recreation Department league must be, for the Sponsor, performed out of a sense of duty to help the community. While sponsorship does afford some benefits (detailed on the back page of this contract), the higher purpose is to help the Winterville Parks and Recreation Department impart the values of teamwork, good sporting behavior, and fair play to the children of the community so that they may someday use these values in becoming good citizens.

Sponsorship of a team in a Winterville Parks and Recreation Department league does not give the Sponsor any rights or responsibilities in the operation of the league or any team in the league. The Sponsor does not have any rights or responsibilities in the selection of managers, coaches, or players for any team in the league. The Sponsor and the Winterville Parks and Recreation Department are independent contractors with respect to one another, and neither shall have any authority to represent or bind the other in any manner or to any extent whatsoever, except as specified herein.

The Sponsor will pay as follows for sponsorships on teams in a Winterville Parks and Recreation Department league:

| Spring sports | | Fall sports | |
| --- | --- | --- | --- |
| Babe Ruth (ages 13-15) | $325 | Fall baseball | $225 |
| Cal Ripken (ages 11-12) | $325 | Flag football | $150 |
| Cal Ripken (ages 9-10) | $325 | Tackle football | $325 |
| Rookie (ages 7-8) | $300 | | |
| Tee ball (ages 5-7) | $250 | | |

Accepted and agreed to by

_____ on _____
Sponsor Representative Signature                                    Date


_____
Winterville Parks and Recreation Department Representative Authorized Signature

## Benefits of a Sponsorship in Winterville

- **Name of business on uniform:** This practice has been in place in youth baseball since its inception in 1939. The name of the business sponsoring the team may be placed on the front or back of the uniform or on the caps. The name of the business must not imply the sale or use of alcohol or tobacco, or any product or activity. For example, Joe's Grocery Store is acceptable, even if Joe's Grocery Store sells tobacco products. However, Joe's Discount Cigarette Outlet is not acceptable. Also, the name of the business must not offend community standards.

- **Recognition plaques or certificates:** The Winterville Parks and Recreation Department produces a plaque with a team photo in honor of the team Sponsor. Each Sponsor receives the plaque along with a certificate of appreciation. These are often displayed by the Sponsor as a matter of community pride.

- **Programs and scorecards:** This season, Winterville is the host to the 10th East North Carolina State Tournament. If you are interested in purchasing an advertisement in this program, please contact the Winterville Parks and Recreation Department at your convenience.

*Remember, sponsorship of a team does not give the Sponsor any rights in the operation of, or the outfitting of, any particular team or the league itself.*

**Figure 8.1** Standard sponsorship agreement used by the Winterville, North Carolina, youth sports program.

Adapted, by permission, from Winterville, North Carolina Parks and Recreation Department.

the title sponsor. This sponsorship level typically ensures exclusive rights within the company's product category. For instance, if Nike were to become a presenting sponsor of the Chicago Marathon, no other sport shoe or clothing merchant could serve as a sponsor for the race.

The third level comprises the official sponsors, whose funding level is approximately 10 percent of that of the title sponsor. Official sponsors are usually smaller companies, and they have a smaller package than presenting sponsors have. They are allowed to sponsor categories not sponsored by the title or presenting sponsor. So, going back to the example of the Chicago Marathon, Gatorade is an acceptable official sponsor as neither Chick-fil-A nor Nike sells sport drinks.

Finally, the fourth sponsorship level is made up of the official suppliers. These sponsors offer goods and services during the event, such as bottled water, first aid equipment, energy bars, and so on.

One example of the use of sponsorships is the annual Share the Spirit Golf Tournament held by the Pickens County YMCA (in Easley, South Carolina). Now in its 14th year, this golf tournament is a major source of income for the YMCA. To recruit sponsors each year, the YMCA approaches past sponsors as well as makes cold calls to community businesses. The YMCA offers a variety of sponsorship levels, ranging from tee sponsors at $100 to hole sponsors at $250 to silver sponsors at $1,000 and gold sponsors at $2,500 (see figure 8.2). In addition to making personal phone calls, the YMCA mails and displays fliers and brochures throughout the community. To recognize sponsors during the tournament, the YMCA displays a large banner with each sponsor's name and logo as well as distributes an appreciation brochure to thank all participants and sponsors. Finally, to thank sponsors after the event, the administrative director sends handwritten thank-you notes to all the

## Example Sponsorship Levels

Pickens County YMCA 13th Annual Share the Spirit Golf Tournament
**Mark your calendar today!**

### When and Where
November 4, 2009
Smithfields Country Club
10:00 a.m.

### Cost
$400 per four-person team
*Lunch will be provided*

### Prizes
First, second, and third place
Hole-in-one
Longest drive
Closest to the pin

### Sponsorship Opportunities
$2,500 Gold Sponsor

*Three teams, two sponsor signs at holes, and one sponsor sign at a tee*

$1,000 Silver Sponsor

*One team, one sponsor sign at a hole, and one sponsor sign at a tee*

$250 Hole Sponsor

$100 Tee Sponsor

Come out and help share the spirit in your community!

**Figure 8.2** Pickens County YMCA Share the Spirit Golf Tournament is supported by numerous sponsors.
Adapted, by permission, from Pickens County YMCA, Easley, SC.

sponsors and the CEO sends appreciation letters to the silver and gold sponsors.

## Gifts

Gifts, another alternative source of funding, are monetary or nonmonetary donations to an agency. One common form of giving is planned giving, which a person has built into his will to be acted upon at his death. Planned giving may involve a monetary gift, a gift of land, or some other gift that the agency can use to better its parks and recreation services to the community.

Gift catalogs can also facilitate giving. In this case, individuals make donations to an agency by purchasing items that can help the agency offer great services. Examples of items that can be found in a gift catalog include trees, park benches, and sport equipment. An agency typically acknowledges the gift giver in some way, whether through

signage or some other recognition. Many public agencies develop nonprofit foundations to provide philanthropic support for the agency by taking on the responsibility of raising funds through grants and giving. With 501(c)(3) status, the nonprofit foundation is able to offer tax breaks to donors.

One example of a park foundation is the Deerfield Park Foundation in Deerfield, Illinois. The foundation secures gifts through bequests (gifts of personal property, including land and cash, by last will and testament), cash contributions, and other forms of gift giving. For example, donors can buy a tree for $250 or a park bench for $700, thus providing the agency and community with needed resources while at the same time having a great deal of control over how their money is spent.

Table 8.2 outlines approaches to gift giving that can be used by the agency in its development strategies. It also provides an agency with a

**Table 8.2** Approaches to Gift Giving

| Donor's goals | Donor's strategy for giving | Donor's benefits |
|---|---|---|
| Maximize tax deduction and minimize gift details. | Give **cash.** | Claim a deduction against a larger portion of adjusted gross income and benefit the agency immediately. |
| Avoid capital gains liability and take an income tax deduction. | Donate **appreciated securities.** | Buy low and give high while avoiding capital gains tax. |
| Avoid capital gains tax on appreciated real estate. | Make an outright gift of **real estate** or consider a **bargain sale** or **retained life estate.** | Avoid capital gains liability and take an income tax deduction. |
| Provide gift for agency's future that costs nothing now. | Include a **bequest** in the will (cash, specific property, or share in estate residue). | Painlessly build the agency's financial strength today and provide resources the agency can put to use tomorrow. |
| Leave more of estate to heirs. | Name agency as beneficiary of **retirement plan** and leave less-taxed assets to family. | Eliminate income tax on retirement plan assets and free up other property to pass to heirs. |
| Create long-term gift that won't draw funds from estate. | Create a new **life insurance policy** or donate a paid-up policy whose coverage is no longer needed. | Increase the ability to make a significant gift to the agency. |
| Get benefits back from assets given to agency and thus afford a larger gift. | Make contribution to a pooled income fund or create a life income plan such as a **charitable gift annuity** or a **charitable remainder unitrust.** | Receive income for life, receive a charitable deduction, and diversify holdings. |
| Reduce gift and estate taxes and leave more of assets to heirs. | Create a **charitable lead trust** to pay income to the agency for a fixed time and then pay the remainder to heirs. | Reduce gift and estate taxes and freeze the taxable value of growing assets before they pass on to family. |
| Reduce high tax liability now and gain additional income later. | Establish a **deferred gift annuity.** | Use the annuity to get a larger deduction and higher income rate than other life income gifts offer. |

©2010, PlannedGiving.Com, Valley Forge, Pennsylvania

rationale for each type of gift that can be shared with potential donors.

# Revenues and Expenditures

An understanding of the various types of revenues and expenditures is critical to the day-to-day management of agency finances. While types and amounts of revenues and expenditures may differ among recreation providers, the basic notions inherent in their management can be applied across the board.

## Projecting Revenues and Expenditures

Certainly an important component of budgeting is projecting revenues and expenditures. Without a good idea of how much money is going to come into and go out of an agency or a program, it is impossible to develop a realistic budget. Participation rates, pricing strategies, and costs all play a role in projecting revenues and expenditures. Revenue for ongoing programs tends to be relatively easy to predict unless the demand changes suddenly due to outside influences such as external competitors (e.g., a new YMCA) or due to drastic increases in costs of supplies. Often programs have a limit on how many participants can enroll. If the program consistently fills up, most programmers budget for this trend to continue.

Anticipating participation rates for new programs can be more difficult. It is assumed that if a new program is developed there is a proven need for the program. The needs assessment that suggested the agency should develop the new program should also provide a reasonable idea of how many participants will enroll. Nonetheless, the anticipated participation rate is still a guess, albeit an educated one. Just because people indicate that they want a new program does not guarantee they will take advantage of it. Conflicting opportunities, costs, and interest level all influence whether a person makes the step from desire to commitment. For this reason, it is prudent to be conservative with budget estimates for new programs.

New facility development and space acquisition may allow existing programs to expand and thus increase participation and revenue—these are situations that also need to be taken into consideration when predicting revenues and expenditures. It is possible that new opportunities may increase expenditures at a faster pace than revenue increases until the program is again maxed out on enrollment and revenue.

Pricing strategies for new programs and pricing adjustments for already existing programs tend to remain consistent from year to year. Pricing strategies are outlined in the following discussion and take into consideration indirect and direct costs associated with a program. Pricing strategies often depend on the philosophy of the agency as well as the individual program. Therefore, programmers need to have a clear understanding of their options when it comes to setting prices and to consider how price can influence the program within the context of the mission of the agency.

## Setting Fees and Charges

As just mentioned, setting fees and charges is often related to the philosophy of the agency with respect to cost recovery and the people who are benefiting from the program. Fees and charges can cover both indirect and direct program costs. Indirect costs are those that cannot be tied directly to a program or an event. They include, for example, the costs of making bond payments on a new multisport facility. Indirect costs are fixed in that they do not vary despite what happens with a program or event; indirect costs remain constant. Direct costs are tied directly to a program or an event and include things such as equipment. Direct costs can be either fixed or variable. For example, the cost of new basketball nets is a fixed direct cost because it is not going to vary by number of participants—it depends only on how many basketball hoops the agency owns. However, costs associated with equipment such as jerseys are variable direct costs in that they change depending on how many participants sign up for the program. Regardless of the types of costs being evaluated, the people setting the fees must prepare specifications and justifications for expenditures so that the participants or customers know how their money is being spent.

Setting fees with respect to covering (or not covering) costs often depends on the program classification. There are three classifications of programs: private programs, public programs, and merit programs (Rossman and Schlatter 2008). Each classification takes a different approach to cost recovery. The classifications are based on who benefits from the program and the appropriate amount to charge the beneficiaries. A private program, such as an adult ski trip, is one in which the primary beneficiary is the individual, and therefore the program is priced to cover all related costs. That is, the pricing strategy is based on full cost recovery and includes both direct (variable and fixed) and indirect costs; the agency is not responsible for subsidizing the program.

On the other hand, public programs serve the entire public. All community members enjoy the related program benefits such as increased leisure opportunities, increased property values, or overall better quality of life. An example of a public program is a community park or perhaps a parade. These programs typically come at no charge to the individual and are paid by the general fund; the program or facility is considered to be for the public good.

Finally, there are the merit programs, which fall in the middle of the continuum. Pricing is based on a percentage and is broken down according to who benefits to what degree. Merit programs are those from which both the individual and the public reap benefits, although often these benefits are reaped at varying degrees. For example, an after-school program benefits individual families by providing after-school care for children—often at a lower cost than that of a private program—while parents work. However, the community also benefits from this program, because it keeps children off the streets and gives them a safe place to go after school. Thus, given this breakdown of benefits, the fee charged for the merit program is a percentage of the total cost and is based on how much an individual benefits from the program. Often the costs to the participant cover only the variable costs associated with the program, such as the money needed for uniforms, sport equipment, or art supplies.

Program classifications are inherently different for nonprofit or commercial programs and services. However, while nonprofit agency programs and services are not classified as public, private, or merit, they may be quite similar to public or merit programs. In the case of a nonprofit agency such as a YMCA or a Boys and Girls Club, the public programs are those that are included with a membership fee. These are programs that do not cost extra for the YMCA member to participate in, as the agency wants the program to be open to all members due to its far-reaching benefits. An example of such a program is a family day drop-in program—in this instance the agency may see the program as a member service or benefit.

Nonprofit agencies often have as part of their mission a desire to meet the recreational needs of their members while not excluding participants with their pricing, because many times youths are their primary audience. They have as their goal beneficial outcomes that are similar to those found in the public sector. Therefore, their pricing structures are often similar to those of public agencies. While some programs may be priced in line with those that are classified as private programs in the public sector, many will be more similar to the merit programs. For nonprofit agencies it is not taxes that help subsidize the programs but membership fees that are paid by all and are more expensive for adult members. In some instances membership rates are actually collected on a sliding scale that depends on the individual's or family's income. These membership fees serve as a general fund for the nonprofit agency. They allow for lower-cost programs, particularly since the agency does not have profit generation as its business model.

On the other hand, the commercial sector certainly has an overarching goal of making a profit. Commercial businesses have owners or shareholders who expect a return on their investments. Therefore, programs and services in the commercial sector are priced to earn money, and the audience is not necessarily an entire membership or community but simply those who can afford the services. However, the prices offered must fit the market so that the company can attract and retain business while still turning a profit. A good example of a price comparison for a similar program offered by a public, nonprofit, and commercial agency is a youth basketball program in Charlotte, North Carolina. The privately owned Yes I Can Youth Basketball Camp and Leagues offers a six-week league for $149 (Yes I Can Basketball 2009), while the YMCA of Greater Charlotte offers a similar program for $80 for members (YMCA of Greater Charlotte 2009) and the Mecklenburg County Park and Recreation Department offers a basketball program for $55 (Mecklenberg County Park and Recreation 2010).

Regardless of the program classification in the public sector, the cost to participate in a public program is often lower than it is to participate in a private program because the public agency may be able to purchase equipment at lower costs, obtain discounts on trips, and negotiate reduced prices in part due to sponsorships, the bidding process, and the nonprofit nature of the agency. These characteristics of public sector programs all help lower the **break-even point** and help reduce costs for the individual participant. Even when providing private programs benefiting the individual, the mission of a public parks and recreation agency is to provide programming for everyone. Although this is not always feasible and is not necessarily even desirable for all activities, for the most part public parks and recreation agencies are the go-to providers of recreation activities that in the commercial sector are unaffordable for many. These public sector programs or facilities may lack some of the amenities for-profit businesses can provide but nonetheless are still good, solid services. In some instances a public agency may feel justified to charge enough to turn a profit on a program. However, this profit is then used to help subsidize programs the agency wants to keep costs down on so that they are affordable for a broader range of participants. This is often the case with youth programs.

Whether public or private, for-profit or nonprofit, an agency always has to start with a good idea of the unit cost for the program or service. Fixed and variable costs must be considered so that the agency has an accurate cost from which to work when determining how much to subsidize a program or service or how much to increase a price to meet pricing goals. The following formula is used to calculate unit cost:

$$P = (F + V) / N,$$

where P = the cost of the unit, F = the total fixed costs, V = the total variable costs, and N = the number of units expected to be sold. Consider as an example a YMCA after-school program that has total fixed costs per week of $500, total variable costs per week of $150, and an expected enrollment of 50 youths per week. Substituting these numbers into the equation gives the following:

$$P = (500 + 150) / 50 = 13.$$

To break even the agency needs to charge $13 per participant per week. Depending on the business model of the agency, the price of the program may be set at $13 or may be either higher or lower.

## Pricing Strategies

Certainly program classification is one way to determine the approach to setting the price of a program. It provides pricing guidance with respect to cost recovery (what percentage of cost to try to recover). However, numerous other pricing strategies go beyond how much of the program cost the agency wants to recover.

Pricing to create new resources is similar to pricing for cost recovery but actually prices a program in order to make a profit. The profit is then used to subsidize other programs or provide additional services.

Pricing to establish value is a strategy used to connote that a program should be valued by the people registering for it. People may not value a program offered free of charge—after all, you get what you pay for. Putting a price on a program indicates the value that participants can expect to receive from that program.

Pricing to influence behavior involves pricing a program or experience in such a way that the price influences a person to act. For example, agencies might charge higher fees for late registration in order to encourage early enrollment or might charge forfeit fees to sport teams in order to encourage them to show up for their games and avoid disappointing other teams who have paid to play. The fees need to be high enough to induce the desired behavior; a forfeit fee of $1 is not going to do it, but a fee of $25 might.

Differential pricing, or matching a price to the characteristics of the participants or the program, can serve several purposes. It allows an agency in the public or nonprofit sector to meet its goal of providing certain classifications of programs to everyone, regardless of their ability to pay. While agencies help people in need with resources such as scholarships, they also use differential pricing to provide assistance as well as promote equity in service provision for groups who may be less able to pay full price, such as seniors and youths. Differential pricing makes concessions in charging full price based on different variables such as the participant, product, place, time, and quantity.

Differential pricing based on participants often focuses on those who have less independent ability to pay, such as youths. However, differential pricing may also be used in the commercial sector to gain market share or to increase profit margins.

League prices for youth sport leagues will often depend on the type of agency that is offering the program.

## Sanctuary Hotel

The Sanctuary Hotel at the Kiawah Island Golf Resort in South Carolina varies the price of its guest rooms throughout the year to reflect the number of island amenities it is able to offer its guests. During the months of June and July, when the greatest number of island amenities are available, a standard oceanfront guest room costs between $545 and $754 per night. From Thanksgiving to March 1st, when the smallest number of amenities are available, the same standard oceanfront guest room ranges from $270 to $405 per night. Given the mild winters at Kiawah Island Golf Resort, many of the island amenities are still available throughout the season, but there are three differences between high season and low season. First, the outdoor pool complexes are closed during the winter months, leaving only the indoor pool amenities. Second, recreation activities such as marsh tours and canoeing expeditions are not offered as frequently during the winter months. Finally, the kids camp for ages 3 to 11 is offered only for half days on Mondays, Wednesdays, and Fridays during the low season as opposed to both half days and full days on Monday through Friday in the high season. In addition to changing its pricing with the season, the resort increases its room rates by 5 percent each year when possible. For example, during the recession period of 2008 to 2009, the resort chose not to utilize the full 5 percent increase.

For example, during slow times of the day a business such as a restaurant may offer reduced prices on menu items. The reduced prices still allow the restaurant to turn a profit but also help it to bring in business. The business gains nothing by sitting empty during open hours—staff, utilities, and so on still must be paid whether the building is empty or full. Therefore, lowering the prices during a slow time brings in additional revenue and entices diners who might not be interested in eating out at regular prices. Some restaurants offer early bird specials that allow people who come in for dinner between 4:30 and 5:30 (for example) to receive a substantial discount on their meal. They are not taking up space from those willing to pay full price, the menu is often limited, and the restaurant is able to bring in additional profits and thus increase its efficiency.

Other commercial businesses such as amusement parks offer differential pricing based on quantity and offer group discounts for their facilities. Resorts often engage in the same practice; see the sidebar on the Sanctuary Hotel.

# Tools for Financial Management

Agencies have a number of tools and formats available to them when setting their operating budget; the overall agency philosophy often dictates the specific budget format. Programs must follow the agency-wide budget format. For all types of budgets, accuracy is key. Therefore, well-designed

systems for collecting accurate financial and operating data on attendance, revenues, expenditures, and maintenance are critical to the development of a useful budget.

## Types of Budgets

Four common types of budgets are addressed in this chapter: object classification line-item budgets, program budgets, performance budgets, and zero-based budgets. In addition, incremental budgeting, which is an approach that can be utilized with many types of budgets, is described.

### Object Classification Line-Item Budgets

An **object classification line-item budget** is a format in which each expenditure, and the dollar amount expended for it, is listed on a separate line within a predetermined coding system. Each line of the budget illustrates the dollar amount budgeted for the classification or code, and often each classification has numerous subclassifications below it. For example, in most budgets there is a line for personnel and a related code, such as 2000. Under that code are subcategories of codes that outline various types of personnel, such as program (2100), maintenance (2200), and so on. Money cannot be transferred from one line to another line or from one program to another program, because budget categories are kept separate. This type of budget focuses on monetary allocations rather than programmatic outcomes such as service benefit outputs, although the classification system could certainly be used in a program budget or a performance budget (Crompton 1999), both of which are described later. This format keeps all expenditures independent, making budget reductions easier in practice. Because the link between money and output is unclear, managers can subtract small amounts from multiple lines without facing how that practice might affect programs and services. Figure 8.3 provides an example of a partial object classification budget. First the classification codes are listed, and then the application of the codes within the fiscal budget is shown.

### Program Budgets

Unlike an object classification line-item budget, a **program budget** outlines expenditures by departmental function or program and thus provides a more outcome-oriented picture of the budget. That is, it focuses more on how money is spent in support of meeting program goals and objectives, and goals and objectives are listed in this budget format. For this reason, the fiscal aspect of the program budget follows the development of the program goals and objectives. Figure 8.4 portrays a program budget for a climbing trip. The budget outlines the program goals and objectives as well as the associated revenues and costs that will allow the goals and objectives to be met successfully. While line-item formatting may be integrated into a program budget, it is done so within the context of each program. For example, while a line-item budget may have an overall salary line for the entire agency, in a program budget the salaries related to each specific program are identified in that part of the budget.

### Performance Budgets

A **performance budget** takes budgeting a step further and really focuses on what expenditures are being made and what effect expenditures have on program outputs. In other words, the budget shows whether money is being spent in such a way that it provides programs and services to the community with valued outcomes and benefits. Figure 8.5 shows a performance budget for an after-school program, identifying efficiency (performance) for the program in light of budgetary figures. Performance standards are utilized to show how much a program or service costs to run at a designated *level* of service and are used for the components of the agency budget that lend themselves to a concise measurement of cost per unit. For example, mowing park grass is one area where a performance budget is appropriate, as cost per acre cut is easy to measure. After identifying mowing as an appropriate component for the

performance budget, the manager should establish a work unit to be measured, which in this case is an acre. The next step is to determine cost per work unit and then to determine the frequency with which the work unit must be completed—in other words, how often does the grass need to be cut? Once this information is collected, the performance budget can be developed.

### Zero-Based Budgeting

**Zero-based budgeting**, a form of program budgeting, requires an agency to start with a zero balance each year when making allocations rather than just modifying the numbers from the previous year. This type of budgeting is very time consuming, as it forces program managers to justify expenditures on a yearly basis. There are two primary steps to zero-based budgeting. First is the development of decision packages, which are the presentations of the proposed budgets for every program. Second is the prioritization of the decision packages, which is accomplished through a cumulative ranking process that is based on priorities across the entire agency. Administrators assign a cutoff point based on available revenue; programs or services that fall below the cutoff point are not funded. Because of the time-consuming nature of zero-based budgeting, few agencies use it other than to prioritize programs and services that are outside of the core services of the agency.

### Incremental Budgeting

**Incremental budgeting** is the process of taking the previous year's budget, determining a percentage increase (or, in some cases, decrease) for the overall budget, and then applying it across the board to the previous year's numbers. Often an agency uses incremental budgeting when revenue forecasts appear to be similar and the agency does not foresee making any great changes to programming yet may increase fees and charges slightly or anticipates greater demand for services.

## Other Budget Types

There are many other types of budget formats available to agencies beyond those discussed in the previous section. Following is a brief description, along with advantages and disadvantages, of six other types of budget formats.

### Activity Budgets

An activity budget divides a budget into activity areas and focuses on the cost to perform a specific function. This allows agencies to have a clearer

# Partial Object Classification Line-Item Budget for an Athletic Department

## Example List of Classification Codes by Object

1000 Personnel services
1100 Salaries, regular
1200 Salaries, temporary
1300 Salaries, seasonal
1400 Salaries, permanent part time
2000 Contractual services
2100 Communications
2101 Postage
2102 Telephone
2103 FedEx, UPS, freight
2104 Internet communications
2105 In-state travel
2106 Out-of-state travel
2200 Printing services
2201 Printing
2202 Photocopying
2203 Word processing
2204 Photography
2205 Marketing and advertising
2206 Blueprints, plans, RFPs
2300 Utilities
2301 Natural gas

2302 Propane
2303 Electrical, outdoor
2304 Electrical, indoor
2305 Water
2306 Sewer
2307 Telephone
2308 Network connections
2400 Repairs
2401 Repairs to equipment
2402 Repairs to buildings and structures
2403 Repairs to playgrounds, equipment, and services
3000 Commodities
3100 Materials
3101 Masonry
3102 Road materials
3103 Lumber
3104 Paint
3105 Sand
3106 Other materials
3200 Supplies
3201 Office
3202 Program

3203 Sport
3204 Craft
3205 Aquatic
3206 Food
3207 Clothing and dry goods
3208 Chemical
4000 Encumbered obligations
4100 Rent
4101 Buildings and spaces
4102 Equipment and vehicles
4200 Insurance
5000 Existing charges
5100 Interest of debt
5200 Pensions and retirements
5300 Grants and subsidies
5400 Taxes
6000 Debt payment
6100 Serial bonds
6200 General obligation bonds
6300 Revenue bonds
6400 Sinking fund installments
6500 Other debt payment

## Partial Object Classification Line-Item Budget

| Object code | Description | Last year annual | This year projected | Next year requested |
|---|---|---|---|---|
| **1000** | **Personnel** | | | |
| 1100 | Salaries, permanent full-time employees | $55,000 | $56,500 | $56,500 |
| 1200 | Salaries, temporary employees | $3,500 | $3,750 | $3,750 |
| 1400 | Salaries, part-time employees | $60,000 | $65,000 | $67,000 |
| **3200** | **Supplies** | | | |
| CONCESSION SUPPLIES | | | | |
| 3206 | Athletics center snack bar | $3,000 | $3,200 | $3,200 |
| 3208 | Cleaning supplies | $250 | $250 | $300 |
| OTHER SUPPLIES | | | | |
| 3202 | First aid kits | $350 | $360 | $375 |
| 3203 | Sport awards, trophies | $600 | $625 | $650 |
| **2200** | **Printing services** | | | |
| 2205 | Marketing | $20,000 | $23,000 | $24,000 |
| 2201 | Brochures | $16,000 | $18,250 | $19,000 |
| **2300** | **Utilities** | | | |
| 2301 | Natural gas | $3,000 | $3,500 | $4,000 |
| 2303 | Electricity | $3,000 | $3,200 | $3,400 |

**Figure 8.3** An object classification line-item budget relies on an agency-specific coding system to track both revenues and expenditures.

Based on Brayley and McLean 2008.

## Program Budget Based on Goals and Objectives

Agency: Extreme Outdoor Adventures

Program budget: Table Rock Climbing Expedition

Program dates: April 1-3

Program length: 3 days

Number of participants: 15

### Goals

1. Introduce climbers to the Table Rock State Park climbing area.
2. Attract intermediate and advanced rock climbers.
3. Provide opportunities for rock climbers to network.
4. Publicize South Carolina state parks as climbing destinations.

### Objectives

1. Climbers will be taken to three Table Rock State Park climbing areas that differ by difficulty level.
2. The trip will be advertised to climbers in the southeast.
3. One social event will be held at the cabin site each night to encourage interaction among rock climbers.
4. Trip leaders will disperse maps and other related climbing information on South Carolina state parks to all participants.

### Description

The climbing event will involve three days of climbing at Table Rock State Park in three different areas of the park—the west, the northeast, and the south face. Climbers will be housed in cabins on-site and will be responsible for their own meals with the exception of snacks, which will be provided. All cabins are equipped with a kitchen and outdoor fire pit. All linens, three climbing guides, and vans for transportation on-site will be provided.

### Budget Summary

| Revenues | | Expenditures | |
|---|---|---|---|
| Program charges | $3,000 | Lodging | $640 |
| | | Snacks | $50 |
| | | Supplies | $75 |
| | | Vehicles | $300 |
| | | Staffing | $1,500 |
| | | | |
| | | | |
| | | | |
| | | | |
| Totals | $3,000 | | $2,565 |
| Total profit = $435 | | | |

**Figure 8.4** A program-based goals and objectives budget format focuses on how revenues and expenditures are used to achieve specified outputs for a program.

## Performance Budget

### After-School Program (40 Weeks)

|  | Last year | This year | Next year |
|---|---|---|---|
| **INPUT** | | | |
| Number of permanent, full-time staff members | 1 | 1 | 2 |
| Number of part-time staff members | 9 | 9 | 12 |
| After-school general fund budget | $60,000 | $62,000 | $75,000 |
| **OUTPUT** | | | |
| Total revenue | $144,000 | $144,000 | $216,000 |
| Total number of participants | 90 | 90 | 120 |
| Number of after-school sites | 3 | 3 | 4 |
| **EFFICIENCY** | | | |
| Percentage of expenditures covered by revenue | 58% | 57% | 65% |
| Estimated cost per participant | $40/week | $40/week | $45/week |
| **EFFECTIVENESS** | | | |
| Percent satisfied on participant survey | 92% | 91% | 93% |

**Figure 8.5** A primary goal of a performance budget is to measure the efficiency of a program in terms of revenue and expenditures.

delineation of the costs associated with different functional activities.

*Advantages*
- Clearly defines services as activities
- Allows for comparisons between activities
- Provides a clear picture of where budget funds are allocated

*Disadvantages*
- Can be difficult to set up and requires detailed accounting system
- May not easily fit some activities
- Reduces some levels of flexibility

### Fee Budgets

A fee budget determines actual cost of services and operations and allocates them to specific categories. This provides a detailed accounting of specific areas.

*Advantages*
- Provides a more detailed account of actual cost
- Shows costs per participant

*Disadvantages*
- Is restricted in use to appropriate areas
- Requires detailed knowledge of needs before initiating
- May not include all actual costs

### Function Budgets

A function budget is similar to the activity budget and allows agencies to group activities under major functions. This tracks activity budgets and allows administrators to view their changes in expenses over time.

*Advantages*
- Provides comparison of functional costs
- Improves knowledge of where funds are allocated

*Disadvantages*
- May not lend itself to easy comparison
- Uses object classification approach and retains similar disadvantages

### Planning, Programming, and Budgeting System

A planning, programming, and budgeting system identifies the relationship between costs and end results (or outcomes) of programs. It measures the outcome of budget expenditures on programs and focuses on the effects of expenditures rather than the cost of the program.

*Advantages*
- Focuses on service goals
- Focuses on end results
- Provides for comparative analysis of programs and services

### Disadvantages

- Requires establishment of an equitable measurement system
- Is difficult to determine importance of need and value
- Does not always allow comparisons across the entire organization

### Running Budgets

A running budget is developed and modified based on income and expenses and is driven by income and limiting income. It allows organizations without stable income to adjust their budget accordingly throughout the fiscal year.

### Advantages

- Is based on daily accounting
- Provides real-time budget accountability
- Ties revenues to income
- Allows a manager to administer or adjust the budget based on fluctuations in revenue and expenditures

### Disadvantages

- Is not a stand-alone system
- Is time consuming to administer

### Unit Budgets

A unit budget is used frequently in large organizations. It groups costs by subunit and allows for use of different budgeting approaches within a subunit. The unit budget is useful for viewing costs across an entire organization; it does not suggest commonality among units but instead depicts where expenditures are.

### Advantages

- Gives clear description of unit expenses
- Is simple to present and comprehend
- Opens budget process to public

### Disadvantages

- Is not a stand-alone system
- Does not give budget detail
- Requires top-down policies

## Other Fiscal Activities

Beyond budgeting, there are other fiscal activities that an employee may engage in to assist with the successful management of financial resources.

While agency managers ultimately may be responsible for many financial activities, they often ask for input on decisions related to payment processing, bidding, and outsourcing.

## Processes for Handling Cash and Other Payments

Because large amounts of cash and other forms of payment move through a parks and recreation agency as it collects rental fees, program fees, admission fees, and other payments, a responsible agency has policies and procedures for processing payments in order to ensure that they are not mismanaged. The procedures should address not only cash payments but also those made by check and credit card and those made online. Policies and procedures need to outline best practices for handling cash with respect to a number of issues. Certainly the policies should institute procedures that include itemizing a list of payments so that it is clear how much people are paying for what. This is especially necessary in an agency where many programs are offered and payments need to be distributed accordingly.

In addition, there should be procedures covering the distribution of petty cash. It is not feasible or efficient for agencies to conduct every transaction through the use of purchase orders or checks—in some instances cash is necessary. Thus agencies keep a small amount of petty cash on hand for small expenses as well as for times when a check will not be accepted. Handling cash, whether it is going out of or coming into an agency, demands an organized set of checks and balances, as cash provides easier opportunities for theft than credit cards or checks provide. Use of forms such as those shown in figures 8.6 and 8.7 can help an agency track the use of petty cash and account for how it is spent.

Agencies whose employees collect money from participants also need to have procedures in place addressing the reconciliation of the cash drawer. That is, they need procedures outlining how employees should count out and record the money as well as the sales receipts at the end of a shift or business day. There should be an even count of receipts and cash; procedures should also describe the steps to be taken if a drawer is either short of cash or has too much cash when compared with sales receipts. Along those same lines, procedures must address how the staff members should close out credit card receipts at the end of the day in order to ensure that they are processed correctly.

## Petty Cash Voucher

Date: _____

Amount: _____

For: _____


Account number: _____

Received by: _____

*Attach receipts immediately following purchase.*

**Figure 8.6**   Agencies use vouchers to track employee use of petty cash.


## Petty Cash Reconciliation Statement

Date: _____

Opening cash on hand:                                          $ _____

*Add*          Payments to petty cash fund:                    $ _____

*Subtract*     Total amount of vouchers paid:                  $ _____

Cash on hand (this should be the same as the amount of cash in the cash box):

                                                               $ _____

**Figure 8.7**   Petty cash reconciliation sheets allow an agency to ensure that the balance of petty cash on hand is accurate.


Figure 8.8 outlines the policies and procedures used by the Naples (Florida) Community Services Department for handling cash and closing out for the day.

The agency should also have procedures outlining how staff members should secure payments made throughout the day as well as at the end of the day. Is a lockbox or a register being used? Should all cash received be deposited in the bank at the end of the day? Procedures answering these kinds of questions ensure that the agency does not run into problems such as theft or misuse of funds.

Purchase orders, or requests for purchase, are another way for an agency to manage expenditures. A purchase order allows an agency to make purchases with approved vendors without having to make payment with cash, check, or credit card. The purchase order serves as a promissory note that the agency will make payment on the bill when it arrives. The paperwork also serves as a tracking device for purchases that are made

by employees in that purchase orders typically require purchaser information as well as a description of what is purchased and for what purpose. Requisitioning a purchase order differs from agency to agency, with guidelines set by anyone ranging from the agency treasurer to a business staff member to—in the case of federal agencies such as national parks—the federal government. Probably the greatest value to using purchase orders is that they allow the agency to follow the trail of how and by whom money is spent.

## Bids

Because public parks and recreation departments are government agencies supported by taxpayer dollars, for many purchases they are required to solicit bids in order to ensure that they are getting the best value for their money. When the public entrusts an agency with its money, it assumes and trusts that the agency will not misappropriate the funds or

## Cash Handling Policies and Procedures

Naples, Florida
Policies and Procedures
Community Services Department

| Policy title: Recreation Centers Daily Cash Handling and Closeout | Policy number: 07-68 Amend: |
|---|---|
| Effective date: February 11, 2008 | Authorization: |

### Purpose
To establish policies and procedures related to the requirement of completing daily cash handling and closeout procedures at all city recreation centers.

### Scope
All Community Services Department personnel (full time, part time, and temporary) assigned to all city recreation centers must be familiar with these policies and procedures.

### Policy
It will be the policy of the city recreation centers to follow cash handling and closeout procedures daily for all activities transacted at the city recreation centers.

### Cash Handling Procedures

A. All payments (especially cash payments, including cash from special events) should be processed through RecWare immediately upon receipt.

B. All payments (especially cash payments) should be placed in the assigned deposit locations (cash drawer, deposit envelope or bag, and so on) immediately upon receipt.

C. All deposits must be locked in the safe overnight.

D. Deposits should never be taken home by employees for overnight safekeeping or for any other reason.

E. All deposits (especially those containing cash) should be delivered to the Finance Department during regular business hours on the next business day.

F. Small sales items, such as snack shack items, retail items, T-shirts, tickets, and so on, may be set up in RecWare as a point of sale for a quick and easy way to record and deposit cash.

G. Under no circumstance should cash payments or deposits be used as petty cash or as cash float.

H. Under no circumstance should cash payments or deposits and cash float or change be used for purchases, payments, loans, personal use, and so on.

I. If the method of payment is cash, the money shall be secured in the cash drawer immediately upon the completion of the transaction. All bills received that are a denomination of $50 or larger must be marked with the counterfeit pen. This must be done before completing the transaction in case the bill proves to be counterfeit.

J. If the method of payment is check, the check must be endorsed with the proper stamp before being placed in the cash drawer. The front of the check must include the complete name and address of the individual or business. If this information is not printed on the check, it must be verified by the staff member and written on the check. The check must be coded by the staff member with the name of the recreational center processing the check. The purpose of the payment (e.g., dance class, camp fee, and so on) should also be included on the check. Checks written on any bank outside of the United States will not be accepted.

K. If the method of payment is credit card, the card must be swiped on the credit card machine or keypad. If the person using the card is unknown to the staff member, the staff member shall require identification. The credit card slip must be signed by the card user before the completion of the transaction. If the payment is made over the phone, the staff member shall write *by phone* on the charge slip and include the name of the person using the card.

*(continued)*

**Figure 8.8** Naples, Florida, has outlined specific guidelines for employees who are responsible for handling payments.

Reprinted, by permission, from City of Naples, Florida.

## Closeout Procedures

L. At the end of each day, the cashier shall run the Cash Distribution By Account (Summary) report from RecWare, which lists the payments by cash, check, and credit card that have been processed for that day and are included in the daily deposit.

M. The daily closeout report must be printed from RecWare at the end of each business day and included in the deposit.

N. If there are any problems or concerns with a daily closeout, the employee should lock the deposit in the safe and notify the supervisor or park manager by note or e-mail. The manager must rectify the situation on the next business day.

O. The daily closeout report must be signed by the employee completing the daily closeout. The employee must then initial the sealed envelope, which contains the deposit and closeout report.

## Cash Drawer Procedures

P. The cash drawer float and change amount is assigned by center: Fleischmann Park = $200.00, Norris Center = $150.00, River Park = $100.00, Skate Park = $100.00, and Tennis Center = $150.00.

Q. The cash drawer float and change should always be at the approved amount and should be verified each day as part of the cash drawer opening and closing procedures. Overages and underages should be reported to the supervisor immediately.

R. The cash drawer float and change should be used only for providing change and should never be used as another form of petty cash.

S. The cash drawer float and change and petty cash funds may be inspected at any time by the administration of the Community Services Department or the Finance Department.

## Special Events Cash Handling Procedures

T. All special events conducted at one of the recreation centers must have a method for accountability if a fee is collected. Wristbands, tickets, stickers, and so on may be used. These items must be prenumbered, and the accountability procedures must be discussed with the Finance Department before each event.

U. All money collected during the special event shall be secured at all times in a designated controlled area.

V. After an event the money should be counted immediately in a secure area with at least two employees present, one of which is a supervisor, and the total amount must be entered into RecWare. The number of tickets (or whatever method of accountability is used) should be verified and noted by the supervisor on the cash report for the event. All money shall be secured in the safe until sent to the Finance Department. All money shall be delivered to the Finance Department by noon the following business day.

## Training

W. All staff members handling money shall receive training on the proper cash handling procedures and the daily processing of cash receipts.

X. No employee without city experience shall be responsible for cash. Experience shall include on-the-job training with a trained staff member on at least two separate occasions.

Y. The Finance Department or Community Services Department will conduct annual training with all available recreation employees to review the forms and processes as needed.

Z. Employees handling cash shall be required to read this policy and sign a receipt acknowledging their understanding of this policy.

**Figure 8.8**  *(continued)*

spend them frivolously. Using quotes and sealed bid processes helps ensure that money is spent appropriately. Quotes and sealed bid processes are used for purchases above a certain dollar amount as dictated by the municipality. Each process requires the agency to seek quotes or sealed bids on items that it would like to purchase. Guidelines are also provided to how many quotes or bids the agency must secure before making the purchase. The primary difference between quotes and bids is the way that each is gathered. When gathering quotes, an employee can contact a preset number of companies directly (e.g., by telephone) and ask for their best price on an item. Although the quotes must be in writing, e-mail or fax usually suffices.

However, a sealed bid requires a public announcement that an agency is soliciting bids for a project so that a greater number of companies can compete for the business. The announcement includes the deadline for the bids, the date the bids will be opened, and the procedures (time and location)

for the opening. Sealed bids typically are required for larger projects such as building construction or vehicle purchases; quotes usually are sufficient for smaller items such as league T-shirts. For example, a parks and recreation agency needing to buy a new lawn mower may be required to get bids from three different businesses that sell lawn mowers. The bid process allows the agency to specify the details of the mower it is looking to purchase (e.g., size, horsepower, and so on). In order for a bid to be considered, it must meet those specifications. Once the bids are secured (by the preset deadline), the agency opens the bids and makes a public announcement as to which bid meeting the specifications outlined by the agency was the lowest.

The use of sealed bids ensures transparency to the processes by which public agencies spend public dollars and helps ward against improprieties in awarding bids such as awarding bids to friends or political allies. Figure 8.9 provides a partial example of an invitation to bid.

## Partial Example of a Request for Bids

### General Specification Bid Documents

Invitation to bid

Instructions to bidders

General requirements

General conditions

Specifications

Bid opening: _____
(date)

Location:    Winnetka Park District Office
             520 Glendale Avenue, Suite 100
             Winnetka, Illinois 60093-2135

### Invitation to Bid

The Winnetka Park District shall receive sealed bids for _____
(item)

in the Winnetka Park District Office, 520 Glendale Avenue, Suite 100, Winnetka, Illinois 60093-2135.
    A public bid opening will be held in the Winnetka Park District Office on (date).
    Bid documents and specifications are available at the Winnetka Park District Office.
    A contract will be awarded at the board meeting of the Winnetka Park District Board of Commissioners

on _____ .
(date)

    The Winnetka Park District Board of Commissioners reserves the right to waive any informalities in the bids received according to its own judgment, reserves the right to accept or reject any or all bids, reserves the right to accept only portions of each proposal and reject the remainder, and reserves the right to combine or separate any section or work if it is in the best public interest.

Winnetka Park District

**Figure 8.9**    The Winnetka Park District uses a standard form for requests for bids.

City of Winnetka, Illinois, Park District.

## Contractual Agreements

For some services an agency may choose to contract for services or privatize or outsource services. While contracting has focused historically on improving efficiency through external management of some services, outsourcing is looked at as a way for an agency to grow (Edginton and Jiang 2000). At its most basic, **outsourcing** is using an outside source to provide a product or a service that traditionally is provided internally. This may be a product or service that is new to the agency or one that can be done more efficiently externally. Outsourcing allows the agency to focus on growing services and products it can provide better internally and thus take advantage of the talents of its staff.

In the right circumstances outsourcing can offer many advantages. Contracting with an outside for-profit business may allow for more cost-effective services, because an outside business may have greater specialization in areas where the agency needs improvement, such as concessions or campground management. Other benefits include increased flexibility, specialized resources, and access to expertise that simply cannot be created (or afforded) internally. Yet despite these benefits, outsourcing—as well as contracting—can bring about difficulties. Certainly quality assurance and supervision while the external company becomes linked with the agency are of high priority. It can

also be difficult for an agency to let go of programs and services that it has a history of offering and controlling internally. Ensuring that the program philosophy of the outsourcing agent matches that of the agency is an important step in successfully navigating this route to services.

There are numerous programs and services for which outsourcing or contracting may be a good option. Recreation programs in general lend themselves to having instructors who work as independent contractors rather than agency employees, particularly given that many programs reflect fads and may not be around long enough for an agency to make a long-term investment in them internally. Guidelines for outsourcing or contracting usually involve examining the cost–benefit ratio of bringing in an external resource. Other situations that lend themselves to outsourcing are services that require highly specialized (and expensive) equipment such as that needed to change the lightbulbs of the outfield lights at a baseball stadium. Since the lightbulbs are changed only about once a year, it makes no sense for the agency to buy an expensive boom truck to reach the lights. Other instances in which outsourcing might be reasonable include building and facility maintenance, facility management (e.g., concession stand or golf course management), fiscal resource management, marketing, park maintenance, support services, and information systems management (Edginton and Jiang 2000).

## Outsourcing Park Accommodations

For years now Xanterra Parks and Resorts has been providing lodging and concessions at some of America's most beautiful destinations—our national and state parks. For example, as the official concessionaire at Old Faithful in Yellowstone National Park, Xanterra is the commercial provider of lodging and meals for guests. No longer wanting to hold responsibility for these types of services, the National Park Service has outsourced the majority of its concessions across the country. Xanterra is a presence not only at Old Faithful but also at the following destinations:

- Bryce Canyon National Park
- Crater Lake National Park
- Death Valley National Park
- Stovepipe Wells Village
- Grand Canyon National Park South Rim
- Mount Rushmore National Memorial
- Petrified Forest National Park
- Rocky Mountain National Park
- Zion National Park
- Additional state parks

Strategies for outsourcing are centered around a cost–benefit analysis within the context of the area that the agency is considering outsourcing. While there may be legal issues that prevent an agency from outsourcing some services, particularly if an agency is unionized, often there are a good deal of services that might be better off when performed by others. Therefore, it is useful for an agency to determine what its core competencies and areas of expertise are—those are the areas for which contracting services out is probably not prudent. However, if there are services, direct or indirect, that the agency feels could be provided more efficiently by others, then the agency might want to explore that option. Outsourcing can open up other avenues of service for the agency to take on as certain services are taken off its plate.

Once areas for outsourcing are identified, an agency needs to research who provides those services as well as outline how it wants the services provided, what it is willing to pay, and how the contract will be written so that everyone, particularly participants, is satisfied. One way to start this process is to issue an RFP. The RFP may be part of a bidding process and should outline what the agency is looking for from the external provider. In this type of relationship it must be very clear what is required from the contractor as well as how supervision and administration will take place to ensure quality control.

From a human resources standpoint, there are additional guidelines as well as liability issues that go along with utilizing independent contractors or outside companies to provide services. The agency should be well versed in financial, managerial, programmatic, and risk management considerations that accompany outsourcing. The sidebar on Xanterra Parks and Resorts on page 157 describes an example of outsourcing that is used by the National Park Service.

## Monitoring Finances

Although agencies typically employ trained accountants to monitor the finances, it is still essential that recreation employees have an idea of how to help ensure that resources are used wisely. There are several financial statements that help keep the finances in check, including balance sheets, income statements, budget statements, and project or program reports. These statements as well as other budgetary reports that are provided to management and programmers help monitor things such as profit margins and program costs on an ongoing basis rather than once a year when a program ends.

Balance sheets show an agency what it owns as well as what it owes so that it has a general understanding of its fiscal solvency at that point in time. An agency's assets equals the sum of its liabilities and equities. Assets are the economic resources that an agency owns or controls, such as cash, facilities, land, and equipment. Liabilities are what an organization owes, such as mortgages, employee wages, and bills to suppliers. Equity is the value of any owner's investment in an agency, which is often not relevant to a publicly owned parks and recreation department but is certainly relevant to a commercial operation. Figure 8.10 shows a sample balance sheet for a swim club.

## Dolphin Swim Club Balance Sheet

As of June 30, 2009

| ASSETS | | LIABILITIES | |
|---|---|---|---|
| **Current assets** | | **Current liabilities** | |
| Cash | $5,000 | Accounts payable | $500 |
| Accounts receivable | $200 | | |
| Inventory and supplies | $2,000 | **Long-term debt** | |
| **Fixed assets** | | Mortgage | $285,000 |
| Pool building | $400,000 | | |
| | | **Equity** | $122,200 |
| Total assets | $407,200 | Total liabilities and equity | $407,200 |

**Figure 8.10**  An agency's balance sheet shows how its assets, or resources, compare to its liabilities and equity.

Income statements are also known as *profit and loss statements* and provide a general picture of how the agency is doing financially during a specific period of time (month, quarter, or year). For the given time period, the income statement outlines all expenditures and revenues as well as identifies the difference between the two as either a profit or a loss. The categories of revenues and expenditures align with those used in the agency's budget document. Figure 8.11 shows a sample income statement for a swim club.

A person examining the balance sheet and income statement for the swim club might assume that the $21,724 profit shown on the income statement automatically increases the equity shown in figure 8.10 by that amount; however, this is not necessarily the case. The balance sheet includes information that reflects future financial activity that does not appear on the income statement. The balance sheet is based on inventory as of June 30th, cash flow for the month of June, and additional economic activity, such as new accounts receivable and accountable. Thus the equation is not as simple as it might first seem.

Budget statements allow an agency to track fiscal performance for a specific period of time, often quarterly, semiannually, or yearly. They allow the budget supervisor to determine whether the agency is staying within its overall budget, and they can be applied at the program, department, or agency level. They allow the budget reader to get a sense of the revenues that have come in over time compared with the expenditures that have gone out and are going to go out. This helps the reader to gain a better understanding of whether the program, department, or agency is on track to stay within its predetermined budget. For example, if the budget report for a program indicates that revenues are down from projections but that expenses are up, the manager needs to get a handle on how to make any needed program adjustments. Figure 8.12 shows an example of a budget statement.

Project or program reports provide detailed fiscal information on a specific project or program such as a day camp or a street festival. Actual revenues as well as actual expenditures are outlined so that the supervisor has documentation that can assist with future planning. These reports (see figure 8.13) can also provide other details about the project or program that may have influenced the fiscal outcome, such as weather conditions, programming conflicts, or other issues that arose that had unanticipated effects on revenues or expenditures.

Finally, a cash flow statement provides a program manager with details concerning the money that is coming into and going out of a program or agency on a regular basis, often monthly. Each month, for example, the cash flow statement gives the projected revenues and expenses and the running cash flow, or the difference between the two amounts, so that the manager can gain a picture of how the program stands overall financially and can adjust spending in a timely manner if

## Dolphin Swim Club Income Statement

For June 2009

| Revenues | | Expenditures | |
|---|---|---|---|
| Season passes | $30,000 | Wages | $8,176 |
| Daily admissions | $2,600 | Supplies | $300 |
| Rentals | $1,600 | Utilities | $1,000 |
| Merchandise sales | $800 | Insurance | $1,000 |
| | | Advertising | $300 |
| | | Mortgage | $2,000 |
| | | Licenses | $500 |
| Total revenues | $35,000 | Total expenditures | $13,276 |
| Net revenue (loss) | $21,724 | | |

**Figure 8.11** To determine whether an agency has a profit or a loss, it outlines all revenues and expenditures on an income statement.

## Sample Budget Statement

Clear Water Rafting Company
Budget Statement, 1st and 2nd Quarters

| | Actual | Budget | Committed | Percent | Balance |
|---|---|---|---|---|---|
| **REVENUES** | | | | | |
| Trips | $42,113 | $72,500 | $0 | 58.1% | $30,387 |
| Concessions | $8,671 | $14,000 | $0 | 61.9% | $5,329 |
| Store receipts | $11,148 | $20,000 | $0 | 55.7% | $8,852 |
| **Total revenues** | $61,932 | $106,500 | $0 | 58.2% | $44,568 |
| **EXPENDITURES** | | | | | |
| Staff | $35,963 | $52,100 | $1,500 | 71.9% | $14,637 |
| Supplies | $2,147 | $3,100 | $0 | 69.3% | $953 |
| Utilities | $1,610 | $2,430 | $0 | 66.3% | $820 |
| Mortgage | $8,051 | $16,000 | $0 | 50.3% | $7,949 |
| Marketing | $2,684 | $4,300 | $500 | 74.0% | $1,116 |
| Maintenance | $3,221 | $4,300 | $0 | 74.9% | $1,079 |
| **Total expenditures** | $53,676 | $82,230 | $2,000 | 67.7% | $26,554 |

**Figure 8.12** A budget statement will assist an agency with tracking revenues and expenditures in comparison to what was allocated in the original budget.

Reprinted, by permission, from A.R. Hurd, R. Barcelona, and J. Meldrum, 2008, *Leisure services management* (Champaign, IL: Human Kinetics), 339.

## Project Report

### Red Hot Fourth Softball Tournament
Event: Slow-Pitch Men's Softball Tournament
Dates: July 3-5, 2009

| | Project budget | Actual |
|---|---|---|
| **REVENUES** | | |
| Corporate sponsorships | $2,500 | $2,250 |
| Registration fees | $800 | $800 |
| Total revenues | $3,300 | $3,050 |
| **EXPENSES** | | |
| Publicity | $100 | $100 |
| Umpires | $840 | $840 |
| Supervisors | $120 | $130 |
| Scorekeepers | $252 | $252 |
| Field crew | $220 | $200 |
| Awards | $320 | $320 |
| Total expenses | $1,852 | $1,842 |
| Net income (loss) | $1,448 | $1,208 |

Submitted by: Alan Rickman

Comments: Sunny weather, no additional field maintenance costs

**Figure 8.13** The project report allows the programmer to gain a clear picture of the fiscal health of a program.

## Cash Flow Statement

| Month | Jan | Feb | Mar | Apr | May |
|---|---|---|---|---|---|
| Projected revenues | $120,000 | $90,000 | $200,000 | $250,000 | $300,000 |
| Projected expenses | $80,000 | $110,000 | $225,000 | $175,000 | $375,000 |
| Cash flow | $40,000 | $(20,000) | $(25,000) | $75,000 | $(75,000) |
| Net cash flow | $40,000 | $20,000 | $(5,000) | $70,000 | $(5,000) |

**Figure 8.14**   A cash flow statement provides a manager with a picture of revenue and expenditures coming and leaving an agency or program.

necessary. Figure 8.14 shows an example cash flow statement. This statement shows that in January the agency had revenues of $120,000 with expenses totaling $80,000. This provided a cash flow (cash available) at the end of the month of $40,000 to carry forward. However, with February expenses exceeding revenues by $20,000, the February cash flow was in the red by $20,000, leaving a running cash flow balance of $20,000 by the end of February ($40,000 January excess – $20,000 February loss = $20,000).

## Conclusion

Whether a leisure services agency is private nonprofit, public, or commercial, having control over its finances is a critical part of its daily operations. This chapter provides the reader with an array of resources to help with general budgeting and then delves into the many financial issues that a manager must oversee in order to handle an agency's budgets from revenues to expenditures. More specifically, the chapter describes numerous sources of funding opportunities, including the more and more popular partnership. In addition, budgeting formats and procedures are outlined, and pricing strategies that can greatly influence program budgeting are examined. The bidding process and outsourcing are described. Finally, the chapter discusses the financial management processes that allow a manager to keep responsible control over the finances of a program or an agency, which is ultimately one of the most important tasks of any employee's job.

## Review Questions

1. Describe sources of funding for leisure services agencies. Which sources are the most likely to be used in each sector?
2. Describe the five types of public–private partnerships. What are the benefits of each type?
3. Discuss the different pricing strategies used in leisure services. Which sectors are the most likely to use each strategy?
4. Describe the five types of commonly used budgeting procedures.
5. Describe the procedures involved in soliciting and awarding bid contracts for purchases and outsourcing.
6. List the uses of the following reports: balance sheet, income statement, budget statement, project or program report, and cash flow statement.

**Visit the online resource at www.HumanKinetics.com/TheParkAndRecreationProfessionalsHandbook for sample documents, keywords, activities and assignments, and more.**

# Human Resources: The Hiring Process

Human resources management, or personnel management, is at its most basic the management of people. This chapter addresses the areas of personnel management that are necessary for an agency to meet the personnel needs of the organization. Specifically, this chapter addresses the planning and processes that take place before an applicant begins a job. These steps include job analysis, job classification, job description development, recruitment, and selection.

# Job Analysis

The job analysis takes place well before candidates apply for the position. In order for an agency to hire the right person for a job, it has to understand what the job entails. Therefore, a job analysis is the starting point of the hiring process. A **job analysis** is the systematic collection of information regarding the knowledge, skills, abilities, and other characteristics (KSAOCs) required to perform a job successfully (Pynes 2009). Certainly a job analysis is critical to the hiring process, but it is also essential to work redesign, human resources planning, training, performance appraisal, career planning, and job evaluation (Noe et al. 2007).

## Components of a Job Analysis

A job analysis involves compiling in-depth descriptions of multiple facets of a particular position. The person in charge of the analysis must gather the following information: job activities, educational requirements, equipment used, working conditions, supervisory and management responsibilities, interpersonal communication skills, agency contacts, external contacts, and KSAOCs.

### Job Activities

The job analysis involves gathering data regarding the specific activities that an employee will need to perform in order to complete required assignments. For example, a youth sport supervisor might have to schedule league play as well as hire officials.

### Educational Requirements

Educational requirements describe the education that an applicant needs in order to be qualified to hold a particular job. In some instances a high school diploma or equivalent may be sufficient, while other positions, such as an administrative position, may require a graduate degree. These requirements may also include certifications that

an individual needs in order to perform a job adequately, such as CPR, first aid, Certified Park and Recreation Professional (CPRP), and Certified Pool Operator certifications.

### Equipment Used

This aspect of the job analysis addresses the equipment and tools that an employee in a particular position will be required to use. For example, a swimming pool manager may need to use a filtration system or a grounds crew member may need to use a mower. In some instances, operating a certain piece of equipment or a tool requires an appropriate license or certification.

### Working Conditions

Working conditions are the conditions under which an employee may need to perform the tasks associated with the successful completion of a job. Working conditions that may be relevant include weather conditions (some jobs may require working outdoors in the heat or cold) and noise conditions (some jobs such as mowing may require ear protection due to noise levels) and may also include travel requirements if an employee is expected to do a great deal of traveling outside of the workplace.

### Supervisory and Management Responsibilities

A job analysis needs to address responsibilities that an employee will have related to managing other employees as well as volunteers, whether they are part time and seasonal or full time. These responsibilities may include hiring, training, scheduling, evaluating, and dismissing employees. In some cases an employee will not have any supervisor or management responsibilities.

### Interpersonal Communication Skills

Most employees in the park and recreation profession must interact with coworkers as well as with the public on an ongoing basis. Depending on the job, communication may be over the telephone, face to face, electronic, or through different forms of public relations materials (e.g., fliers, press releases, and so on). This section of the job analysis needs to address the degree to which communication (type as well as frequency) will be a part of the job.

### Agency Contacts

This area of the job analysis outlines the people within the organization the employee will come into contact with when completing job tasks.

Agency contacts include supervisors and subordinates as well as any other employees the person may need to contact in order to perform the job duties successfully. For instance, a pool manager must be able to work well with lifeguards and maintenance staff members in order to perform successfully.

### External Contacts

As mentioned previously, professionals in the parks and recreation field have a great deal of contact with community members as well as with other agencies, both private and public. A complete job analysis uncovers the degree to which a particular employee will have to maintain these contacts and what responsibilities maintaining these contacts will involve. For example, a marketing manager must maintain contact with local media outlets.

### KSAOCs

Job knowledge is the information that a person must possess in order to perform a job. For instance, a pool manager needs to have a working knowledge of pool chemicals in order to provide a safe and enjoyable aquatic experience for customers. Skills are specific observable competencies required to complete the tasks associated with a job. For example, a lifeguard must be able to swim the length of a 50-yard pool. Abilities are an employee's aptitude for tasks—that is, how well the employee can complete tasks. One example is an administrative assistant who not only knows how to type but also can type 70 words per minute. Finally, other characteristics may include personality, fit, attitude, or other variables that lend themselves to successful job completion. For example, flexibility is a good characteristic for a day camp director (Pynes 2009).

## Data Collection Methods

A thorough job analysis produces a great deal of data. Because the type of data collected and the best or easiest method for data collection can differ greatly depending on the job being analyzed, there are numerous ways to collect data for a job analysis. Regardless of which method is used, accuracy is important to ensure the validity of the job analysis and the subsequent job description.

Jobs in the recreation field can require a broad set of KSAOCs in order to successfully meet the requirements of a position.

The job analysis must truthfully measure what it purports to be measuring—information relevant to the successful completion of a job.

A manager can use one or more of the following formats to gather information about a job: interviews, questionnaires, structured checklists, observations, or diaries and logs. Figure 9.1 is one example of a form that can be used to document data. The sample form provides space for the reviewer to document the duties; time spent on different tasks; degree of supervision required; necessary skills, knowledge, and abilities; and other traits necessary to perform the job. While not all jobs require a form this detailed, this sample provides a thorough representation of the types of data that may be collected for a job analysis.

### Interview

During the interview, the person conducting the job analysis sits down with the person currently in the position, that person's supervisor, and possibly another expert in the area in which that person works in order to determine the functions of the position (Pynes 2009). The various people may be interviewed separately or together as a group.

# Job Analysis Form

1. Title of position
2. Name of agency
3. Brief description of agency mission
4. Summary of duties and responsibilities of position related to (a) agency mission, (b) data, (c) people, and (d) things
5. Description of tasks

Percentage of time                                                    Importance of task to agency mission

(specify if daily, weekly, monthly, or annually)

| Task | Essential | Important | Supportive |
|------|-----------|-----------|------------|
| 1. _____ | _____ | _____ | _____ |
| 2. _____ | _____ | _____ | _____ |
| 3. _____ | _____ | _____ | _____ |
| 4. _____ | _____ | _____ | _____ |
| 5. _____ | _____ | _____ | _____ |

6. Relationship to other jobs
    a. Transfers
    b. Promotions
        From
        To
    c. Supervision received
    d. Supervision given
7. Skills required for machines, equipment, and work aids

| Skill | Needed immediately | Can be acquired through postentry training |
|-------|--------------------|---------------------------------------------|
|       |                    |                                             |
|       |                    |                                             |

8. Knowledge and abilities needed for task accomplishments

| Knowledge and ability | Needed immediately | Can be acquired on the job |
|-----------------------|--------------------|----------------------------|
|                       |                    |                            |
|                       |                    |                            |
|                       |                    |                            |

**Figure 9.1** A job analysis form will help a supervisor identify all of the required components of a position.

From A.R. Hurd and D.M. Anderson, 2011, *The park and recreation professional's handbook* (Champaign, IL: Human Kinetics). Figure 8.2, pp. 158-160 from PERSONNEL MANAGEMENT IN GOVERNMENT AGENCIES AND NONPROFIT ORGANIZATIONS, by D.L. Dresang. Copyright © 2009 by Pearson Education, Inc. Reprinted by permission.

9. Worker traits
    a. Aptitudes
    b. Temperaments
    c. Interests
    d. Physical traits
    e. Licenses and certificates required
    f. Vocational or educational preparation required
    g. Experiences required

10. Traits, skills, knowledge, and abilities necessary for career advancements

    a. _____

    b. _____

    c. _____

11. Social representation of workforce in this position classification (complete after position is classified if this is a new position)

    a.  Men                    _____

        Women                  _____

        Total                  _____

    b.  Caucasian              _____

        African American       _____

        Spanish surname        _____

        Native American        _____

        Other                  _____

        Total                  _____

    c.  Person with disability  _____

12. General comments _____

    _____

    _____

13. Basis of analysis
    a. Interviews
    b. Documents
    c. Literature reviewed
    d. Other

14. Analyst _____

15. Reviewed by
    a. Agency personnel_____

    b. Personnel office supervisor _____

**Figure 9.1** *(continued)*

### Questionnaire

For this method of data collection, those with expertise regarding a specific position complete an open-ended questionnaire. The questions might cover essential activities and tasks and percentage of time spent on tasks as well as ask for information about contacts within and outside of the agency.

### Structured Checklist

The structured checklist is a type of questionnaire on which an expert checks all listed items or tasks relevant to the analyzed job. In short, the structured checklist is a document that lists the potential tasks that the employee may perform, and the person completing the checklist rates how important each task is to the job. For example, an agency's standard form might include a task such as word processing. The person completing the checklist would identify how important word processing is to the position, typically rating it on a scale ranging from "Very important" to "Not important at all."

### Observation

When using observation for data collection, the person conducting the job analysis watches the incumbent performing the tasks necessary to complete the job. Certain jobs are more suited to this type of analysis; examples are lifeguarding and officiating. However, jobs that require a great deal of cognitive processing, such as being an executive director, are difficult to analyze solely through observation.

### Diary or Log

This analysis method requires incumbents to keep track of their daily activities and the time spent completing those activities. These data inform the job analysis on the percentage of time each activity takes, thereby giving the person doing the job analysis an indication of the general nature of the position and what it entails with respect to workload (Pynes 2009).

Regardless of the analysis technique used, the final product should be a written job analysis. The job analysis should include the information outlined previously as well as information about who conducted the job analysis and when the analysis was completed. The final job analysis is a working document—over time the nature of certain jobs evolves, and thus from time to time the analysis will need to be updated or completely revised.

# Job Classification

An agency uses **job classifications** to categorize job positions by *function level* or *ability*. Many government positions fit within a civil service structure that influences hiring practices, as the structure classifies positions based on required qualifications, responsibilities, and level of supervision. When hiring, the agency will also consider the ability level at which an employee can perform the responsibilities of the job within the context of the civil service guidelines. This classification system groups employees into positions; classes; vertical classifications, or series; and horizontal classifications, or grades (Edginton, Hudson, and Lankford 2001; Kraus and Curtis 2000). A job's classification indicates where the job falls within the organizational structure of the agency. Positions are specific jobs that require identified tasks to be completed as outlined in a job description. Classes are groups of positions that have comparable responsibilities and qualifications. Positions in the same class may have very different content responsibilities (e.g., a cultural arts supervisor versus an athletic supervisor), but they tend to be subject to the same policies and guidelines regarding pay, benefits, promotion, and other personnel issues (Kraus and Curtis 2000).

A **vertical job classification,** or series, is the vertical ascendancy of a position—the levels a person must work through to climb the ladder of management within a particular department or specialization, gradually earning greater status as well as higher pay. Figure 9.2 provides an example of the vertical classification of positions for the Lincoln (Nebraska) Parks and Recreation Department. The director is the most senior administrator of the department, and there are two areas falling beneath the director: (1) aquatics and recreation centers and (2) natural resources and outdoor education. The chart illustrates the chain of command in each area; the lines connecting the boxes show direct levels of supervision and accountability. For example, the assistant recreation manager reports directly to the recreation manager, and recreation manager is the position that the assistant manager ascends to in a direct promotion. The assistant manager does not report directly to the department director but reports indirectly through the recreation manager.

The **horizontal job classification,** or grade, arranges classes of positions in terms of responsibility, supervision given and received, and complexity of work. The grade rises as work

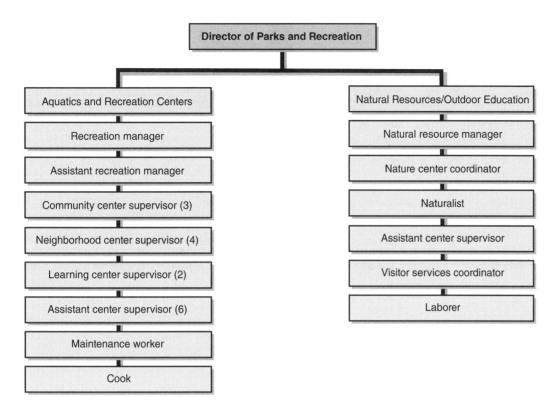

**Figure 9.2**   A vertical classification chart will provide a visual representation of management levels within an agency.
From Department of Parks and Recreation, Lincoln, NE.

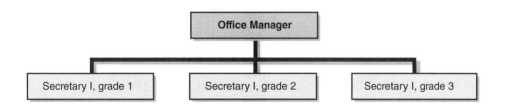

**Figure 9.3**   A horizontal classification chart is used to illustrate the levels of responsibility for the different classes of one type of position—a secretary, in this example.
Adapted from Edginton, Hudson, and Lankford 2001.

becomes more difficult and responsibilities grow in number. For example, a secretary position may be classified as secretary I, II, or III, but a secretary I, grade 3 position may have more responsibility than a secretary I, grade 1 position. Figure 9.3 provides an example of a horizontal classification (Edginton, Hudson, and Lankford 2001).

Within the classification system there are guidelines that dictate requirements for positions; these requirements may include experience, education, and testing (e.g., civil service exam). In addition, the classification system outlines pay structures and benefits by class and series. For instance, often there are pay grades for each class of positions; these pay grades dictate how much (or how little) an agency can pay an employee for a position.

Government agencies, such as municipal parks and recreation departments, may be required to utilize civil service requirements to place people into positions. Typically, these requirements are a combination of education, experience, and examination scores; military veterans are then given preference (Kraus and Curtis 2000). There are some positions, such as frontline positions and top management positions, that are not filled according to these guidelines. However, these requirements often apply to middle-level management positions. Historically, because the exams used as part of these requirements are not profession specific, they have been less than adequate in meeting the needs of the parks and recreation field. Therefore, state agencies have been working to have adjustments made within the municipal sector of parks and recreation (Kraus and Curtis 2000).

There are three levels of management that all jobs, regardless of class, fall into. The first level, frontline personnel, includes the people who provide direct leisure services, such as recreation leaders, instructors, and program volunteers. The second level, middle-level managers, includes employees who have a higher level of responsibility and thus greater authority to make decisions. These employees typically supervise the frontline employees, and so they must have greater experience and in some cases higher education than the people in the frontline positions have.

The third level, top-level managers, includes the people who are responsible for planning, policy development, and organizational structure as well as for managing the middle-level employees. Top-level positions include park superintendents, recreation directors, and chief executive officers, among others (Kraus and Curtis 2000).

After completing the job analysis and classification, the agency is on its way to hiring a new employee. Once the hiring process officially begins, the job description is often the point of departure for each step that follows, including recruitment, screening, and selection. While the specifics of the hiring process differ from agency to agency, there is overlap in the types of activities that are conducted. Figure 9.4 depicts a flowchart an agency might use when hiring, starting with obtaining permission to hire for a position and concluding with making the hire upon successful negotiation with the candidate. The remainder of this chapter outlines the steps taken to complete this process.

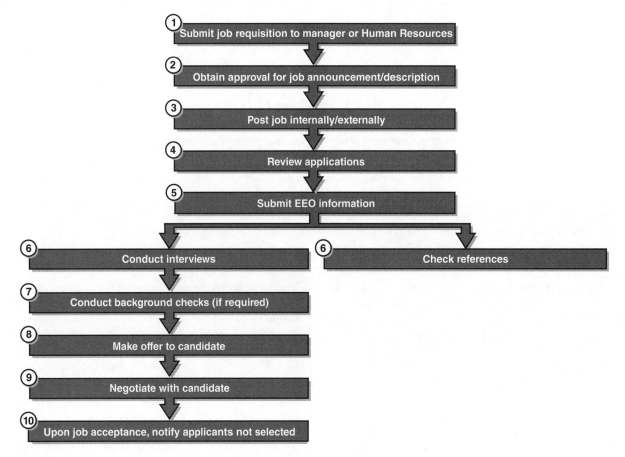

**Figure 9.4**   A hiring flowchart can help managers stay on track during the hiring process.

# Job Description

Developing a job description is an important step in the personnel planning process. A **job description** is a list of the tasks, duties, and responsibilities that an employee must complete successfully within the context of a specific job (Noe et al. 2007). Tasks, duties, and responsibilities are observable actions; examples are an after-school supervisor conducting a tutoring session or a dance instructor teaching dance steps.

While the specific format of a job description may vary by agency, there are some items that are essential to include, because they influence both candidate selection and ongoing human resources management issues, such as performance evaluations, training, and dismissal. A well-designed job description provides the following information: title, administrative information, summary, essential duties, additional responsibilities, and job specifications. Figure 9.5 shows a sample job description for an Outdoor Recreation Coordinator for the Charleston County (South Carolina) Park and Recreation Commission.

## Title

The title should be descriptive of the job as well as indicate the management level that the position holds within the organization (e.g., assistant athletic coordinator, athletic coordinator, executive director). In the example from figure 9.5, the title is *Outdoor Recreation Coordinator.*

## Administrative Information

In some cases the job description includes the division and department that the position is in as well as the completion date of the job analysis that informed the job description. Information provided in this section also includes the history of the ongoing development of the job description. The example job description in figure 9.5 identifies *Recreation* as the division for the position.

## Summary

The summary is where an agency lists the details related to the responsibilities of the job. This may include types of responsibilities, tools and equipment used, and level of authority. In the example from figure 9.5, the summary section is called *General Statement of Job.*

## Essential Duties

Listed in order of importance, the essential duties include details such as physical strength necessary to perform a job, types of people the employee must interact with, and outcomes of tasks that are necessary for the successful completion of the job. Essential duties listed in the example from figure 9.5 include promotion, training, and budgeting.

## Additional Responsibilities

Often stated as "all other duties as assigned," this section of the job description allows for the introduction of additional job responsibilities as a job evolves and thus spares the agency from having to constantly update the job description. The job description in figure 9.5 addresses these additional responsibilities simply by stating, "Performs other related duties as required."

## Job Specifications

These specifications provide information on the knowledge, skills, abilities, and other characteristics required to complete a job successfully. A solid job description provides guidance for the next logical step in the hiring process—recruiting potential staff members. The example description in figure 9.5 lists the job specifications under the section titled *Required Knowledge, Skills, and Abilities* and includes things such as the ability to use standard office equipment and software and knowledge of outdoor programs including safety regulations.

# Recruiting Potential Staff Members

Once a job analysis and job description have been completed or updated, the next step in the personnel planning process is to hire staff members as necessary; one of the primary tools to do this is recruitment. Recruiting is the practice of identifying and attracting potential employees (Noe et al. 2007). Recruitment can be internal when the agency is looking to promote from within or external when the goal is to bring in new talent and ideas. Whether an agency recruits internally or externally, and in many cases agencies do both, there are benefits and drawbacks to doing either. Irrespective of internal versus external recruitment, the recruitment puzzle comprises several

# Job Description

## Charleston County Park and Recreation Commission Classification Description

Classification title: Outdoor Recreation Coordinator      Grade: 209

Division: Recreation      FLSA Status: Exempt

### General Statement of Job

Under the direction of the Outdoor Recreation Program Manager, the Outdoor Recreation Coordinator is a catalyst to ensure that the needs for outdoor programming in the areas of land, challenge course, water, climbing, and youth programs are met for the Charleston community. The Outdoor Recreation Coordinator will accomplish this by designing and implementing new programs; by recruiting, supervising, and training part-time staff members and volunteers; by coordinating programs and activities; by providing technical assistance to other divisions within the Charleston County Park and Recreation Commission and to outside groups; by providing ongoing evaluation of programs and activities to ensure high quality; and by formulating and administering related portions of the outdoor recreation department budget. This position requires weekend, evening, and holiday work.

### Specific Duties and Responsibilities

Develop, implement, and assist with promotion and oversee all outdoor recreation programs in assigned programming area. Hire, plan, assign, direct, train, evaluate, and supervise work of outdoor recreation part-time staff members, volunteers, and interns to deliver a wide variety of outdoor recreation and adventure services in the specific area of programming. Depending on the position, this may include water programs, land programs, climbing wall programs, youth programs, and festivals.

Plan, research, conduct, evaluate, and assist with the development, promotion, and coordination of outdoor recreation and adventure programs. Within assigned area of programming, prepare and control annual budgets, perform strategic planning, analyze monthly budget reports, and oversee expenditures for the specific area of outdoor recreation services. Keep current on safety and risk management in the outdoor recreation field.

Research and procure equipment for outdoor recreation according to accepted procurement standards. Respond to requests for information. Monitor and respond to participant and customer complaints, concerns, criticisms, and feedback. Plan and implement programs in a way that protects the natural resources and environmental quality of county park facilities. Assist the outdoor recreation department as a training resource for the Charleston County Park and Recreation Commission and the region. Assist with maintaining compliance of the outdoor recreation team's accreditation requirements through the Association for Experiential Education (AEE).

Maintain training in the fields of outdoor recreation, risk management, and personnel management and establish professional affiliations in recreation programming and related fields. Provide input and assistance in the development of lands and facilities for multiple uses as requested. Help marketing with the solicitation of sponsors for programs as requested. Fulfill duties of the Outdoor Recreation Program Manager as needed or requested in manager's absence. Performs other related duties as required.

### Required Knowledge, Skills, and Abilities

- Broad knowledge of general recreation principles and in-depth knowledge and experience in outdoor adventure philosophy and programming
- Knowledge of outdoor programs, including safety regulations
- Ability to use standard office equipment and software
- Ability to present clear, concise, and comprehensive oral and written reports
- Ability to manage time effectively and to establish good work habits
- Ability to establish and maintain effective working relationships with Charleston County Park and Recreation Commission staff members and officials and the public

**Figure 9.5** Sample job description for an Outdoor Recreation Coordinator in Charleston County, South Carolina.

Adapted from Charleston County Park and Recreation Commission.

- Ability to accept constructive criticism and to demonstrate good judgment, tact, and courtesy
- Ability to plan, direct, and evaluate work of subordinates and to coordinate the activities of assigned staff members
- Ability to plan, initiate, and execute programs, including during evening and weekend hours
- Ability to obtain and maintain Wilderness First Responder certification and other certifications related to the program area (e.g., American Mountain Guides Association, Leave No Trace, American Camp Association, Association for Challenge Course Technology) and the needs of the program
- Knowledge of principles and practices of budget preparation and administration
- Ability to possess and maintain a valid South Carolina driver's license

## Minimum Training and Experience

A bachelor's degree from an accredited college or university, preferably in outdoor recreation or a related field, is required. In addition, at least three years of professional experience in a specific area of outdoor programming with at least one year of supervisory experience is desired.

## Working Conditions and Physical Abilities

The physical demands described here are those that must be met by an employee to perform the essential functions of this job. Physical demands are in excess of those for sedentary work; work involves walking, standing, pushing, pulling, stooping, crouching, balancing, and so on. This position also requires good listening skills and occasional lifting of up to 50 pounds. This position requires regular travel to central and remote locations throughout Charleston County and beyond.

Outdoor recreation employees must also be comfortable in water up to and including class III white water and ocean conditions up to and including the U.S. Coast Guard small craft advisory. Employees must also have the ability to ascend and descend a 50-foot climbing wall and must be comfortable working in confined spaces.

The work environment characteristics described here represent those an employee encounters while performing the essential functions of this job. While performing the duties of this job, the employee is exposed regularly to extreme heat, humidity, rain, cold, wind, and sun. The noise level in the work environment is variable.

**Figure 9.5** *(continued)*

important pieces, including the job announcement and the job application process.

## Internal Recruitment

Internal recruitment involves searching for people already employed by an agency to fill a position for which their skill set is an ideal (or at least good) match. Typically the position is one that involves advancement or is newly designed, though in some agencies it may simply be a job that provides new challenges for an employee in a different area of work. In unionized agencies, internal candidates are preferred, keeping in line with a collective bargaining agreement (Pynes 2009).

There are both benefits and drawbacks to internal recruitment. From a financial perspective, internal recruiting often costs less and takes less time. Internal recruitment does not require paying for advertisements or paying to bring in job candidates for interviews. In addition, internal recruitment can be good for morale, as employees see that there are opportunities for advancement within the agency. This not only has a positive effect on those already working for the agency but also can be a recruitment strategy in that it draws in new external hires who see the agency as a place where advancement is possible. A promising job candidate may be less excited about a position that is considered to be a dead end within the agency. Internal recruitment may also incentivize employees to increase their skill sets in order to qualify for different positions, at a minimum resulting in more highly skilled and motivated employees. Internal recruitment also provides an agency with a known product; the agency knows that the employee is a good fit with the company culture and also has a good idea whether the employee can do the job.

External recruitment can be an effective way for an agency to reduce stagnation in operations as new ideas are brought in by new employees.

On the other hand, internal recruitment can lend itself to stagnation as well as prevent growth in agency diversity, not only in gender, race, religion, and other demographics but also in ideas. In addition, internal recruitment can create resentment among employees as coworkers receive promotions. Finally, internal recruitment can prevent the agency from hiring the best person for the job if that best person is not currently working for the agency. Therefore, an agency has to determine if the benefits of exclusively utilizing internal recruitment outweigh the potential costs. Regardless, internal recruitment for an existing opening leaves another position open within the agency. At some point the agency must hire an external candidate, though perhaps at a lower level. However, an alternative to externally hiring someone is to promote a part-time employee to a full-time position. Figure 9.6 illustrates an internal position announcement for an Outdoor Recreation Coordinator for Water Programs that would report to the open position described in figure 9.5.

## External Recruitment

External recruitment, or seeking job candidates outside of the agency, has its own set of positives and negatives (see table 9.1). On the positive side, external recruitment can help increase the staff diversity, can introduce skill sets that cannot be found among current staff members, and can bring in new energy to an agency. In addition, a new hire also comes without any type of agency history—whether it be positive or negative. On the other side, external recruitment is more costly, because an agency must pay advertising fees. Also, an agency may sometimes pick up the cost of bringing in applicants to interview, especially when hiring upper management. In addition, it is more difficult to predict how a new employee will fit into an agency.

Before external recruitment begins, an agency must identify the labor market. The labor market is the geographic area in which workers compete for jobs and employers compete for workers. The level of the position dictates whether

# Charleston County Park and Recreation Commission Internal Position Announcement

Position title: Outdoor Recreation Coordinator for Water Programs

Grade: 209                                                                Salary: $37,460-$49,634

Location: Headquarters

## General Duties

Under the direction of the Outdoor Recreation Program Manager, the Outdoor Recreation Coordinator for Water Programs is a catalyst to ensure that the needs for outdoor programming, particularly water programming, are met for the Charleston community. This will be accomplished by designing and implementing new programs; by recruiting, assisting with training, and overseeing part-time staff members and volunteers; by coordinating programs and activities; by providing technical assistance to other divisions within the commission and to outside groups; by providing ongoing evaluation of programs and activities to ensure high quality; and by formulating and administering the outdoor program's budget.

## Qualifications

A bachelor's degree from an accredited college or university, preferably in recreation or outdoor recreation, is required. In addition, at least three years of professional experience in outdoor adventure programming with emphasis in water-based sports is required. American Canoe Association Instructor certification is desired. Supervisory experience is also necessary.

## Required Knowledge, Skills, and Abilities

- Broad knowledge of outdoor adventure philosophy and activities, including in particular canoeing and kayaking skills
- Experience in challenge course, backpacking, and camp programming
- Knowledge of principles and practices of administration and budget preparation and control
- Ability to exercise mature judgment and function within broad guidelines with a minimum of direction
- Ability to plan, direct, and evaluate work of subordinates and coordinate the activities of assigned staff members
- Ability to communicate clearly and concisely, both orally and in writing; ability to address large groups of people
- Ability to present ideas effectively and to develop related reports
- Extensive knowledge of the principles of safety and risk management
- Ability to establish and maintain effective working relationships with other employees, with agency officials, and with the public

## Eligibility

Any Charleston County Park and Recreation Commission employee who has been employed with the commission a minimum of six months is eligible to apply.

## Deadline

Submit an application for internal job posting (attached) and resume to human resources. Will begin reviewing on November 13, 2008. The position is open until filled. Equal opportunity employer.

**Figure 9.6** Internal recruitment can provide new opportunities for part-time staff to secure a full-time position within an agency.

Adapted from Charleston County Park and Recreation Commission.

**Table 9.1**    Benefits and Drawbacks of Internal and External Recruitment

|  | Internal | External |
|---|---|---|
| Benefits | • Lower financial cost<br>• No advertising<br>• No travel costs<br>• Faster hiring process<br>• Increased employee morale<br>• Incentive for skill development<br>• Employee is a known entity | • More diverse staff and ideas<br>• New skill sets<br>• New energy<br>• Lack of history that internal candidate may bring |
| Drawbacks | • Stagnation<br>• Lack of diversity (people, ideas)<br>• Might prevent hiring of best available candidate | • Can be costly<br>• Sometimes difficult to predict fit of potential employee |

the labor market remains local or is broadened to include the state, region, or entire nation. While the labor market for frontline staff members typically is limited to the local level, more management-oriented positions, depending on the size of the agency, may be opened up to a wider market. Strategies for both types of recruitment may overlap. Internal recruitment strategies can include internal publications such as newsletters, e-mail announcements, personal invitations, and postings. External applicants can be attracted through internships, Web sites, electronic mailing lists, local papers, college or university departments, invitations, and word of mouth.

## Job Announcement

An agency uses the job announcement, which is culled from the job description, to publicly kick off the job search. A crucial piece of the recruitment puzzle, job announcements need to be very clear and must be descriptive enough that potential applicants understand the position for which the agency is hiring. The announcement should provide the job title; salary (even if it is commensurate with experience); job description; job location; education, certification, and experience required; any examination required; an equal employment opportunity statement; and administrative information such as application deadlines, how to apply, and so on (Dresang 2007). With so many job postings online today, many job announcements do not look much different from the official job descriptions, as agencies are posting them on their own Web sites and thus

avoiding the word cost of newspaper postings, which in turn allows for more descriptive job announcements. Figure 9.7 illustrates two job announcements for the Charleston County Park and Recreation Commission Outdoor Recreation Coordinator—one for print media and one illustrating what an agency would place online. Because print media announcements can come at a significant financial cost, brevity is becoming the norm, as is illustrated in figure 9.7a. When an interested applicant goes to the referenced Web site, a much more complete job announcement is available, as is shown in figure 9.7b.

## Job Application

The job application is the written (and in today's world, often electronic) form that an applicant completes to formally enter into consideration for a job. While applicants typically submit a resume for full-time positions, most agencies require a standardized application to be on file as well. For part-time and seasonal employees, typically the job application is the only paperwork necessary. There are guidelines for what an agency can and cannot ask on the job application form. Standard requested information includes contact information for the applicant (name, address, phone, e-mail), work experience (companies, job titles, dates of employment), and educational background. The applicant is also required to sign the application in order to attest to the accuracy of the information provided. In many instances the application also has a section for references.

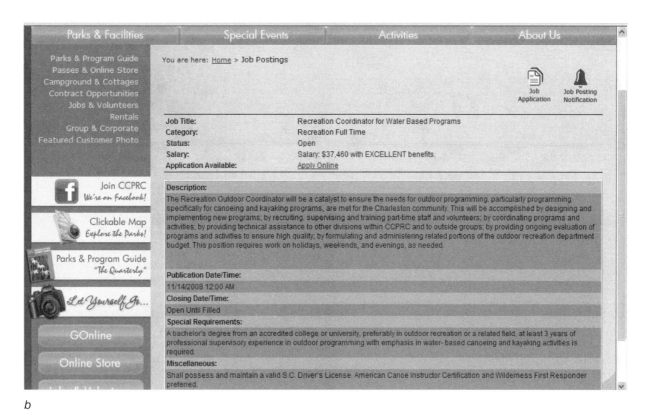

a

b

**Figure 9.7** Because of the related costs, many agencies will only publish (a) short job announcements in print media with a (b) Web site link to a more complete online announcement.

Reprinted, by permission, from Charleston County Park and Recreation Commission.

Questions that violate the guidelines of equal employment opportunity legislation are not permitted. For example, the application should not ask a candidate for a birth date, although it can ask if the applicant is over the age of 18 if that is a requirement of the position. Table 9.2 lists job application questions that might be considered discriminatory.

The agency may want to have steps in place to confirm receipt of the application with the applicant and to request any additional needed materials. Good communication with an applicant throughout the application process only enhances the reputation of the agency.

## Hiring Process

The logical first step in beginning the hiring process is gaining approval to hire for the position. Even if a position is not new, hiring freezes and restructuring can prevent an agency from filling positions. In the case of a new position, human resources personnel often have to fully vet job descriptions and recruitment measures with an eye toward personnel law before releasing them to the public.

Once an agency approves a position, the next step is determining who will do the hiring for the particular job. In some cases direct supervisors hire their own staff members, especially in cases

**Table 9.2**  Job Application Guidelines

| Job application category | Likely not discriminatory to ask: | Might be discriminatory to ask: |
|---|---|---|
| Name | Any other names that applicant has worked under | Applicant's birth name if he or she has changed it legally |
| Age | If age of applicant is less than 18 or 21 (if a minimum age is a requirement for the position) | • Birth date<br>• High school graduation date |
| Place of residence | • Applicant's place of residence<br>• Alternative contact information | • Location of birth or parents' birth<br>• Length lived at current or previous addresses |
| Race or color | If collected for affirmative action purposes, but only if retained separately from application such as with a tear-off sheet and not tracked by name | Race or color of skin |
| Citizenship, birthplace, and national origin | If the applicant is either a U.S. citizen or an alien authorized to work in the United States with only "yes" or "no" as options | Applicant's lineage, ancestry, national origin, parentage, or nationality or nationality of applicant's parents or spouse |
| Marital or family status | | • Marital status of applicant<br>• Dependents of applicants<br>• Pregnancy status<br>• Child care arrangements<br>• Employment status of spouse<br>• Name of spouse |
| Creed or religion | Only when a BFOQ exists (e.g., Catholic priest) | • Religious affiliation<br>• Church, parish, mosque, or synagogue<br>• Holidays observed by applicant |
| References | Names of work references or character references | References that would lead to potential charges of discrimination related to another category (e.g., name of applicant's religious leader or references related to political affiliation and contacts) |
| Organizations | Information about memberships in any professional, service, or trade organization | Social organizations, political parties, or social clubs in which applicant is active |
| Arrest record and convictions | Inquiries into convictions if job related | Inquiries about conviction unrelated to job requirements |
| Height and weight | Only when a BFOQ exists | Any inquiries unrelated to job requirements |
| Physical limitations or disability | • Whether applicant can perform essential functions of the job in question<br>• Questions related to accommodation if reasonable to believe an accommodation would be necessary because of an obvious or voluntarily disclosed disability | Any questions that ask applicant to list or describe any disability or physical limitation |
| Education | Level of education earned if deemed a requisite requirement for a position (e.g., college degree) | Date of high school graduation |

| Job application category | Likely not discriminatory to ask: | Might be discriminatory to ask: |
| --- | --- | --- |
| Military | Questions related to military experience or training | Military discharge details or military service records |
| Credit or financial status | Must follow Fair Credit Reporting Act, which requires notification if interviewer uses outside sources to provide information to make adverse decisions about applicants | Using information gained from sources outside the hiring organization without notice to the applicant |
| Gender | Only when a BFOQ exists | Questions about applicant's sex or gender |
| Medical questions/exams | • If job can be performed and how they would perform the job<br>• Job offer can be conditioned upon answers to certain medical questions or successfully passing a medical exam, but only if all new employees in same job have to answer questions or pass exam<br>• If started work, can only ask medical questions or require medical exam if needed to document request for accommodations or reason to believe job cannot be performed successfully or safely because of a medical condition | • If applicant has a disability or the nature of an obvious disability<br>• Medical questions or a medical exam before making job offer |
| Security check for certain religious or ethnic groups | If all applicants must undergo background checks before being offered a position | Subjecting only particular religious or ethnic groups to heightened security checks |

Adapted from R.L. Mathis, Mathis & Associates, L.L.C.

of part-time and seasonal help. However, a hiring committee may take on the responsibility of hiring for positions in higher levels of management, such as a recreation director.

It is vital that the people doing the hiring are versed in the major areas of employment law that pertain to hiring, including affirmative action, equal opportunity, and interviewing. While managers should utilize a human resources professional to make sure they are adhering to applicable employment laws, the individuals responsible for hiring personnel still need to be aware of what is legal and illegal in the hiring process.

## Employment Law

The employees who play a role in hiring should have a working knowledge of equal employment opportunity (EEO) law. The following sections provide definitions and guidelines with respect to the legalities designed to protect the rights of equal consideration for all applicants, specifically with regard to the EEO law and general employment law.

### Equal Employment Opportunity Laws

EEO laws are concerned with the information that is collected on applications as well as in interviews. Questions that even indirectly collect information about a person's protected status (e.g., race, ethnicity, religion, marital status, sexual orientation, color, disability, age, and so on) are prohibited. Other bases for protection include gender and military experience. In addition, EEO laws are concerned with discrimination in general. Two types of employment discrimination are disparate treatment and disparate impact. Disparate treatment is when a person or an agency treats individuals in a protected class differently, while disparate impact is when members of a protected class are underrepresented due to employment decisions that disadvantage them, such as the use of testing that has a negative effect on minorities

## EEO Policy

Reviewed and approved October 13, 1999

The Champaign Park District prohibits discrimination on the basis of race, color, religion, sex, age, national origin, veteran status, or disability. All employees, managers, supervisors, and job applicants are guaranteed the same employment opportunities. No person or employee, no matter title or position, has authority, whether expressed, actual, apparent, or implied, to discriminate against another employee of the Champaign Park District.

The Champaign Park District will not discriminate against any employee, manager, supervisor, or applicant on the basis of race, color, religion, sex, age, national origin, veteran status, or disability. The general managers, department heads, supervisors, and staff members will base all recruitment, placement, selection, training, and layoff decisions solely on job-related qualifications and abilities without regard to race, color, religion, sex, age, national origin, veteran status, or disability. The Champaign Park District prohibits verbal, physical, or visual conduct that belittles or demeans any individual on the basis of race, color, religion, sex, age, national origin, veteran status, or disability.

(Mathis and Jackson 2008). Agencies need to have steps in place to avoid both types of discrimination when hiring; see the sidebar for an example of EEO policy.

### Civil Rights Acts of 1866 and 1871

The Civil Rights Act of 1866 prohibits racial discrimination with respect to entering into contracts, including employment contracts. Nonprofit and private employers, unions, and employment agencies all fall under its coverage. The Civil Rights Act of 1871 extended that coverage to include state and local governments (Pynes 2009).

### Title VII of the Civil Rights Act of 1964

Title VII of the Civil Rights Act of 1964 covers discrimination in employment due to race, color, religion, sex, or national origin. The Civil Rights Act of 1964 also created the Equal Employment Opportunity Commission to investigate and resolve complaints of discrimination. Title VII allows for discrimination on the basis of identified bona fide occupational qualifications as defined in this chapter.

### Civil Rights Act of 1991

An employer who uses a selection procedure that has a disparate impact on a protected group is obligated to prove the validity of the selection procedure and to prove there is a business necessity for using that method (Noe et al. 2007). One example of procedures that have been called into question in the past is the use of standardized tests such as an intelligence test. The act also prohibits preferential treatment that favors minority groups.

### Protected Groups

There are laws that protect people who share a common characteristic that has often led to discrimination in the past. Groups that fall into this category include women, minorities, and individuals with disabilities, among others.

### Bona Fide Occupational Qualifications

While employment law protects against discrimination in hiring, Title VII of the Civil Rights Act of 1964 does allow for discrimination on the basis of sex, religion, or national origin if the characteristic is determined to be a *bona fide occupational qualification* (BFOQ). That is, the qualification must be "reasonably necessary to the normal operation of the particular business or enterprise" (Mathis and Jackson 2008, 103). For example, a person needs to be a Catholic in order to become a priest in the Catholic church.

### Americans with Disabilities Act of 1990

Employers must make reasonable accommodations for people with disabilities. The ADA restricts many types of questions during the hiring process that may expose a disability when it is not relevant to the successful performance of a job. While employers can gather information about whether a person can perform job duties, they cannot investigate disabilities.

### Equal Pay Act of 1963

This law, amended by the Equal Employment Opportunity Act of 1972, addresses inequities in pay between men and women. Employers can pay different wages to men and women, but only if the difference is based on job-related factors such as

The Americans with Disabilities Act has gone a long way toward ensuring the rights of persons with disabilities in the workplace

seniority or quantity and quality of performance. Differences in pay cannot be based on gender.

### Lilly Ledbetter Fair Pay Act of 2009

To amend Title VII of the Civil Rights Act of 1964, the Age Discrimination in Employment Act of 1967, the Americans with Disabilities Act of 1990, and the Rehabilitation Act of 1973, the Lilly Ledbetter Fair Pay Act was signed into law. The act clarifies that a discriminatory compensation decision or other practice that is unlawful under such acts occurs each time an organization pays a person pursuant to the discriminatory compensation decision or other practice and for other purposes. Earlier rulings had ruled that plaintiffs had to file wage claims within 180 days of a company's decision to pay the plaintiff less than it paid a counterpart doing the same work. In short, this act resets that clock with each issued paycheck.

### Age Discrimination in Employment Act of 1967

This law protects employees over the age of 40 with respect to hiring, pay, recruitment, and benefits. The only time age can be taken into

consideration when it comes to older employees is if an employer can prove that being a younger employee is a BFOQ, something that is relatively difficult to do in the parks and recreation field.

### Pregnancy Discrimination Act of 1978

This law protects women who are pregnant or affected by pregnancy-related medical conditions against discrimination. This includes discrimination in hiring and firing practices, pay, and benefits.

### Family and Medical Leave Act of 1993

The Family and Medical Leave Act (FMLA) provides protection from job loss to qualified employees who need time off for family and health reasons. The time off (up to 12 weeks during a 12-month period) is unpaid and can cover diverse circumstances such as childbirth, adoption of a child, acquisition of a foster child, or serious medical conditions affecting the employee or an immediate family member.

## Screening Applicants

Once job applications have been collected, the screening process begins. Screening can involve a multitude of steps, such as tests ranging from aptitude tests to screening tests for drugs and physical ability as necessitated by the job for which the person is applying. In addition, most hiring involves an interview as a final step. Different tests or tools that can be utilized for screening include cognitive ability and aptitude tests, achievement tests, interest inventories, experience and training ratings, structured exams, work samples or performance tests, in-basket tests, leaderless group discussions, assessment centers, drug tests, and physical ability tests.

### Cognitive Ability and Aptitude Tests

Cognitive ability tests measure intelligence. However, research has found that these tests have a propensity for adversely affecting protected groups. While there are strategies to overcome these adverse effects, many question the legality of those strategies. On the other hand, aptitude tests measure the ability of a person to perform the KSAOCs required for the job, including things such as verbal skills, quantitative skills, and motor skills.

### Achievement Tests

Achievement tests determine if an applicant has learned and mastered the specific skills necessary to do a job. A lifeguard certification test is one example of an achievement test.

## Interest Inventories

Interest inventories are not concerned with job performance but instead investigate whether a job is a good fit for a potential applicant. Basically, the inventories match an applicant's job preferences with specific types of jobs. A career counselor often utilizes the inventories to help individuals looking for jobs.

## Experience and Training Ratings

These ratings quantify what an applicant can bring to a job in terms of education, experience, training, and achievements. These are all data that are relevant to meeting the demands of a particular job.

## Structured Exams

These exams ask job-related questions to measure job requirements that many standard exams cannot measure. Skills tested may include interpersonal, verbal, and supervisory skills.

## Work Samples or Performance Tests

These measures require applicants to actually show that they can perform the tasks necessary for a job. Asking a person applying for a business office position to read a budget and having an applicant for a grounds crew use a mower are both examples of performance tests.

## In-Basket Tests

These tests simulate administrative tasks. They measure task prioritization, written communication, and judgment in that the applicant must examine a list of potential duties related to a job and address each task in a set amount of time (Pynes 2009).

## Leaderless Group Discussions

These discussions measure oral communication, leadership, persuasiveness, adaptability, and tolerance for stress (Pynes 2009). These skills are measured by having applicants work in a group to solve a defined problem with no group leader assigned.

## Assessment Centers

These centers utilize a number of different types of screening tests to obtain a well-rounded measurement of an applicant's abilities. Trained assessors make judgments about the applicant's behaviors and abilities.

## Drug Tests

Agencies often use drug testing as a screening tool, particularly when public safety is at risk, such as when hiring bus drivers. By law, an agency does not have to guarantee applicants the same testing rights that are granted to employees. While an agency may be able to test applicants, it does not necessarily have the same right to do so with current employees.

## Physical Ability Tests

These tests are for positions that require physicality. Therefore, physical ability tests may be implemented as part of the screening process to ensure that an applicant can, for example, lift 50 pounds if that is a requirement of the successful completion of a job-related task.

While not a screening test per se, preemployment testing can be used to ensure that an applicant can perform the duties of a job. The difference is that preemployment testing is used after a conditional job offer is made in order to allow the employer to ensure that a person can complete job tasks. Once the agency makes a job offer, it may then require a medical examination as well as make disability-related inquiries and ask the applicant to describe how he or she can complete job tasks with or without reasonable accommodations. According to ADA guidelines, if the exam screens out a person with a disability, then the employer must prove that the exclusionary criterion is job related and must also show that the job could not be completed with reasonable accommodations (Pynes 2009). Different types of preemployment tests include medical examinations, physical agility and physical fitness tests, and psychological examinations.

## Employment References

Verification of credentials (checking references) is also an important part of the screening process. The references that the applicant provides are a good starting point for ensuring that the applicant's employment history is accurate, particularly if they are employer references. Unfortunately, if past employers fear that they will be charged with defamation if they provide a negative reference for an employee who left on negative terms, you may receive only minimal information from those references. However, as Pynes (2009) notes, the potential of avoiding risks related to significant problems that the employee had in a previous job outweighs the possibility of getting a minimal level of information.

A second type of credential check that many parks and recreation agencies use is the background check. A background check allows an organization to determine whether applicants are representing themselves accurately. A paid outside company conducts the background check; the agency decides what type of information it wants confirmed (criminal history, education level, and so on). The level of background check requested will dictate its cost as well as the length of time it takes to complete. An agency must outline, in its policies and procedures, how it will handle negatives that may turn up in a background check. For instance, an arrest for driving under the influence that happened 20 years ago when an applicant was a 22 year-old-college senior may be deemed not a concern if the rest of the record is clean and especially if transporting others is not a job requirement. However, an agency should not consider an applicant for a volunteer youth soccer coach if the background check turns up a conviction for child abuse.

## Interviewing

While supervisors may not always be involved in the initial screening of applicants, they are most certainly involved in candidate interviews. There are a number of interview styles an agency might use. Nondirective, structured, situational, behavior description, and panel are five types of interview styles.

A nondirective interview allows the interviewer a great deal of latitude with respect to the questions asked. While the interviewer may ask questions from a standard list related to strengths, weaknesses, or experiences, often the applicant's answer will drive the follow-up questions. The drawback is that if the interviewer is not skilled in questioning or does not have a strong knowledge of the legalities inherent in interview questioning, the interview could produce irrelevant or unreliable information at best and lead to a lawsuit at worst.

A structured interview uses set questions that pertain to the KSAOCs necessary to complete the job. While a structured interview sometimes discourages alternative questions that are based on what comes up in the interview, it has the likelihood of producing more strongly valid and reliable data (Noe et al. 2007). In addition, it ensures consistency in questions asked among all applicants.

Situational and behavior description interviews measure how someone might react to a particular situation relevant to the job. The primary difference is that the situational interview forces candidates to project how they may respond in a possible scenario, while the behavior description

interview asks candidates how they handled a situation in the past. One example of a situational question might be, "How would you handle a youth sport coach who requests that you put her neighbor's child on her team to help with carpooling despite the fact that a draft is used to make up teams?" An example of a behavior description question might be, "When was the last time you lost your temper, what was the situation, and how did you deal with it?"

In a panel interview, the candidate meets with a number of representatives of the organization in a group setting. Agencies are starting to use panel interviews more often, as they can be less time consuming for both the agency and the job candidate. If the candidate can meet with five agency representatives from different departments all at one time rather than one at a time, the interview process can become more efficient and can cost less in terms of personnel time. It is important, however, for those doing the interviewing to be on the same page with regard to questioning, and thus formal, prepared questions tend to be the norm in order to retain a controlled interview environment. In addition, it is important for the committee to make the candidate comfortable, as interviewing with five people at one time can be quite intimidating.

Although used in almost all hiring situations, interviewing has its benefits and drawbacks. Some agencies may choose to use group interviews, in which an agency interviews multiple candidates at the same time. This type of interview allows the agency to compare the responses of candidates as well as the interactions among candidates. It also shows who has leadership skills or how candidates manage conflict that may arise during the interview. This type of interview can save time, as it allows the agency to give job-related information to all the candidates simultaneously. In some instances the interviewers give the group a job-oriented task to complete so that they can see how the candidates work with others. Some agencies use an assessment center to conduct interviews. An assessment center uses multiple evaluations (e.g., job-related simulations, interviews, and psychological tests) to provide a standardized evaluation of candidate behavior. In the past, as well as occasionally today, agencies have used phone interviews to screen candidates without incurring (either on their part or the candidate's part) the expense of travel. Without a travel budget, hiring can be limited to candidates in the immediate area or candidates willing to pay for their own travel. A phone interview can at least help make the initial cut for a position and spare the expensive costs of bringing everyone in for an interview. However, with today's technology the Internet interview is taking the place of the phone interview, particularly with the growing popularity of Skype, a Web-based program that allows for free video calls (www.skype.com). Through the use of a Webcam, companies can now see the candidate they are interviewing and so can observe facial expressions and body language in addition to hearing the words spoken.

Certainly an interview gives the agency a chance to meet the applicant in person and assess interpersonal and communication skills. The interview also allows the applicant to expand on the information provided on the resume or job application. Some people are more impressive in person than they are on paper (and vice versa). However, there are issues that an agency needs to consider to ensure that interviews are valid, reliable, and nondiscrimina-

tory. It is essential that interview questions follow guidelines designed to protect both the employer and the applicant. Reducing the subjectivity of the process is a good starting point. Interviews that are focused on the job, are structured, and are standardized for all applicants can go a long way in increasing the objectivity of the interviewer and agency. In addition, interviewers need to be aware of the legality of certain questions. Again, a structured interview format, approved by human resources, will help prevent an interviewer from crossing the line with questioning. A poorly done interview can cost a company in time lost as well as good candidates lost.

## Employee Selection and Negotiation

With the applicants fully vetted, the next step is selecting which applicant to hire for the job. Once the people responsible for choosing the applicant make their selection, they must communicate that decision to the applicant. The job offer includes information such as pay and starting date and any other relevant information that the person has not already received. It might also behoove the person making the offer to restate important information that the applicant has already received but will need to consider in deciding whether to accept the offer.

Negotiation of job terms is an inevitable part of the final hiring procedures. The agency and applicant must come to agreement on salary, benefits, and other forms of compensation before a hire is completed successfully. Most organizations have salary ranges into which a job position falls, and the negotiation will take into consideration relevant applicant qualifications in determining where the employee will start within the salary range. Relevant qualifications may include education, years of experience, and previous salary. Benefits may include insurance (health, dental, life), retirement, and vacation time. Other forms of compensation may include flex time, paid maternity leave, personal leave, and sick days.

Once the applicant accepts the offer, the human resources department needs to be notified so that the process of completing necessary paperwork can begin. Unfortunately, upon making a successful hire many agencies fail to complete the hiring process by notifying the applicants that

Hiring practices for part-time staff need to follow many of the same guidelines set for full-time staff.

were not hired that the position has been filled. This lack of communication can distract from an agency's reputation and can possibly cost quality employees in the future. On the other hand, good communication can enhance an agency's reputation among the workforce.

## Contracting With Seasonal and Part-Time Staff Members

Recreation providers hire a number of seasonal and part-time staff members. A parks and recreation agency with an outdoor aquatic facility does not need to hire lifeguards to work all year. Likewise, a concert venue does not need to hire ushers as full-time employees when they work only during events. Therefore, part of the hiring guidelines for most recreation providers are tailored toward staffing events and programs with seasonal and part-time staff members.

While many of the same elements of the hiring process for full-time employees apply to part-time and seasonal employees, they are performed on a smaller scale in most cases. Whereas an agency may recruit regionally for a full-time aquatic programmer or manager, the same agency will recruit locally for lifeguards. Other hiring procedures, including the application process and interviewing, also change due to the difference in the investment an agency makes with a full-time hire versus a part-time or seasonal hire. In fact, in some instances an agency may forego hiring and contract out some of its seasonal or part-time staff. The agency may be interested in managing only its full-time staff and may not feel that it has the expertise or time to manage hiring and supervising 100 lifeguards. Therefore, it may choose to contract out this part of staff management to a company that focuses on finding good part-time and seasonal employees. However, the agency must still be careful to contract out to a reputable company, as ultimately that company will represent the agency. An agency needs to monitor the work that the contractual staff members perform to forestall any difficulties with the provision of services. See chapter 8 for a more detailed discussion on outsourcing.

## Conclusion

There is no resource more valuable to an agency than a good employee. From the job analysis to the final stages of hiring, finding the right match between the position and the applicant is critical to the ongoing success of any agency. Therefore, ensuring that the hiring process for part-time and full-time employees, as well as volunteers, is well thought out and adhered to goes a long way in ensuring an effective workforce.

## Review Questions

1. Define job analysis. Describe the eight components of a job analysis.
2. What are five methods for collecting data for a job analysis?
3. Describe horizontal and vertical classifications of job positions.
4. Discuss the legislation related to fair hiring practices (e.g., the Age Discrimination in Employment Act of 1967).
5. Outline the standard components of a job description.
6. Describe the positives and negatives of internal and external recruitment.
7. Compare and contrast the testing procedures that can be used to select new employees.

**Visit the online resource at www.HumanKinetics.com/TheParkAndRecreationProfessionalsHandbook for sample documents, keywords, activities and assignments, and more.**

chapter 10

# Human Resources: Employee Management

The role of human resources management does not end upon the successful recruitment of a new employee. From orientation to performance evaluation, managers are responsible for ensuring that their personnel are well versed in both the nature of the job and the expectations for performance. Good recruiting goes a long way in ensuring that an agency hires the right person for a job, but if the agency does not invest in the employee's development, it will likely not reap the full benefits of a good hire. This chapter outlines the steps needed to ensure effective employee management.

## Employee Orientation

Once employees have been selected and subsequently hired, their transition into the agency should start with a well-designed orientation. A well-designed orientation can positively contribute to both the short-term and long-term success of the new employee. Orientation is training that introduces new employees to the agency, including its rules and organizational culture, in order to help them do their job well. The orientation should provide information about the company and the employee's department as well as other information related to the workplace. At the company level, the orientation should include the company's mission (figure 10.1), vision (figure 10.2), and goals. In addition, other areas to be covered include policies and procedures (figure 10.3), compensation, benefits (table 10.1) and services, safety information, employee and union relations (if relevant), facilities, and customer relations.

At the department level, information should include department functions and philosophy; job duties and responsibilities; policies, standards, procedures, and rules; and performance expectations. A tour as well as an introduction to the departmental employees should also be provided. Other orientation information, particularly for new employees who have just transferred to the area, may include information on the community.

Effective orientation serves five purposes. First, it helps establish a favorable impression of the organization and the job. Second, it provides organization and job information. Third, it enhances interpersonal acceptance by coworkers. Fourth, it helps accelerate the socialization and integration of the new employee. Finally, it ensures that employee performance and productivity begin more quickly (Mathis and Jackson 2008).

Certain organizations also use less traditional orientation programs such as mentoring programs, which are also discussed in chapter 13. Formal mentoring programs give new employees someone they can immediately go to with questions about the organization and the job. This way employees do not have to wait for an informal mentoring relationship to develop. Formal mentoring programs typically involve a person at the agency, perhaps a manager or someone in human resources, identifying an appropriate mentor for a new employee. The program may match the two on criteria such as their positions within the agency or their past experiences. Demographic data such as gender or age may also be given consideration. Obviously the mentor

## Indianapolis (Indiana) Parks and Recreation Mission Statement

Indy Parks and Recreation shall provide clear leadership and well-defined direction for enhancing the quality of life for Indianapolis and Marion County residents by providing parks and recreation resources and services that

- provide and facilitate quality recreation and leisure opportunities;
- encourage and support natural and cultural resources stewardship and environmental education;
- include safe, clean, and well-maintained park facilities for the community's fun and enjoyment; and
- promote and facilitate mutually beneficial county-wide partnerships.

**Figure 10.1**    The Indianapolis (Indiana) Parks and Recreation mission statement gives its employees a clear idea of what the agency stands for.

should have more experience within the agency. The mentor does not have to be from the same department if there are other reasons for picking a mentor from elsewhere in the agency, such as overall management experience or a potential good personality fit.

Sometimes formal mentorship works well; however, other times the two individuals may not click and may be unable to take full advantage of the program. Informal mentoring also has a great deal to offer employees who are able to cultivate this type of relationship. Because an informal mentoring relationship develops more naturally, it tends to offer the benefit of fit and comfort to both the mentor and the mentee. Mentors can provide ongoing career support and give advice on career development, promotion, and agency politics. New employees can learn a great deal from mentors who can show the ropes associated with the particular career track they have experienced.

While most people tend to think of the benefits that mentoring provides the mentee, there are also benefits to the mentor that make developing the relationship worthwhile. Engaging in mentoring can increase productivity as well as reputation if the mentee succeeds in the agency. Positive mentoring can also reap benefits for the agency. Good mentoring has been tied to an increase in organizational commitment, orga-

nizational citizenship, and job satisfaction—all outcomes that are of benefit to an agency and that certainly illustrate how mentoring influences employee motivation.

## Employee Motivation

Part of being a supervisor is motivating employees. This motivation ultimately ties closely to how successful the employees are in their positions. There are a number of techniques that a supervisor can utilize to increase motivation among employees, starting by modeling desired behaviors. It is difficult for employees to be motivated to act in a particular manner if they do not see their own supervisor also displaying those same behaviors. In addition, praise and recognition go a long way toward motivating employees. While not all agencies have formal recognition programs, a supervisor's attention to employee performance and subsequent acknowledgment of exceptional performance (beyond just during the evaluation period) can lead to continued good performance and high employee morale.

Feedback is also an important component of motivation. Feedback must be quick and specific if it is being used to produce more of the same behaviors. A supervisor who provides positive

## Camas (Washington) Parks and Recreation Vision Statement

Through provision of recreation and parks services, we enhance the quality of life and nurture the health and well-being of our people, our community, our environment, and our economy.

We are community driven. Together, and often in partnership with related fields and organizations, we do the following:

- **Help individuals reach their potential,** ensuring healthy, active, and balanced lifestyles; providing a fit foundation for productive lives; and stimulating holistic growth and development
- **Strengthen the social foundations of our society,** building strong relationships; collaborating to support families of all kinds, nurturing leadership, and developing self-reliant communities; and creating understanding and harmony through shared leisure lifestyles
- **Serve as stewards of the environment,** creating environmental awareness and encouraging ecosystem approaches to planning and protecting, preserving, and restoring significant natural areas and corridors
- **Build and renew local economies,** reducing dependencies on health and social services through building a fit and productive workforce; stimulating the leisure industries; and attracting economic development to our community known for our high quality of life

**Figure 10.2** The Camas (Washington) Parks and Recreation vision statement describes what the agency hopes to accomplish through its programs, services, and facilities.

## Example Code of Conduct

Portland (Maine) Recreation and Facilities Management
Recreation Division
Staff Code of Conduct
Revised May 2008

### Seasonal Employees

#### Purpose

This policy is intended to set professional expectations and standards for the Recreation and Facilities Management employees at work. Employees are expected to provide a safe and appropriate recreation experience for program participants. Employees are also expected to maintain professional relationships with participants and their families at all times. Employees will sign and date the Code of Conduct. A copy of this document will be kept on file in the Recreation Division office.

### Staff

#### Personal Appearance

In order for staff members to be appropriate role models for the children in our care, it is necessary to have a dress code that promotes professionalism. Therefore, dress will be neat and clean in appearance. Appropriate attire is required for specific work assignments. Sneakers should be worn in the gym; sandals are appropriate for beach field trips only. Inseams on shorts must be a minimum of a three-and-a-half inches. Tank tops and bikini bathing suits are not to be worn. Graphics and logos on clothing must be in good taste, not vulgar or suggestive. Hair, skin, and fingernails should be well groomed.

#### Purchasing Card

The following is a partial list of the employee's responsibilities for obtaining and using the city's purchasing card:

- Maintain card security.
- Purchase materials and services for city business purposes only.
- Obtain a sales receipt for each purchase made.
- Give vendor notice that the purchase is to be tax exempt.
- Forward receipts to the financial officer (or designee) daily.
- Obtain account credit for returns and exchanges.
- Respond to disputed charges.

**The purchasing card is not transferable and may not be used by any other person other than the employee whose name appears on the card.**

Employees must sign the Purchasing Card User Agreement.

**Figure 10.3**   Portland (Maine) Parks and Recreation uses an employee code of conduct to outline professional expectations and standards for its staff.

Reprinted, by permission, from City of Portland, Maine; Department of Recreation and Facilities Management; Recreation Division.

feedback only once a year during a performance evaluation is unlikely to get the same results as the supervisor who utilizes feedback throughout the year as appropriate. When the feedback immediately follows the act, it is much more likely to affect an employee's motivation and subsequent behaviors. If the feedback comes eight months after the performance, the employee may not even remember what was done to deserve

it. For example, if a hotel desk clerk appeases a difficult customer who is attempting to check in five hours early by offering to store luggage until check-in time and providing a map and list of activities to pursue in the meantime, the manager should acknowledge the good work immediately.

Delegation of responsibilities can be another tool used to motivate employees. Employees who

**Table 10.1**  South Carolina Department of Parks, Recreation, and Tourism Benefits

| Fringe benefits | Value for single coverage | Value for full family coverage |
|---|---|---|
| 15 days annual leave | $1,730.77 | $1,730.77 |
| 15 days sick leave | $1,730.77 | $1,730.77 |
| Health, dental, life, and disability insurance | $2,663.88 | $5,784.96 |
| Holidays | $1,384.62 | $1,384.62 |
| Retirement match | $2,265.00 | $2,265.00 |
| Social security match | $2,295.00 | $2,295.00 |
| Workers' compensation | $300.00 | $300.00 |
| Total dollar amount of fringe benefits | $12,370.04 | $15,491.12 |
| Annual salary | $30,000.00 | $30,000.00 |
| **Total compensation package** | **$42,370.04** | **$45,491.12** |
| **Fringe benefits as a percentage of annual salary** | 41% | 52% |

From South Carolina Department of Parks, Recreation, and Tourism.

feel they are trusted members of the staff take that trust to heart and are motivated by it. A similar idea is to increase employee involvement in decision making. Again, if employees feel that they have a vested interest in an agency's decisions, they are more likely to feel motivated to see those decisions come to fruition. Simply put, giving employees ownership of tasks and decisions can be instrumental in motivating them because it helps them to feel like important contributors to the agency's success.

Perhaps the most often overlooked motivational tool is fun. An environment that is fun while still promoting work efficiency can reduce stress as well as make the agency a place where people want to work and therefore perform better.

Different things motivate different employees. Extrinsic rewards such as pay, recognition, and advancement motivate some employees. Other employees are motivated intrinsically and put forth extra effort for outcomes such as feelings of increased self-worth and pride in a job well done. Most employees are motivated by both extrinsic and intrinsic rewards. In fact, according to Herzberg's two-factor theory, there are some job characteristics that, while not motivators per se, lead to lack of motivation and unhappiness if they are absent or unsatisfactory. These are labeled *hygiene factors* and are job-related factors such as salary, policies, technical issues, and so on. However, happiness and satisfaction with hygiene factors do not motivate employees. There are other factors, called *motivators,* that can increase satisfaction. Motivators are tied into the nature of the work and how meaningful the work is, such as work that is challenging, rewarding, or exciting (Herzberg 1968).

# Employee Evaluation

Not long after employees are hired, evaluations become a very real part of their lives. Agencies use employee evaluations in order to make a wide variety of personnel management decisions, including advancement, salary increases, retention, and termination. In addition, evaluations can provide information on employee training needs and career planning.

## Evaluation Methods

There are several employee evaluation methods that can be used, including a trait rating or graphic rating scale, a behaviorally anchored rating scale, an essay, productivity data or work standards, management by objectives, critical incidents, and personnel data. The choice of methods may be

## Working for the Best: SAS Ranks as #1 Place to Work in America

Identified as One of the Best Companies to Work For in every one of the 13 years that *Fortune* magazine has been conducting the rankings, software company SAS offers its employees superior perks: low cost, high-quality child care, 90-percent coverage of the health insurance premium, unlimited sick days, and a medical center staffed by 4 physicians and 10 nurse practitioners (at no cost to employees). On the recreation side of things (the fun factor), a free 66,000-square-foot fitness center and natatorium, a lending library, and a summer camp for children are among the additional benefits available to SAS staff. This kind of treatment has paid off for SAS, which is highly profitable, boasts a turnover rate of only 2 percent, and ranks as the world's largest privately owned software company (*Fortune* Magazine 2010).

determined at the agency level or at the departmental level and typically reflects the purpose of the evaluation.

### Trait Rating or Graphic Rating Scale

When completing a trait rating or graphic rating scale, the evaluator is provided with a list of character traits that are relevant to job performance (e.g., cooperation, creativity, attitude, initiative) and asked to rate the employee on a scale that ranges, for example, from "Poor" to "Excellent." These types of evaluations are very subjective and often not really related to successful job completion. Their reliability and validity are often called into question (Pynes 2009).

### Behaviorally Anchored Rating Scale

When completing a **behaviorally anchored rating scale (BARS),** evaluators use behavioral descriptions to measure performance. The descriptions are examples of behaviors reflecting unacceptable performance to outstanding performance, and the evaluator rates the employee based on the behavior that the employee comes closest to displaying. While the employee does not have to exhibit the exact behavior being described on the evaluation form, the descriptions provide an idea of the level of performance that is necessary for positive ratings. Although the BARS is highly valid, its scale development can be excessively time consuming because a new scale needs to be developed for most job titles. Thus this type of evaluation is rarely used. Figure 10.4 provides an example of a BARS that might be used for employees working the front desk.

### Essay

This evaluation method requires the rater to write an essay describing the employee's performance. This type of evaluation can be highly subjective and thus less valid and reliable. In addition, the reliability and validity depend greatly on the time the evaluator puts into writing the essay as well as the writing skills of the evaluator.

### Productivity Data and Work Standards

When an agency uses these types of standards, it evaluates employees on the quantity and quality of their output. In order for the standards to be acceptable to the evaluated employee, the process for setting the standards needs to be clear. An example of a standard for a front desk employee might be the ability to process 30 program registration forms in 60 minutes with fewer than three errors.

### Management by Objectives

During the first step of **management by objectives (MBO),** the supervisor (the rater) and the employee determine the employee's goals and objectives for the evaluation period as well as figure out a plan for achieving them. At the conclusion of the evaluation period, the employee is rated on the completion of the goals and objectives. However, without good objectives, the MBO process becomes meaningless. Too often the written objectives are too easy or the plan for achieving them is not given due consideration. A highly valid approach to writing objectives is to ensure that they are tied to the specific duties outlined in an employee's job description. The achievement of goals and objectives is important, but so is the means for achieving them. In other words, while it may be great when an employee increases participation by 20 percent, if the increase results in lower participant satisfaction, then it is not indicative of positive growth. A supervisor may also want to incorporate a qualitative measurement of performance. These

## Behaviorally Anchored Rating Scale

Job: Front desk
Dimension: Process walk-in program registrations, greet public, and answer phones
Check the rating that describes this person's job performance most accurately.

_____ **Superior:**   Correctly processes cash, check, and credit payments for registration. Ensures all registration forms are complete and entered into computer system by the end of the day. Answers questions accurately and in a pleasant manner both in person as well as on the telephone; finds answers to questions not known quickly. Answers telephone within four rings and quickly and accurately directs calls to the appropriate staff member. Keeps staff members apprised on commonly asked questions regarding programs and facilities to assist with better meeting the needs of the public and the participants through face-to-face communication. Maintains a log of questions.

_____ **Very good:**   Correctly processes cash, check, and credit payments for registration. Ensures all registration forms are complete and entered into the computer system within two days. Answers all questions to the best of his or her ability or takes a message for the answer to be returned at a later time. Answers the telephone professionally and directs calls to staff members as appropriate.

_____ **Good:**   Rarely has any difficulty with processing cash, check, and credit payments for registrations. Collects completed registration forms and enters them into the computer system in a timely manner. Professionally answers the telephone, directs calls, and answers questions as appropriate.

_____ **Needs improvement:**   On occasion is not able to reconcile registration receipts with revenue collected. Collects registration forms but often has to make follow-up phone calls to obtain missing information; data entry into the registration system can take up to a week.

_____ **Unsatisfactory:**   Consistently unable to reconcile registration receipts with revenue collected. Does not review registration forms for accuracy or completeness and does not follow up on incomplete forms. Often allows phone to ring numerous times before answering and often disconnects callers before they can be transferred to appropriate staff member.

Comments: _____

_____

_____

_____

Rater's signature: _____

**Figure 10.4**   Example of a behaviorally anchored rating scale for a front desk employee.

standards can be useful when numerical measurement cannot adequately capture what an employee accomplishes or when circumstances outside the employee's control prevent the employee from reaching the target numbers.

### Critical Incidents

When using this method, the evaluator records specific work actions, both successful and unsuccessful, and uses those incidents to evaluate the employee. An example of a successful incident might be when a meeting planner for a conference center handles an equipment issue, in a timely manner, when technical support does not deliver laptops to the correct meeting rooms. An example of an unsuccessful incident might be when an after-school program leader spends too much of the budget on craft supplies and doesn't have enough money left over to purchase healthy snacks for the youths in the program.

### Personnel Data

For this method, the evaluator records objective data such as being absent and coming to work late.

Parks and recreation employees' ability to work well with participants is an important area to consider in a performance evaluation.

A supervisor may use this information to evaluate an employee's conformance to organizational policies; however, this type of information typically says little about how well an employee is performing the job duties.

### Employee Ranking

In some instances raters compare employee performances. In other words, they rank employees from best to worst. There are three ways to rank employees. The first, simple ranking, is to rank employees from the highest performer to the lowest performer. The second, forced distribution, is to put a certain percentage of employees into each performance category. The third, paired comparison, is to compare every employee to every other employee. This last method is obviously very time consuming for a large workforce—and even when there are just 15 employees an evaluator has to make 105 comparisons (Noe et al. 2007). When done well, comparisons may lead to positive competition among employees, but when comparisons are done poorly, they can lead to hard feelings and negative competition that threaten the morale of the employees.

## Rating Errors

While conducting an evaluation properly is important from a legal standpoint, it also has implications for employee morale. Preparation

is an important part of the evaluation process. A supervisor who arrives for an evaluation unprepared or who completes an evaluation with no data (or, more commonly, with invalid or unreliable data) with which to make judgments often is unable to provide accurate, thorough, or well-conceived feedback. Preparing to conduct an evaluation means more than walking into an employee's office and giving a thumbs-up or thumbs-down. Preparation in the way of ongoing observation and review throughout the year is necessary in order to gain a complete picture of an employee's work performance. Paying attention to performance only once the evaluation is impending or ignoring performance throughout the year can lead to a number of rating errors.

### Halo Effect

The halo effect occurs when an evaluator rates an employee as excellent in one performance category and this perception of excellence flows into other areas of performance that may not be so excellent. For example, a lifeguard who is excellent at giving swimming lessons but only average at completing end-of-day closing duties may receive excellent marks for both duties. In many instances the halo effect is due to poor evaluator training. The evaluator is not able to distinguish adequately among different categories of evaluation.

## Central Tendency

Central tendency occurs when the employee performance scores all fall around the midrange, or average, score. Because it is easier to rank most employees as average, this error prevents a valid evaluation and fails to distinguish between low and high performers.

## Strict Rating

Strict rating occurs when a supervisor rates an employee consistently lower than the norm or average. While there may be justification for the lower scores, supervisors need to be aware of any biases they may have that could lead to an invalid strict rating tendency.

## Lenient Rating

Opposite of strict rating is lenient rating, which may occur when a supervisor consistently rates an employee higher than the norm or average. Again, the rating may be warranted, but it behooves supervisors to be aware of potential biases that might allow this to happen in error.

## Latest Behavior

The latest behavior error occurs when a recent event influences a rating and so the rating does not take into account behavior over the entire time period that the evaluation is measuring. Good or bad, the employee's latest behavior has undue influence on the evaluation.

## Initial Impression

The first impression of an employee can be negative or positive and can sometimes be quite strong. The initial impression error occurs when the evaluator bases the appraisal on that first impression of the employee and thus fails to recognize behaviors the employee consistently demonstrated during the evaluation period.

## Spillover Effect

The spillover effect occurs when past performance appraisals, whether good or bad, unfairly affect the current evaluation. The supervisor is not taking into consideration improvements or declines in performance that may need to be documented in the current evaluation.

## Same as Me

As humans we are drawn to individuals like ourselves. This can lead to an evaluation error when employees receive a better rating than deserved because they are like the rater in some way that is sometimes job related but often not. The shared characteristics may be somewhat relevant to work, such as punctuality, or may be unrelated to work, such as race, gender, or age.

## Different From Me

Just as we are drawn to people who are like us, we are often turned off by those who are different. These feelings can lead to the different-from-me error when an employee receives a lower evaluation than deserved because she is not like the rater or has characteristics that the rater does not hold in high regard. Again, these characteristics may be job related, but often they are not relevant to the job or the evaluation (Pynes 2009).

# Feedback on Evaluation

It is important to allow the evaluated employee an opportunity for feedback on an evaluation. To limit misunderstandings, it is valuable to have the feedback in writing. In some evaluation systems an employee completes an independent self-evaluation as part of the process. The agency uses this information to discover where there may be misunderstandings about expectations. Self-evaluation also helps employees gain greater insight into their performance based on their own understanding of their job. In many instances there is an official evaluation form that the supervisor completes for the employee to review. The form includes space for the employee to provide feedback on whether he agrees or disagrees with the evaluation. However, even with a written evaluation, it is still important for the supervisor and employee to meet face to face as part of the evaluation process, especially when the employee is a full-time or permanent part-time staff member. A face-to-face meeting may be less feasible for seasonal staff members, who in some agencies may number in the hundreds. Meeting in person allows for greater clarity in the evaluation process as well as facilitates conversation about past and future performance. Sometimes there may be misinterpretation of the written word; supplementing a written evaluation with a meeting can help alleviate this potential problem.

Regardless of how the evaluation is conducted, both the supervisor and the employee should sign the evaluation signifying that it has been completed and that both parties are aware of the outcome. If the evaluation is negative, an employee may be hesitant to sign it; often the evaluation form provides the option for employees to check a box indicating that they either agree or disagree with the evaluation and provide a written statement explaining why before signing on the signature line. Regardless of how it is used, the signature line is very important in that it signifies that the employee is aware of what is going into the personnel file with respect to performance evaluations.

# Employee Discipline

The outcome of a performance evaluation may necessitate discipline for poor performance or unacceptable behavior. Typically a disciplinary action is progressive and follows these four steps: verbal warning, written warning, intervention, and termination (Hurd, Barcelona, and Meldrum 2008).

## Step 1: Verbal Warning

A verbal warning typically occurs upon the first instance of a disciplinary problem. This step traditionally involves a meeting between the supervisor and the employee and a conversation covering acceptable behavior and consequences for further incidents. While no written documentation is placed in the employee's file, the supervisor should still keep notes for future reference should additional problems arise.

## Step 2: Written Warning

A written warning occurs when the verbal warning fails to prevent a reoccurrence of the problem. In this step the supervisor formally documents the incident, outlining the incident as well as the initial verbal warning. The supervisor asks the employee to sign the written warning; if the employee refuses, the supervisor should document the refusal in writing and place all forms in the employee's file. The supervisor should give the employee the opportunity to write a response to the warning and should include the response in the file. In addition, a conversation similar to the one held in step 1 should also take place to clarify acceptable behavior and consequences for further incidents.

## Step 3: Intervention

An intervention occurs when the written warning has not produced the desired change in the employee's behavior. Intervention involves the development of an employee improvement plan, which should follow these steps:

1. Identify and define the performance problem.
2. Explain the effects of the problem (on participants, other employees, and so on).
3. Define expected performance standards.
4. Explore ideas for a solution to the problem.
5. Write the improvement plan.

These steps should take place in consultation with the employee so there is no question about the expectations held for the employee.

## Step 4: Termination

Unfortunately there are times when a supervisor must terminate an employee. Supervisors cannot have too much documentation in this type of situation. In addition, the supervisor should plan on meeting with personnel such as human resources or the agency attorney before carrying out the termination in order to ensure that there are no legal liabilities to be aware of regarding termination and to ensure that proper protocol is followed. Other issues to keep in mind are the location of the termination, which should depend on the emotions that might surround the situation (e.g., if the termination might make the supervisor feel threatened), involving a witness in the proceedings, relaying the finality of the termination to the employee, outlining the progressive disciplinary steps that were taken, and outlining pertinent details related to the termination (including pay and benefits) in writing. The employee should sign this termination letter to acknowledge its receipt. Then the agency should allow the employee to collect personal belongings (the agency may also offer to send them), should collect all keys, and should suspend access to computer systems and any other systems the employee was able to access.

It is important to collect and retain information related to disciplinary actions should the discipline reach the termination stage. An agency must have thorough documentation. The supervisor needs to keep the details of each progressive disciplinary action in the employee's personnel file so that they can be easily accessed when needed. Personnel retain the right to examine the contents of their file at any time—there should be no secrets as to what is in the file. While discipline for specific instances can occur at any time during the year (and should not be saved up for the evaluation period if it needs to be handled earlier), in some cases the evaluation provides a formal venue to address ongoing general concerns.

## Performance Plan

For more general concerns of underperformance, the evaluation is an opportunity to develop a performance plan in partnership with the employee. The **performance plan** includes goals and objectives that the supervisor feels the employee needs to meet in order to perform the job to the agency's standards. In addition, the performance plan will often include an outline of the work products (outputs) that are expected, any additional work assignments and responsibilities, and expectations for what the employee needs to do in order to maintain (or acquire) qualifications. Basically a performance plan is a plan for what the employee is expected to achieve during an assessment period.

Follow up on progress must be ongoing. If a supervisor does not address a lack of progress toward meeting goals and objectives until an annual evaluation, there is no chance to redirect the employee's performance at an earlier date and prevent the problem from worsening. Conversely, if the employee is doing an exemplary job of meeting and perhaps exceeding the goals and objectives, feedback needs to come sooner than a year later. The most effective feedback is immediate, specific, and direct.

## Dismissing Employees

Unfortunately, there comes a time when a supervisor must dismiss an employee for either lack of performance or inappropriate action. Regardless of the reason for dismissal, an agency needs to have clearly defined policies and procedures in place in order to avoid finding itself in legal hot water over an unjustified firing.

### Policies

When it comes to firing, policies on what constitutes a fireable offense and on what performance standards must be met for job retention need to

be defined and stated clearly. In some instances fireable offenses may be severe enough that the action taken by the employee is illegal, while in other cases offenses may simply be actions that violate the personnel code of the agency. Examples of both instances include sexual harassment, embezzlement, fraud, immoral conduct, and bribery.

### Procedures

The employee policy manual needs to outline clearly the procedures for dismissal. There are steps that must be taken in order for a dismissal to be processed appropriately. These steps address protocol for documentation, meetings, and procedures related to how an employee will actually leave the agency (e.g., time frame, final pay, cashing in of benefits, and so on). The procedures should also include guidelines for what steps dismissed employees should take in order to appeal what they may feel is an unjust firing. In short, the procedures must outline the steps

An employee performance plan can be used to address a wide variety of concerns with performance, such as interaction with participants or program administration.

the agency must take in this type of situation in order to ensure that the dismissal is justified and handled in a way that avoids legal repercussions.

### Documentation

The documentation needed for dismissal must provide a valid paper trail of the behavior that led to the dismissal. For instance, if an agency dismisses an employee for sexual harassment, it needs to ensure that it has documentation of the complaints as well as the handling of the situation, whether it was immediate dismissal or it was censure followed by repeated harassment and then dismissal. If an agency fires an employee due to poor performance, the agency generally documents the performance multiple times to show a consistent pattern of poor performance despite opportunities for improvement. This type of situation is where having signed paperwork along the way to illustrate that the employee was aware of complaints, poor evaluation results, or other reports that were utilized in the dismissal helps to prevent litigation associated with the dismissal.

### Exit Interviews

It is important to conduct an exit interview with a departing employee when practical. Certainly this is much easier to do when an employee leaves on good terms. However, when an agency dismisses an employee, the employee may be unwilling to participate in an exit interview. Exit interviews can provide valuable information regarding the work culture within the agency and may provide valuable insight into rehiring for positions.

### At-Will Employment

The term **at-will employment** refers to the right of employers to fire employees for any reason or for no reason at all. It also gives employees the legal right to quit their jobs at any time for any reason. This terminology is not relevant in a situation where there is a signed contract of employment terms between the individual and the agency. An agency that utilizes at-will employment needs to make this stipulation clear to its employees and needs to emphasize, in writing, that documents such as employee manuals do not constitute an employment contract. Despite this legal doctrine, employers may not fire employees in a way that discriminates, violates public policy, or conflicts with written or implied promises they made concerning the length of employment or the grounds for termination.

## Employee Supervision

Employees who are in supervisory positions have a number of responsibilities related to staff management, including scheduling and delegation of responsibilities as well as general supervision tasks such as holding meetings, handling grievances, and working with unions when relevant. In addition, the supervisor needs to be aware of management style and how it can affect employee performance.

## Staff Scheduling

Scheduling staff members, particularly seasonal staff members, can be a large part of the supervisor job duties. Some agencies utilize scheduling software to help with what can be a monumental task if the part-time and seasonal staff is large, particularly in the summer season. Software programs can be used to schedule staff at multiple sites such as swimming pools, recreation centers, and athletic fields. Employees in charge of staff scheduling, particularly for part-time help, should develop policies and procedures related to requests for time off, employee substitutions, and overtime pay, because these are areas where scheduling can get tricky and make employees angry if they feel they are being treated unfairly.

## Delegating Responsibilities

Delegation, or assigning subordinates tasks that you as a manager have ultimate responsibility for, is a skill that can free up time to take care of tasks that should be confined to management. Delegation can allow managers to use the skill sets that uniquely qualify them to be in management positions rather than spend time on tasks that others can easily handle. Effective delegation can also be used as a motivational tool for subordinates, as it can help them develop new skills, can decrease the monotony in their job tasks, and can give them a sense of ownership. Unfortunately, when delegation is not done well, a manager spends a lot of time engaged in work tasks that take time away from other essential duties that only the manager can perform.

There are numerous reasons why some managers are unwilling to delegate responsibilities. First, they may feel that they are the only ones who can do a job correctly. Second, they may be concerned by the fact that they hold ultimate responsibility for the delegated tasks. Third, they may simply

A manager's duties when supervising employees can include taking responsibility for employee training.

feel that they cannot take the necessary time to teach someone how to do the job. Finally, they may feel guilty for passing on tasks if they perceive their employees to already be overworked (Straub 1998).

However, there are many reasons—beyond those already mentioned—why delegation can be beneficial. Certainly delegation can allow a manager to unload routine, noncritical work, although this does not mean that subordinates should get only the junk or trivial work, because this can cause resentment. Effective delegating can also help a manager groom a successor. Managers are often looking to move into higher levels of authority, and for the health of the organization managers can use delegation to prepare promising employees to take over their position once they move up. Delegation not only can empower and motivate ambitious employees but also can be an integral part of a career development program as long as agencies give employees meaningful work to complete. This in turn can reduce turnover (Straub 1998).

Regardless of the rationale for delegation, it will not be effective without the right match between employee and task. The manager must consider what level to delegate the task to, keeping in mind that those who deal with the problems and issues daily are often the best people to complete related tasks. Other issues to consider include the

deadline for completion, the level of coordination needed for the task, how the task can help the employee grow, and how much innovation is involved in completing the task.

After choosing a person for delegation, the manager must understand how to set up the situation for success rather than failure. Setting the person up for success can start with the understanding that delegating a complete task is easier for everyone. It is easier for someone to have control over a delegated task from beginning to end, and it is easier for the manager to track progress. In addition, the manager needs to focus on results and not on the methods used to attain the results (unless, of course, the methods are unethical). If employees are trustworthy enough to have tasks delegated to them, then they should be trustworthy enough to choose their own work habits. Without this trust, delegation is inefficient and loses its positive outcomes such as career development and motivation. Other important things to remember include a willingness to micromanage (a micromanager is not a delegator) and to explain the value of an assignment so that it is not seen as busywork or grunt work. It also behooves both the supervisor and the subordinate for the subordinate to have enough authority to accomplish the task without constantly needing to consult the supervisor. However, the supervisor also needs to be able to give the resources that are necessary to complete the task as well as be willing to accept the mistakes that inevitably will occur, especially when completing the task involves developing new skills.

In short, when delegating tasks, a supervisor needs to set up the employee for success and make sure everyone is on the same page with regard to what is expected. Steps to ensure successful delegation include calling a meeting, providing clear direction, defining limits of responsibility and authority, giving the employee a role to live up to, establishing deadlines, getting a commitment, letting others know that the task has been delegated, and following up so that everyone stays on the same page (Straub 1998). Delegation is an acquired skill. Only through a willingness to venture into that territory will a manager become effective at delegation and reap the rewards of its success.

## General Supervision

General supervision of employees is more an art than a science. A manager needs to know how to avoid micromanaging employees while still providing direction and supervision as needed. This section addresses issues inherent in supervision, such as balancing between too much and too little control over an employee's work; conducting meetings; managing time cards, payroll, and employee records; recognizing staff work; and handling grievances. In some agencies, including commercial, private nonprofit, and public agencies, supervision can also extend to interns or fieldwork students.

### Micromanagement

**Micromanagement** is excessive control over people or projects. It is characterized by a manager's preoccupation with work that needs to be done, particularly work that has been delegated, as well as a manager's anxiety over how the work is being done. What is deemed to be excessive control may well be in the eyes of the beholder, but if employees perceive management to be controlling, they may begin to feel as if they have no autonomy in their job and that they are not trusted to complete their job. In both cases they are likely to lose motivation. One example of micromanagement is the manager who gives an athletic supervisor the task of seeking bids for equipment and then proceeds to dictate how to write the bid request, who to send the request to,

and what specifications to include and then reads through all of the bids. While the manager has gone through the motion of delegating a responsibility that the athletic supervisor should be able to handle, the manager has not relinquished any control over the task. Thus the athletic supervisor is unable to seek the bids in an efficient manner and likely feels that there is a lack of trust. One of the most effective ways to avoid micromanagement is to delegate authority for projects and then follow the guidelines given earlier with respect to effective delegation.

### Meetings

Orchestrating meetings is another task that most supervisors complete on a regular basis. There are some essential elements involved in holding a successful meeting. First, a well-informed agenda is important for keeping a meeting on track and running efficiently. Meetings that waste time because they are unfocused, run long, or are unnecessary will be viewed harshly by employees.

The first step in running a good meeting is to start the meeting on time. If employees have made the effort to clear their schedules for a meeting, it is only fair that the person running the meeting does not waste their time or disrupt their schedules by starting the meeting late. The leader should then review the agenda and desired outcomes for the meeting. This sets the stage for the upcoming discussions and focuses the meeting from the outset. In fact, sending the agenda to employees ahead of time can help them to prepare for the meeting and can lead to a more efficient meeting.

The person running the meeting needs to make sure someone has the responsibility of taking notes for the meeting. Often this may be an administrative assistant, although in certain situations another meeting participant may need to complete this task. Without accurate notes, miscommunication often leads to inaction or wrong action following the meeting. With respect to formal meetings, such as monthly staff meetings, notes may be distributed as minutes and approved at the start of the next meeting with any corrections being made as necessary.

The person running the meeting also needs to deal with disruptive behavior in order for a productive meeting to take place. Disruptive behavior may include side conversations, inappropriate comments, ringing cell phones, text messaging, and other behavior that takes the focus away from the meeting. By setting a tone that discourages disruptive behavior, the meeting facilitator can run a more effective and efficient meeting because employees will be less distracted.

Depending on the formality of the agency or the meeting, *Robert's Rules of Order* (Robert et al. 2000) may be used to facilitate the meeting process. This book outlines parliamentary procedures developed for smooth, orderly, and fairly conducted meetings.

### Managing Time Cards, Payroll, and Employee Records

While it is ultimately the responsibility of the employees to ensure that time cards are accurate, a supervisor who handles any degree of payroll is responsible for accuracy in this area of expenditures. Training staff members on how to process time cards and the importance of signing in or out accurately can emphasize to staff members the degree to which discrepancies in time cards and ultimately payroll will or will not be tolerated. It is up to a supervisor to ensure that staff members are following the guidelines established by the agency with regard to payroll. Payroll is one form of an employee record, and a supervisor must be prepared to handle issues related to a variety of employee records. The supervisor must ensure that these records, such as disciplinary reports, commendations, vacation requests, and requests for sick leave, are handled with confidentiality when necessary and are up to date and accurate.

### Establishing Staff Recognition Programs

General supervision always includes employee motivation and retention. Good employees are an agency's most valuable resource. Without good people, it is impossible to produce a good product regardless of the type of recreation services offered. A staff recognition program allows a supervisor to privately or publicly acknowledge the good work that employees are doing. However, in order for the program to help motivate or retain employees, it must be perceived as fair and valuable and be appreciated by employees. For example, if an agency recognizes all its employees to make sure that no one feels left out, the program tarnishes the efforts of those who really go above and beyond. On the other hand, if the program is so cheesy that no one wants to be associated with it, the program will fail.

An agency may recognize employees for a wide variety of accomplishments, such as years of service or exemplary work. Recognition may include

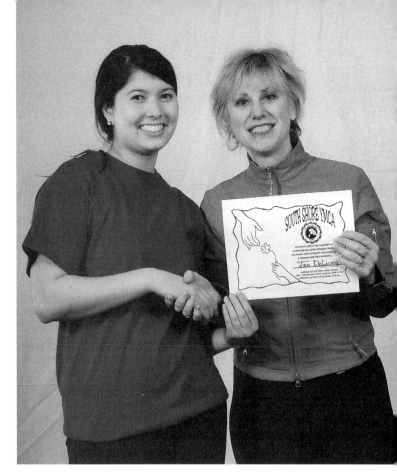

When designed well, employee recognition programs can serve as a motivator for strong job performance.

awards, increased benefits such as an extra day off with pay, or simply a public announcement. For example, the Logan (Utah) Parks and Recreation Department has an Employee Recognition Award that formally recognizes employees for outstanding performance in the workplace. The award recipient is selected by a committee of employee representatives from each of the divisions within the Logan Parks and Recreation Department, and the recipient's picture and biography are posted on the department's Web page.

### Employee Grievances

Just as agencies must outline procedures for employee dismissal, they must also develop policies and procedures to handle employee grievances, which may or may not be in response to a dismissal. A **grievance** is a complaint that is filed in response to treatment felt to be unfair and worthy of action. A grievance may be in response to issues as varied as sexual harassment claims, unsatisfactory performance evaluations, or failure to be promoted.

When an employee and supervisor cannot come to an agreement over a grievance, then a neutral arbitrator may need to come in to resolve the issue. In many cases this person is an ombudsman, either internal or external to the agency, who provides mediation between the employee with the grievance and the person the grievance is against. The hope is that the mediation can forestall legal action. If the mediator is unable to help the two parties settle the grievance, then the less-than-desirable step of legal action is the employee's next recourse. Legal action should be sought only after all other options are exhausted, because it can have numerous negative effects, ranging from financial to psychological, on both the employee and the employer.

### Supervising Interns and Fieldwork Students

Because parks and recreation degree programs require students to complete a specified number of hours in the field, in the form of practicums and internships, it is highly likely that a parks and recreation professional will at some point be responsible for supervising a student. Because the experience is meant to be a learning experience, the supervisor should ensure that the student gains exposure to and experience in a wide variety of areas.

The student's academic department provides the guidelines covering what is expected of the student and the reports and other assignments that must be completed as part of the experience. This paperwork also includes evaluation reports that a supervisor must complete on a set schedule. Often this fieldwork experience is the final real-world experience that a student has before graduating and entering the job market. Therefore, it is important to ensure that the student is allowed the opportunity to apply what was learned in the classroom. This application of knowledge will hopefully help the student to navigate the job market upon graduation and to succeed once hired into a position.

## Learning by Doing With the Charleston County Parks and Recreation Commission

The Charleston County Parks and Recreation Commission (CCPRC) has long had a strong reputation as a parks and recreation agency dedicated to providing university students with a quality internship experience. The agency's goals for its internship program are threefold:

- To assist the student in gaining experience and knowledge of leadership in program areas by involving the students in as many of these areas as possible.
- To assist the student in gaining experience working in their area of expertise while in a park and recreation setting.
- To assist the student in developing an understanding of human relations and to develop skills to work with others.

CCPRC's internship program is 12 weeks (480 hours) of paid, intensive experience designed to provide university students with hands-on experience in the field in preparation for a professional position upon graduation. Interns are exposed to aspects of the profession outside of their area of expertise through participation in staff meetings, commission meetings, and group activities with other interns (thus helping further build their professional network), along with day-to-day park and recreation operations. Specific areas of focus (divisions that offer internships) include marketing, capital improvement projects, outdoor recreation, general recreation, and operations.

The operations interns are facility based and experience all park facility operations, including water parks, beach parks, day parks, and special facility areas, which could include concessions, lifeguarding, office management, employee management, human resources skills, and everything involved in the day-to-day operation of parks. All recreation interns are involved in recreation programming, while outdoor recreation interns work primarily with summer camp, the climbing wall, the challenge course, water-based programs, land-based programs, sailing, and other outdoor programs. General recreation interns primarily work with group services, festivals, special events, environmental education, and community education (Charleston County Parks and Recreation Commission 2010).

From networking opportunities to training and development to hands-on labor, the supervisor should be able to create a work and study plan that provides the student with a true learning experience within an environment that is a little more safe than being on a paid job. The supervisor should recognize that this is a learning exercise for the student and thus should expect some growing pains and should help the student advance as much as possible as related to the chosen profession.

## Organized Labor

**Labor unions** are organizations formed for the "purpose of representing their members' interests and resolving conflicts with employers" (Noe et al. 2007, 459). Unions protect the interests of members, as well as improve wages, working conditions, and hours. In the days of the industrial revolution, when workers, including children, had to contend with terrible working conditions, the labor movement was the impetus for better employee rights and safer working conditions. Labor unions are one offshoot of the labor movement.

The premise of a union is that a large body of employees, known as a *bargaining unit,* can be more effective than individuals when it comes to bargaining for employee rights. In order for employees to be represented by a union, either the employer must voluntarily recognize the group as a bargaining unit or the majority of the employees must vote for representation. While it is not illegal for a company to try to persuade employees not to unionize, a company cannot use threats to prevent it from happening. With the ability to strike, or stop work, the union can cause hardship to its employer if its members feel that their workplace is treating them unfairly.

The outcome of negotiations between unionized employees and their employer is a collective bargaining agreement that outlines benefits, work hours, and salaries, among other things. These are set for a predetermined number of years and an employer cannot change them without the union representative's approval.

Unions are a touchy subject in many areas of the country due to notions that they lead to higher consumer costs by demanding higher pay and benefits for employees who may not deserve them. For those protected by the strength of a union, unions are an emblem of employee protection that guarantees fair pay for fair work. Unions have a strong history in certain geographic parts of the country, such as the Midwest, and are virtually nonexistent in other areas, such as the south.

## Volunteers

Volunteers make up a substantial part of the staff members of recreation providers in the public sector as well as the private nonprofit sector. Public parks and recreation departments as well as private nonprofit recreation providers such as the YMCA and Boys and Girls Club simply could not offer the services they do without the help of volunteers. These volunteers serve in

In some recreation agencies, volunteers make up a large part of the work force.

every capacity from volunteer coach to special event help. Agencies use volunteers with specific skills to help with services such as answering telephones, bookkeeping, and instructing. While volunteers are plentiful in the public and private nonprofit sectors, the commercial sector typically does not use volunteers but instead relies on part-time staff members to produce their services.

Because of their importance to the agency, volunteers should be treated with the same respect that part-time and full-time staff members receive. In fact, many of the issues already discussed in this book with regard to paid staff—recruitment, hiring, supervision, evaluation, and motivation—also apply to volunteers. Agencies who utilize volunteers would be well served to develop a volunteer personnel management system to provide guidelines for working with different groups of volunteers.

Before volunteer recruitment begins, an agency should try to get an idea of the organization's need for volunteers. The assessment may ask questions about where volunteers are needed, how many volunteers are needed, and in what types of jobs volunteers may appropriately replace or supplement paid staff members.

The second stage of volunteer management recognizes that, much like paid staff positions, many volunteer positions require a job analysis and a job description. For instance, while an agency might not need a detailed job description for someone who hands out hot cider at a tree lighting event, it certainly may want one for a youth sport coach. The job description should include a title and a function statement and should describe who the volunteer reports to, the staff liaison, tasks, time commitment, training, evaluation, benefits, and necessary qualifications. A youth sport coach is an important position within recreation programming, and its job description should convey its importance to the volunteer. Without this information it is difficult to use volunteers as effectively as possible and it is more difficult for volunteers to understand how they are contributing to an agency.

## The Importance of Volunteers: City of Phoenix Parks and Recreation

The City of Phoenix Parks and Recreation Department is reenergizing its volunteer efforts through a comprehensive approach to volunteer recruitment and recognition. Individuals interested in volunteering for the parks and recreation department can choose from a wide array of opportunities in which to get involved. Volunteers who long to wear a whistle around their necks have multiple opportunities to work as youth sport coaches in one of the many sport leagues that are offered by the department, including soccer, kickball, and baseball. Those with more of a bent toward the outdoors might find themselves building and maintaining trails, conducting outdoor programs in the parks, tending flower beds, or serving as park stewards. In fact, a group of volunteers can choose to adopt or sponsor a park and take responsibility for the amenities in it, which may include sport fields, flower beds, trails, sport courts, benches and tables, playgrounds, urban lakes and waterways, trees and shrubs, parking areas, and exercise courses. It's a big job not meant for one individual but for a group looking for a regular volunteer activity, and park adoption is a good way to give back to the community. Phoenix also uses volunteers as docents and guides at its museums, as staff at special events, as golf course starters and attendants, and as customer service representatives in community centers by answering questions at the front desk.

With all this attention to volunteers, Phoenix is also working on further developing its volunteer recognition program. One example of a recognition tool is the presentation of volunteer lapel pins that are coded by number of hours served (e.g., 100 Club, 250 Club, 500 Club). In addition, the department also dedicates the San Diego Padres' first spring training baseball game to its volunteers. They invite the volunteers to attend for free and announce the department's appreciation throughout the game. Other recognition activities include appreciation dinner events, press releases, announcements of appreciation at the governing parks and recreation board, and certificates of appreciation and a letter from the parks and recreation director (City of Phoenix 2010).

Once the job analyses and descriptions are complete, the agency will have a clearer picture of how to recruit volunteers, as the job analysis defines the skills that the volunteers should possess. In some instances the job skills are quite minimal, while in other instances they may require higher skill levels. Recruiting volunteers can be time consuming. Convincing someone to give their time and talent for free is often difficult. There are many ways to approach recruitment. One way is to "grow your own," which means to cultivate volunteers from participants. Additional recruitment tactics include asking current volunteers or employees for referrals, having staff members make personal contact, speaking to friendship groups, asking for family involvement (how many parents do you see coaching youth sports?), and using the media.

Once volunteers are recruited, it benefits both the volunteer and the agency to have an orientation and training program in place to explain the organization's philosophy; the program content; the organization, history, bylaws, and ethics of the agency; the benefits; and the contact information. Again, the depth of orientation and training depends on the volunteer position. Onetime volunteers may need to know only what they are doing that day, while long-term volunteers may be better served by a more in-depth training and orientation, particularly for positions that require greater skill.

Many agencies forget the importance of evaluating volunteers. Too often agencies consider themselves lucky to get a warm body. But what does an agency do with a volunteer who does not perform adequately? How does the agency recognize the exceptional volunteer? Without an evaluation process (again, depending on the volunteer position), it can be difficult to manage volunteers as well as their effects on programs and services. There will be times when an agency must dismiss a volunteer; documentation of poor performance or behavior makes this task easier. However, most of the time the agency has occasion to recognize and reward volunteers, which are two steps that are critical to retention. A supervisor should consider both public recognition and private recognition as part of the process of retaining good volunteers. Figure 10.5 outlines different ways to recognize volunteers. Although volunteers are not paid staff members, many of the same management techniques used for paid staff members can also be applied to them.

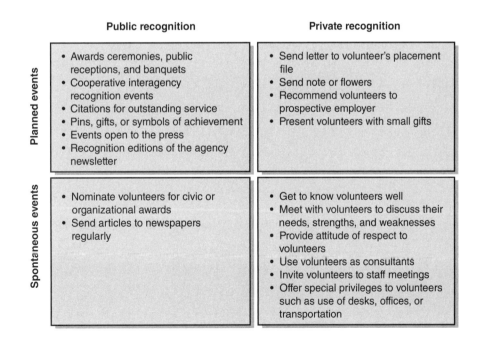

**Figure 10.5** Volunteer recognition can go a long way in ensuring volunteer commitment to an agency.

## Conclusion

While the successful hiring of a new employee may end the actual hiring process, a supervisor still has much work to do to ensure the success of the new employee, starting with a well-designed orientation. The orientation can go a long way in setting the tone for the employee's tenure with an agency, from introducing the new employee to the culture, policies, and procedures of the agency to ensuring that the new employee knows where to go to ask questions. Other supervisory responsibilities for managing and supporting employees include evaluating employees, scheduling employees, supervising meetings, handling employee grievances, and delegating

tasks. Within the public and private nonprofit sectors, these tasks also apply to volunteers, and thus policies and procedures should reflect this.

While hiring the right people is necessary for an agency to fulfill its mission, managing people effectively is vital to retaining employees. Management starts on day one with orientation and continues with other managerial duties such as developing and enforcing policies and procedures, conducting performance appraisals, recognizing performance, motivating employees, and in some cases disciplining employees. Armed with the necessary management tools, a strong administrator can be invaluable when it comes to the successful retention of employees.

---

### Review Questions

1. What are the five purposes of orientation for new employees?
2. Explain how employee motivation, employee evaluation, and employee performance are related.
3. List the methods of employee evaluation described in this chapter. Develop a list of pros and cons for each method.
4. Explain the primary concepts behind organized labor.
5. Differentiate between networking and mentoring. What are the benefits of each?

---

 **Visit the online resource at www.HumanKinetics.com/TheParkAndRecreationProfessionalsHandbook for sample documents, keywords, activities and assignments, and more.**

# Marketing

chapter 11

Marketing is an increasingly important aspect of management given today's economy and the growing trend of entrepreneurship in all three sectors of leisure services. Whether an agency is in the public, commercial, or nonprofit sector, the competition for business is strong. This chapter presents marketing and the multitude of elements it encompasses. This book takes a different approach to marketing than many texts take by presenting the material in the form of a marketing plan. A **marketing plan** is a documented guide that details customers, products, and means to achieve marketing goals and objectives.

Marketing plans have several purposes, including to

- provide a written document demonstrating how resources are used,
- position the agency among its competitors,
- critically examine both the internal and the external environments of the agency and how they affect products and services, and
- communicate to the entire staff the role of marketing within the agency and the responsibilities of each staff member related to marketing.

Marketing is a far broader and more complex concept than advertising and publicity. Many view these terms as synonymous, but you will learn quickly that this is not the case. Marketing is complex and involves all aspects of leisure services delivery.

## Definition of Marketing

Marketing is the "purposeful planning and execution of the pricing, place, and promotion of ideas, goods, and services to create an exchange of time or resources that results in the satisfaction of individual needs and organizational objectives" (Hurd, Barcelona, and Meldrum 2008, 167). Figure 11.1 illustrates this definition of marketing.

This definition demonstrates how multifaceted marketing is. The definition can be dissected into three components, the first of which is the marketing mix. The marketing mix, sometimes called the *4 Ps* (Product, Price, Place, Promotion), is the foundation of marketing. The marketing mix is concerned with the product itself, how much it costs, where the product is available, and what forms of communication are used to inform potential customers about the product. Each of these elements is manipulated to best meet the needs

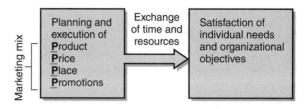

**Figure 11.1** Marketing is a complex process that extends beyond promotions and advertising.

Reprinted, by permission, from A. Hurd, R. Barcelona, and J. Meldrum, 2008, *Leisure services management* (Champaign, IL: Human Kinetics), 167.

of the customers. The marketing mix is explained in detail within the marketing plan presented in this chapter.

The second component of marketing is the exchange of time and resources. In the leisure services industry, we seek participation and purchase of products and services. People must use their discretionary time for participation and often must pay for the services they receive. Part of marketing is convincing people that the product is valuable and will meet their needs. Meeting the needs of the customer is a portion of the last component of marketing—satisfying customer needs and organizational objectives. Chapter 2 on programming demonstrates the importance of this component. Agencies should develop programs that customers want, but the programs should also adhere to the values, vision, and mission of the agency itself. All programs should meet organizational objectives or not be offered.

## Marketing Plan

Developing a marketing plan is a highly sought-after skill in the parks and recreation profession. Many professionals become overwhelmed at the thought of developing a marketing plan, but much of that can be attributed to a lack of knowledge about what goes into a marketing plan. This chapter presents a five-part marketing plan with subsections. A marketing plan includes the following:

1. Executive summary and introduction
2. Situational analysis
   - Product and services analysis
   - Demand trends and economic climate
   - SWOT analysis
   - Competitor analysis
   - Branding and positioning

3. Customer analysis
   - Market research
   - Market segments
   - Target markets
   - Consumer behavior
4. Marketing goals and strategies
   - Use of the marketing mix to develop goals and strategies
   - Communication
5. Implementation, monitoring, and evaluation
   - Plan for implementation
   - Budget
   - Evaluation of marketing effectiveness

# Executive Summary and Introduction

The executive summary is the first section to appear in the marketing plan and the last section to be written. It summarizes the entire plan and gives an overview of its contents. The executive summary can be considered a stand-alone document, with greater detail found in the plan itself. It is the first (and possibly only) part of the plan that is read. Do not mistake the executive summary for the introduction. The introduction to the marketing plan introduces the contents of the plan. It details what the reader should expect to find in the plan itself. Chapter 5 provides more detail on the executive summary along with writing tips.

# Situational Analysis

The situational analysis is the compilation of information needed for planning and implementing the marketing mix (Stotlar 2005). This section of the marketing plan examines the internal and external environments that can affect marketing. The situational analysis includes a product and services analysis, a discussion on demand trends and economic climate, a SWOT analysis, a competitor analysis, and a discussion on branding and positioning.

## Product and Services Analysis

The product and services analysis requires the agency to answer the question, "What business is the agency in?" Hopefully this is fairly easy to answer and the products match the mission of the agency. However, analyzing products is not always that straightforward. Agencies have core products and product extensions to consider. The **core products** are the central products or services that the agency produces. The **product extensions** enhance the core product. For example, a tennis center provides tennis lessons, tournaments, and leagues as the core products and concessions and a pro shop as the extension products. The extensions do not have to be tangible products—they can also be the benefits derived from a product or service (table 11.1).

In addition to determining what the products are, this section of the marketing plan addresses the location of the product within the product life cycle. The product life cycle is a five-phase model of the stages that a product moves through from creation to termination (figure 11.2).

A product enters the introduction stage once it is developed and released to the market. At this stage there are few customers and little profitability since resources were spent to establish the program. As the product receives promotion, it moves into the growth phase and participation increases. Sometimes participation demand outgrows the supply as people become aware of the product. Then the growth stage levels off somewhat and the product moves into the maturation phase. Maturation is often the longest phase of the life cycle, and some products stay here for

**Table 11.1**  Sample Core and Extension Products

| Core products | Product extensions |
|---|---|
| County park with camping, swimming, and boating | Canoe rentals, firewood sales, grocery store |
| Fitness facility with classes and fitness and weight equipment | Concession area, personal training, opportunities for socialization |
| Youth soccer league | Skill building, wellness, socialization, positive sport behavior |

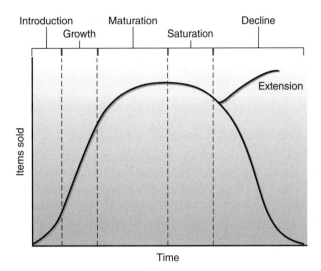

**Figure 11.2**  All products move through a life cycle, but the rate of movement differs with each product.

Reprinted, by permission, from A. Hurd, R. Barcelona, and J. Meldrum, 2008, *Leisure services management* (Champaign, IL: Human Kinetics), 174.

many years. Participation numbers still grow, but they do so at a much slower rate. In the saturation phase, people who stop participating are replaced by new participants so the numbers stay steady rather than increase or decrease.

The last phase in the life cycle is decline. As the number of participants decreases, decisions are made about what to do with the product. Three options are available: petrification, death, and extension. With petrification, a product is simply left to decline to the point of no participants and is phased out. A program can also experience death if it is stopped before it has a chance to decline completely. Programmers see a decline and decide that the program must end, usually because of the drain on resources. The last option, extension, is quite elaborate and involves examining both the market and the product from the perspective of the existing product and market and new products and markets (figure 11.3).

Extension strategies require the marketing team to manipulate either the product or the market. Sometimes manipulating both makes sense. The following list describes the manipulations aimed at extending the life cycle of the product.

- *Market development:* Market development is the extension strategy used when an existing product is opened to a new market. This may mean promoting the product to a different group of potential users, such

as a population that is slightly older than the population the program was originally designed for.

- *Market penetration:* Market penetration is keeping an existing product in its current form and aiming the marketing deeper into the target market. Marketing strategies can attempt to attract nonusers or customers of competitors within the same target market.

- *Product development and product replacement:* Sometimes new products are developed to meet the needs of an existing market. When this occurs, either product development or product replacement is being employed. Product development is when the declining product is replaced by a new product for the same market. In product replacement the old product is replaced by a new and improved version of the same product.

- *Diversification:* When an agency chooses to go in a completely different direction by providing new products for a new target market, it has chosen diversification as the extension strategy. The new product begins the life cycle at the introduction stage.

Conducting a product and services analysis involves identifying what products and services are being offered and what product extensions

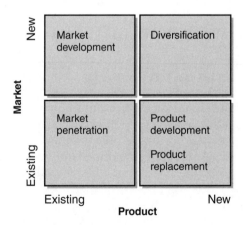

**Figure 11.3**  Extension strategies can lengthen the life of a product by changing either the product or the target market.

Reprinted, by permission, from A. Hurd, R. Barcelona, and J. Meldrum, 2008, *Leisure services management* (Champaign, IL: Human Kinetics), 175. Adapted from D.R. Howard and J.L. Crompton, 1980, *Financing, managing, and marketing recreation and park resources* (Dubuque, IA: Wm. C. Brown Publishers), 397, by permission of The McGraw-Hill Companies.

**Services or Experiences?**

The birth of service marketing boded well for parks and recreation. We are a service-based industry rather than a product-based one. However, O'Sullivan and Spangler (1998) suggest that although we are a service industry, we are in the business of providing experiences. They describe an experience as something that a person is involved in during consumption; the state of being physically, mentally, emotionally, socially, or spiritually engaged; and having a conscious perception of intentionally encountering an event.

Think about the difference between a service and an experience in terms of this example. Getting a haircut or an oil change is a service provided to the customer. An experience is zip lining through the rain forest, playing in a state championship game, or running a marathon. Although we call many parks and recreation activities *services*, it is the experience itself that we are offering and enticing people to exchange their resources for.

exist, analyzing whether they meet the mission of the organization, examining their stage in the product life cycle, and assessing the quality of each of these elements. This analysis may uncover products that should not be offered or that need marketing attention. Understanding where products fall in the life cycle dictates the level of marketing that needs to be done. This first part of the marketing plan lays the foundation for the remaining sections of the document. In chapter 5, the MacMillan matrix was presented as a means to analyze programs. This technique can also be used to analyze programs in a marketing plan.

## Demand Trends and Economic Climate

Accurately predicting demand for products is a challenging yet important part of developing a marketing plan. Low-demand programs require different marketing techniques than high-demand ones do. Demand is influenced by trends and fads, economic factors, and past supply and demand. Trends and fads were discussed in chapter 2 on programming. Watching them helps the marketing staff assess demand. Fads have a shorter demand time frame than trends have. The difficulty comes in predicting what will be a trend versus a fad and how long the trend or fad will last.

Often it is a guessing game, but there are indicators that can help. For example, the economic climate influences demand. A recession can limit what people buy and how they spend their money. Travel and tourism, for instance, increase in times of economic growth and decrease during a recession (Middleton and Clark 2001). During a recession people tend to stay closer to home

and enjoy so-called *staycations* or take day trips (daycations). During a recession, the demand for products can shift. For example, the NRPA has seen a decline in its annual conference attendance that matches the current economic decline. However, it has seen an increase in use of its Web-based educational opportunities as people look to increase their skills but lack the money to travel to conferences.

Probably the most common predictor of demand is past records of supply and demand. Agencies diligently track attendance and use figures on programs, facilities, and events. These numbers are compared with supply, or how many opportunities for the activity are available. Supply is measured both internally and externally by looking at what is offered by the agency and its competitors.

Using just one of these techniques to predict demand is insufficient. Demand predictions require examining a multitude of data sources to make the best decisions possible.

## SWOT Analysis

A SWOT analysis is a common planning tool in management. The strengths and weaknesses focus on the internal environment of the agency, whereas the opportunities and threats examine the external environment. A detailed description of a SWOT analysis is given in chapter 5.

## Competitor Analysis

An agency's competitors are those who compete for the same customers. To identify competitors, think about consumer choices. If people were not using your services or buying your products,

Events such as road races must consider their competition at the local and state levels. Some larger races expand to include regional and national competition.

where would they go, what would they do, or what would they buy? Analyzing competitors means thinking outside the box. There are direct competitors who do the same thing as you do, and then there are indirect competitors who have a share of the leisure services market. For example, Boulder Parks and Recreation sees Longmont Parks and Recreation and Broomfield Parks and Recreation as direct competition based on proximity and programs offered. The YMCA, 24 Hour Fitness, Flatiron Athletic Club, and RallySport could be considered both direct and indirect competition depending on the services offered. Some are the same services as those offered by Boulder Parks and Recreation, and others are different but can compete for people's time and money.

A competitor analysis identifies who is out there and what services they offer compared with yours. Identifying the strengths and weaknesses of the competition helps in determining a marketing strategy that will make your services a priority over the competition and give your agency the needed competitive advantage.

## Branding and Positioning

Agencies seek to make their products stand out in a positive way to consumers. This requires attention to both branding and positioning. These two concepts are closely intertwined and are often erroneously used as interchangeable concepts. Branding is the use of a name, logo, symbol, or color associated with a product that invokes feeling, emotion, and attitude about the product

(Mullin, Hardy, and Sutton 2007). Positioning refers to how a product is perceived in the minds of the consumers compared with the products of competitors. The difference is that positioning looks at the overall image of the brand whereas branding relies on logos, names, symbols, and colors to create that image.

The sport and leisure field has an advantage of invoking feelings, emotions, and attitudes because its product is often an experience. This is especially true with sport products such as the Indianapolis Colts or the Duke Blue Devils. Although many public and nonprofit agencies do not have a national brand like these examples, they establish their brand within the community they serve. So, branding is not just a strategy for large commercial agencies to undertake.

### Branding Process

Developing a brand can increase attendance, participation, and sales. However, before this can happen, the organization must go through the four-step branding process: brand awareness, brand image, brand equity, and brand loyalty (Shank 2005).

First, you must establish brand awareness. Consumers in the desired target market must be aware that the brand exists. This is done in the introduction stage of the product life cycle.

Second, you must establish the brand image. Brand image is a consumer's beliefs and attitudes about a product. Companies work hard to associate their products with the right image. This can be done by designing advertisements to reflect the desired image or associating the product with a desired image through sponsorship. For example, Home Depot, Lowe's, Budweiser, and Red Bull are all NASCAR sponsors and associate themselves with this target market. Brand image can be affected by "product features or characteristics, product performance or quality, price, brand name, customer service, packaging, advertising, promotion, and distribution channels" (Shank 2005, 229).

Once a positive brand image is created, the third step in the branding process is establishing brand equity. Brand equity is the increased value the product has over its generic equivalent. There are a number of advantages of brand equity (Middleton and Clark 2001; Mullin, Hardy, and Sutton 2007):

- A losing sport team results in less revenue loss because of the value associated with the team.

- Agencies can charge premium prices for their products.
- There is an increased chance of attracting corporate sponsors.
- Recovery time after a crisis is lessened.
- Customers feel their risk of purchase is reduced because of the known quality of the brand.

Finally, the ultimate goal in marketing is brand loyalty. A brand-loyal customer repeatedly buys a particular brand of product and is committed to using that product over other products. Companies strive for brand loyalty because it is unlikely customers will be lost to the competition, and their purchase becomes habit rather than the result of an extensive decision-making process. Brand loyalty is a competitive advantage over the competition and thus increases brand equity along the way.

Sport is a good example of brand loyalty. Indiana University (IU) basketball has a rich history steeped in tradition. In the past several years the program has experienced some difficult times. However, there are loyal fans who continue to buy season tickets regardless of the quality of the team. IU knows the loyalty level and understands that its loyal fans will not defect and begin supporting its in-state rival, Purdue. The Chicago Cubs have not won a World Series since 1908, and yet the team has an extensive and loyal fan base whose slogan is, "Wait until next year." These fans remain loyal and refuse to defect to the Chicago White Sox or the St. Louis Cardinals.

Someone who is brand loyal does not buy the product that is cheapest but instead buys the one they are loyal to. In terms of recreation equipment, avid runners may be brand loyal to a type of shoe, skiers may be loyal to a brand of ski, and cyclists may have a brand of bike that they prefer.

### Positioning Process

Positioning takes branding a step further as branding begins to create the position of the product in the mind of the consumer. Positioning is the place a product holds in the mind of the public and elected officials and is the process of maintaining a valued and distinctive position (Crompton 2009). New products on the market seek to position themselves to be seen as better than their competitors, and once a product is positioned, it may need to change its position over time. When an agency deliberately attempts to change its existing position, it is **repositioning** itself. If a public parks and recreation agency is seeing decreased budget allocations from the city council, it may question its position in the minds of the council members. Decreases in funding often come from the view that parks and recreation provides nonessential discretionary services. When this is the case, the agency needs to reposition itself in the minds of the council and community. The agency needs to demonstrate its role in the community in terms of health and wellness and economic, community, and youth development, among other things.

Crompton (2009) outlines four strategies agencies can use to reposition themselves. These are real repositioning, associative repositioning, psychological repositioning, and competitive repositioning.

- Real repositioning requires the agency to determine what position it wants in the market and then to create services to achieve that desired position. For example, if an agency wants to be known for youth development, then it may need to create programs in youth development to reposition itself as a quality youth-serving agency.
- Associative repositioning requires the agency to partner or associate with an agency that has a positive position in the community. The hope is that being associated with a positive agency makes the other agency also look positive.
- Psychological repositioning relies on the ability of an agency to alter its stakeholders' perception of what it does. Because a position is established from past experience and perception, psychological strategies are used to change perception. Strategies might include providing scientific evidence, including research, facts, and statistics; providing testimonials from opinion leaders and experts; changing the perception of value by finding a new way to demonstrate the value of the agency, such as presenting the cost of the after-school program as cost per hour in addition to total cost, and changing nomenclature to better appeal to or educate consumers, such as using the term *investments in leisure* rather than *tax subsidy* or using the term *low-maintenance areas* rather than *natural areas* (so that the areas are not perceived as unkempt).
- Competitive repositioning requires the agency to demonstrate how resources given to other agencies would be better utilized

in the one doing the repositioning. Crompton argues that "competitive repositioning may be conceptualized as 'depositioning' another agency since it is challenging the legitimacy or authenticity of that agency's positioning claims and trying to demote them" (Crompton 2009, 105).

The best repositioning method is to combine the methods just described to achieve the desired repositioning goals. As you will see throughout the rest of this chapter, branding and positioning are critical components of marketing, and many marketing activities are directed at building the brand and creating a good position in the minds of the consumers.

## Customer Analysis

Since the customer is the cornerstone of marketing, it is imperative to answer these two questions: Who are our customers? What do we know about them? This section of the marketing plan delves into market research, market segmentation, target marketing, and consumer behavior.

### Market Research

Market research is the systematic process of collecting, analyzing, and reporting information to enhance decision making throughout the mar-

keting planning process (Shank 2005). Market research is used to answer any number of questions about products and customers, including the following:

***Product Information Needs***

- What do customers want from our products?
- How do they view our products?
- What products do they use?
- How big is our market?
- Where and when do customers register for programs?
- How often do they participate in programs?

***Customer Information Needs***

- What is the customer's contact information (e.g., name, children, age, address)?
- How far do customers drive to use our products?
- Where do customers hear about our products?

Market research data are either primary or secondary. Primary data come directly from consumers. Data can come from surveys, interviews, observations, focus groups, or Internet surveys. The process for collecting these data is much like that for collecting evaluation data (see chapter 4). Secondary data, on the other hand, are compiled

An agency will use market research data to help them better promote programs through media sources that attract the same customer groups.

by market research firms and are available for purchase. These data include demographics, psychographics, product use, advertising preferences, and so on.

Primary data can come from internal and external sources. Good sources of internal data come from registration systems because customers must complete basic information about themselves and their families. Amazon.com tracks purchases for customers logging into their accounts. Amazon asks for basic demographic data, tracks purchases, and then recommends books or materials that are similar to those of past purchases. Customer loyalty cards are another source of information. Grocery stores promote these cards as a way of giving discounts, but they are really using the cards to track purchases and gain a demographic profile of purchasers and their products. External primary data can be gathered from the Census Bureau, a local chamber of commerce, or libraries. Much of these data are demographics, but demographics can prove valuable when determining the target market.

Market research is essentially gathering data so that marketing decisions can be made. Without data on customers, good decisions become guesses. Poor guessing results in wasted resources.

## Market Segments and Target Markets

Market research provides the ability to segment markets. Market segmentation is the process of dividing a large and heterogeneous group of people into smaller, more homogenous groups with similar wants, needs, and demographic profiles. Market segments divide the population into groups who are likely to respond to a certain marketing mix (Mullin, Hardy, and Sutton 2007). Target marketing then selects one or more of the market segments to direct its efforts toward.

Some parks and recreation agencies, especially those in the public and nonprofit sectors, feel they must provide services for everyone. Thus they direct their marketing efforts to the general public instead of a targeted group. Known as *mass marketing,* this approach is often a waste of resources. Selecting a target market does not mean that people outside the target market are excluded from participating. Target marketing means that the marketing mix is aimed at a group of people most likely to participate and most likely to respond to that particular marketing mix. For example, the Manhattan Beach Parks and Recreation Department in Manhattan Beach, California, offers a trip to the Catalina Silent Film Festival. The trip is designed and promoted as a trip for people 55 years or older, but this does not mean that a 50-year-old would be excluded from the trip (City of Manhattan Beach 2009).

There are five bases of segmentation, or means to segment a market. These are demographics, geography, psychographics, behavioral characteristics, and benefits (Hurd, Barcelona, and Meldrum 2008).

### Demographics

Demographics are characteristics used to define a population. They include age, race, family income, and education level, among others. Demographic data are relatively easy to access through the Census Bureau and are commonly used by many parks and recreation agencies. For example, the Burlington (Connecticut) Parks and Recreation uses age to classify its programs (Burlington Parks and Recreation 2010). Its brochure has activities for children and youths, adults, and older adults.

### Geography

A second segmentation base, geography, focuses on geodemographics and proximity. The premise behind geodemographics is that people who are similar in income, culture, and perspectives naturally gravitate toward one another. Once these people move to their neighborhoods, they become even more alike and share similar consumer behaviors (Carroll 2009). When a store asks for your zip code when you make a purchase, it's using geodemographics as a segmentation technique.

One example of segmentation is the PRIZM lifestyle segmentation system, which divides every U.S. neighborhood into 1 of 62 clusters. Variables such as demographics, lifestyle, urbanization, and socioeconomic status are used to cluster these neighborhoods. Here are few examples of the clusters (Claritas 2000):

➤ Blue Blood Estates—People aged 45 to 64, predominantly White and Asian, established executives, old-money heirs, used to luxury and privilege, one-tenth are multimillionaires.

Urban Gold Coast—People aged 45 to 64, predominantly White and Asian, highly educated, live in urban apartments and condos, few have children or own cars, very busy and affluent, many live in places like New York City.

American Dreams—Mixed age and ethnically diverse, immigrants, descendents from multicultural backgrounds, multilingual neighborhoods, married couples with and without children, high school education with some college, work in trades and public service jobs.

Another common geography-based segmentation strategy is proximity, or how close people live or work to a service. A person living or working 10 minutes from a fitness center is more likely to use that location than someone 30 to 40 minutes away (especially if there are other options that are closer). Some agencies locate facilities based on proximity so as to serve an entire community. For example, the Houston Parks and Recreation Department has a multitude of branches because it serves such a large community. Today, the Houston Parks and Recreation Department manages 350 parks and 56 community centers located throughout the city to accommodate its users (Houston Parks and Recreation Department 2009).

## Psychographics

A third base of segmentation is psychographics. Psychographics are lifestyle and personality descriptors. There is a relationship between lifestyle and consumer behavior (Fullerton 2007), so people with similar lifestyles buy similar products. Lifestyle descriptors are often categorized as activities, interests, and opinions. Table 11.2 depicts psychographics that can be used to segment a market.

## Behavioral Characteristics

Behavioral characteristics are based on the product consumption habits of the consumers, the skill level of the users, and the product loyalty of the consumers. Agencies must be cognizant of use levels and understand how products should be offered to meet the needs of a multitude of user levels. Think about how companies are increasingly recognizing their high-level users, such as with the Hilton Honors rewards program and airline frequent-flier miles. The Chicago White Sox offer a variety of ticket packages, including a single-game package, a seven-game package, and season tickets. Also, for mid- to high-level users they offer premium seating in areas such as the LG Skyline Club, Jim Beam Club, and Diamond Suites. High-level users who purchase season tickets also receive many benefits such as gift packages, lower-priced parking, resell opportunities, and discounted suite prices (Chicago White Sox 2009).

Here are a few things to keep in mind when segmenting by behavioral characteristics (Mullin, Hardy, and Sutton 2007):

- It is wise to offer programs at all use levels so that light users can possibly increase to medium or heavy use over time. This ensures a steady stream of users.
- Levels of consumption will vary from product to product and by age group.
- Sales volume is more likely to increase by moving light and medium users up to medium and heavy users than by attracting first-time users.

**Table 11.2** Sample Psychographics Categories

| Activities | Interests | Opinions |
|---|---|---|
| Work | Family | Themselves |
| Hobbies | Home | Social issues |
| Social events | Job | Politics |
| Vacation | Community | Business |
| Entertainment | Recreation | Economics |
| Club membership | Fashion | Education |
| Community | Food | Products |
| Shopping | Media | Future |
| Sport | Achievements | Culture |

From SHANK, M.D., SPORT MARKETING: A STRATEGIC PERSPECTIVE, 2nd ed. pg. 195. 2005. (Upper Saddle River, NJ: Pearson Education), 195.

**Addams Family Market Segmentation**

The Ford Center for the Performing Arts in Chicago ran a pre-Broadway production of the *Addams Family* with Nathan Lane and Bebe Neuwirth. Knowing the psychographics of some of its customers, the theater hosted a benefit on one evening of the production for Equality Illinois. The mission of Equality Illinois is "to secure, protect and defend equal rights for lesbian, gay, bisexual and transgender people in Illinois" (Equality Illinois 2009). The theater felt that the lesbian, gay, bisexual, and transgender (LGBT) community has an interest in theater and that Nathan Lane has an LGBT following, so identifying this community as a market segment was based on solid psychographic variables.

Understanding the skill level of consumers is valuable in knowing what products to offer to meet their needs. Agencies can offer softball leagues for various skill levels or golf leagues for various golf handicaps.

### Benefits

Finally, markets can be segmented by product benefits, because consumers seek certain qualities in a product. For example, Nike has shoes for basketball players, dancers, lacrosse players, and walkers. Each line of shoes offers the benefits the consumer is seeking. For instance, the lacrosse shoes offer traction, comfort, support, and speed. Trek makes bikes for roads, triathlons, mountains, and bike paths, among others. Each bike has unique features, from the size of the tire and seat to how upright the rider sits. These two companies thus use benefits as one way to segment their markets.

### Combining Segmentation Methods

Most agencies use one or more of the five market segmenting methods. The more data the agency has, the more able it is to select the best market and to utilize a marketing mix to reach that market. Once the market is segmented, the agency selects which market to target. Market segmentation and target marketing are keys to all aspects of marketing and ensure that agency resources are put to best use. Haphazard marketing and mass marketing rarely attract the number of consumers sought.

## Consumer Behavior

Consumer behavior involves the decision making and buying patterns of users. Although much information can be gathered through the segmentation process, there is still the matter of how customers decide to buy the products

they buy. Understanding consumer behavior is enhanced by knowing the consumer decision-making process.

Consumers move through a four-step decision-making process (figure 11.4). First, they identify a need through media exposure, friends, family, self-awareness, or environmental factors. Next, they seek ways to meet the need through products and services, and they evaluate their options. Once the options are evaluated, they make a purchase or experience a service. Afterward, the product or service is evaluated. Customers evaluate their satisfaction with the purchase decision and weaknesses of this choice. People mentally perform a cost–benefit analysis, measuring the costs of the product (such as time or money) in relation to the benefits they receive. If the benefits outweigh the costs, the consumer is satisfied with the product purchase. If the costs outweigh the benefits, then the consumer is dissatisfied.

Marketing can affect all levels of the consumer decision-making process. For example, an agency

**Figure 11.4** People follow a four-step process when making purchasing decisions.

## Diffusion of Innovation

In the introduction phase of the product life cycle, it is challenging to attract new customers. There is much research on this concept, which is properly titled *diffusion of innovation*. Diffusion of innovation explains how people learn about a new product and how use spreads throughout a market. Christ (2009) identified five categories of people who adopt new products:

- Innovators—This small segment of the population is at the forefront of adopting new products. Innovators are eager to try new products, regardless of price. They are not usually brand loyal since they are looking for the newest things on the market.
- Early adopters—People in this group also enjoy new products, but they are often more practical about their buying decisions than the innovators are. They also like to communicate their experiences to the next group, the early majority. Early adopters are key in marketing because they are considered opinion leaders since they like to share their experiences.
- Early majority—The early majority adopters account for up to one-third of the entire market. They tend to wait until they get feedback on the product from others before buying. Because of the size of the market, the future of a product may completely rely on acceptance by this group.
- Late majority—This group is just as large as the early majority. These adopters take a wait-and-see approach before trying the new product. Once the late majority enters the market, the product is likely to see high profits.
- Laggards—This is the last group to adopt a product, and many of these people do so because they do not have another choice. Because of their reluctance, not much marketing is directed at the laggards.

can launch an advertising campaign to convince a potential consumer that a need exists, can make information readily available so the customer can make an informed decision about which product to buy, can make the purchase easy and can build the anticipation of the experience via e-mail messages or photos of past experiences, and can send reminders of the experience that has passed by giving certificates, providing photos, or making phone calls to follow up on the experience.

The customer analysis part of the marketing plan is all about market research and gathering data that provide insight into who the customer is, how to segment the market, and how the customer behaves. These data are the impetus for the next section of the marketing plan.

## Marketing Goals and Strategies

The action part of the marketing plan is the goals and strategies. All of the information from the first three parts of the marketing plan was gathered so this part of the plan could be developed. The market research has been completed, the results

of the SWOT analysis are known, the status of branding and positioning has been identified, and the place of the product on the life cycle has been determined. From this information, the goals and strategies are developed to provide the direction and directives for what will be accomplished in the future.

In chapter 2, goals and objectives were discussed. It may be beneficial to review that chapter to refresh your memory about the proper way to write them. Marketing goals are broad statements depicting what should be accomplished. The strategies (sometimes termed *objectives* and *tactics*) are the nuts and bolts of how a goal will be achieved. Always keep in mind that marketing goals must be consistent with agency goals and objectives and adhere to the mission of the agency. Sample marketing goals might include the following:

- Increase youth sport sponsorship.
- Increase revenue at the Rialto Theatre.
- Target the 55+ age group for fitness programs.
- Establish a media campaign for the opening of the new recreation center.

Although these goals are a good start, it is the strategies that provide the detail for the plan. In addition to the strategies, assignments and deadlines are created to designate responsibility. In some instances, a budget figure is assigned to the strategy. This helps the marketing staff develop the budget for the upcoming year and shows where money will be spent.

Goal: Target the 55+ age group for fitness programs.

Strategy: Develop three new fitness programs for 55+ residents.

Deadline: Third quarter 2011

Responsibility: Programming staff in consultation with marketing staff

Strategy: Create advertisements to run on targeted radio and television stations.

Budget: $2,000

Deadline: Third quarter 2011

Responsibility: Marketing staff

The goals and strategies can be extensive and take a great deal of time to develop. However, having a solid foundation of data helps in the development of the strategies.

In the beginning of the chapter we defined marketing, but thus far the marketing mix has not been a major topic of discussion. The marketing mix is a major contributing factor to the marketing strategies and is also called the *4 Ps*—Product, Place, Price, and Promotion. Remember that marketing is the planning and execution of the marketing mix to create the exchange of time and resources that results in the satisfaction of individual needs and organizational objectives. As such, the marketing plan addresses the marketing mix and uses the elements within the 4 Ps to precipitate that exchange. The effects of the 4 Ps on marketing are discussed in the following sections.

## Product

Product was discussed as part of the product analysis within the marketing plan, and examples were given for marketing during the phases of the product life cycle. In addition to the life cycle, there are many aspects of the product that are considered marketing strategies. For example, a product can be modified to better meet the needs of the consumer (product replacement), a more thorough understanding of program benefits can be used in the promotion of the product, a needs

assessment can drive programming development decisions, a gap in service provision for a select target market can be filled so needs are met, or a high-quality program can be offered to enhance the brand.

## Place

Place, sometimes referred to as *distribution,* is the location where consumption or purchase of the product takes place. This could be a recreation center, dance studio, theater, hotel, or sport arena. In some situations the place is also the product, such as the Grand Canyon, Everglades, or Fenway Park. For other services, the place may not seem overly important since it is just a building or location where people take classes or buy equipment. However, place has a major influence on marketing and is a legitimate part of the marketing plan.

Place has four parts to consider—community composition, distribution channels, atmosphere, and location. Community composition has been discussed at length within the customer analysis section. It affects place in that it describes the neighborhoods and the community around the location.

Distribution channels describe how products and services reach the customer. They are either direct or indirect (figure 11.5). Direct distribution occurs when the product moves directly from the producer to the consumer. For example, Holiday Inn provides rooms directly to its customers, and the YWCA provides programs for its members. Direct distribution is found in all three sectors; however, it is arguably more prevalent in the public and nonprofit sectors.

When there is an intermediary party involved in the distribution of products, indirect distribution is being used. The intermediaries are commonly wholesalers, retailers, or intermediary agencies. Retailers sell products directly to the final customers, whereas wholesalers purchase products from the manufacturers and sell them to retailers or other wholesalers who then sell them to the consumer. Sporting goods stores are an example of indirect distribution. They are the retailer who receives products from a wholesaler or directly from the factory and then sells the products to the consumer. In some situations an intermediary agency is used to distribute a company's products. For example, Disney sells tickets at its parks, which is direct distribution. In addition, it uses intermediary travel agents to book trips and purchase tickets. From a marketing perspective, Disney is concerned about its intermediary

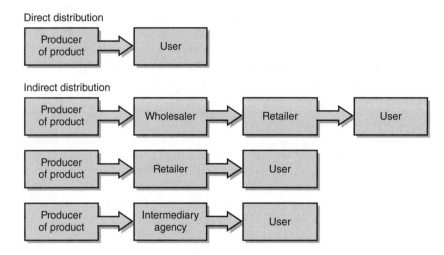

**Figure 11.5**   Although most services in parks and recreation are direct, some agencies will use indirect channels of distribution.

Reprinted, by permission, from A. Hurd, R. Barcelona, and J. Meldrum, 2008, *Leisure services management* (Champaign, IL: Human Kinetics), 177.

distributors in that these distributors must provide good customer service and information. These agencies reflect positively or negatively on Disney and have an effect on its brand. The more entities involved in the distribution process, the higher the product price and the less control the producer has over the customer service.

The look of a facility both inside and outside contributes to the atmosphere that people experience, and the atmosphere can attract or eliminate customers. Think about a restaurant. If it is dirty on the outside or the inside, would this influence your decision to patronize it? Many people would be influenced by the restaurant appearance, while others might argue that as long as the food is good, they would go there. Few businesses have the luxury of turning potential customers away because of the atmosphere of the facility, and few would lose customers because their facility is too clean or too nice. Small things can be done to improve the atmosphere, such as applying fresh paint inside and out, providing a clean facility, adding color to rooms, making rooms bright by adding natural or artificial light, or establishing the tone of the facility by manipulating color, light, smell, or sound. For example, Las Vegas casinos are known for manipulating the atmosphere for gamblers. Although these are design elements, they are also marketing techniques that increase consumption:

- The internal structures have a theme such as New York or Paris.
- The high-rollers' gambling area has more luxuries than the regular tables have.

- Bright lights are everywhere inside and out.
- There are no windows so gamblers do not know if it is day or night.
- There are no clocks so people lose track of time and stay in the casino.
- The casinos are designed like mazes so it is difficult to get out, encouraging people to sit down and play if they are lost.
- Loose slot machines are placed in high-traffic areas so spectators see more payouts.
- The uniforms of the staff members contribute to the image of the casino.

Any realtor or businessperson will say that the key to business success is location, location, location. People have to be able to find the business or agency before they can patronize it. Customers see high-visibility locations more often, and they commit the business to memory. In addition to being able to find the location, customers need to easily access it. Accessibility is affected by modes of transportation, parking, availability of roads to the location, and distance traveled.

The type of business dictates modes of transportation. For example, a recreation center in a major metropolitan area relies on the city bus system, trains and subways, and personal vehicles to transport customers. Hotels such as Super 8 or Motel 6 are located near interstates because they know their customers will be driving to their destinations and seek to pull off the interstate for the night. High-end hotels such as Hilton or Hyatt

## Mets Promote Alternative Parking Options

The New York Mets opened Citi Field in 2009. It is located in Queens, just minutes from the heart of New York City. The new stadium has a capacity of 41,800 people and 8,300 parking spaces. This means that each car must have at least five people in it to accommodate a sold-out game. Knowing that parking and transportation are an issue, the Mets have an extensive Web site promoting all of the transportation options, including the subway, Long Island Rail Road, New Jersey Transit, city buses, and New Jersey ferry. In addition, the Mets use players to do online minicommercials encouraging one of these modes of transportation for faster, easier, and greener access to the park (New York Mets 2009).

cater to business travelers and build locations in downtown business districts where taxis transport customers from the airport. Even though not all customers drive, when customers do drive, they expect to have ample parking available. Sufficient parking can increase the number of customers coming to the business.

The availability of roads and the distance of travel influence facility use. A major attraction such as an amusement park or a stadium is not located at the end of a two-lane road. It would take entirely too long for people to get in and out of the parking lots. For example, the Kings Island Theme Park is located just off of Interstate 71 northeast of Cincinnati, Ohio. As another example, outlet malls rely heavily on tourists, so outlet malls in places such as Branson (Missouri), Myrtle Beach (South Carolina), and Park City (Utah) are located on major highways that provide easy access. Along with transportation, people are concerned with how far they have to travel, or their drawing radius. Mullin, Hardy, and Sutton (2007) outline key pieces of information that affect the drawing radius:

- Demographics such as age, income, stage in the life cycle, and discretionary time can increase and decrease the drawing radius.

- People will drive farther for a onetime event than they will for a program that is offered more than once a week.

- Emotional commitment to the event extends the drawing radius; parents will drive farther to watch their child participate in an event.

- In sport, the big game or a top-name player increases the drawing radius.

In addition, the amount of competition, the quality of the location and product, and brand loyalty can influence the drawing radius. Market research will provide the data to determine what the drawing radius is for a city. A known drawing radius affects advertising—advertising money is spent predominantly within the drawing radius rather than outside of it.

Many young marketers in leisure services ignore the place aspect of marketing, yet there is much that can be done to improve place. Here are a few examples:

- If relying on wholesalers and retailers, monitor the quality of those distributors for customer service. Poor customer service on their end can lead to a damaged brand name.

- Enhance the atmosphere of facilities if needed. Promote major changes to the community so that people are aware of them.

- If a facility is poorly located, advertise the driving directions to increase the likelihood of customers finding it. Use signage strategically with the company logo to build the brand.

- Advertise alternative modes of transportation or parking lots and garages if parking is limited.

- Take a map of the drawing radius. Use the radius to target advertising and select the target market. Determine if it is possible to expand the drawing radius through promotions or programming.

## Price

Pricing is the only aspect of marketing that generates any revenue, and it is often the least understood aspect of the marketing mix. Charging too much drives away customers, and charging too little leaves a shortfall in revenues (Kotler, Bowen, and Makens 2010). Given this, pricing

If a fitness club has low membership fees but is always crowded, how might members perceive the faciliity's cost and value?

is a complicated part of marketing. Chapter 8 details how to set prices. This chapter discusses the marketing implications of price, namely cost and value, pricing strategies, psychology of pricing, and price changes.

## Cost and Value

The term *price* conjures the visual of dollar signs because it is the monetary amount assigned to a product. While monetary amount is important for marketing, another factor that must be considered with price is value. Value is the "perception of benefits received for what someone must give up" (Christ 2009, 282). Value not only includes the monetary cost of the product but also the opportunity, effort, and psychological costs associated with it (Brayley and McLean 2008).

To demonstrate costs, let's assume you are going to a concert with your mother. Monetary costs go beyond the price of the program itself. The monetary costs of the concert include the tickets, transportation, parking, dinner beforehand, and souvenirs. Opportunity costs are the opportunities that are given up to go to the concert. They might be an evening with friends, time spent studying, or tickets to a play. Effort costs encompass the physical and mental energy it takes to participate. If the show is far away, then it requires the energy of driving a long distance, the energy of getting from the far-away parking space to your

back-row seats, and the effort it takes to plan for the evening out with Mom. Lastly, psychological costs are the feelings and emotions felt from the experience. These can be both positive and negative. Fun, excitement, and a sense of closeness with your mother are positive aspects. Negative aspects might include the embarrassment of telling your friends what concert you are attending if your mother's taste in music is different than your own. Pricing is far more complicated than what is seen on the surface, and it extends beyond the cost of the product alone.

The costs associated with a product are directly related to the value of the product. Costs influence how much a person values an experience. In marketing terms, exchange theory becomes evident. The consumer takes into consideration all of the costs associated with the concert and then determines if the costs are a good value or if the costs outweigh the benefits. If the costs exceed perceived benefits, no exchange is made. If the reverse is true, then a purchase is made. Marketing efforts are designed to help consumers see the value, or benefits, of the product so that they are more likely to make a purchase.

## Pricing Strategies

Prices are set with a purpose in mind. Some prices are set to break even, be subsidized, or make money. Agencies know which of these purposes applies to each program based on their philosophy and pricing structure. Commercial agencies predominantly want to make a profit, whereas nonprofit and public agencies subsidize some programs, break even on some programs, and turn a profit on other programs.

Pricing is often set with the purpose of establishing the value of a product. An exceptionally low price often causes consumers to question the value. If the price is low for that particular item, then the value must be low, too. Market research and an understanding of consumer behavior help agencies know the perceived price–value relationship for their products. Prices are also set to influence behavior. They are set low in off-peak times for services such as hotel rooms, ski resorts, or movie theaters. These lower prices are used to smooth demand by moving people from high-demand times to low-demand times. Damage deposits, early registration discounts, and discounts for paying via direct deposits are other means of using price to influence behavior.

Product-line pricing is another pricing strategy used. Agencies offer a spectrum of prices for products in order to appeal to a range of consumers. For example, the Broadway play *Jersey Boys* offers tickets at a range of prices depending on the seats, the day of the week, and whether the play is on a holiday. The higher-priced tickets start at $360 for premier seats and $152 for seats in the orchestra section on a holiday. The lower-priced tickets start at $97 for seats in the mezzanine section on a Tuesday or Thursday. Ticket options are also available for large groups and matinees (Broadway.com 2009). Lower prices appeal to those who are price sensitive and higher prices target a more affluent market (Shank 2005).

A bundling strategy is used when products are grouped together and offered for a price. All-inclusive vacations such as Apple Vacations; golf vacations with room, meals, and golf included; and group ticket sales for ball games or theater productions are examples of bundling.

### Psychology of Pricing

Pricing has a multitude of psychological implications. In addition to enlisting pricing strategies, marketing also uses these psychological factors in setting prices. Two common psychological aspects to pricing are price–quality relationships and odd–even pricing.

Price dictates quality for many consumers. They view a higher-priced item as having more value. Take restaurants, for example. A higher-priced restaurant is perceived to be better than a lower-priced one. Hotel rooms priced at $75, $175, or $475 per night have different levels of quality and services associated with them. The perceived quality of the restaurant can also demonstrate value and dictate price. An $8 piece of cheesecake at McDonald's would be unacceptable to most consumers. However, if that same cheesecake were offered in a high-end restaurant, many customers would readily pay the price and value the dessert.

Odd–even pricing is the perception of price differences based on how the numbers are presented. People perceive $29.99 to be cheaper than $30 and $199 to be cheaper than $200. These slight differences are perceived as greater than they actually are. Notice how stores use odd–even pricing techniques for their products. Rarely is a price an even dollar amount.

### Price Changes

Marketing is involved in setting prices, but it is also a part of changing prices. Prices do not remain the same and must be adjusted over time. People have a price set in their minds that they expect to pay for a product (the reference price). There is the actual price of the item (objective price), and then there is the perception of whether the actual price is cheap, about right, or expensive (subjective price). When the reference and objective prices are out of balance, price adjustments need to be made or promotional aspects need to be changed. If the reference price is higher than the objective price, the product is seen as inexpensive and the price can be raised so that the reference and objective prices are aligned. Conversely, if people perceive the product as expensive, then steps need to be taken to align perception and reality through price change or promotion.

In terms of promotional efforts, agencies can do the following:

- Explain the reasons for the price change and the benefits associated with the product. This technique is an attempt to increase the value of the product in the mind of the consumer.
- Compare the product with that of the competitors to show how the price increase is in line with other prices.
- Make changes to the program to enhance it and promote the positive changes in order to increase the value of the program.

Pricing strategies, value implications, psychological aspects, and price changes all contribute to the complexity of pricing as part of the marketing mix. Determining the correct price for a product is part science and part art. Knowing consumers and their behaviors helps in setting the right price. However, price is just one part of the marketing mix that can be used to market a product. Here are some examples of how price is used in marketing:

- If free programs are offered, emphasize quality or the reason for no cost, such as community appreciation.
- Design ads that espouse the benefits of the product so potential consumers see the value.
- Offer off-peak time discounts such as reduced rates for golf rounds starting after 5:00 p.m.
- Give a 10 percent discount to fitness club members who pay all 12 months in advance or pay via automatic withdrawal.
- Bundle the hotel, flight, and rental car for trips.

## Promotion

Promotion is the best-known aspect of the marketing mix and is often used interchangeably with marketing. However, promotion is a small part of the entire concept of marketing. It is the communication piece of the marketing mix that is used to positively position the product in the mind of the consumer and ultimately create brand loyalty. Promotion encompasses advertising, sales promotion, publicity, and personal selling. These four components are often referred to as the *promotions mix*. For the promotional aspect of the marketing mix to be successful, it should follow the AIDA approach (Mullin, Hardy, and Sutton 2007):

A = increase Awareness.

I = attract Interest.

D = arouse Desire.

A = initiate Action.

Various promotional techniques are used to accomplish each of these four things. The AIDA approach begins with promoting general understanding of the product so people know about it. The next levels increase knowledge and interest until actual participation ensues. Many companies spend large amounts of money just moving people from desire to action. There are many products and experiences that people desire but never actually purchase. A good promotional campaign moves people through the entire process. A good campaign uses one or more elements of the promotions mix, which are described next.

### Advertising

Advertising is paid communication offered through some form of media. It includes signage at events, print and broadcast media, billboards, bus signs, Web sites, and blogs, among other things. By paying for this advertisement, the purchasing

## Marketing to Boomers

Baby boomers in the United States were born between 1946 and 1964 and represent 79 million people. This is a major sector of the population that influences marketing in leisure services. They have $1 trillion per year in spending power, they are well educated, and they want quality experiences. Here are a few points to remember when promoting programs to this group (Cochran, Rothschadl, and Rudick 2009, 39):

- Motivate boomers by emotional rather than rational messages.
- Once boomers are emotionally hooked, then provide rational information.
- Appeal to the rational side and offer options where consumers can go to get more information.
- Build relationships with customers and show you care about them.
- Do not insinuate that boomers are old or label them as *seniors*.
- Don't use photos of people who look like traditional seniors since boomers see themselves as 10 to 15 years younger than they are.
- Use multiple media sources to reach boomers. Don't leave out the Internet, and realize that word of mouth is powerful with this group.

agency controls the message by designing the content of the commercial, bus sign, or radio advertisement. When designing the ads, the benefits of the product are a focus. Since many parks and recreation products are services and lack the tangibility of a true product, the advertisements have the additional challenge of making the service more tangible in the customer's mind. This is done by advocating the benefits of the product. This goes back to the concept of creating product value so that people see the value as greater than the total cost. In addition to promoting the benefits of the product, the advertisement should develop an advertising appeal. Shank (2005) identified these common appeals, or means to attract consumers, in sport that are also applicable to other leisure services.

Selecting which type of advertisement to buy is dictated by the preferences of the target market, the cost of the medium, and the message to be conveyed. Market research provides the data on the preferences for the target market, and these preferences dictate what media to buy. For example, buying ads on the Internet is not a good choice if the target market is males aged 65+ who have lower incomes. The message will miss them completely. If you are targeting college students in a community, then the university newspaper or Facebook advertising is ideal.

Cost is the second deciding factor in advertisement selection. Some forms of advertisement can be quite expensive. The cost of advertising is based on the number of exposures and the production of the message. The more people who will see or hear the ad, the higher the cost will be. The cost of airing a television commercial during the Super Bowl is much higher than the cost of running the same ad at 2:00 a.m. during the week.

The last factor in selecting advertising media is the message that is to be conveyed. A simple message can be displayed on a billboard, on the side of a bus, or on a dasher board in the local hockey rink. A more complicated message is better served by another type of medium. If a visual is needed, television might be the best choice. If the advertisement copy can make the product stand out from the description, radio or newspaper ads are favorable. If extensive detail is needed, a blog, newsletter, or direct-mail piece might be a better option.

Regardless of the message and the cost, arguably the most important aspect of choosing media is what part of the target market the media can reach. If you are incorrect on that part of the equation, then the other two do not matter, because your target market will not see the advertisement regardless of the cost or message.

## Sales Promotions

Sales promotions are coupons, trinkets, prizes, and other items that draw customers to a product (Kotler, Bowen, and Makens 2010). Sales promotions fall into four categories (Hurd, Barcelona, and Meldrum 2008):

- Promotional pricing: Coupons and gimmicks give consumers discounted products. They involve things such as half-priced tickets, discounted admission with a soda can, and early bird discounts.
- Free offers: These allow participation at no cost, such as free classes, free admission or parking, or free admission for children with adult admission.
- Prizes: These are trinkets of value that are given for participation. Prizes include bobble-head dolls, T-shirts, and door prizes.
- Celebrities: Celebrities are used to endorse products or attend events. People may participate because of this endorsement or opportunity to meet the celebrity.

Sales promotions are used in the short term to expose people to a product or to increase declining sales. Although they stimulate product use, the results are short lived and they do not build brand loyalty.

This event is being advertised in the park where it takes place. The purpose of this low-cost banner is to remind people of the event in hopes of initiating action.

## Personal Selling

Personal selling is direct, face-to-face communication with a person or group of people. Personal selling allows for relationship development with potential customers. It is useful for products that require detailed information or for customers who have questions about a product. Although selling has a negative connotation to some, it is a part of the service industry. Employees at the front desk, instructors, and leaders all use personal selling. Leisure services professionals do not use the same techniques that are used by a sales director for a major hotel or a local travel agent, but they do use personal selling in that they answer questions and help customers understand the value of the products at the agency.

## Publicity

Publicity is exposure for an agency that is not paid for or controlled by the agency itself. The agency can provide information to the media in the form of a **news release** (for print media) or a **public service announcement** (for broadcast media). The media then choose whether or not to use the information. The media dictate if, when, and how they run the information. Media staff also come upon information from other sources and may utilize it. This can include taking photos at programs and events for the newspaper or creating a story about the program after it occurs, describing what happened. Although this does not help attract attention to the program, it gets the agency name in front of the public and helps build the brand. In addition to positive publicity, negative publicity is also a reality. The media cover events such as a drowning at a pool, a camp bus accident, or the arrest of a staff member. This sort of publicity is beyond the direct control of the agency and requires the agency to have a crisis communication program (discussed later in the chapter).

Here are some examples of how promotions are used in marketing:

- Paying for advertisements on billboards, in newspapers, and on the radio
- Sending news releases to the local newspaper about an upcoming special event such as the Delray Beach Garlic Fest
- Giving the first 100 people in the gate for the ball game a free ball with the team logo
- Having the head softball coach from the local university throw out the first pitch at the state softball tournament

The marketing mix is powerful and requires much creativity to shape the message and select the means to promote the product. The marketing plan culminates in doing just that, and the promotions mix is the bulk of the marketing goals and strategies. It will change as the product moves through its life cycle (see table 11.3).

## Communication

The promotion part of the marketing mix is the communication piece. Many examples of how information can be communicated have already been given. However, there are a few other communication issues and tools that need to be discussed. The first issue is that all communication, whether it is a news release or newspaper ad, must adhere

**Table 11.3**   Marketing Strategies for the Product Life Cycle

| Product life cycle | Marketing strategies |
| --- | --- |
| Introduction | Use heavy promotions to expose people to the product, use free sessions and other coupons, and direct promotions toward educating the consumer. |
| Growth | Use word of mouth and continue heavily promoting the program to increase exposure. Begin advertising, especially as competition enters the market. |
| Maturation | Use advertising campaigns, focus on exposure and creating loyalty to the product, cut back on advertising and use reminders to loyal customers that the product still exists. |
| Saturation | Change advertising and promotional strategies so customers see something new. |
| Decline—death | Limit promotions to occasional reminder advertising. |
| Decline—petrification | Do minimal marketing, if anything at all. |
| Decline—extension | Combine introduction, growth, and maturation marketing strategies depending on the extension strategy used. |

Source: Hurd, Barcelona, and Meldrum 2008

to the values, vision, and mission of the agency. Furthermore, it has to help build the brand. Putting out information that is inconsistent with the agency can cause confusion about the brand and the true purpose of the agency. For example, a public parks and recreation agency would most likely not associate itself with an event that the community perceives to be a wild, out-of-control, alcohol-fueled party. Such an event does not adhere to the values, vision, and mission of parks and recreation agencies, and many people would question why taxpayer dollars are being used in this way. In another example, a YMCA prides itself on its Christian values. Running ads that appear to be risqué would be out of character and would confuse and possibly anger its members and the public.

Leisure services agencies in all three sectors are expected to respond to the needs of the public through programming, parks, facilities, product development, and much more. The public also expects to receive information and have contact with the agency when requested. The following sections describe the means of communication that agencies use on a regular basis.

### Public Meetings

Public meetings are held to provide information to the public and to get feedback from the public. This is an open forum for discussion on issues. Public meetings have an agenda and a staff person or another person associated with the agency on hand to facilitate the discussion.

### Speakers Bureaus

Agencies provide speakers who attend meetings and events to discuss various topics. An agency might have people who can talk about environmental ethics, playground safety, sustainable tourism, or general programs within the agency.

### Information Packets and Media Kits

Information packets and media kits are prepared for major events or for an agency as a whole. The purpose is to provide information to those needing it. It may be for newspaper articles, visitors in town for a softball tournament, or new residents to the community. Media kits include news releases, fliers, and in-depth background or historical information.

### News Conferences

News conferences are held when a major issue arises that is of concern to the media. It could be a crisis that requires the agency to make a statement, a new acquisition of land, or a company expanding or closing. News conferences often contain a prepared statement made by a spokesperson and occasionally involve a question-and-answer session.

### Social Media Marketing

Social marketing is rapidly changing and becoming increasingly more popular. Social media are Web-based marketing tools that allow for interaction and social development, such as Facebook, Twitter, blogs, YouTube, and others. Agencies use these elements in various ways. For example, the Plano (Texas) Parks and Recreation Department has a presence on YouTube; the Champaign (Illinois) Park District communicates with its volunteers via Facebook; there is a Facebook group for TR professionals to discuss issues in the field; the Sierra Rock Climbing School has a blog that discusses upcoming trips, certifications, and opportunities for lessons; and Nash County, North Carolina, uses Twitter to communicate with residents.

## Implementation, Monitoring, and Evaluation

Once the marketing plan has been developed, it must be implemented, monitored, and evaluated. Implementing the plan is not just the job of the marketing staff. It is the responsibility of all staff members, especially those who are assigned tasks within the goals and strategies section of the plan. Stotlar (2005) suggests a four-step process for implementing the marketing plan:

1. Identify the strategies to be completed that are detailed in the plan.
2. Establish the sequence in which the strategies are to be accomplished.
3. Estimate the amount of time each strategy will take.
4. Develop a calendar with the tasks and the allotted time built in. This calendar will show when things are to be accomplished and when work flow is lighter and heavier.

Hopefully, everything will go as planned, but that expectation is usually unrealistic in a changing profession like parks and recreation. The marketing plan is monitored throughout the time period that it covers and adjustments are made as needed. A key aspect of monitoring progress is to hold people accountable for their assigned responsibilities. Without this accountability, marketing goals will not be achieved.

The last piece of the marketing plan is evaluation. The monitoring aspect is a form of evaluation, but a formal evaluation of the plan and marketing efforts is needed. The plan can be evaluated monthly, quarterly, semiannually, or annually. Depending on the size of the agency, this time period will differ. Many agencies evaluate their marketing plans on a quarterly basis. This gives staff members ample time to implement some of the outlined strategies and to assess how well they are working.

Though the entire marketing plan is evaluated, certain aspects of it are evaluated more regularly for effectiveness. This is sometimes an overlooked aspect of marketing, but it is not overly complicated. Here are some ways to evaluate marketing:

- Hold focus groups with users and nonusers to ascertain how programs are meeting needs. Focus on the marketing mix and its effects.

- Use longitudinal program registration data if they are available for each program. They may show increases or decreases that can be aligned with marketing efforts.

- Track sales by using coupons. Use different coupon designs to mark different distribution routes and areas. This will indicate where people are seeing promotions about the product.

- Establish a phone line that people call for information on a specific product and advertise that number for the product. All calls on that line are known to derive from a specific advertisement. If a separate phone line is not available, place a line in the advertisement that says, "For more information, call Madison" (assuming that there is no Madison at the agency). All calls to this fictitious person are a result of the advertisement.

Marketing plans are extensive documents that are necessary to direct marketing efforts over a period of time. They aid leisure services providers in thoroughly understanding their community, their product, and their product promotion. A marketing plan is a time-consuming venture, but it is valuable to the agency if it is done well and implemented as designed. Following the steps described in this chapter will help with the planning process.

# Public Relations

Some aspects of marketing are not encompassed directly within the marketing plan. Public relations is one of those things. Some texts have 5 Ps in the marketing mix so that it includes public relations. From the description of the functions of public relations, it is easy to see how much of it does fit within the marketing mix, although other parts do not fit as well. **Public relations** is communication used to create a positive image for the agency's internal and external publics (Hurd, Barcelona, and Meldrum 2008). The external public comprises the community members, customers, and other stakeholders, whereas the internal public encompasses the staff members, board members, and volunteers associated with the agency. Public relations has three major elements: communication with the public, media relations, and crisis communication.

## Communication With the Public

Many topics within marketing come back to building the brand. Communication with the public is another means to create the brand and position it within the community. In addition, community relations helps to build the brand. Community relations involves outreach activities that are designed to create goodwill in the community and develop a positive relationship and image. For example, the National Basketball Association (NBA) has developed NBA Cares, a program that has NBA athletes go out into the community and raise money for various organizations. Some players also help support their own charitable organizations through NBA Cares. For example, Carlos Boozer of the Utah Jazz started a youth basketball camp in his hometown of Juneau (Alaska) for NBA Cares. To participate in the camp, children must pay a fee of $150, with part of the proceeds going to Boozer's Buddies, which supports families affected by sickle cell disease and funds treatment (Associated Press 2009).

Another organization that has many community outreach programs is the YMCA. For example, the YMCA of Southwestern Indiana has many programs to benefit the community, including a college prep program to help high school juniors and seniors navigate the college admissions process, a college tour program, a compute and shoot program that teaches the importance of school and living actively, and many others (YMCA of Southwestern Indiana n.d.). These are examples of positive activi-

Some agencies will hold special events, such as a race for visually impaired runners, in order to enhance their own image in the eyes of the community members.

ties in the community that also promote a positive image of and support for the agency.

Recreation agencies often serve as a resource center for all recreation opportunities in a community. If community members are not sure where they can find recreation services, they may begin by calling the agency that they think might have answers. Agencies should be prepared to offer information and suggestions on the various recreation opportunities in the community, even if the agency does not provide them. This means that if someone requests information on karate programs, the agency should give information about its own karate programs but also provide information on area karate studios if they better meet the needs of the constituents.

Much of marketing is focused on the external public, but this does not mean that the internal public should be ignored. Maintaining a constant stream of communication with employees is a way to enhance employee morale. In addition, it makes better-informed employees who can answer questions from the public, show that they are happy working for the organization, and promote the agency to the public themselves. Internal communication avenues include newsletters, blogs, meetings, reports, trainings, and e-mails.

Agencies must provide solid customer service. This means ensuring that the agency is customer

focused and that it responds to complaints, disputes, and protests. To address these situations, agencies should establish a process such as the following (Hurd et al. 2007):

1. Thoroughly listen to the customer's complaint or concern without making excuses and causing an argument. Sometimes customers just want to be heard by a staff member.

2. Let the customer know the complaint will be dealt with by the appropriate staff member and within a specific time frame. Complaints must be handled quickly. It shows the customer they are important to the agency.

3. Give the complaint to the appropriate staff member to handle. Complaints should be sent to the appropriate department. One person handling complaints agency-wide does not always result in the best solution to the situation.

4. Resolve the complaint to the best of the agency's ability.

5. Notify the customer of the resolution.

Keep in mind that not all customers will walk away happy with how their complaints are resolved. Following agency policy and using good judgment help an agency to succeed more often in terms of customer complaints.

## Media Relations

Creating a good working relationship with the media can go a long way in receiving positive publicity and fair handling of a crisis situation. Agencies can take a proactive, reactive, or interactive approach when working with the media (Gonring 1997).

A proactive approach to working with the media is used when the agency provides information to the media before an event or program. This includes news releases about upcoming activities, a press kit containing detailed information on a new product, or an advance tour of a new resort that is opening. All of these are designed to provide information so that the media will develop a story for their particular outlet.

A reactive approach to the media involves responding to requests. The media may request information on a program or issue, request an interview with a coach, ask for background information on a refurbished facility, or ask for a photo session with a star player. A quick and friendly response to requests enhances the relationship between the agency and the media.

Lastly, an interactive approach to the media involves cultivating a mutually beneficial relationship between the agency and the media. Television, radio, and print media have different deadlines. Therefore, when working with the media, it is important to consider these deadlines when planning news conferences or providing information prior to the news conference to media members who have early deadlines. This ensures all media members have information they can use. For example, the Mecklenburg County (North Carolina) Park and Recreation Department (MCPRD) hosts the Bark in the Park Dog Festival each year. It partners with a local television station, Cox Broadcasting, to offer the event. The following is a sample of some of the responsibilities of Cox Broadcasting and the MCPRD:

### Responsibilities of Cox Broadcasting

- Produce four commercials for the event with its anchors.
- Air approximately 200 spots for approximately a month before the event during higher-rated, prime-time broadcasts such as the 10 p.m. news and college basketball games.
- Place a link to the event on its Web site.
- Provide talent to emcee various portions of the event.
- Pay the MCPRD one-third of every event-related advertising package Cox Broadcasting sells to businesses who wish to receive the event TV spot tagged at the end with the message: "This spot is brought to you by. . . ."

### Responsibilities of MCPRD

- Place the TV sponsor logo on T-shirts, posters, billboards, banners, sponsor boards, and so on.
- Include TV sponsor in the event as much as possible.
- Provide TV sponsor with a 20- by 20-foot space at the event for them to set up a tent.
- Put a link to the TV sponsor's Web page on the official Bark in the Park page.
- Announce four times during the event that Cox Broadcasting is the official television sponsor of the event.
- Help advertising representatives sell airtime for the event to businesses who might want to have the TV spots tagged with their name at the end as a commercial sponsor.

## Crisis Communication

Crisis communication and media relations go hand in hand. A crisis is a situation that has the potential to cause unusually high media concern. An agency should always have a crisis management plan to help deal with negative situations. Here are some real-life headlines in which the situation required crisis management:

➤ A 32-year-old Shawnee Man Died Monday Saving a Drowning Child at the Chickasaw National Recreation Area (Staff Reports 2009)

➤ Zambelli CEO Talks About Worker's July 4th Fireworks Death: 19-Year-Old Father Dies in Accident at Park Display (The Pittsburgh Channel 2009)

➤ Coast Guard Hoists Injured Hiker From Olympic National Park (Kirotv.com 2009)

A crisis management plan has three distinct sections and serves as a guide in dealing with a crisis situation. These three sections include the

## Spokesperson Dos and Don'ts

Here are a few pointers to keep in mind when speaking to the media during a crisis:

- Do: Admit that a crisis has occurred but do not accept guilt until details are known.
- Do: Speak truthfully, authoritatively, and sincerely.
- Do: Have a prepared, written speech to read.
- Do: Highlight safety and rescue efforts made.
- Do: Anticipate questions and plan your responses to them.
- Don't: Be afraid to say "I don't know."
- Don't: Say "No comment." It looks as though you are guilty.
- Don't: Speak off the record.
- Don't: Become defensive when asked difficult questions.
- Don't: Speculate about what happened.
- Don't: Cover up or mislead the press.

following: Create a crisis management team, identify a spokesperson, and develop response strategies.

### Create a Crisis Management Team

The crisis management team is a compilation of upper-management employees who have authority to make decisions and can organize people in an efficient and effective manner. The team often consists of the CEO, department heads, and other key personnel such as marketing and risk management personnel. Sometimes external agencies, such as the insurance company, hospital, or police force, have representation on the crisis management team. This group follows preestablished response strategies and may be called upon to set up a news conference, serve as experts in certain situations, collect information, or monitor publicity. The group members must be well versed in the crisis management plan and put it into action immediately.

### Identify a Spokesperson

The crisis management team includes an assigned spokesperson. This person is often the CEO, public information officer, or sport information director. The spokesperson does not have to be the top person in the organization but should be the person best able to handle the media in a crisis. The media will ask difficult questions, and the spokesperson must remain calm and answer the questions as well as possible. The spokesperson should be comfortable in front of a camera, skilled at directing responses to another topic, respectful of the role of the reporters, believable, credible, and calm in stressful situations (Clawson Freeo 2009). In a crisis the spokesperson is the only person who speaks to the media on behalf of the agency. Too many people talking can make the agency look as though it does not know what is going on with the situation.

### Develop Response Strategies

The main purpose of the crisis management plan is to develop response strategies, or means to deal with the crisis. Response strategies outline how the crisis management team is contacted, how staff members are contacted, how the media are contacted, how victims' families are notified, what information needs to be collected, how to deal with specific situations (e.g., hurricanes, chemical spills, lockdown of a facility), what are the roles of each crisis management team member, and how to set up a news conference. Each of these sections is outlined in detail so the crisis management team knows what to do. All team members have responsibilities within these response strategies that they must carry out.

No agency wants to experience a crisis, but it is bound to happen at one point or another. When it does, the agency must be prepared. Having a good working relationship with the media will help the agency to better maneuver through the crisis.

## Conclusion

Marketing is a complex process that requires careful research and planning. It requires agencies to know who their customers are, what their customers want, and how to reach their customers. A haphazard approach is inefficient and ineffective because of the waste of resources. Marketing is challenging because of these same things, but it also allows for extreme creativity in designing messages and selecting media that reach the target market. Whether you have a marketing department or have to do it all as a programmer, you will benefit from a knowledge base in marketing. It allows you to design and implement the marketing plan yourself or to work with the marketing team. It is always helpful if the programmers can speak the language of the marketers and vice versa.

### Review Questions

1.  List the sections of a marketing plan and give a brief description of each section.
2.  What is market research? Why does an agency need to do market research?
3.  Define and differentiate branding and positioning. Explain the four-step branding process.
4.  Define public relations. What are the three main parts to public relations? Define them.
5.  Explain each step in the crisis communication process.

 Visit the online resource at www.HumanKinetics.com/TheParkAndRecreationProfessionalsHandbook for sample documents, keywords, activities and assignments, and more.

chapter 12

# Policies
# and Decision
# Making

**OUTCOMES**

- Distinguish among policies, standards, procedures, and rules.

- Demonstrate the policy development process.

- Apply the decision-making process.

Policies and decision making are implicitly intertwined. Policies are established to guide organizational behavior and are referred to when major decisions are made. Policies guide decisions in areas such as personnel, governance, facility use, and staff and participant conduct. This chapter details the process of establishing policies as well as the process of making decisions.

## Policies, Standards, Procedures, and Rules

Policies, standards, procedures, and rules are different levels of an established framework developed to guide actions and behaviors within an organization (see figure 12.1). These different levels have varying administrative controls and development processes. Some levels require board approval, whereas others are developed by middle and frontline staff members. Each level has a higher degree of authority within the organization and requires a higher approval process. Policies require board approval, whereas rules can be established at the staff level.

### Policies

Policies are the highest level of directives the agency can establish. They are "broad statements that provide direction for an organization and flow from its goals and objectives" (Hurd, Barcelona, and Meldrum 2008, 120). Situations within an organization often require standardized and consistent responses that come from an established policy. Policies also protect staff members and ensure they make the correct decisions. For example, the University of New Hampshire Department of Campus Recreation sport policy states that "all aquatic-oriented clubs (sailing, rowing) require members to pass a swimming skills test which is administered and certified by a Department of Campus Recreation employee. Members must also view a film reviewing hypothermia training" (University of New Hampshire Department of Campus Recreation 2009). This policy clearly states that no one is exempt from taking and passing the swimming skills test, regardless of claimed swimming experience.

Since policies guide processes and decision making, it is easy to question how policies differ from **administration** of the organization. This is a particularly difficult issue in public and nonprofit parks and recreation agencies when a governing board is involved. Boards have the ultimate responsibility to set policies and yet should be removed from day-to-day operations and management of the organization. The board sets policies that are in the best interest of the entire organization over the long term. The CEO of the organization carries out the policies set by the board and is responsible for the daily operation of the organization. Table 12.1 shows a few examples to help clarify the difference between policy and administration (Municipal Research and Services Center of Washington 2009). Because of the power of policies, there is an established process on policy making that is detailed later in the chapter.

### Standards

Standards are benchmarks established to indicate when a desired level has been achieved. It is difficult to set standards for things such as programs and events. However, standards can be implemented within programs and events. Standards of safety, cleanliness, staff attire, and respect for the environment can be implemented. For example, the **Leadership in Energy and Environmental Design (LEED)** has established standards for environmentally sustainable construction. The University of Maine recently opened a LEED-certified student recreation and fitness center. The university received certification due to design and construction practices such as using locally harvested stone, a customer service desk made of 100 percent recycled materials, low-flow plumbing fixtures, and recycled rubber sport floors (University of Maine Campus Recreation 2009).

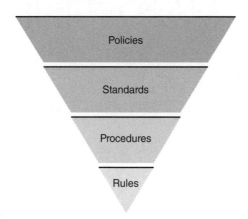

**Figure 12.1**    Policies have the highest level of authority within an organization, followed by standards, procedures, and rules.

**Table 12.1** Policy Versus Administration

| Policy | Administration |
|---|---|
| Set hiring practices. | Hire staff members. |
| Define the powers, functions, and duties of officers and employees. | Fill positions consistent with local ordinances. |
| Establish rental policies and regulations. | Implement rental policies and regulations. |
| Establish the staff dress code. | Implement the staff dress code. |

Here are a few more examples of standards that can be found in leisure services:

- ACA accreditation standards outline policies, procedures, and practices for camp operation, program quality, and the health and safety of campers and staff members (American Camp Association 2009).

- Starfish Aquatics Institute, an organization dedicated to aquatic safety and training, has standards for aquatic risk management, swim lesson instruction, lifeguard training, and water quality and management (Starfish Aquatics Institute 2010).

- State health boards set standards for safe food handling that should be implemented in restaurants and concession areas.

## Procedures

The next level of the policy framework is procedures. Procedures are specific steps or actions taken to implement a policy. For example, Ball State University Recreation Services has a detailed policy manual stating unacceptable behaviors within the Office of Recreation Services (figure 12.2). Within this policy are procedures that must be followed to ensure the policy is not broken (Ball State University 2009).

Many agencies have standard operating procedures that they follow. These standard operating procedures are detailed steps on how to handle specific situations. The procedures are rarely, if ever, deviated from. The Fort Benning (Georgia) Directorate of Family, Morale, Welfare, and Recreation has standard operating procedures for checking in and out rental equipment (figure 12.3).

Procedures are more expansive in that they result in a variety of manuals within an agency. These manuals are often labeled *operations manuals* and can cover safety and security, facilities, programs, and general operations. Individual manuals are developed for these areas because there are differences in each area that warrant individualized procedures. The following is a list of possible topics covered in a general operations manual (Hurd et al. 2007):

- Security issues such as opening and closing, emergency response, and evacuation

- Staffing issues such as number, qualifications and certifications, and patterns

- Utilization issues such as appropriate use of facilities and equipment and rental processes

- Inspection issues such as schedules, checklists, correction processes, and room-by-room participant counts

- Hazard issues such as removing or correcting real and potential hazards

Policies, standards, procedures, and rules should be a major topic during staff orientation and training.

### 6.2 Recreation Services Disciplinary Procedures

When a violation occurs within or adjacent to facilities of the Office of Recreation Services or in the context of programs sponsored by the Office of Recreation Services, the following disciplinary procedures apply.

#### 6.2.1 Preliminary Meeting

a. Pending results of an investigative review of an incident, the student's ID or recreation privilege card will be turned off and the student will not have the privilege of utilizing facilities or programs within Recreation Services.

b. A preliminary meeting will be convened in a timely manner with the student in question and a designated Recreation Services staff person (Graduate Assistant or Assistant Director for Recreation Services) to discuss the incident.

c. The student may plead responsible for the behavior and the staff member may assign sanctions.

d. If a student pleads not responsible for the behavior, the case will be referred to an administrative hearing.

e. Students who fail to appear for a preliminary meeting will have their case referred to an administrative hearing.

#### 6.2.2 Recreation Services Administrative Hearing

a. Administrative hearings are conducted by a designated Recreation Services staff person (Assistant Director or Associate Director for Recreation Services). Students will be given the opportunity to present witnesses or other evidence to support their claims. The staff person conducting the hearing will determine responsibility and, if necessary, assign sanctions.

b. A written notice indicating the findings of the hearing and sanctions will be mailed to the student's known address.

c. When a violation is believed to be a team violation, that team may be represented at the administrative hearing by the team captain or another designated team member. Sanctions may be administered collectively to the team or individually against team members.

#### 6.2.3 Sanctions

Final disciplinary decisions may result in any combination of the following:

a. Official reprimand—Statement of warning provided verbally or in writing stating that the continuation of or repetition of unacceptable behavior may lead to further disciplinary action.

b. Suspension—Suspension from Recreation Services facilities or programs for a predetermined period of time.

c. Forfeiture—Forfeiture of any outcomes of previous activities.

d. Restitution—Requirement to provide monetary reimbursement for restoration or replacement of public or private property damaged or for medical bills related to injuries to another person.

e. Disciplinary probation—A specified period of time during which the student must demonstrate a willingness and ability to conform to all university regulations. Any violation of university policy while on disciplinary probation may result in referral to the university review board with the possibility of suspension or expulsion from the university.

**Figure 12.2** Ball State University details its Recreation Services disciplinary process.

### 6.2.4 Appeal Process

a. Students have an opportunity to appeal any decision of discipline from any member of the Recreation Services staff.

b. All appeals of disciplinary decisions *must* be made in writing within three business days of the receipt of the original decision and must be sent directly to the Associate Director of Recreation Services.

c. A student may appeal based on the following reasons:

1. A substantial procedural error that unreasonably impaired the student or the hearing body

2. An unduly harsh sanction against the accused student

3. New and substantive information not available at the original hearing

4. Information of substantial bias on the part of the disciplinary body hearing the case

d. An appeal may be resolved in one of the following ways:

1. The original decision may be upheld.

2. Modified sanctions, either greater or lesser, may be imposed.

3. The case may be remanded back for a new hearing.

4. All allegations may be dismissed.

e. Appeal decisions shall be based solely upon the written documentation of the incident and a written statement of appeal from the patron.

f. The appellate decision shall be final and will not be subject to any further appeal.

### 6.2.5 Referrals to the Office of Student Rights and Community Standards

Any case may be referred to the Office of Student Rights and Community Standards for adjudication or for consideration of additional sanctions when the following occurs:

a. Violations are of a more serious nature and may warrant consideration of probation, suspension, or expulsion from the university.

b. The complexity and nature of the violation warrant referral.

**Figure 12.2** *(continued)*

An operations manual is updated regularly and requires input from many levels within the organization. For example, staff members who have the responsibility of opening and closing a facility should be involved in reviewing and adjusting these procedures.

## Rules

Rules are derived from policies and procedures and guide specific behaviors within a program, facility, league, and so on (figure 12.4). For example, games and sports have rules, and these rules detail what can and cannot be done as well as what happens when rules are broken.

It is not uncommon to have different sets of rules governing different activities within the agency. Not all programs, events, or facilities could adhere to only one set of rules. Rules are specific to the activity at hand.

As you can see, there are different levels within the umbrella of policy making. Each level has different power and responsibilities in guiding behaviors and decision making. Policies direct all other levels, have the most power, and are set by policy-making boards in the nonprofit and public sectors. Procedures detail how a policy is carried out; rules pertain to individual programs, events, and facilities and outline acceptable and unacceptable behavior and associated consequences. Lastly, standards delineate benchmarks to achieve and can be determined internally or externally. Not all situations that arise can be addressed by referring to one of these policy levels. However, these policy levels guide staff members in making informed

## Sample Equipment Check-In Procedure

a. Each customer must take all rental items to the warehouse to check the items back in with a recreation assistant.

b. The customer is responsible for unloading all items from their vehicle to the warehouse or storage area.

c. A recreation assistant will inspect all rental items to note any damage, missing parts, or lack of cleanliness.

d. If there is any damage or missing part or if items need to be cleaned, the recreation assistant will inform the customer that there will be a cleaning or damage fee, whichever applies.

e. A recreation assistant may reject any rental item being returned due to lack of cleanliness. If the customer wishes to keep items to clean them, the items are still due by the date and time stated on the receipt. Late fees will apply to all rental items that are returned after the due date and time.

f. A recreation assistant will give the customer the warehouse copy of the receipt if the customer doesn't bring the customer copy when returning items. This copy will be stamped by a recreation assistant as received and noted with any damages, cleaning, or missing parts.

g. The customer and recreation assistant will review and sign off the checklist for campers and inflatables at the time of check-in.

h. The customer must return to the ODR office to close out the rental items with the ODR front desk. If the customer fails to confirm with the front desk that the rental items have been received by ODR, the customer will accrue late fees until it is confirmed that the customer has returned all rental items in satisfactory condition.

i. The customer must present government ID to the ODR Front Desk Staff and the copy of the stamped receipt. If a refund is due to the customer, the ODR staff will process it accordingly; the refund will be the same form of payment as the deposit. The only exception is checks; checks are given back as cash. Cash refunds up to $100 will be issued from ODR. Cash refunds over $100 will be processed through Red River; the first $100 is given to the customer as cash, then the remaining amount is issued in check form by Red River within two weeks and is mailed directly to the customer's address currently on file.

j. If money is owed to ODR, payment must be made at that time by the customer.

k. The customer will receive a final receipt showing the transaction and show a $0 balance.

l. A copy of all rental receipt transactions will be kept by the ODR office.

**Figure 12.3**    The Fort Benning Directorate of Family, Morale, Welfare, and Recreation Outdoor Recreation (ODR) and Equipment Resource Center (2009) has a check-in procedure for rental equipment.

Reprinted from Fort Benning Directorate of Family, Morale, Welfare, and Recreation, 2009, *Standard Operating Procedures (SOP)*, Available: http://www.benningmwr.com/documents/crd/Equipment%20Check-in%20Procedures.pdf

decisions. Employees can refer to past acceptable behaviors and similar policies to make decisions in the absence of clear policy.

# Policy Development Process

If a board exists within a leisure services agency, as it does in public, private nonprofit, and some commercial agencies, it will have the ultimate policy-making responsibility. However, in most cases the board does not actually develop the policy. The staff members have this responsibil-

ity, with final approval coming from the board. In situations where the agency is a small commercial entity, policies are set by the business owners. The following sections outline a seven-step process for policy development (figure 12.5). Depending on the sector and the board, this process may be adapted to fit an agency's needs.

## Step 1: Assess Needs and Existing Conditions

When discussion begins about the need for a policy, it is usually the result of a few situations that have occurred and need to be addressed.

## Elk Meadow Lodge and RV Resort Rules for Visitors

### Check-In and Check-Out
Check-in for RV sites is 12 p.m., and check-out is 11:00 a.m. If you are staying in a cabin or cottage or renting the RV, please note that check-in begins at 3:00 p.m. and check-out is at 10:00 a.m.

### Fireworks
For the safety of all guests, fireworks are prohibited on all resort property.

### Quiet Time
Everyone deserves a good night's sleep. Please move about quietly between the hours of 10:30 p.m. and 7:00 a.m.

### Vehicle Repair and Washing
Please refrain from washing your vehicles or RVs on-site. Our knowledgeable staff can direct you to nearby facilities. Also, no repair work, including changing the oil, is permitted on resort property.

### Cancellations
Need to cancel your trip? Deposits are nonrefundable. However, you will receive a credit equal to the amount of your deposit that is valid for up to 14 months from the date of cancellation.

**Figure 12.4** The Elk Meadow Lodge and RV Resort in Estes Park (Colorado) has rules to guide visitors (Elk Meadow Lodge and RV Resort 2009).

Adapted from Elk Meadow Lodge & RV Resort, 2009, *Resort Policies* (Estes Park, CO). Available: http://essentialcoloradorv.com/elk-meadow/resort-policies.cfm

Policy needs can be dictated by a change in technology, the building of a new facility, growth in the community, or the need to change the way business is being done. If policy is going to be developed or revised, then an issue should be present. Policy is not created for the sake of having a policy. There must be some existing condition that needs to be addressed to justify policy making. To illustrate the process, let's walk through an example that addresses an issue that has been prevalent in all sectors lately: personal computer use at work.

*Example*
Need and existing condition: The technology department has determined that staff members spend an average of an hour a day on Facebook. While some staff members have a need to use this Web site for their work responsibilities, most are using it for personal reasons.

## Step 2: Define Goals and Objectives

Goals and objectives are a recurring theme throughout the leisure services field, from programming and planning to decision making and policy making. In policy making goals are developed to give overall ideas of what should be accomplished with the policy. The goals take into consideration the need for the policy and what is currently happening. The objectives are a means to measure the success of the goal. Going back to our Facebook example, here is a sample of a goal and its objectives:

*Example*

Goal: Develop a policy to manage staff member use of Facebook.

Objective: Regulate use of Facebook to enable marketing staff members to use this social medium.

Objective: Limit personal use of Facebook during work hours.

Objective: Include other forms of social networking that should be regulated.

Remember that ultimately a policy needs goals and objectives so that its relevance is clear. If a policy does not have a purpose, then it should not exist.

## Step 3: Involve Stakeholders

When it comes to policy formation, **stakeholders** can include the general public, specific users or participants, staff members, and board members.

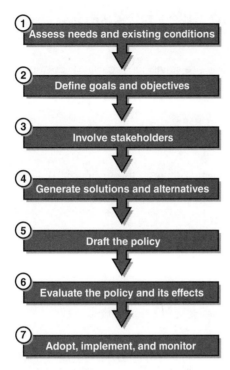

**Figure 12.5** Policy development requires working through a seven-step process.

Selecting the stakeholders to involve in the process depends on the situation at hand. For example, the Facebook situation would probably not benefit from getting input from the general public. It is an issue best handled internally. Policy changes that affect user groups, such as field rental policies, should involve the affected groups. Groups affected either positively or negatively should be included. A one-sided representation can lead to poor policy making.

Stakeholders can be involved in several ways. Here are a few examples (Hurd et al. 2007):

- Citizen advisory groups such as the Fairfax (Virginia) Parks and Recreation Advisory Board, the Parkland (Florida) Teen Advisory Group, and the Calgary Community Advisory Group for the Northwest Calgary Recreation Centre Project
- Citizen task forces that investigate a specific issue and provide a report to the agency
- Public hearings and meetings to give community members an opportunity to share their thoughts
- Questions placed on the ballot for voters to decide (this is the ultimate form of public

input and is done for major issues rather than small policy decisions)
- Focus groups held with selected stakeholders
- Surveys of community members conducted through e-mail, mail, telephone, or personal interview

The staff members listen and gather information that can be used to develop solutions. Different stakeholder groups can bring numerous perspectives to issues that the staff members alone may not foresee. Furthermore, if the public is involved in the process, there is a base of support the agency may be able to count on as the policy moves through the process of implementation.

## Step 4: Generate Solutions and Alternatives

Once the goals, objectives, and public input have been completed, solutions are generated. Developing only one solution may be appropriate, but if the policy has the potential to affect a wide number of people, several solutions should be developed. If the policy is important enough to involve stakeholders, then it probably requires several alternatives.

A common mistake that committees make—and policy development is not exempt from this—is to lock into one solution right away and get busy developing that solution rather than looking at alternatives. If the solution is clear cut, then this is acceptable practice. In general, parks and recreation agencies are quite willing to share resources and ideas with each other. Policies are no different. When investigating possible solutions, ask agencies like yours for their sample policies. These samples can help you see how other agencies handle similar situations.

If multiple solutions are developed, they each need to be evaluated based on the goals and objectives established. In addition, budget, available resources such as staff and technology, and the ability to enforce the policy should be considered. In our Facebook example, if the policy requires strict monitoring of employee computers or requires software prohibiting Facebook access, then the agency needs to consider whether it has the staff hours and knowledge to implement this policy as well as the money to purchase the software. Each solution is considered and the best solution is selected.

## Step 5: Draft the Policy

Once a solution is determined, the policy is drafted. Drafting policy can be tedious and time consuming. After all, it dictates future processes and decision making within the organization.

There are a couple of different approaches to drafting a policy. First, look at the existing policy manual to understand how current policies are written. Usually policies follow a set format and are written in a consistent language. Second, decide who will draft the policy. Will it be drafted by a committee or by one or two individuals? Lastly, review the draft. Rarely does one person draft the policy and then send it directly to the board. Usually one or two people draft the policy, have key staff members or a policy committee review it and make suggestions, and then redraft the policy.

The specific situation will dictate how to handle the drafting process. Major policy changes can require review by stakeholders, just as their input was gathered when initially writing the policy. It can also be beneficial to ask staff members not involved in the drafting process to examine the policy. An outsider's perspective can provide good insight into potential weaknesses.

### *Example*

Using the Facebook example, the staff committee developed the following policy: No staff other than marketing staff and select administrative staff will have access to any social networking Web sites (e.g., Facebook, MySpace). Staff members with access to these sites may use these sites if they are doing so as part of their duties as a member of this agency.

## Step 6: Evaluate the Policy and Its Effects

Once the draft is complete, a final evaluation of the policy and its effects are undertaken. This process ultimately depends on the staff members. They are asked to review the policy and uncover any potential effects it may have on the agency and the stakeholders. It is imperative to analyze the policy from many different perspectives while considering what happened in the past that triggered the need for a policy, what could happen in the future, and how this new policy might conflict with any existing policies within the organization.

Ultimately there are trade-offs with a new policy or a policy revision. Usually there are some

Implementing a new policy sometimes results in changes to standards, procedures, and rules.

people who do not like the policy, but if it betters a situation, streamlines a process, or is in the best interest of the agency and community, then it is warranted. Furthermore, policies are designed to last several years and are not just a short-term solution to fix a fleeting problem.

## Step 7: Adopt, Implement, and Monitor the Policy

Within an agency, the policy-making process should be clearly outlined within the policy manual. When a board is the ultimate policy-making body, the drafted policy is presented to the board for feedback. Once the policy is acceptable to the board members, they formally adopt it. Once the policy is adopted, the staff members have the responsibility for determining how to implement the policy. Any new policy should be monitored closely to ensure it is working properly. The evaluation process, feedback on the draft, and initial consideration of possible solutions often expose potential pitfalls within a policy. However, this is not always the case. If a policy needs to be adjusted, it is redrafted and sent before the board for approval once again.

An important element of the implementation process is informing the general public, especially those affected by the policy, that a change has been made. The general public does not need a copy of the entire policy manual from an agency—nor is providing everyone in the public with a copy a feasible task. Here are several means of informing the public of a policy (Hurd et al. 2007):

- Place of copy of the policy manual online for the public to read.
- Post selected rules, policies, and procedures in facilities and in program brochures.
- Have a copy of the policy manual available for those who are interested in reading it.
- Train staff members on the rationale behind policies so that they can convey the rationale to the public

## Policy Review and Revision

The policy-making process detailed in this chapter thus far has focused on developing new policies. However, much of policy making is reviewing and revising existing policies. For example, the Commission for Accreditation of Park and Recreation Agencies has policy review as one of its fundamental standards:

➤ **1.4.1 Policy Manual**
    *Standard:* There shall be a manual setting forth the agency policies, which is kept up-to date, reviewed systematically, at least every five years, by the administration, and made available to pertinent administrative and supervisory personnel. (Commission for Accreditation of Park and Recreation Agencies 2009, 4)

As with most other agency processes, policy dictates how often policies are reviewed and revised. The leisure services profession is always changing, and policies can easily become outdated. When this happens they must be revised or removed. The revision process is essentially the same as the development process, but it is often done internally by staff members or a conglom-

eration of staff members and stakeholders. They draft a new policy that is reviewed and ultimately approved by the board. Keep in mind that, with the exception of standards, when moving down the policy framework, the likelihood of revising each level increases.

# Decision-Making Process

Decision making is a much-needed and important competency for everyone in a leisure services organization, from the entry-level employee to the CEO (Hurd 2005). We face different decisions every day. Some are simple or routine. Others require a lot of thought, investigation, and weighing of the pros and cons of specific actions. Policy making, decision making, and problem solving are discussed together because they are so interrelated. Policies are established to guide staff members in decision making and problem solving. However, not all decisions and problems are policy driven.

Decision making and problem solving are closely intertwined. Problem solving is moving from a current state to a more desirable state. Decision making, on the other hand, is selecting a solution from possible alternatives to a problem or situation. While problem solving requires decision making in order to reach a desired state, not all decision making addresses a problem. For example, students have many decisions to make before going to their first class—what time to get up, whether to shower, what to wear, what to have for breakfast, and how to get to class. Decisions like these are routine and do not take much thought, and they do not address problems. It is the decisions that are not routine or easy that require much more contemplation, most often because they require trade-offs and carry a risk of failure.

The leisure services industry is going through many changes right now due to the economy, technology, and aging baby boomers, among other things. Leisure services professionals are a tightly networked group who rely on each other for advice in solving problems and making decisions. Sometimes decisions require investigating what others do in order to gain guidance. For example, the Center for Parks and Recreation (www.cprpcenter.org) is an online forum for leisure services professionals to discuss issues and get advice on things happening in their community. Current issues under discussion include budget cuts, branding, legal liability, diversity in the outdoors, and training entry-level professionals. Contributors give advice; recommend resources; or share articles, books, and other sources of information.

Although there are numerous resources available, there is a need to organize the available information in order to come to a good decision. The decision-making process is one mechanism for accomplishing this task (figure 12.6).

The six steps of the decision-making process are described in the following sections. To better illustrate this process, each section addresses a problem and the decisions to be made using the decision-making process. Following this process and meticulously gathering information to make the best decision possible are key to obtaining a quality result.

## Step 1: Identify and Define the Problem

Identifying and defining the problem may sound overly simplistic. However, doing so is the key to getting to the proper solution. The difficulty of this step lies in determining what the real problem is. Our experiences, perspectives, and job demands can distort our views of a situation. Two people

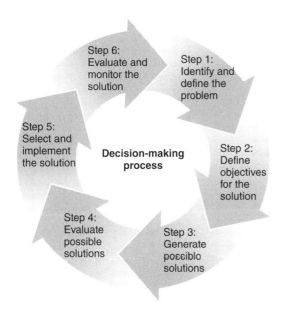

**Figure 12.6** The decision-making process is a six-step process that moves a person through all aspects of decision making.

Reprinted, by permission, from A. Hurd, R. Barcelona, and J. Meldrum, 2008, *Leisure services management* (Champaign, IL: Human Kinetics), 157.

observing the same issue can see it under a completely different light. These differences can cause people to solve the wrong problem or attempt to correct the wrong element.

Suppose, for example, that a manager observes that the agency registration line is always too long and that staff members are talking with customers about many different things, thus increasing each customer's stay at the counter. The manager's perspective is that there are not enough staff members available to handle the customers and that the staff members are spending too much time on idle chitchat. The manager feels the staff members should be courteous but not so engaging. However, had the manager looked more closely at the situation and asked the staff members about the problem, they would have shared that the computer server is slow and delays processing. During the delay, the staff members talk with customers so they do not realize how slow the system is. Imagine the resources wasted if the manager ends up hiring new staff members instead of upgrading the server.

Good managers observe the situation, but they also gather information to determine what the deep-seated issue is so that they can solve the correct problem. Uncovering the real problem requires three actions. The first is to examine the situation from an outsider's perspective (Harvard Business Essentials 2006). That perspective might come from the customers, board members, or staff members involved in the issue. For example, the manager described earlier might ask a trusted colleague to go through the registration process. The colleague will have an unbiased opinion and will probably notice the inability of the server to keep up with the demands of the agency. The second action is to talk with staff members about the situation and to ask a lot of questions to help reveal the problem as it is rather than as it is perceived. The last action is to try to find dissenting opinions on the problem. This means seeking a multitude of perspectives. Information gained from each may lead to the true core of the problem.

### Example

A new 170,000 square-foot student recreation center is being built on campus. The total cost is $44 million and will be funded by student fees and bonds issued by the university. Once the facility is open, it is expected that the facility will break even. A large portion of the revenue will come from membership fees. Students are paying their membership through a mandatory student recreation fee that is part of their tuition bill. There

Managers constantly seek ways to better serve customers. Some issues require simple solutions while others require extensive problem solving and a major decision.

are 25,000 students on campus, and the budget is limiting the size of the facility and its ability to meet the needs of the students. The new facility will be a vast improvement over the old one, but the recreation services staff is afraid the facility will be too small before the doors even open two years down the road.

The facility is being built on the main thoroughfare in the community, so the whole city is anxiously awaiting its opening. Already alumni and community members are questioning whether they will be allowed to use the facility.

The recreation services staff has been charged with developing a use plan for the building. This plan should address student, faculty, staff, alumni, and community access to the fitness portion of the facility.

## Step 2: Define Objectives for the Solution

The objectives for the solution are the benchmarks that determine whether the solution is achieved. The objectives focus on the end results and are used to evaluate each of the potential solutions. Essentially, the objectives answer the question, "What are we trying to achieve?" Objectives can include the following:

- Make a decision that is in the best interest of the community.
- Use resources efficiently.
- Maintain quality programs and an expected level of service.
- Enhance public perception of the agency.

Good objectives take into account all stakeholders, including the staff, community, and board members (and owners, if there are any).

### Example

The following are objectives for the solution to the new facility use plan the recreation services staff must create:

- Meet the recreation needs of the students.
- Consider financial feasibility of increasing and decreasing user groups.
- Develop a policy that is in the best interest of the university.

## Step 3: Generate Possible Solutions

If a manager is faced with a difficult decision, then it must have more than one solution. If there is only one solution, then going through the decision-making process is not very useful, because there is no decision to make. Good decision making requires examining several possibilities. Some of these possibilities will be better than others, and sometimes an unlikely solution will have more merit than originally thought.

The need to generate numerous solutions cannot be overstated. There is a popular management term called **groupthink** that describes how idea generation can be stifled within a group. Groupthink occurs when group members readily agree on a solution without thoroughly analyzing other options due to the need to conform and agree. When groupthink happens the group members look at fewer alternatives, are not critical of each other's ideas, do not gather enough information to make good decisions, hide the information that goes against the group decision, feel infallible and take excessive risks, pressure dissenters into remaining quiet, and assume that the majority view is unanimous (Janis 1972).

To prevent groupthink, group members need to keep an open mind and look for alternative solutions. Generating ideas for a solution can be challenging. There are three techniques that are commonly used in business to generate ideas: the nominal group technique and the Delphi technique, which are discussed in chapter 4, and brainstorming. All three of these can be used to generate solutions to problems, develop ideas for programs, or plan for the future.

Brainstorming is best done in a small group of no more than 10 people. The facilitator, who is a neutral party, asks the group members to give ideas about a certain topic. The group members give suggestions, and often the suggestions build on the ideas of others. There are two rules in brainstorming: Generate as many ideas as possible, and never evaluate ideas during the brainstorming session. Evaluation comes later in the process. The facilitator carefully monitors the session to stop any criticism, as criticism can stifle creativity. Knowing that the risk of being criticized is minimal, people can be freer with their ideas. The facilitator must also ensure that the group does not get stuck on one train of thought or wander away from the intended topic. This can happen if the group has too much fun with this exercise.

Brainstorming can result in many ideas, which are then categorized so they may be discussed by the group. As discussion ensues, some ideas may be eliminated or combined and improved upon. Brainstorming is used not only to generate solutions to problems but also to create new programs, enhance special events, and develop program or facility names.

*Example*

The following solutions were generated to solve the problem of creating a facility use plan for the new student recreation center:

- Allow students to use all aspects of the facility, including programs and events, for free. Charge faculty and staff members a monthly membership fee and exclude alumni and community members.

- Charge students a reduced rate for programs and faculty and staff members a full rate for programs in addition to a monthly membership fee. Exclude alumni and community members.

- Have a three-tiered membership system in which students use the facility for free, faculty and staff members pay a reduced membership rate, and alumni and community members pay the full monthly rate.

## Step 4: Evaluate Possible Solutions

Once possible solutions are identified, they are evaluated based on the objectives established in step 2. This requires the people involved to look at the solutions from many different perspectives, play devil's advocate, and think beyond the current situation to the future of the organization. Harvard Business Essentials (2006) lists several variables to consider when assessing the quality of the potential solutions:

- Costs and finances: Consider how the solution will affect the current and future budgets. Look at the total cost and any hidden costs that might arise. Also look at the monetary costs and benefits and how the solution will affect cash flow. Finally, consider the cash investment needed to implement the solution.

- Benefits: Determine what benefits the solution brings in terms of products and services, staff members, and customers.

- Intangibles: Evaluate how the solution will affect company image, employee motivation, and customer satisfaction.

- Time: Consider the length of time needed to implement the solution. Anticipate expected and unexpected delays.

- Feasibility: Evaluate how realistic the solution is, what obstacles will impede its implementation, and what resistance may arise among staff members and customers.

- Resources: Beyond the issue of costs, consider other resources needed, namely staff resources.
- Risk: Measure the risk that is an inherent element in many solutions. Take the time to determine how to reduce this risk, because doing so can make a difference in the solution choice.
- Ethics: Evaluate whether the solution will help the agency to uphold its responsibility

to do what is right and in the best interest of itself and the people it serves. In some situations a solution may not be one that the agency wants to share with its constituency. If so, contemplate whether it is a good solution.

Keeping all of these variables and the stated objectives in mind, the decision makers must evaluate each solution by measuring pros and cons. This process brings the positives and negatives to the forefront and examines the trade-offs that are made for the solution. Let's go back to our

**Table 12.2**   Pros and Cons of Possible Solutions

| Solutions | Pros (+) | Cons (–) |
|---|---|---|
| Allow students to use all aspects of the facility, including programs and events, for free. Charge faculty and staff members a monthly membership fee and exclude alumni and community members. | 1. Takes into consideration that students already pay fees to support the building<br>2. Provides opportunities for university employees<br>3. Minimizes the number of people utilizing a facility that is already too small<br>4. Provides added benefit to working at the university | 1. May still need to consider that student fees do not cover the entire cost of the fitness area<br>2. May anger faculty and staff members by asking them to pay membership fees<br>3. May anger alumni and community members by preventing them from using something that is a part of the community<br>4. May alienate potential donors to the university<br>5. Students who do not use the facility still have to pay for it |
| Charge students a reduced rate for programs and faculty and staff members a full rate for programs in addition to a monthly membership fee. Exclude alumni and community members. | 1. Makes it so that students who use the facility are the ones actually paying for it<br>2. Students pay for "extras" such as programs if they want them<br>3. Provides opportunities for university employees to use the facility<br>4. Minimizes the number of people utilizing a facility that is already too small | 1. May anger students because they already pay fees that should cover all programs<br>2. May anger faculty and staff members by asking them to pay membership and program fees<br>3. May anger alumni and community members by preventing them from using something that is a part of the community<br>4. May alienate potential donors to the university<br>5. Students who do not use the facility still have to pay for it |
| Have a three-tiered membership system in which students use the facility for free, faculty and staff members pay a reduced membership rate, and alumni and community members pay the full monthly rate. | 1. Reduces cost for a group who has minimal resources (students)<br>2. Gives faculty and staff members a benefit of working at the university<br>3. Enhances relationships with the community and alumni<br>4. Increases revenue | 1. May lead to potential overuse of a facility that is already too small<br>2. Students may feel they cannot fully use a facility they are not required to pay for<br>3. Students who do not use the facility still have to pay for it |

## Decision-Making Scenario

The CEO of an agency assembles a group of staff members to be on the hiring committee for the new recreation director. The recreation director reports directly to the CEO, who has the ultimate decision on whom to hire. The hiring committee follows the hiring process outlined in the policy manual and selects two candidates to bring in for interviews. One candidate is internal to the agency and one is external to the agency. The committee feels that both candidates would do the job well but that the internal candidate is a stronger candidate for the position, since she has been doing the job well for two years as the interim recreation director. The committee puts together a list of pros and cons for each candidate. The committee members assume they know who the CEO will choose based on their recommendations. However, the CEO chooses the external candidate. The hiring committee is shocked and angered at the decision, but given the chain of command, the CEO has the ultimate decision-making authority.

registration example. Improving the speed of the server will make the registration line go faster, but a trade-off is that the staff members will not have time to chat with customers as much. Some customers value that face time, because it makes them feel important to the agency.

Thoroughly evaluating each solution is imperative to selecting the right one or at least to improving the chances for success. Even with a well-constructed evaluation process, many decisions still have an element of uncertainty that is unknown until the decision is implemented.

### Example

To help the decision makers, table 12.2 lists the pros and cons of the solutions for creating a facility use plan for the new student recreation center.

## Step 5: Select and Implement the Solution

The fifth step in the decision-making process is to select and implement the solution. Once the evaluation process is complete, a solution may become obvious. If there is no obvious solution, the decision makers will have to select the one they feel is best for all stakeholders. There may be extensive discussion, debate, and sometimes a range of emotions preceding that decision, but ultimately a decision must be made based on the information available.

If a group has the responsibility of making a decision, selecting one that every group member agrees with can be difficult. As such, a decision-making process is implemented. Decisions can be unanimous or can be made by a majority vote. On the other hand, the leader of the group can make the decision after discussion with the group (Kaner et al. 2007). While unanimous decisions appear to have the full support of everyone involved, they can fall victim to groupthink. A majority vote produces a win–lose solution in which those who won the vote feel they were successful and those who lost the vote feel they were disregarded. The last option when making a group decision is for the person in charge to make the final decision. This option is used quite often, especially if the person in charge has a high level of authority in the organization. This person is the one who controls the resources and has the responsibility of failure and success (Kaner et al. 2007). If the person making the decision follows the recommendation of the group, the group members are happy and supportive. They feel that their input was valued by their leader and that the decision was a true collaborative effort. However, the leader might go against the group as well. If this happens, the group can become angry, feel their opinions do not matter, and question if this assignment was a good use of their time.

Once the decision is made, it is implemented. Key to implementation is communication. Major decisions often involve people with varying opinions who can be upset when they believe that a wrong decision is made. The person in charge of the decision-making group or agency must communicate with everyone involved—especially those included in the process and those directly affected by the decision. Communicating the decision involves developing an action plan, anticipating resistance, and explaining the solution.

First is developing the action plan, which outlines how the decision will be implemented. A solution can go into effect right away, can be phased in, or can be implemented on a specified date.

Second is addressing resistance. Some resistance to the decision is inevitable. Change brings about a variety of emotions in people. Some people are committed to the change and are eager to embrace the decision. Others are compliant. They know and accept the decision but hold back any opinions until the decision is implemented and they can see for themselves that it was the right thing to do. These people make up the wait-and-see group. Finally, there are some people who resist the decision. These people may make many claims, such as "We have always done it this way." "We did this before and it didn't work." "It won't work here." "The customers won't like it." Some people in the resistance group never come around to embrace the decision, while others take some time getting used to the change and then accept it.

Moving people from resistance to commitment or compliance requires the decision makers to communicate the solution. Here are some suggestions for communicating a decision to all groups involved (and not just those who are resisting):

- Make known the pros and cons of the decision. There is no doubt that staff members will question some of the negatives, just as the decision makers did during the decision-making process. Demonstrating to the staff members that the negatives were considered in the decision-making process can build support for the decision.

- Use facts to support the decision. It is essential to be honest about the effects the decision will have on the agency and its customers. Providing the facts can help clarify the reasons for the decision in terms of economics, benefits, and resources, among other things.

- Build on the support of those who are committed to the decision. Ask these people to discuss the decision with those who are resistant. This may lead to a lively discussion, but it also can help both sides see the decision from a different perspective.

- Do not rush and push compliance and commitment. Provide information and facts and allow those resisting to mull over the decision based on what they know. Some people naturally start with resistance but are open to gathering information and making their own decision once they have all of the information.

### Example

The university has decided to charge students a reduced rate and faculty and staff members a full rate and to exclude alumni and community members. Once this decision is made, recreation services must have a plan in place for implementing the policy and communicating the decision to students, faculty, staff, community members, and alumni.

## Step 6: Evaluate and Monitor the Solution

The last step in the decision-making process is to evaluate and monitor the solution. Simply implementing the solution and forgetting about it assumes that it was the absolute right thing to do. This is a rare situation. Once a decision is implemented, its effects should be observed to see whether it meets the initial objectives, achieves the proper outcomes, and is in the best interest of the agency and its customers. If the decision is not doing what it is supposed to do, the decision makers may have to go back through the decision-making process to look for a new solution or a modification to the current decision.

### Example

The recreation services staff members will monitor use patterns. If they find that occupancy rates are too low, then they can consider allowing alumni and community members to use the facility. Likewise, if revenue goals are not being met, they can consider including alumni and community members in order to increase revenue.

A new facility such as a recreation center will require many decisions to be made. Not all of them will be popular with users, staff, and board members.

## Conclusion

Policy making and decision making are closely related issues that affect how an agency operates. Policy formation and implementation influence how decisions are made and what processes are followed within an organization. Often major policies and decisions involve more than one staff member. Involving many people provides a multitude of perspectives. Both policy making and decision making can rely on just staff members or can interject the perspectives of the users or stakeholders. Once implemented, both policies and decisions are monitored to ensure they are effective. If they are not effective or they fail to deliver the intended outcomes, they can be changed to make them work for the agency. Regardless of the sector in which the leisure services agency operates, policy making and decision making are keys to success that greatly affect both the day-to-day operations and the long-term stability of the agency.

### Review Questions

1. Differentiate problem solving and decision making. Give examples of each in the leisure services field.
2. Define policies, standards, procedures, and rules. What are the major differences among them?
3. Describe the decision-making process.
4. What is the role of board members and stakeholders in the policy-making process?
5. Explain the concepts of brainstorming and groupthink.
6. What are variables to consider when evaluating possible solutions to a problem?

**Visit the online resource at www.HumanKinetics.com/TheParkAndRecreationProfessionalsHandbook for sample documents, keywords, activities and assignments, and more.**

# chapter 13

# Professional Development

**OUTCOMES**

- Identify the elements of career development.

- Define ethics and morals.

- Formulate solutions to ethical dilemmas.

- Identify and describe ethics theories.

- Understand ecotourism, environmental ethics, and sustainability.

- Examine the role of social responsibility in leisure services.

Many of the chapters in this book describe step by step the processes needed to accomplish the responsibilities of being a leisure services professional. This chapter is a bit different. It focuses more on a philosophy rather than a clearly defined process of professional development. **Professional development** refers to skills and knowledge attained for both personal development and career advancement. A discussion on professional development is not complete without including ethics and the ethical dilemmas that professionals face. The day-to-day activities of a professional require adherence to a strict code of ethical conduct. Without ethical conduct, the other parts of professionalism are greatly diminished.

# Professional Development Process

Professional development encompasses numerous facilitated learning opportunities, from college degree programs to formal course work to conferences and informal learning opportunities situated in practice (Speck and Knipe 2005). Motivation for professional development can be multifaceted and may include career preparation, advancement, networking, skill development, increased compensation, and self-fulfillment.

## Career Preparation

One of the first stages of professional development is career preparation. That is, what is needed to be qualified for a career in the leisure services? While it has not always been the case, today's entry-level leisure services professional often has a college degree in parks and recreation or a related field. Currently there are 89 programs that are accredited by the NRPA as well as many more that are not accredited. The NRPA **accreditation** process recognizes programs as meeting or exceeding standards of academic quality as related to parks and recreation education.

As students prepare for a leisure services career, they must complete course work that meets standards identified by the NRPA as necessary for preparing a student to work in the profession. This course work includes financial management and programming as well as a working knowledge of the history of the profession. Part of this career preparation also involves completing practicums and internships while still a student. This hands-on experience provides students with the opportunity to perform the tasks associated with

Learning is an ongoing process. Students spend four or more years preparing for a career and then their entire career developing into a quality professional who makes a solid contribution to the field.

working in the profession, including programming, staff supervision, maintenance, budgeting, management, and risk management, among others.

Students also have the option to gain multiple certifications or other credentials that may enhance their status as a professional. One of the most recognized certifications for individuals working in public parks and recreation is the Certified Park and Recreation Professional (CPRP). Other relevant certifications include Certified Pool/Spa Operator, Certified Playground Safety Inspector, and Wilderness First Responder as well as certifications in CPR and first aid. The following lists include more certification options.

### Aquatics

- Aquatic Facility Operator (AFO)
- Water Safety Instructor (WSI)
- Jeff Ellis and Associates Certifications
- Certified Pool/Spa Operator

### Meetings and Events

- Certified Festival and Events Executive
- Certified Meeting Professional
- Certified Special Events Professional (CSEP)

### Public Parks and Recreation and Therapeutic Recreation

- Certified Park and Recreation Professional (CPRP)
- Certified Playground Safety Inspector (CPSI)
- Certified Therapeutic Recreation Specialist (CTRS)

### Fitness

- Personal trainer certifications (via the American Council on Exercise, American Fitness Professionals and Associates, Aerobics and Fitness Association of America, National Strength and Conditioning Association)
- Primary Group Exercise Certification
- Group Fitness Instructor Certification

### Outdoor Recreation

- Leave No Trace Master Educator
- Wilderness Education Association National Standard Program
- American Canoe Association Instructor
- American Canoe Association Swiftwater Rescue

- American Mountain Guides Association Certification
- National Association for Search and Rescue Courses
- Professional Ski Instructor
- Certified Heritage Interpreter
- Certified Interpretive Manager
- Certified Interpretive Planner

### Tourism

- Certified Destination Management Executive

### Camping

- American Camp Association Professional Certification

Further professional development that should begin as soon as a student considers a career in leisure services is participation in professional associations and conferences. Most professional associations and conferences offer students discounted rates to join and attend both conferences and workshops. In fact, this type of involvement can facilitate overall career preparation, because students can learn more about certification exams and can network with professionals who may be helpful in the search for an internship or a job.

There are multiple professional associations in the leisure services field, including the NRPA; state professional associations such as the Illinois Park and Recreation Association and the North Carolina Recreation and Park Association; the American Alliance for Health, Physical Education, Recreation and Dance; and the National Alliance for Youth Sports, among many others. The following lists name a variety of professional associations.

### Public Parks and Recreation

- National Recreation and Park Association (www.nrpa.org)
- State parks and recreation associations (e.g., Illinois Park and Recreation Association, North Carolina Recreation and Park Association)
- American Alliance for Health, Physical Education, Recreation and Dance (www.aahperd.org)
- World Leisure and Recreation Association

### Therapeutic Recreation

- American Therapeutic Recreation Association (www.atra-online.com)
- National Therapeutic Recreation Society (www.nrpa.org/ntrs/)

### Sports
- National Intramural-Recreational Sports Association (www.nirsa.org)
- North American Society for Sport Management (www.nassm.org)

### Commercial Recreation and Tourism
- Resort and Commercial Recreation Association (www.rcra.org)
- World Tourism Organization (www.unwto.org/index.php)
- World Travel and Tourism Council (www.wttc.org)

### Outdoor Recreation
- American Camp Association (www.acacamps.org)
- Association for Experiential Education (www.aee.org)
- Wilderness Education Association (www.weainfo.org)
- National Association for Interpretation (www.interpnet.com)
- North American Association for Environmental Education (www.naaee.org)
- University of New Hampshire Outdoor Education (www.unh.edu/outdoor-education/resources/index.htm)
- Outdoor Industry Association (www.outdoorindustry.org)
- Student Conservation Association (www.thesca.org)

### Event and Meeting Management
- International Festivals and Events Association (www.ifea.com)
- International Association of Assembly Managers (www.iaam.org)
- International Special Events Society (www.ises.com)
- Professional Convention Management Association (www.pcma.org)

## Continuing Education

Once immersed within the field, professionals may choose to engage in continuing education so they can further build competencies and facilitate career advancement. These competencies may include technical and functional expertise related to the job they are in or the job they want to attain. Examples include skills in new technology, personnel management, grant writing, program development, and technical abilities. There are a variety of avenues that a professional can take to learn in these areas.

Professional conferences are one venue through which professionals can engage in continuing education and earn **continuing education units (CEUs),** which are required to maintain professional certifications. For instance, a one-hour educational session typically earns a CPRP .1 CEUs; a CPRP must earn 2.0 CEUs over a two-year period in order to retain certification. Sessions must be approved by the certifying body before they can award CEUs. Approval is based on the background of the speaker, the length of the session, and the objectives of the session. Sessions cover a variety of topics relevant to today's professional, including customer service, risk management, program design, partnership, leadership, teamwork, and personal effectiveness. Regardless of the topic, sessions awarding CEUs must be conducted professionally by a qualified speaker with well-defined learning objectives.

Professionals may also attend educational workshops that are strictly focused on one particular topic such as playground safety or aquatic facility management. Often these workshops cover a great deal of material on the topic and conclude with a certification exam for which the professional should then be prepared. These workshops often last multiple days due to the amount of material that must be covered in order for the professional to be prepared for the certification exam.

Other opportunities for continuing education may occur in more traditional educational settings such as colleges and universities and may include online as well as traditional classes. Often these learning opportunities are a good fit for employees interested in increasing their understanding of the parks and recreation field, particularly employees whose previous educational background is outside of the parks and recreation field. Others may be seeking an advanced degree in parks and recreation or in a related field such as public administration or youth development in order to gain more opportunities for advancement.

## Career Progression

Most professionals are not content with indefinitely remaining in the same career position that they started in; most professionals ultimately look to advance to jobs with greater responsibili-

The NRPA Ahrens Institute is home to the National Recreation and Park Association. NRPA has as one of its main purposes to advance the profession and the professionals within it through networking, education, research, and resources.

ties and certainly greater rewards. There are two ways to advance throughout a career: external advancement and internal advancement. While there may be opportunities for career progression within larger agencies (internal advancement), often career progression requires an employee to transfer outside of the current agency in order to advance (external advancement). Regardless of the path a person takes, networking often provides the first entree into a new position.

## Networking

Starting as early as college, or even high school, networking is an effective way to make contacts with people who may be able to help with career progression either immediately or in the future. Although many high school students may not think a full-time career in leisure services is an option, part-time jobs can help students learn about the profession and make early contacts that can open doors with respect to both future jobs and college programs to prepare for a full-time career in leisure services. Building a solid network of contacts can help young professionals not only find a first job or a new job but also address issues that come up in the current job.

A diverse network of contacts is beneficial. In this sense, diversity refers to variety in the types of positions contacts hold, the education levels contacts have obtained, and the geographic locations in which contacts work. Think about it: If

you are working as a youth sport coordinator and your entire network comprises other youth sport coordinators in a small section of your state, who can you go to when you are looking for a position with more responsibility, such as a facility coordinator, or when you are looking to move out of state? A homogenous network of professional contacts does not serve a person nearly as well as a network with some variety.

Networking can take place at many locations, but often professional conferences provide the most successful venue, because they provide a great opportunity to interact with a wide variety of professionals. However, networking opportunities can present themselves in numerous ways, not only in professional life but also in personal life. Being aware of opportunities and willing to extend your professional contact can go a long way to cultivating those opportunities, wherever they are discovered. Remember, the people you keep in touch with can serve as an entree into new positions down the road or as a resource for solving problems in your current position.

## Internal Advancement

Internal advancement typically does not rely on external networks, although internal relationships can be an important component of advancement within an agency. Internal advancement is just as it sounds—advancing into a position of greater responsibility within the same organization a professional is already working in. The new position comes with a title change as well as a pay increase and possibly new benefits such as use of an agency vehicle.

There are different ways that an employee may become eligible for internal advancement. While some agencies may not want to advance internal candidates, preferring instead external hires who will bring in new ideas, many agencies groom current employees to take on more responsibilities over time. These opportunities may arise through formal recruitment strategies that entice numerous internal applicants to interview for a position or through a promotion for which the person does not have to apply.

Success in internal advancements can be facilitated through positive performance evaluations, continuing education, and other indicators that a person is a hardworking employee with potential. An agency's history of internal advancement can motivate employees, because those who are interested in living (and remaining) in a specific geographical area or staying with an agency they love working for appreciate the opportunity to advance without relocation. This type of agency history can go a long way in helping to recruit good employees.

### External Advancement

As mentioned earlier, often career progression requires changing employers. A current agency may have no opportunities available for advancement due to size or very low turnover or due to a philosophy that prefers to hire externally for open positions. Networking can certainly be a way of learning about external advancement opportunities in the field, particularly in geographic areas the professional is unfamiliar with.

Information sources that can help professionals look for new jobs include career sites such as the NRPA online career center and listservs that post relevant job openings. In addition, a person may attend job fairs at universities and other locations when looking for a first position or a new position. Conferences can also be a good way to find out about new opportunities because they often feature an area known as a *job mart* where job postings are listed for attendees to peruse what is currently available on a state, regional, or national level. In addition, there are often representatives from the hiring agency available to discuss the jobs further.

# Training and Development

Training and development are important to personnel development. Whether done in-house or at a conference or some other venue, well-designed training and development can benefit both the agency and the employee.

## In-Service Training

While continuing education often takes place outside of an agency, in-house opportunities for training and development can play a large role in preparing employees for future advancement. Training improves the performance of an employee in a current job. Often it is designed around information gained from the job analysis as well as the results of performance appraisals. On the other hand, development is the overall focus on additional skills that can lead to career progression. A developmental orientation to training provides employees with opportunities to gain new skills and background in areas that can progress their careers either in the current organization or in a new organization.

Initial job training for many positions begins when the employee is still a student completing a practicum or internship experience. However, job training in the workplace may also be necessary after the person has been hired. Often it starts with orientation and continues as the employee is trained in specific areas of the organization. For example, while new employees may be familiar with budgeting, they will still need to be trained on the specifics of the organization's budgeting procedures, because these procedures can differ greatly among agencies. Other areas that lend themselves to training include planning, communication, conflict management, and so on. Employees who manage other employees, whether seasonal, part time, or full time, may benefit from training in staff motivation, performance evaluations, and supervision. This type of training can also provide support for an employee who is not currently managing people but hopes to do so in the future and thus can contribute to employee development. Regardless of the specific topics addressed, an agency must remember that the training is for adult learners who will present their own set of demands as learners.

## Adult Learners

Adult learners are different from traditional learners. They bring different concerns, expertise, and goals to the training environment. One concern held by adult learners is that participating in training will make them look weak and will signal that they are not qualified for their current job or for a promotion. For this reason, mandatory training may be helpful so that employees do not feel singled out for attending training. On the other hand, mandatory training may be less effective if employees are not motivated to attend and do so just because they have to. It is recommended that attendance at training and subsequent skill development be tied into the agency's reward system. If employees do not see the benefit of training, both from an everyday perspective and a long-term perspective, their motivation to attend may wane and both the employer and the employee will lose out on the benefits.

Adult learners bring experience and knowledge to training that are often quite relevant to the topic at hand. Their input can make the training more enriching for everyone involved. Because adult learners are decision makers and self-directed learners, their learning style typically differs from that of traditional students. Given the knowledge, experiences, and desire for active learning dis-

played by adult learners, training sessions can be developed to take advantage of what they bring to the table and exploit it for the greater good of the training.

There are various training formats that may work well for adult learners as long as the formats are suited to the topic. Training can include lectures or can be more active and involve experiential learning. Group initiative training is one type of experiential learning that can help employees improve skills such as communication and cooperation through active team-building exercises with learning objectives that can be transferred to the workplace. Another format that employees may find useful is role-playing, particularly when training is centered on a skill required for working with the public, such as conflict management. Case studies, audiovisual training, equipment simulations (e.g., realistic, computerized mannequins used for CPR and first aid training), and videoconferencing can also work for training and development purposes if the agency has access to these resources.

## Mentoring

While mentoring is described in chapter 10 as part of the discussion on human resources management, it is also relevant to a discussion on professional development. Mentoring is a relationship

In order for adults to learn and develop their careers, they need to be engaged in the topic and the training methods used. Ideally, their engagement leads to interaction and discussion about the topic.

in which a person with more experience guides a person with less experience. The mentor may or may not be the inexperienced employee's supervisor—either way, the mentor will have greater experience in the workplace and can assist the junior employee's professional development. Both formal mentoring, which is arranged by the agency, and informal mentoring, which occurs when a senior employee happens to develop a mentoring relationship with a junior employee, can contribute to the professional development of both mentor and mentee.

The relationship can provide the mentee with access to broader networks and with opportunities to learn new skills either directly from the mentor or indirectly through the mentor's ability, in some cases, to delegate responsibilities. Mentors may also encourage and support their proteges in attending workshops and conferences as well as in continuing education within an academic setting. The mentor can serve as a voice within an agency that speaks on behalf of the mentee when it comes time for promotions or other benefits that the mentee may be interested in, such as travel funds.

A mentor is not left out in the cold when it comes to benefiting from the relationship. A recent hire who is a new graduate may bring up-to-date knowledge that the mentor can learn from and use to increase her own skill set. In addition, when a mentee within a mentoring relationship shows real potential, this success can shine a glowing light on the mentor as well.

## Ongoing Development

Supervisors often play a strong role in the professional development of their staff members. Orientation may be the first stage of an employee's professional development within the context of a new employer, but professional development should not stop there. From providing networking to continuing education, supervisors should constantly encourage and facilitate professional development opportunities for their staff members. As employees continue to develop, an agency can only reap the benefits of the resulting performance improvement.

## Ethics and Morals

A true professional will have a solid set of ethics and morals that guides their career. Ethics are never clear cut, because they are quite personal. While the law may dictate some ethical decisions, such as embezzling agency funds, the law guides rather than serves as a mandate for ethical behavior. In other situations personal beliefs and ethics will guide behavior. Personal ethics vary from person to person and make teaching a clear-cut ethical approach to the leisure services profession quite difficult. This chapter examines what ethics and morals are, why people do unethical things, and how to resolve ethical dilemmas. In addition, this chapter discusses social responsibility and environmental ethics.

Some people may wonder why ethics even need to be discussed, because we should always do what is right. However, doing what is right is not quite that lucid or easy. Leisure services professionals face ethical decisions on a daily basis. They are accountable to clients and constituents and sometimes have involvement in the political arena. Because of this accountability, leisure services professionals have a responsibility to do what is right and in the best interest of the agency. Furthermore, the leisure services profession is charged with protecting the natural environment, preserving historical and cultural resources, and promoting sustainable tourism. A professional ethical standard must be developed to help leisure services professionals carry out these responsibilities.

Before going any further in this discussion, the terms *ethics* and *morals* need to be defined. **Ethics** are standards, behaviors, and principles that guide behaviors. Ethics can be derived from professional associations, the profession itself, the community in which the agency is located, and agency practices and policies. **Morals** also guide behavior, but they are a matter of personal opinion often driven by society or religion. Thus ethics are more professionally driven, while morals are more personally driven. For example, imagine a public parks and recreation employee is hiring summer staff members for youth programs. A highly qualified candidate applies for the position and is perfect for the program. It is obvious the candidate is obese. While morally, the employee feels that someone who is obese will send the wrong message to youth and impact the image of the agency, ethically the employee knows to hire the best person for the job. Because of this gray area between ethics and morals and the professional focus of this text, the term *ethics* rather than *morals* is emphasized throughout the chapter.

## Unethical Behavior

Unethical behavior happens every day. Sometimes it is grossly wrong behavior, such as sexual harassment in the workplace, while other times it is a lesser transgression, such as surfing the Web for personal reasons during work time. Measuring the degree of transgression is difficult, if not impossible. Before examining the different ethical transgressions, let's examine why people do things that are unethical. Maxwell (2005) provides some reasons for unethical behavior.

First, people do what is most convenient. Some people behave unethically because it is the easiest or fastest thing to do. Copying a homework assignment, keeping the extra change inadvertently given at a restaurant, and watching the movie rather than reading the book for an assignment are matters of convenience.

Second, people do what they must do to win. Business and politics are often tagged with the stereotype of winning at all costs. Some people feel the only way to get ahead is to cheat the system or make undesirable decisions. If a board of park commissioners keeps an important yet controversial issue off the agenda because elections are coming up soon, the commissioners are doing this to protect their position rather than do what is right for the agency.

Third, people rationalize their choices with relativism. This means that ethical dilemmas are solved based on the circumstances of the dilemma. Everyone has their own ethical standards that will change from situation to situation. Furthermore, people have a tendency to be easy on themselves and to compare their actions with the actions of others who seem to be less ethical. In reality, how many people truly feel they are unethical?

Howard and Korver (2008) give one additional reason for behaving unethically—people desensitize themselves to unethical behavior. In some situations, unethical behavior becomes the norm. It is accepted because people have desensitized themselves to the wrong involved. For example, the University of Illinois used to have a special admissions category for students who were connected to donors or alumni or who had political connections to trustees, the governor, or other politicians. For years these applicants were given preferential consideration for admission. Not until the practice was brought to the public's attention by the media was it stopped.

## Ethical Transgressions

Ethical transgressions often fall within four categories: lying, deceiving, stealing, and causing harm (Howard and Korver 2008). While there are many other areas of ethical transgressions, most unethical behaviors can be grouped into these four categories.

### Lying

Lying is "telling someone something we know not to be true with the intention of misleading them" (Howard and Korver 2008, 13). Lying is quite prominent in our lives. This is indicated by our many different variations of the word, such as *fib, embellish, stretch the truth, overstate, distort,* and *dupe,* among others (Howard and Korver 2008). Lies can range from one causing a lot of damage to one known as *a little white lie.* White lies are deemed as innocent and innocuous, such as telling a child that Santa Claus or the tooth fairy really exists. Lying occurs more often in the leisure services industry than most people would like to believe. For example, an employee calls in sick to attend a friend's party, a lifeguard tells a fellow lifeguard that he can't work for her because he has a doctor's appointment when in reality he doesn't want to take the shift, or a part-time employee is told he is being let go because the end of the season is nearing when really he is being dismissed for poor performance. Even small lies can foster an atmosphere of distrust, and distrust among bosses and coworkers is detrimental to a positive work environment.

### Deceiving

Deception is similar to lying and is "failing to correct an inaccurate impression, feigning ignorance, not telling the whole truth, withholding information, sugarcoating the truth, or overusing tact" (Howard and Korvar 2008, 17). Given this definition it is easy to see that deception occurs quite often in the workplace and in our personal lives. For example, a supervisor evaluating a mediocre employee might stretch the list of strengths to keep the employee from feeling quite so badly about all the weaknesses listed. A staff member might justify using a pub sponsor by promoting that the pub sells food rather than alcohol since alcohol sponsorship is against agency policy. Or perhaps the agency allows a nonalcoholic beer sponsor knowing that the same distributor sells traditional beer as well. Deception often occurs to make others feel better, to lessen hurt feelings, or to enhance the image of the agency or the professional.

### Stealing

Stealing has a very negative connotation. It is the procurement of property that does not belong to the procurer that is taken without permission from the owner. This may mean overbilling for services, underpaying at a store, or putting the same copy of software on multiple computers. In the leisure services field, professionals pad their travel expense accounts by collecting money on meals they did not eat, agencies are not billed for softball equipment received because of a vendor mistake that the agency fails to report, and staff members take home office supplies for their personal use. Stealing is not confined to taking large amounts of money or valuable equipment. It also includes the small-ticket items that can eventually add up to a large amount of money. Stealing within a company, regardless of the amount, often leads to termination.

### Causing Harm

Harm is putting a person or business at risk of injury or damage. An agency offers a wine tasting without providing transportation options. People are harmed because they must choose whether to participate or drive under the influence. A marketing manager has a favorite printer in town, so when receiving print bids, the manager selects agencies that will submit higher bids rather than businesses that will be more competitive. The businesses that miss out on the opportunity to bid on the project are harmed because they are losing out on potential revenue.

Ethical transgressions, whether lying, deceiving, stealing, or harming others, happen all the time in business. How we deal with these situations is an important aspect of becoming a trustworthy and competent professional.

# Ethics Theories

The field of ethics is an expansive area of study. With it comes a defining framework of theories. Although a complete overview of ethics theories is beyond the scope of this chapter, a few of the more common ones are discussed here, including Kohlberg's stages of moral development, consequences theory, Kant's duty-based ethics, and virtue ethics.

## Kohlberg's Stages of Moral Development

Much has been written on human development (see chapter 3). Kohlberg's stages of moral development show how people develop morally. People go through the stages at different rates, but they must achieve one stage before moving to the next stage because the stages are progressive. As shown in table 13.1, Kohlberg outlines three levels and six stages (Cherry 2009):

- Level 1: Preconventional morality. This level is usually experienced by children. It involves focus on self and egocentrism.
  - Stage 1: Obedience and punishment. In this stage children understand the concept of punishment and behave so that they avoid punishment and the negative ramifications of their actions.

**Table 13.1**　Kohlberg's Theory of Moral Development

| Level | Stage | Typical behavior |
|---|---|---|
| Level 1 Preconventional morality | Stage 1 Obedience and punishment | Avoid punishment |
| | Stage 2 Individualism and exchange | Earn rewards |
| Level 2 Conventional morality | Stage 3 Interpersonal relationships | Seek approval from others |
| | Stage 4 Maintaining social order | Seek approval from society |
| Level 3 Postconventional morality | Stage 5 Social contract and individual rights | Expect certain basic rights to be protected; want a democratic procedure for improving society |
| | Stage 6 Universal principles | Do the right thing, even if it conflicts with unjust rules |

○ Stage 2: Individualism and exchange. The concept of rewards is learned in this stage. They behave in a way that will garner them rewards. They want to know what is in it for them and will do whatever is in their own best interest.

- Level 2: Conventional morality. This level is experienced by adolescents and adults. Moral reasoning is focused on comparing actions with societal views and expectations.

  ○ Stage 3: Interpersonal relationships. In this stage individuals try to meet social expectations so they are perceived as good and are liked by others.

  ○ Stage 4: Maintaining social order. This stage moves beyond individual approval to societal approval. There is an expectation that laws, rules, and order will be followed when making decisions.

- Level 3: Postconventional morality. Experienced by adults, this level is where people realize that their principles may be different from society's principles.

  ○ Stage 5: Social contract and individual rights. In this stage, adults realize that people have different views and values. Laws are designed as social contracts and maintain order, but they are also designed to do the greatest good for the greatest number. People should agree on these laws. It is this stage of moral development that leads to a democratic society.

  ○ Stage 6: Universal principles. Based on abstract reasoning and universal ethical principles, this final stage is where people follow internalized principles of justice even if they conflict with laws and rules. A conflict with laws and rules can occur when the laws are unjust. People take certain actions because it is the right thing to do.

## Consequences Theory

Ethical behavior within consequences theory is dictated by the outcomes, or consequences, of actions. Actions are chosen because they have the best possible outcomes for those involved. There are consequences for the person making the decision as well as others connected to the decision.

Should a scuba diving instructor allow extra students to join a full class even if it might compromise the group's safety?

For example, a scuba instructor is paid contractually and receives a percent from each person enrolled in the class. The class maximum is set at 10 participants due to the one instructor and the available equipment. The class fills and two additional people ask to register. The instructor has two older sets of scuba equipment she can use and has to decide whether to accept the additional participants. The consequence for the instructor is that she makes more money on the class. The consequences for the participants are that two people have to use old equipment, instructor time is divided among 12 people rather than 10, and safety might be compromised by the one instructor taking on two extra participants.

This situation has both positive and negative consequences. The instructor can add the two participants and make more money, which is self-serving. The instructor can also do what is in the best interest of the first 10 people who registered and adhere to the class maximum. If the instructor goes with the latter option, she is choosing to seek the maximum good for the greatest number of people. This motive is labeled as **utilitarianism,** which is an aspect of consequences theory (McLean and Yoder 2005).

Utilitarianism may seem like a good theory to follow in the decision-making process. However, one of its major weaknesses is that it may ignore the interests of minority groups. In this context the term *minority* is not equated to race. The minority is simply the group with the smallest numbers. For example, utilitarianism may dictate that national parks should cater to recreationists over conservationists because more people use the parks for recreation and thus catering to recreationists does the greatest good for the greatest number of people.

Here is another example. A community has two pools in town. Both were built at approximately the same time, and both need major renovations and repairs. One pool is in a middle- and upper-income neighborhood that also has a YMCA pool, two country-club pools, and a pool managed by a housing association. The second community pool is in a low-income neighborhood that does not have access to any other pool. This pool also has half the annual attendance, has fewer programs, and loses 40 percent more money each year. When it comes time to choose which pool to renovate first, a utilitarian approach would select the pool in the middle- and upper-income neighborhood because it serves more people. If decisions are constantly made like this, the lower-income neighborhoods would disproportionately lose out (table 13.2).

## Kant's Duty-Based Ethics

Immanuel Kant's perspective on ethical behavior is quite different from that of consequences theory. It is a viable alternative to consequences theory and does not discount minority interests or consider consequences. Kant's theory, often labeled as *deontological ethics,* is duty or obligation based (McLean and Yoder 2005). The theory states that good and right actions should be taken regardless of the consequences. Actions should be morally right and well intended. For example, you ask a friend to work in the activity center at the resort for you. Your friend has inferred that he needs the money and you want the day off, and he agrees to work for you. While on your shift your friend falls, gets hurt, and is off work for a week. Your intentions in this situation were good and should not be judged as being bad simply because the outcome was negative. The decision was made from a sense of duty to your friend, and you meant well.

Since duties exist in our everyday and professional lives, they will affect our approach to ethical behavior. As public employees we have a duty to use the taxpayers' money efficiently and effectively. A trip leader has a duty to provide a safe experience. Everyone has a civic duty to treat each other fairly and not violate human or civil rights. Simply following rules, regulations, and laws is not enough to determine what our behaviors should be. People have to consider the obligations and duties they have toward others regardless of consequences (McLean and Yoder 2005).

## Virtue Ethics

Virtue ethics focus on character and virtue rather than consequences and duty. Someone who has high character acts accordingly in ethical situations, and character influences decision making. The YMCA is a prime example of virtue ethics. The organization promotes caring, respect, responsibility, and honesty in all of its programs. The YMCA of Topeka gives Character Values Awards to community members who exhibit these qualities (YMCA of Topeka 2009). The Oahe Family YMCA prominently displays a statement on the importance of character:

➤ The Oahe Family YMCA is committed to the idea that each person is unique and special. It is also committed to the idea that each person should display certain characteristics and positive values towards themselves and others. We expect that all of our members, program participants, volunteers and staff follow the YMCA Character Development program that emphasizes the core values of "Honesty, Caring, Responsibility and Respect". Please demonstrate these values in all that you do at the YMCA. (Oahe Family YMCA 2009)

**Table 13.2**    Pool Comparisons

| Middle- and upper-income neighborhood | Low-income neighborhood |
|---|---|
| Area pools include a YMCA pool, two country-club pools, and a pool managed by the housing association | No other pools in the area |
| 10,000 visitors per year | 5,000 visitors per year |
| 20 programs per year | 10 programs per year |
| Breaks even | 40% subsidized |

The YMCA of Greater Cincinnati has a character development initiative with programs designed to develop decision-making skills and critical-thinking skills among youths. The initiative helps youths reflect on their beliefs about what is the right thing to do and on ways to demonstrate the YMCA core values (YMCA of Greater Cincinnati 2009).

McLean and Yoder (2005) suggest that our positions in the leisure services industry affect how we behave and set a standard for our level of character. They argue that the higher the position in the organization, the more that is expected in terms of ethical behaviors. For example, two employees at a multimillion dollar hotel chain are arrested for driving under the influence. One of them is the vice president of the chain and the other is a part-time staff member at the front desk. Both commit the same crime, and yet chances are that the vice president's arrest will be newsworthy, whereas the other person's arrest will go unnoticed until listed in the weekly arrest reports. In addition, the reprimands handed down by the president may be quite different for each of these employees. Likewise, a major sport star arrested for driving under the influence will be highly criticized for the arrest compared with a guy who plays pickup basketball in the park with his friends.

People grow and develop morally over the life span. In any given situation we can look at the consequences of our actions to guide our behaviors. We can also turn to the law, to rules, or to a professional code of conduct to guide us in adhering to our duty. We can use our inner character to tell us intuitively what is right. Most leisure services professionals do all three when deciding what actions to take.

## Code of Ethics

Individual businesses and organizations as well as professional associations often adopt a code of ethics. The terms *code of conduct* or *code of ethical conduct* are also used. A code of ethics is a written document that outlines professional responsibilities, principles, values, and standards that are used to guide decisions and procedures. It directs professionals in a way that is in the best interest of the constituents. The following are a few examples from the leisure services field.

The National Therapeutic Recreation Society (NTRS) code of ethics has six sections and several issues within each section. Figure 13.1 includes the six sections and sample subsections.

The International Olympic Committee has a three-page document that discusses uses of resources, dignity, and integrity, among other things (International Olympic Committee 2007). Under Section A, which is on dignity, these statements can be found:

➤ 2. There shall be no discrimination between the participants on the basis of race, gender, ethnic origin, religion, philosophical or political origin, marital status or other grounds.

3. All doping practices at all levels are strictly prohibited. The provisions against doping in the World Anti-Doping Code shall be scrupulously observed.

5. All forms of participation in, or support for betting related to the Olympic Games, and all forms of promotion of betting related to the Olympic Games are prohibited.

The NRPA has a succinct code (NRPA staff member, personal communication, August 3, 2009):

➤ The National Recreation and Park Association has provided leadership to the nation in fostering the expansion of recreation and parks. NRPA has stressed the value of recreation, both active and passive, for the individual's growth and development. Its members are dedicated to the common cause of assuring that people of all ages and abilities have the opportunity to find the most satisfying use of their leisure time and enjoy an improved quality of life.

The association has consistently affirmed the importance of well-informed and professionally trained personnel to continually improve the administration of recreation and park programs. Members of NRPA are encouraged to support the efforts of the association and profession by supporting state affiliate and national activities and participating in continuing education opportunities, certification, and accreditation.

Membership in NRPA carries with it special responsibilities to the public at large, and to the specific communities and agencies in which recreation and park services

## NTRS Code of Ethics Excerpt

### I. The Obligation of Professional Virtue

Professionals possess and practice the virtues of integrity, honesty, fairness, competence, diligence, and self-awareness.

A. Integrity: Professionals act in ways that protect, preserve, and promote the soundness and completeness of their commitment to service. Professionals do not forsake nor arbitrarily compromise their principles. They strive for unity, firmness, and consistency of character. Professionals exhibit personal and professional qualities conducive to the highest ideals of human service.

### II. The Obligation of the Professional to the Individual

A. Well-being: The foremost concern of professionals is the well-being of the people they serve. They do everything reasonable in their power and within the scope of professional practice to benefit these people. Above all, professionals cause no harm.

### III. The Obligation of the Professional to Other Individuals and to Society

A. General welfare: Professionals make certain that their actions do not harm others. They also seek to promote the general welfare of society by advocating the importance of leisure, recreation, and play.

B. Fairness: Professionals are fair to other individuals and to the general public. They seek to balance the needs of the individuals they serve with the needs of other persons according to principles of equity.

### IV. The Obligation of the Professional to Colleagues

A. Respect: Professionals show respect for colleagues and their respective professions. They take no action that undermines the integrity of their colleagues.

B. Cooperation and support: Professionals cooperate with and support their colleagues for the benefit of the persons they serve. Professionals demand the highest professional and moral conduct of each other. They approach and offer help to colleagues who require assistance with an ethical problem. Professionals take appropriate action toward colleagues who behave unethically.

### V. The Obligation of the Professional to the Profession

B. Respect: Professionals treat the profession with critical respect. They strive to protect, preserve, and promote the integrity of the profession and its commitment to public service.

C. Reform: Professionals are committed to regular and continuous evaluation of the profession. Changes are implemented that improve the profession's ability to serve society.

### VI. The Obligation of the Profession to Society

A. Service: The profession exists to serve society. All of its activities and resources are devoted to the principle of service.

Note: For a complete copy of the NTRS Code of Ethics, contact NRPA.

**Figure 13.1**   A complete version of the NTRS code of ethics can be found on the NRPA Web site (National Therapeutic Recreation Society 2001). This example demonstrates a portion of the professional standards that guide TR professionals.

Reprinted, by permission, from National Therapeutic Recreation Association, 2009, *National Therapeutic Recreation Society Code of Ethics*. Available: http://www.nrpa.org/uploadedFiles/Connect_and_Share/The_NRPA_Network_(Socnet_Function)/NTRS%20code%20of%20ethics.pdf are offered. As a member of the National Recreation and Park Association, I accept and agree to abide by this Code of Ethics and pledge myself to:

- Adhere to the highest standards of integrity and honesty in all public and personal activities to inspire public confidence and trust.

- Strive for personal and professional excellence and encourage the professional development of associates and students.

- Strive for the highest standards of professional competence, fairness, impartiality, efficiency, effectiveness, and fiscal responsibility.

- Avoid any interest or activity which is in conflict with the performance of job responsibilities.

- Promote the public interest and avoid personal gain or profit from the performance of job duties and responsibilities.

- Support equal employment opportunities.

Reprinted, by permission, from NRPA.

These code of ethics examples are relatively short. There are other codes of ethics that are quite long and detailed. For example, the International Cricket Council has three codes of ethics, including one for players and officials, one for umpires, and one for developing program events. The 29-page document for players and officials addresses activities such as gambling, offenses and penalties, referee duties, reporting and notification procedure, disciplinary procedure, and guidelines for offenses (International Cricket Council 2007).

Pfister and Tierney (2009, 177) provide a list of topics to include in a code of ethics:

- General employee conduct
- Conflicts of interest
- Outside activities and employment
- Relationships with clients and suppliers
- Gifts, entertainments, and favors
- Kickbacks and secret commissions
- Organization funds and other assets
- Organization records and communications

- Dealing with outside people and organizations
- Prompt communications
- Privacy and confidentiality
- Service to the community
- Protection and conservation of natural resources

# Resolving Ethical Dilemmas

Ethical dilemmas arise regularly in the parks and recreation profession. Each situation requires a different method of dealing with it. In some cases you might simply work through the decision-making process outlined in chapter 12. In other cases an issue may need more in-depth analysis from an ethical standpoint. One method for analysis is to utilize the ethical dilemmas resolution process depicted in figure 13.2 and described in the following sections (Sabbach 2010).

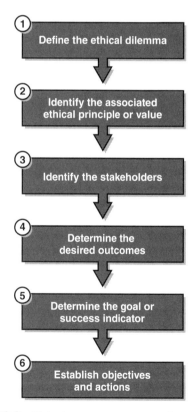

**Figure 13.2**  This six-step process examines an ethical dilemma from many different perspectives and requires the development of a solution.

Adapted, by permission, from Jamie Sabbach, 110% LLC.

## Step 1: Define the Ethical Dilemma

In this initial step, the issue is examined from all perspectives and a current state is identified. The manager asks questions such as, "What is happening?" "Why is this happening?" "Who is involved in the situation?"

## Step 2: Identify the Associated Ethical Principle or Value

In order for an issue to be an ethical dilemma, an ethical principle or value must be involved. The Josephson Institute is a nonprofit agency that is considered by many to be the preeminent leader in character and ethical behavior. The institute created a program called *Character Counts!* (Josephson Institute 2009), which is based on the six pillars of character: trustworthiness, respect, responsibility, fairness, caring, and citizenship (see figure 13.3). These pillars of character drive ethical behavior and cannot be separated from one another. It is not enough to adhere to one pillar and sacrifice the others. Ethical behavior requires adherence to all pillars. The YMCA has adopted this program and centers much of its activities and guiding principles on the six pillars (Josephson Institute 2009).

### Trustworthiness

Trustworthiness is an encompassing term that includes honesty, integrity, reliability, and loyalty. The Josephson Institute asserts that honesty is demonstrated in the way we communicate with people and in the way we behave. Honest communication means telling the truth, being sincere, and being candid when needed. Demonstrating honesty in our behaviors implies that we will not cheat, steal, commit fraud, or trick people.

In addition to honesty, integrity is required for ethical behavior. People with integrity remain consistent in their actions by adhering to their values in an honest and trustworthy manner.

Reliability is keeping promises, accepting responsibility, and following through on responsibilities. Not following through on responsibilities and promises makes others question who we are ethically and makes us appear dishonest in our actions.

Lastly, loyalty is demonstrated in the relationships we establish with people. We have relationships in our personal lives with our husband or wife, partners, parents, and siblings. We also have relationships with coworkers that require loyalty. Loyalty is problematic when it conflicts with other ethical behaviors. For example, imagine that your coworker and best friend Alex is stealing money from petty cash. You confront this person and he promises that it is a short-term loan that he will pay back before the boss finds out. Loyalty exists between you and your friend, but there is also loyalty between you and the organization and your integrity says that Alex's action is against the law and must be reported. Loyalty can be difficult when it requires people to prioritize their loyalties and do what is right.

### Respect

We often hear phrases such as, "Respect your elders" and "Respect is earned and not given." In addition to elders, all people should be treated respectfully. Even though you may disagree with the actions of a person, you must treat that person with respect. If you do not uphold this principle, you will compromise your own values by treating a person poorly.

The Phoenix Parks and Recreation Department has a policy on codes of conduct for all of its programs and facilities. Many aspects of this policy are consistent with the ethical pillar of respect (Phoenix Parks and Recreation Department 2009):

➤ **Policy on Codes of Conduct**
  When using facilities for, or participation in, youth programs and activities, managed or allowed by the City of Phoenix everyone is responsible for:
  - Conducting themselves in a proper and socially acceptable manner.
  - Exhibiting behavior that supports the health, safety and well-being of others.
  - Providing a drug free environment.
  - Refraining from the use of profanity or offensive language and ethnic slurs.
  - Abiding by all laws, rules, regulations and ordinances whether city, state or local.
  - Abstaining from any type of conduct intended to humiliate or intimidate others.

### Responsibility

Exhibiting responsible behavior requires people to be accountable for their own actions regardless of whether they are right or wrong. Responsible people who are wrong in their actions admit wrongdoing and accept responsibility for the consequences rather than blame others. Exhibit-

## Six Pillars of Character

**Trustworthiness**
- Honesty
- Integrity
- Reliability
- Loyalty

**Respect**
- Respect for all people

**Responsibility**
- Accountability
- Admitting wrongdoing
- Following through

**Fairness**
- Impartiality
- Equality
- Consistency

**Caring**
- Concern for others
- Treating others well

**Citizenship**
- Civic duty
- Volunteerism
- Community involvement

**Figure 13.3** The six pillars of character present the values that all people can agree on regardless of political, religious, or cultural views.

ing responsible behavior also requires individuals to follow through on what they are supposed to do and to perform required duties to the best of their abilities. The human resources person must hire quality people, the accountant must pay bills on time and monitor the agency's financial position, and the recreation therapist must develop an individual plan of care to meet each participant's needs. Imagine what would happen if these people did not take responsibility on the job and hired inept people, went well over budget, and developed a harmful plan for a participant.

### Fairness

Treating people fairly involves being impartial, treating people equally, and being consistent in treatment of situations and people. Impartial treatment requires eliminating favoritism of one person or group. For example, assume your agency is building playgrounds in neighborhood parks. The last three playgrounds have been built in affluent neighborhoods whose residents were quite vocal in their desire to have a playground and demonstrated a great need for a playground. The parks in the low-income neighborhoods have not had new equipment in at least 15 years; however, the residents there are not complaining. Is this fair treatment? If the lower-income communities are not expressing a need, why give a playground to them? Most people would feel this scenario is unfair and inequitable, as the low-income neighborhoods did not receive impartial or equitable treatment.

Consistency is also an aspect of fairness. Consistency becomes a common issue when a professional begins supervising employees. Employees must be treated fairly and consistently. All employees should follow the same policies and procedures and should be reprimanded consistently for the same misconduct in the work-

place. For example, all supervisors who are late turning in payroll should be disciplined in the same manner. However, differences may occur depending on whether the payroll is being turned in late for the first time or for the third time. The first offense for every employee should have the same repercussions, as should the offenses beyond the first one. Policies and procedures often dictate how these situations are handled and enforce the idea of consistency.

### Caring

Caring is both a pillar and an underlying reason for behaving ethically. Caring, or showing concern for others, is the emotional aspect of ethics. Treating people well and minimizing how much we hurt others are ethical actions. Caring does not mean that you will never hurt people. It is more realistic to cause as little harm as possible while still behaving ethically. Caring also drives honesty, accountability, and respectful actions. People exhibit honesty because they care about others. The same can be said for accountability, respect, fairness, and integrity. Many other behaviors are driven by caring for people.

### Citizenship

Citizenship is your civic duty to do your part in the community. Good citizenship is obeying laws, volunteering, and staying informed of community issues. Citizenship shows itself in many different facets of the leisure services field, including the 5,000+ volunteers needed for the Ironman World Championships, the 7,000+ volunteers who average seven hours each at the Boston Marathon, the Genesee County (Michigan) Parks and Recreation Commission adopt-a-park program, the Tennessee State Parks recycling program, and the Yosemite National Park shuttle bus amenity. Good citizens

Events and programs can sometimes have ethical dilemmas associated with them that are difficult to solve. Using a systematic process to study the issue from many perspectives can help solve it.

give back more to the community than they take from it. Many public and nonprofit agencies count on the citizenship of others to operate.

## Step 3: Identify the Stakeholders

Stakeholders are individuals, groups, or agencies who are affected by or interested in an organization's actions. Stakeholders can include staff members, a whole department, the board, or the community. In an ethical situation, there will be people who are affected by the results of decisions made and actions taken. When developing an ethics action plan, an organization should identify those stakeholders so the ramifications of the decision and action are clear.

## Step 4: Determine the Desired Outcomes

In any ethical situation there is a desired outcome, or what the organization wants to achieve. After considering the dilemma, the ethical principles, and the stakeholders involved, the organization formulates an outcome. The outcome is broad and is an overarching desired state. At this point no goals or objectives are formed, as they are developed in steps 5 and 6.

## Step 5: Determine the Goal or Success Indicator

Once the desired outcomes are known, goals can be established for what is to be accomplished. Remember from chapter 2 that goals are clear statements of what a program is intended to achieve. Several goals can emerge based on the outcomes identified. These goals, once achieved, should indicate that success and the desired outcomes were reached.

## Step 6: Establish Objectives and Actions

This part of the action plan lists the steps that are to be taken in order to achieve the goals and desired outcomes. This section identifies step by step the tasks to be completed, the deadlines for completing the tasks, and the people responsible for completing the tasks. It is hoped that once all action steps are completed, the ethical situation will have been dealt with positively and the stakeholders involved will have deemed the solution to be in the best interest of all involved.

To get a better understanding of the organizational ethics action plan, look at table 13.3, which illustrates the ethical dilemma that might occur when board and council members pressure

**Table 13.3** Organizational Ethics Action Plan

| Ethical dilemma | Current state: Staff members are feeling pressured to hire friends and family members of past and current board and council members. Low morale is resulting from this pressure and staff members feel a sense of inappropriateness and unfair practices. |
|---|---|
| Ethical principles | Fairness, respect, accountability |
| Stakeholders | Staff members, friends and family members, board and council members, community as a whole |
| Outcomes | Policy that mitigates political pressures to hire certain individuals for reasons other than predetermined selection criteria and qualifiers such as experience, skill and ability, and personality |
| Goals and success indicators | Implement a nepotism and fair hiring practices policy that states that family members of board and council members are ineligible for hire by the department and that outlines fair hiring practices that apply to all candidates. |
| Objectives and actions | 1. Meet with human resources and legal representatives by March 31, 2011, to gather information and recommendations about the formulation of such policy.<br>2. Develop an outline of social, political, and legal consequences that can arise from the hire of relatives, friends, and so on of board or council members by April 30, 2011. This should include rationale for the development and implementation of a policy that addresses fair hiring practices.<br>3. Meet with board and council representatives about such a strategy, including the rationale (i.e., social, political, and legal consequences) by May 31, 2011.<br>4. Develop a nepotism and fair hiring practices policy by July 31, 2011.<br>5. Implement a nepotism and fair hiring practices policy by September 30, 2011. |

Reprinted by permission from GreenPlay, LLC, www.greenplayllc.com.

staff members into hiring friends and family. The ethical principles, the stakeholders, the outcomes, the goals and success indicators, and the objectives and actions are defined to show how this ethical issue can be solved. In this instance, the staff members want to stop political pressure to hire people who are not qualified. To do this, they develop a nepotism and fair hiring practices policy and meet with the board to discuss the policy and its reason for creation.

## Ethical Issues

An important aspect of the leisure services profession is the relationships that are established with constituents, fellow professionals, and community partners. Conflicts of interest and gifts, bribes, and kickbacks go beyond ethical behavior and can get an employee into difficult or undesirable situations. Such behaviors can have severe consequences. Religion also affects the ethics, morals, and values people adhere to, even in the workplace. Key ethical issues affecting the agency itself include social responsibility and environmental ethics. Each of these issues is discussed in more detail in the following sections in order to show how each relates to leisure services.

## Conflicts of Interest

A conflict of interest occurs because of the roles we play. A leisure services professional is an agency employee but also may be a parent, a business owner, or a volunteer or donor to another agency. When one of these roles is at odds with what is in the best interest of the agency, a conflict of interest occurs. Here are a few examples of conflicts of interest:

- A board member's husband owns a local T-shirt printing business that has submitted a $12,000 bid for the annual T-shirt contract
- The nephew of the resort's CEO is contracted to do landscaping for the resort, even though for the past 10 years a different company has held this contract and has received positive reviews each year until suddenly terminated
- A board member at the YMCA calls the CEO to put in a good word for a neighbor who has applied for a much-coveted position in aquatics

While many of these situations are not illegal, there is a public perception about them. Other T-shirt businesses might be angered by the husband's bid, the landscape company dropped in favor of the nephew might feel unfairly treated, and the staff members might feel the board is overstepping its boundaries. Conflicts of interest should be stopped immediately if there is any question of the legality of the situation. If the concern is more about image and doing what is in the best interest of the agency, then further action should be taken. First, the agency should establish a policy that prevents board members and staff members from entering into such situations. Second, all conflicts of interest must be disclosed as soon as they occur. Third, the person involved in the conflict should be required to disengage from the situation (so, for example, the board member would not vote on the T-shirt bids). Fourth and last, agencies should put policies in place that require bids and quotes to minimize conflicts of interest (Board Source 2009).

The following is an example policy addressing a conflict of interest:

➤ **Ashland Area Recreation Association Conflict of Interest**
If any officer has a potential conflict of interest in any transaction of the Ashland Area Recreation Association in which the officer has a financial interest, direct or indirect, the officer shall inform the other officers of that conflict of interest. The officer shall not vote on or otherwise

participate in the decision on that transaction. If the amount of such transactions exceeds $500.00 in a fiscal year, those transactions must be approved by a two-thirds vote of the disinterested officers. If the amount of such transactions exceeds $5,000.00 in a fiscal year, the Association shall also publish a notice of the proposal in a local newspaper and shall inform the state director of charitable trusts of the proposal before making a final decision on the transactions. The Association shall follow all relevant state laws on conflicts of interest, including those prohibiting the loan of money or property to any officer. (Ashland Area Recreation Association 2009)

## Gifts, Bribes, and Kickbacks

Although gifts, bribes, and kickbacks are often associated with politicians, they affect leisure services as well. McLean and Yoder (2005, 95) define gifts, bribes, and kickbacks as follows:

- Gifts: Items of value or something given without an expectation of return.
- Bribes: Cash or other items of value given to persuade or induce an action. Bribes can be given to win contracts, sway a vote, or influence a decision.
- Kickbacks: Illegal paybacks from a previous exchange. Kickbacks occur when a sum of money is given after a contract has been awarded.

Accepting gifts can be acceptable or unacceptable depending on the policies of the agency and the laws of the state. For example, Illinois has an ethics test mandated by the governor for all state employees. A large section of that test focuses on state employees accepting gifts. Following are two situations to consider. Think about whether they should be considered a gift, bribe, or kickback.

Through a sealed bid, a major cola company receives the two-year contract for providing all beverages within the agency. The agency's marketing director is building a strong working relationship with the cola company in hopes of getting it to sponsor more events. The vice president of the cola company invites the marketing director to play golf one afternoon and covers the greens

If an agency or employee becomes involved in conflicts of interest and other ethical issues, a public relations problem can result.

fees and cart rental through her own contractual agreement with the golf course. The marketing director feels this is a good opportunity to get to know the cola company staff better.

It is one-and-a-half years later and the cola contract is coming up for the next two years. The vice president invites the marketing director and her family to join her at a swanky resort for the weekend. The cola company will pay for the weekend. While at the resort the vice president suggests that the cola contract be extended rather than rebid since the company has treated the agency and the marketing director quite well these past two years.

It is fairly clear that the resort invitation is an unethical situation as it appears to be a bribe. The free golf game is not as easy to discern. It appears to simply be a gift. Agency policy will dictate what, if any, gifts are acceptable. Here is a sample gift policy from the Jewish Community Foundation:

➤ **Acceptance of Gifts**
Board and Committee members will not accept (other than *de minimus* awards and honoraria) gifts, gratuities, free trips, personal property or any other items of value from any outside persons or organizations that might be provided as an inducement to support their organizations or interests. (Jewish Community Foundation 2006)

## Religion and Ethics

Religion plays a prominent role in shaping values and guiding behaviors. However, there are many religions and a wide variety of beliefs. Some religions are more conservative, and some are more liberal. When organizations develop ethics statements, they must be careful to avoid religion as a basis for the statement. While most religions do provide guidance on ethical conduct, such as forbidding people to steal, murder, or commit adultery, ethics do not require a religious foundation. Rather, ethics use "reason and experience to determine what is good and bad, right and wrong, better and worse" (MacKinnon 2001, 4).

The phrase *separation of church and state* is often cited as being in the U.S. Constitution. This is untrue, as the phrase is not in there. The First Amendment to the U.S. Constitution does say that "Congress shall make no law respecting an establishment of religion, or prohibiting the free exercise thereof." This is interpreted as saying that the government cannot establish a national religion or prohibit a religion. In 1802 Thomas Jefferson sent a letter to the Danbury Baptists

using the phrase *wall of separation between the church and the state* (MacKinnon 2001). This phrase was used to insinuate protection of the church from government involvement rather than prevention of church involvement in the government.

In the United States, there is much separation between church and state. However, sometimes these lines are blurred:

- Prayers are said at the presidential inauguration.
- The U.S. Pledge of Allegiance, National Anthem, and Declaration of Independence all mention God.
- The words *In God We Trust* are written on all U.S. currency.
- The President of the United States is sworn in with a hand on the Bible, and the speech ends with, "So help me God."

All of these examples and more suggest that the United States is based on Christianity and a belief in God rather than some other higher power. Think about a time when a President does not recognize God as the higher power or when a minority religion that does not recognize God becomes very powerful and influences standards in society. Parks and recreation agencies have experienced some of this already. For example, many agencies no longer hold Easter egg hunts or Christmas programs. Here are a few leisure services ethical situations to consider in terms of religion:

- Should the local parks and recreation department have a gospel night in the park since the gospel choirs in town are all affiliated with a church?
- A miniature golf course has a loudspeaker that pipes radio music over the course. Should the golf course be allowed to play the local religious station? Does it matter if the golf course is a public, nonprofit, or commercial agency?
- A youth soccer coach asks her team to pray before the start of the soccer game each Saturday. The league is run through the local YMCA. Should the coach be allowed to pray with the team?
- A youth soccer coach asks his team to pray before the start of the soccer game each Saturday. The league is run through the local parks and recreation department. Should the coach be allowed to pray with the team?

## Social Responsibility

Social responsibility is an ethical philosophy or approach to doing business in which decisions are made and actions are taken to contribute to the welfare of the community. An organization dedicated to being socially responsible seeks to improve quality of life for people and communities. When an organization is committed to social responsibility, its employees feel pride in their work and their company. The socially responsible company strategically selects its issues to support. This strategy should be well developed and defined as the operational strategic plan for the company. A company can also increase its business by being socially responsible, as people who have the same beliefs are more inclined to patronize those businesses. The following are a few examples of socially responsible corporations.

Starbucks builds its corporate responsibility around the farmers who grow the Starbucks coffee. The company makes sure that the growers get a fair price for their coffee, provides loans to farmers, encourages environmentally sound growing practices and socially responsible working conditions, helps farmers establish sustainable coffee production, and funds projects that benefit coffee communities. In addition, Starbucks launched a new green retail strategic initiative in 2008 that continues to grow (Starbucks Corporation 2008).

L.L. Bean supports conservation, recreation, culture, education and health, and human services. This company partners with nonprofit organizations that are committed to the same ideals. L.L. Bean partners include the Mount Washington Observatory, New England Nordic Ski Association, Friends of Acadia, Appalachian Trail Conservancy, and National Park Foundation, just to name a few (L.L. Bean 2009).

Timberland has a tree as its logo and has socially responsible programs and policies dedicated to eliminating the company's carbon footprint and upholding a vision of an accountable, sustainable enterprise. The Timberland Web site explains the company's dedication to this effort:

➤ For a bunch of folks wearing lug sole boots, that may sound like a hard thing to do. But when a boot is made of recyclable and renewable materials, bound by water-based adhesives, manufactured with energy generated by wind and sun, transported by green freight and sold in 100% recyclable packaging distinguished by an industry first nutritional label . . . you'll understand a bit about what we strive for as an enterprise.

It's simple—we have a passion for the outdoors and embrace our responsibility to preserve our natural resources. And, every day—by planting trees, erecting solar panels, developing sustainable products and encouraging civic action to preserve our planet—we express our deep reverence for nature and our commitment to a sustainable future. (Timberland 2009)

Often social responsibility is associated with commercial organizations because they have the resources to commit to helping the community. However, a public or nonprofit agency can also be socially responsible in the way it treats employees and the community. These types of agencies can coordinate volunteer efforts in the community, help raise funds for projects, or reduce their carbon footprints. Even small steps contribute to a socially responsible ethic.

## Environmental Ethics

There is much talk about becoming a greener society, conserving natural resources, and reducing carbon footprints. All of these elements are part of environmental ethics. Environmental ethics embrace responsible conduct that is in the best interest of the natural environment. An organization with strong environmental ethics is concerned with future generations and protecting the natural environment for their experience.

People often develop their own set of environmental ethics. What can an individual do to become more conscience of the environment and raise the collective consciousness about the natural environment? Creating and adhering to your own environmental ethics is as simple as stating a personal philosophy about the natural environment and what can be done to enhance it. Personal environmental ethics might include the following (Trask 2006):

### For the Office

- Work four 10-hour days during the week to reduce commuting.
- Buy a laptop rather than a desktop computer because laptops use less energy.
- Use both sides of the paper.
- Save files on the computer rather than print hard copies.
- Use recycled items such as paper and toner cartridges.

### For Home

- Install water-saving devices in the bathroom.
- Buy concentrated products because of the reduced packaging.
- Wash clothes in warm or cold versus hot water.
- Buy phosphate-free detergent.
- Buy products made from recycled materials.
- Be a locavore and buy locally grown food.

The tourism industry is increasingly espousing its environmental efforts through ecotourism, sometimes called *sustainable tourism*. Ecotourism is responsible travel to natural areas that promotes conservation of nature and sustains the well-being of those in the community. The International Ecotourism Society (TIES) suggests that ecotourism activities should follow six principles (International Ecotourism Society 2009):

- Minimize environmental effects.
- Build environmental and cultural awareness and respect.
- Provide positive experiences for both visitors and hosts.
- Provide direct financial benefits for conservation.
- Provide financial benefits and empowerment for local people.
- Raise sensitivity to political, environmental, and social climates in host countries.

The surge in ecotourism over the past 20 years has occurred for several reasons. First, there has been an increased demand in nature tourism. With this came the realization that conservationists and the local community should work together to protect the resources and manage the oncoming growth. Second, there is an increased interest in environmental issues and a desire to conserve the natural environment. This is quite evident with the demand in ecotourism destinations and consumers' willingness to pay more for green products. Lastly, travelers want to escape and seek remote destinations in which to do it (Drumm and Moore 2005).

Ecotourism focuses on destinations and their practices, but there are behaviors that make travelers more respectful of the environment as well. The American Society of Travel Agents (ASTA) has its Ten Commandments of Ecotourism, which serves as a code of conduct (see figure 13.4).

## ASTA Ten Commandments of Ecotourism

1. Respect the frailty of the earth. Unique and beautiful destinations may not be here for future generations to enjoy unless we all are willing to help in their preservation.
2. Patronize organizations (hotels, airlines, resorts, cruise lines, tour operators, and suppliers) that advance energy conservation, promote water and air quality, provide recycling, manage waste and toxic materials safely, practice noise abatement, encourage community involvement, and provide experienced and well-trained staff members dedicated to strong principles of conservation.
3. Learn about and support conservation-oriented programs and organizations working to preserve the environment and the local culture. Consider a volunteer vacation where you can volunteer to help the local community during a portion of your vacation.
4. Walk or utilize environmentally sound methods of transportation whenever possible.
5. Encourage drivers of public vehicles to stop engines when parked.
6. Leave only footprints. Take only photographs. No graffiti! No litter! Do not take away souvenirs from historical sites and natural areas.
7. Educate yourself about the geography, customs, manners, and cultures of the region you visit in order to make your travels more meaningful. Take time to listen to the people. Encourage local conservation efforts.
8. Respect the privacy and dignity of others. Ask before photographing people.
9. Do not buy products made from endangered plants or animals, such as ivory, tortoise shell, animal skins, and feathers.
10. Always follow designated trails. Do not disturb animals or plants or their natural habitats.

**Figure 13.4**  The ASTA believes that travel is a right for all people and that travel destinations should be protected and environmental impact minimized.

**Top Five Ecotourism Destinations**

Planet Green named its top ecotourism destinations for 2009. The top five include the following (Peterson 2009):

1. Costa Rica
2. Kenya
3. Northwest Canada and Alaska
4. Belize
5. Hawaii

Environmental ethics and ecotourism will continue to grow in the future. North Americans are increasingly realizing the value of natural resources and are developing their own environmental ethics to protect their resources.

## Conclusion

Professional development encompasses how employees grow and enhance their skills and all-around performance within their profession. Professional development can be influenced strongly by the individual's agency, supervisor, or formal or informal mentor. Professionalism requires continuing education, involvement in professional associations, and enhancing credentials through certification, among other things.

A major element of professional development is establishing yourself as an honest, ethical, and credible individual and employee. Of course, one chapter on ethics cannot provide all the answers to the plethora of ethical dilemmas that occur throughout a career in the leisure services or any other field. Addressing ethical issues comes from experience, practice, and the desire to do what is right. Begin by developing your own code of ethics and your own environmental ethics statement. Examine the code of ethics of your place of employment. These codes will dictate behaviors and help you solve tough ethical decisions.

## Review Questions

1. What are the elements of career development? Explain each element.
2. Define morals and ethics.
3. Differentiate among ecotourism, environmental ethics, and sustainability.
4. Describe the four ethics theories presented in this chapter.
5. Describe the process you should follow to resolve an ethical dilemma.
6. Define social responsibility. Find an example from a leisure services agency.

 **Visit the online resource at www.HumanKinetics.com/TheParkAndRecreationProfessionalsHandbook for sample documents, keywords, activities and assignments, and more.**

# appendix

# NRPA Council on Accreditation Standards

The Council on Accreditation of Parks, Recreation, Tourism and Related Professions (COAPRT) reviews and grants accreditation status to universities with curricula that meet the established criteria. These criteria were established to ensure continued improvement and quality of undergraduate education in the profession. Prior to the establishment of COAPRT, the Council on Accreditation (COA) administered the accreditation process. This group established the COA Standards 2004, which will be phased out and replaced with the newer COAPRT standards in 2013. Because of this transition, this appendix includes both sets of standards.

## COA Standards 2004

The following standards delineate the professional competencies for all students. For ease of identifying areas of competence, the standards are clustered into seven topical areas, shown as headings, below. Please note: The Council on Accreditation has included "Content to consider" after each 8.0 series standard. This is provided to aid understanding of the standard but does not constitute a list of content that a program must include to address the standard. Programs are encouraged, where appropriate, to address each standard through their own individual area(s) of specialty. Therefore, programs with a focus in diverse areas such as therapeutic recreation, tourism, youth services, outdoor recreation, or others may address the standards through their particular focus and are not to be bound by one specific area of recreation, park resources, and leisure services.

### Conceptual Foundations

**8.01** Understanding of the conceptual foundations of play, recreation, and leisure. *Content to consider:* A substantive exploration and understanding of the various concepts of play, recreation, and leisure, and the role that these concepts have in the delivery of recreation and leisure services.

**8.02** Understanding of the significance of play, recreation, and leisure in contemporary society. *Content to consider:* An understanding of the relationship between the three concepts and historical, multicultural, technological, economic, political, social/psychological, international, physical, philosophical, and environmental perspectives.

**8.03** Understanding of the significance of play, recreation, and leisure throughout the life span. *Content to consider:* An understanding of how the importance and influence of play, recreation, and leisure change across various life stages. This understanding may include the developmental, preventive and therapeutic role of these concepts.

**8.04** Understanding of the interrelationship between leisure behavior and the natural environment. *Content to consider:* An understanding of how the natural environment will influence one's leisure behavior, as well as how the natural environment facilitates the achievement of a state of leisure.

**8.05** Understanding of environmental ethics and its relationship to leisure behavior. *Content to consider:* An understanding of environmental protection and preservation in park or recreation facility development and program provision.

### Profession

**8.06** Understanding of the following as they relate to recreation, park resources, and leisure services:

**8.06.01** History and development of the profession. *Content to consider:* Events and milestones in the development of the profession.

**8.06.02** Professional organizations. *Content to consider:* Evolution of the current professional organizations that relate to the field of recreation, park resources, and leisure services, as well as the accredited options.

**8.06.03** Current issues and trends in the profession. *Content to consider:* Issues currently affecting the profession may include, but are not limited to, certification and accreditation, tourism, violence, substance abuse, video games, computers, aging, leisure-based businesses, use of open space, environmental impact, gender, sexuality, and private vs. public enterprises.

**8.07** Understanding of ethical principles and professionalism. *Content to consider:* Presentation of information discussing philosophy and the relationship of values, morals, and judgment to professional practice. The importance of following a professional code of ethics and standards of conduct, and how these two areas are critical in defining leisure services as a profession may be addressed.

**8.08** Understanding of the importance of maintaining professional competence and the available resources for professional development. *Content to consider:* The importance of credentialing and contributing to the advancement of the profession. Certification processes, the maintenance of those credentials through attending national, regional, and local educational programs, and service via leadership positions in professional organizations. Competence in the provision of professional services and programs as an asset to the community and the prevention of consumer harm may also be addressed.

### Delivery Systems

**8.09** Understanding of the roles, interrelationships, and use of diverse delivery systems addressing recreation, park resources, and leisure. *Content to consider:* An understanding of the public, private, profit, and not-for-profit delivery systems that address the leisure needs of the public, how they work together, and their importance.

**8.10** Understanding of the importance of leisure service delivery systems for diverse populations. *Content to consider:* The impact of leisure service delivery systems on a wide diversity of populations (i.e., mental, physical, aged, youth, multicultural etc.).

**8.11** Understanding of inclusive practices as they apply to:

**8.11.01** Operating programs and services. *Content to consider:* How agencies are addressing inclusiveness within the operation of programs and services; including the policies, practices, philosophies, and benefits.

**8.11.02** Design of areas and facilities. *Content to consider:* Location, environmental issues, populations to be served, programs to be housed, and fiscal and political implications of specific sites and settings.

**8.12** Understanding of the roles, interrelationships, and use of diverse leisure delivery systems in promoting:

**8.12.01** Community development. *Content to consider:* The impact that program/plans will have on the immediate and surrounding communities, duplication of services, growth, and population(s) to be served.

**8.12.02** Economic development. *Content to consider:* The impact that leisure service delivery systems have on the economic development of a community, including the costs and benefits of program provision.

### Program and Event Planning

**8.13** Understanding of the variety of programs and services to enhance individual, group, and community quality of life. *Content to consider:* Content and purpose of programs and services that relate to individual and group goals and values, benefits of the leisure experience, theories of programming, knowledge of participant behavior, and participant-driven programs that promote quality of life.

**8.14** Ability to implement the following principles and procedures related to program/event planning for individual, group, and community quality of life:

**8.14.01** Assessment of needs. *Content to consider:* The variety of assessment techniques and their use.

**8.14.02** Development of outcome-oriented goals and objectives. *Content to consider:* Development of outcome-oriented goals and objectives based upon formal needs assessment.

**8.14.03** Selection and coordination of programs, events, and resources. *Content to consider:* Availability and accessibility of programs, resources and facilities; the social and physical environment of the setting within the greater community; and the integration and coordination with public, nonprofit and private sectors of programs within and outside the direct service area.

**8.14.04** Marketing of programs/events. *Content to consider:* Advertising, publicity, sales promotion, pricing, positioning, product, place, personal selling, and public relations.

**8.14.05** Preparation, operation, and maintenance of venues. *Content to consider:* Planning, organizing, developing, and scheduling of routine, preventive, and emergency maintenance and operational tasks; managing of operational and maintenance personnel; and maintenance and replacement of equipment, natural resources, and structure and systems maintenance.

**8.14.06** Implementation of programs/events. *Content to consider:* Based upon outcome oriented goals and objectives, knowledge of participant-leader interface; customer service considerations; program registration procedures; managing participant complaints, and actual implementation of programs for individuals and groups.

**8.14.07** Evaluation of programs/events. *Content to consider:* Participant-oriented evaluation, program-oriented evaluation, and organization-oriented evaluation processes; evaluation approaches and models; data collection instruments and methods; and ethical responsibilities of evaluation of programs for individuals and groups.

**8.15** Understanding of group dynamics and processes. *Content to consider:* Facilitation of positive group interactions; developing group goals and identities; creating, promoting, and maintaining positive group atmosphere and communication; and establishing an environment within the group for effective programming outcomes.

**8.16** Ability to use various leadership techniques to enhance individual, group, and community experiences. *Content to consider:* Utilizing ethical considerations, leadership models, motivation techniques, team leadership, and self-managed team concepts in providing programs for individuals and groups.

### *Administration/Management*

**8.17** Ability to apply basic principles of research and data analysis related to recreation, park resources, and leisure services. *Content to consider:* Application of appropriate research methodology and statistical analysis for assessment, planning, and evaluation processes; application to evidence-based decision making.

**8.18** Understanding of the fundamental principles and procedures of management. *Content to consider:* Organization philosophy, goals, and objectives; planning systems; policy and procedure formulation; governance and oversight; power and politics; organizational design and structures; and information technology management.

**8.19** Understanding of the principles and procedures of human resource management. *Content to consider:* Human resource planning and staffing, compensation, staff development, labor relations and collective bargaining, conflict resolution and negotiation, decision-making models, employment law, grievance management, and workplace diversity.

**8.20** Understanding of the principles and procedures of supervisory leadership. *Content to consider:* Interpersonal communication; motivation; managing employee performance; supervisory leadership; discipline and separation; ethics and standards of conduct; managing volunteers, part-time, and seasonal staff.

**8.21** Understanding of the principles and procedures of budgeting and financial management. *Content to consider:* Financing, budgeting methods, fiscal accountability, fiscal policies, purchasing, and inventory control.

**8.22** Understanding of the principles and procedures related to agency marketing techniques and strategies. *Content to consider:* Writing principles; consumer buying behavior; segmentation, targeting, and positioning; product life cycles; advertising; various forms of media, including print, broadcast and online; media planning and buying; copyrighting; planning and programming public relations events; implementing public relations strategy through various forms of media; and media relations.

**8.23** Ability to utilize the tools of professional communication. *Content to consider:* Technical writing, public speaking, and audio-visual/multimedia resources.

**8.24** Ability to apply current technology to professional practice. *Content to consider:* Application of current technology separately and in integrated formats for professional practice. Examples of technology include the following: word processing, spreadsheets, database management, presentation and graphic software, and web page development. An example of applying current technology in an integrated format is the use of presentation software to include spreadsheet components.

**8.25** Knowledge of the following principles and procedures of developing areas and facilities:

**8.25.01** Assessment. *Content to consider:* Social, environmental, and physical assessment and impact of the environment to determine its suitability for the development of recreational areas and facilities.

**8.25.02** Planning. *Content to consider:* Basic planning models and principles as they relate to the development and construction of recreational areas/facilities.

**8.25.03** Functional Design. *Content to consider:* Principles of functional design to maximize participation while maintaining a sound environment.

**8.25.04** Evaluation. *Content to consider:* Principles and procedures for evaluating the appropriateness and functionality of a recreation area/facility.

**8.25.05** Operation and maintenance. *Content to consider:* Basic operation and maintenance principles and procedures as they relate to the operation of a recreation area/facility.

### Legal Aspects

**8.26** Understanding of the following related to recreation, park resources, and leisure services:

**8.26.01** Legal foundations and the legislative process

**8.26.02** Contracts and tort law

**8.26.03** Regulatory agents and methods of compliance. *Content to consider:* Enabling laws; public and private control; national, state, and local agencies and regulations; creation and enforcement of legislation; human rights; property law.

**8.27** Understanding the principles and practices of safety, emergency, and risk management related to recreation, park resources, and leisure services. *Content to consider:* Components of risk management planning; emergency procedures; safety/law enforcement.

### Field Experiences

**8.28** Formal field experience(s) of at least 100 total documented clock hours in appropriate professional recreation organizations/agencies prior to internship. *Content to consider:* May include a variety of experiences in required courses, in-depth experiences of greater duration, and required community service.

**8.29** Internship, full-time continuing experience in one appropriate professional recreation organization/agency of at least 400 clock hours over an extended period of time, not less than 10 weeks. If an option is accredited, the internship must be directly related to such option.

# COAPRT Standards 2013

The 7.0 series standards are distinctly different from the standards in the 1.0-6.0 series. In contrast to the "Facts about the Program" that are embedded in the 1.0-6.0 standards, the 7.0 series standards address the "Learning Outcomes" of the Program. These standards describe the goals of student learning for "foundational" professional preparation in recreation, park resources, leisure services, and other elements of the human service and experience industries.

### Foundations

**7.01** Students graduating from the Program shall demonstrate the following entry-level knowledge: a) the nature and scope of the relevant park, recreation, tourism, or related professions and their associated industries; b) techniques and processes used by professionals and workers in those industries; and c) the foundations of the profession in history, science, and philosophy.

**7.02** Students graduating from the Program shall demonstrate the ability to design, implement, and evaluate services that facilitate targeted human experiences and that embrace personal and cultural dimensions of diversity.

**7.03** Students graduating from the Program shall demonstrate knowledge of the scope of the profession, professional practice, and the historical, scientific, and philosophical foundations of the relevant recreation, park resources, leisure experiences, or human service industries.

**7.03.01** Students graduating from the Program shall demonstrate entry-level knowledge of the scope of the profession that is the focus of the Program, along with professional practices of that profession.

**7.03.02** Students graduating from the Program shall demonstrate entry-level knowledge of the historical, scientific, and philosophical foundations of the profession(s) for which the Program prepares students.

**7.03.03** Students graduating from the Program shall demonstrate the ability to apply relevant knowledge of professional practice and the historical, scientific, and philosophical foundations to develop valid and sound arguments on which to base decisions about professional policies, procedures, practices, techniques, and related ethical and professional issues.

*Provision of Services and Experiences for the Public, Guests, Visitors, and Clients*

**7.04** Students graduating from the Program shall demonstrate the ability to design, implement, and evaluate recreation, park resources, leisure, and human service offerings facilitating targeted human experiences that embrace personal and cultural dimensions of diversity.

**7.04.01** Students graduating from the Program shall demonstrate the ability to design experiences clearly reflecting application of knowledge from relevant facets of contemporary professional practice, science, and philosophy.

**7.04.02** Students graduating from the Program shall demonstrate the ability to facilitate recreation and leisure experiences among diverse clientele, settings, cultures, and contexts.

**7.04.03** Students graduating from the Program shall demonstrate the ability to evaluate service and experience offerings and to use evaluation data to improve the quality of offerings.

*Management/Administration*

**7.05** Students graduating from the Program shall be able to demonstrate entry-level knowledge about management/administration of recreation, park resources, and leisure services.

**7.05.01** Students graduating from the Program shall be able to recognize basic facts, concepts, principles, and procedures of management/administration, infrastructure management, financial and human resource management, and marketing/public relations.

**7.05.02** Students graduating from the Program shall be able to apply entry-level concepts, principles, and procedures of management/administration, infrastructure management, financial and human resource management, and marketing/public relations to a specific setting.

Reprinted, by permission, from NRPA.

# glossary

**access control**—Systems in place that allow or limit entry to a facility or an amenity within a facility.

**accreditation**—Certification that standards, competencies, and quality have been reached within a degree program.

**administration**—The process of planning, leading, controlling, and organizing activities within an organization.

**administrative equipment**—Equipment that supports the administrative and executive operation of the facility.

**at-will employment**—Employment status that gives employers the right to fire employees for any reason or for no reason at all and gives employees the legal right to quit their jobs at any time for any reason.

**behaviorally anchored rating scale (BARS)**—An evaluation tool that uses behavioral descriptions to measure performance. The descriptions are examples of behaviors reflecting unacceptable performance to outstanding performance, and the evaluator rates the employee based on the behavior that the employee comes closest to displaying.

**break-even point**—When revenues equal expenditures.

**building maintenance**—Maintenance of indoor facilities.

**capital budget**—A budget that outlines the larger expenses of an agency that do not recur on an annual basis. An example of a capital expense is the construction of a new recreation center.

**capital improvement plan (CIP)**—A plan to address high-cost equipment, facility, and other agency needs. The CIP includes prioritized projects, projected completion dates, and estimated costs.

**Civilian Conservation Corps (CCC)**—Federal agency organized during the Great Depression to provide jobs to unemployed workers on projects such as state parks and trails.

**commodity outlets**—Spaces in a facility where users can purchase items such as equipment, apparel, food, or gifts. Commodity outlets can be excellent sources of revenue for a facility.

**continuing education units (CEUs)**—A measure of time spent advancing professional knowledge. A one-hour educational session typically earns a workshop attendee .1 CEUs.

**coordination**—Planning and organizing all of the details associated with a program or event.

**copyright**—Legal ownership of an original work such as a book, magazine article, or song.

**core products**—The primary products or services an agency produces.

**cyclical maintenance**—Scheduled maintenance activities that are performed on a schedule and typically have numerous processes involved in completing the full cycle of the maintenance activity.

**delivery equipment**—Equipment used to run programs or allow users to participate in the primary activities of the facility.

**demographics**—Descriptors of the population, such as age, race, income, and geography.

**developmentally appropriate practices**—Planning programs to meet the needs of participants given the participants' ages and current abilities and the appropriateness of the task.

**efficiency system equipment**—The electrical and mechanical equipment systems that support the overall use of the facility.

**emergency preparedness**—Procedures that are implemented when emergency situations arise.

**equipment**—Anything in a facility that contributes to administrative and program operations.

**equipment maintenance**—Maintenance of items that participants and employees utilize during facility operations.

**equity investments**—Investments in a privately owned company in which the investors do not expect the money to be paid off as they would with a loan but instead expect to gain a percentage of ownership and hopefully a percentage of earned profits.

**ethics**—Standards, behaviors, and principles that guide behaviors. Ethics can be derived from professional associations, the profession itself, the community in which the agency is located, and agency practices and policies.

**evaluation**—A systematic method of assessing the strengths and weaknesses of a program, policy, or employee.

**existentialism**—The branch of philosophy that believes that reality is living and that individuals are responsible for developing themselves and are responsible only to and for themselves. Thus personal choice and freedom are of great importance.

**expendable equipment**—Equipment purchased on a regular basis that is used in day-to-day administrative operations and in running programs.

**fiscal year**—The financial year of an agency.

**fixed equipment**—Equipment attached permanently to a facility. Fixed equipment is usually installed during construction.

**formative evaluation**—An evaluation that provides feedback on a program while it is ongoing. A programmer can use the formative evaluation to guide program improvement before the program ends and thus can adapt the program midstream.

**fundamental motor skills**—Foundational movement skills upon which all other physical activities are based.

**Gallahue's hourglass model of motor development**—A visual representation of motor development across the life span.

**general obligation bonds**—A common type of municipal bond issued by city or other local governments that is secured by the government's pledge to use legally available resources, including tax revenues, to repay bondholders. The general obligation bond is a form of long-term debt funding for which the leisure services agency must obtain voter approval to borrow money.

**goal**—A broad statement of what the program or project is intended to achieve.

**grievance**—A complaint that is filed in response to treatment felt to be unfair and worthy of action.

**grounds maintenance**—Maintenance of outdoor spaces.

**groupthink**—A situation that occurs when group members readily agree on a solution without thoroughly analyzing other options due to the need to conform and agree.

**hardscape maintenance**—Maintenance of paved or unnatural growth areas such as sidewalks, playgrounds, or bike trails.

**horizontal job classification**—Classification system in which positions are organized in terms of responsibility, supervision given and received, and complexity of work. The classification, or grade, rises as work becomes more difficult and responsibilities more numerous and important.

**humanism**—A branch of philosophy focused on human interests and values that has no concern with the idea of a divine being such as God.

**idealism**—A branch of philosophy focused on self-defined ideals influenced by what is perceived as excellence or perfection.

**incremental budgeting**—The process of taking the previous year's budget, determining a percentage increase (or, in some cases, decrease) for the overall budget, and then applying it across the board to the previous year's numbers.

**inventory process**—The process of recording the receipt and ownership of equipment.

**job analysis**—The systematic process of collecting information on the knowledge, skills, abilities, and other characteristics (KSAOCs) required to perform a job successfully.

**job classifications**—Categories in which job positions are organized by function level or ability.

**job description**—A list of the tasks, duties, and responsibilities an employee must complete successfully within the context of a specific job.

**kinesiology**—The study of human movement.

**labor unions**—Organizations formed to represent their members' interests and to resolve conflicts with employers. Unions protect the interests of their members and improve wages, working conditions, and hours.

**Leadership in Energy and Environmental Design (LEED)**—A green building certification issued by a third party ensuring that a building was designed and built using practices that save energy and natural resources.

**leisure delivery system**—A system of businesses and agencies that provide leisure services through public, private nonprofit, and private or commercial entities.

**maintenance equipment**—Equipment used to keep facilities and equipment in proper working condition.

**maintenance projects**—Unforeseen maintenance that includes larger-scale maintenance activities such as major repairs or renovations to spaces in a facility.

**management by objectives (MBO)**—An employee planning and performance tool in which the supervisor (the rater) and the employee determine the employee's goals and objectives for the evaluation period as well as figure out a plan for achieving them.

**marketing plan**—A documented guide detailing customers, products, and means to achieve marketing goals and objectives.

**micromanagement**—Excessive control over people or projects. It is characterized by a manager's preoccupation with work that needs to be done, particularly work that has been delegated, as well as a manager's anxiety over how the work is being done.

**mission statement**—A statement of purpose that an organization develops outlining who its customers are, what services it offers, and how it delivers its services.

**morals**—Personal principles and values that guide behavior and are often driven by society or religion.

**motor development**—Continuous changes in a person's movement abilities across the life span, brought about by interactions among the individual, the environment, and the task.

**news release**—A standardized form of communication sent to print media that details information about a product or service.

**nonequity investments**—An investment in which the money borrowed (invested) must be paid back over time. The investor does not own any part of the company unless the loan is in default. Lines of credit, installment loans, and home equity loans are all nonequity investments.

**object classification line-item budget**—A budget system in which each expenditure, and the dollar amount expended for it, is listed on a separate line within a predetermined coding system.

**objectives**—Specific and measurable statements defining how a goal will be achieved.

**opening and closing procedures**—Daily or seasonal procedures followed uniformly by any employee opening or closing a facility.

**operating budget**—A budget outlining and tracking the day-to-day revenues and expenses of a business or agency. It includes items such as salaries, supplies, and utilities.

**outsourcing**—The use of an outside source to provide a recreation product or service that traditionally has been provided internally.

**partnership**—Collaboration in which two or more agencies work together to accomplish a mutually desirable goal. Each partner reaps the rewards of a successful partnership but also takes on the risks associated with the partnership.

**patent**—Legal ownership of a product invention.

**performance budget**—A budget focusing on how expenditures directly affect program outputs.

**performance plan**—Goals and objectives that a supervisor feels an employee needs to meet in order to perform the job to the agency's standards.

**permanent equipment**—Equipment not affixed to the facility but necessary in order for the facility to operate.

**pragmatism**—A branch of philosophy in which the worth or value of something is determined by its consequences or outcomes.

**preventative maintenance**—Scheduled maintenance used to protect areas and equipment from wearing out or breaking down and to extend the life of spaces and equipment.

**privatization**—The transfer of government-owned services or assets to the private sector.

**product extensions**—Products and services that enhance core products.

**professional development**—Skills and knowledge attained for both personal development and career advancement.

**program budget**—A budget in which expenditures are outlined by departmental function or by program. It provides a more outcome-oriented picture of the budget.

**public relations**—Communication used to create a positive image for the agency's internal and external publics.

**public service announcement**—A standardized form of communication sent to broadcast media that details information about a product or service.

**qualitative data**—Data that are nonnumerical and typically expressed in narrative or description.

**quantitative data**—Numerical data.

**realism**—A branch of philosophy focused on the natural order of the world, believing that objects are defined not only by the individual but also independently by reality. The realist focuses on the practical rather than the ideal or theoretical.

**records**—Documentation of routine maintenance, preventative maintenance, inspections, cyclical maintenance, unforeseen maintenance, maintenance projects, and maintenance manuals that allows an agency to monitor the amount of resources required to maintain facilities and equipment.

**reliability**—The quality describing a measurement in which the same data are collected repeatedly when a phenomenon is measured multiple times. In other words, the measurement is a consistent measurement of a program or some other unit of observation.

**repositioning**—Changing the place a product currently holds in the mind of the consumer.

**resources**—The financial, physical, technological, and human assets needed by an organization to operate.

**routine maintenance**—Scheduled maintenance that includes daily and weekly activities that preserve or improve the appearance of a facility or piece of equipment.

**scheduled maintenance**—Maintenance activities that are planned in advance and are part of a schedule of maintenance activities.

**scheduling**—The assignment of time, place, and people for facility use.

**services portfolio**—A document of all the services, products, and facilities offered by an agency. This document may also contain information such as evaluations of services, descriptions of competitors and the target markets, and the overall value of the services, products, and facilities to the agency.

**shared vision**—A statement explaining where an agency wants to be or what an agency wants to look like at some point in the future that is agreed upon and supported by the entire organization.

**stakeholders**—People or organizations who may be affected by a decision, process, or service.

**standards**—Guidelines established so an agency can determine the amount of work necessary to make an area aesthetically appealing and safe.

**structural equipment**—Fixed equipment installed during facility construction.

**subsidized program**—A program priced so that its expenditures exceed the revenues it generates. It must obtain funding from a source other than program fees.

**summative evaluation**—An evaluation conducted at the conclusion of a program summarizing how the program performed.

**trademark**—Legal ownership of a sign, symbol, logo, design, image, name, or phrase.

**triangulation**—Utilizing different forms of evaluation in order to attain data from different perspectives, such as utilizing a focus group or interview, a survey, and a suggestion box.

**unforeseen maintenance**—Unscheduled maintenance that is the response to an area or a piece of equipment that has failed and requires repairs.

**unscheduled maintenance**—Maintenance activities that are not regularly scheduled.

**utilitarianism**—An aspect of ethics in which an individual chooses to do what will result in the greatest good for the greatest number of people.

**validity**—The quality describing a measurement tool that accurately measures what it purports to be measuring. Valid data are a true measurement of a concept, attitude, or preference and a true representation of reality.

**values**—Standards and beliefs that guide the behaviors of an organization's members.

**vertical job classification**—Classification system describing the vertical ascendancy of a position, or the levels a person must work through to climb the ladder of management within a particular department or specialization, gradually earning greater status as well as higher pay.

**vision statement**—A statement explaining where an agency wants to be or what an agency wants to look like at some point in the future.

**work order**—A formal document used to evaluate a maintenance issue, determine the required steps of action, prioritize the steps, and assign maintenance staff members to complete the steps.

**Work Projects Administration (WPA)**—Federal agency organized during the Great Depression to put the unemployed to work on useful projects throughout the country, including community parks and recreation centers.

**zero-based budgeting**—A budget system that requires an agency to start with a zero balance each year when making allocations rather than just modifying the numbers from the previous year.

# references and resources

Abrams, R. 2005. *Business plan in a day.* Palo Alto, CA: The Planning Shop.

Allegheny College. 2010. Mission statement. www.alleghenysports.com/sports/2009/6/9/FB_0609091854.aspx?tab=missionstatement.

American Camp Association. 2006. *American Camp Association's accreditation process guide.* Martinsville, IN: American Camp Association.

American Camp Association. 2009. ACA accreditation and standards. www.acacamps.org/accreditation/.

American College of Sports Medicine. 2007. ACSM survey predicts 2008 fitness trends. www.acsm.org/AM/Template.cfm?Section=ACSM%20News%20Releases&CONTENTID=9207&.

Anderson, L., and C. Brown Kress. 2003. *Inclusion: Including people with disabilities in parks and recreation opportunities.* State College, PA: Venture.

Anderson, L.W., and D.R. Krathwohl (Eds.). 2001. *A taxonomy for learning, teaching and assessing: A revision of Bloom's taxonomy of educational objectives.* New York: Longman.

Area Connect. 2010. Kokomo City, Indiana statistics and demographics (US Census 2000). http://kokomo.areaconnect.com/statistics.htm.

Arlington Virginia Parks, Recreation and Cultural Resources. 2009. Therapeutic recreation: Vision and mission. www.arlingtonva.us/departments/ParksRecreation/scripts/assistance/ParksRecreationScriptsAssistanceTrVision.aspx.

Armstrong, M. 2006. *A handbook of human resource management practice.* 10th ed. Philadelphia: Kogan Page.

Ashland Area Recreation Association. 2009. The Ashland Area Recreation Association conflict of interest policy. http://ashland.nh.gov:8080/ashland/departments/park-and-recreation-department/ashland-area-recreation-association-aara/AARA%20conflict%20of%20interest%20policy.pdf.

Associated Press. 2009. Boozer hosting Alaska camp to help fight sickle cell disease. *Deseret News,* July 13. www.deseretnews.com/article/705316527/Boozer-hosting-Alaska-camp-to-help-fight-sickle-cell-disease.html.

Babbie, E. 2009. *The practice of social research.* 12th ed. Belmont, CA: Wadsworth.

Bach, G., and A. Schilling. 2008. Combating the overuse epidemic. *Parks and Recreation* 43(8): 24-7.

Baertlein, L. 2009. Recession takes bite out of brand loyalty: Study. www.reuters.com/article/businessNews/idUSTRE55L0SD20090622?feedType=RSS&feedName=businessNews.

Ball State University. 2009. 6.2: Recreation services disciplinary procedures. http://cms.bsu.edu/About/AdministrativeOffices/StudentRights/PoliciesandProcedures/StudentCode/62RecServDisProc.aspx.

Ball State University Disabled Student Development. 2008. *Accessibility checklist for programs and events.*

Barnes, P. 2007. Physical activity among adults: United States, 2000 and 2005. Centers for Disease Control and Prevention. www.cdc.gov/nchs/data/hestat/physicalactivity/physicalactivity.htm.

Beeler, C. 2005. Human resources employment. In *Management of park and recreation agencies,* ed. B. van der Smissen, M. Moiseichik, and V.J. Hartenburg, 399-435. Ashburn, VA: National Recreation and Park Association.

Beeler, C., and S. Perkins. 2005. Supervision. In *Management of park and recreation agencies,* ed. B. van der Smissen, M. Moiseichik, and V.J. Hartenburg, 469-91. Ashburn, VA: National Recreation and Park Association.

Blankenship, D.C. 2010. *Applied research and evaluation methods in recreation.* Champaign, IL: Human Kinetics.

Bloom, B. 1956. *Taxonomy of educational objectives.* New York: Longman.

Board Source. 2009. What is a conflict of interest? www.boardsource.org/Knowledge.asp?ID=3.382.

Boccaro, J.N., and R.J. Barcelona. 2003. University and community park and recreation department partnerships: Tips for unlocking the potential of collaboration. *Parks and Recreation* 38(10): 50-5.

Bocarro, J.N, and M.S. Wells. 2009. Making a difference through parks and recreation: Reflections on physical activity, health and wellness research. *Journal of Park and Recreation Administration* 27(3): 1-7.

Brayley, R.E., and D.D. McLean. 1999. *Managing financial resources in sport and leisure service organizations.* Champaign, IL: Sagamore Publishing.

Brayley, R.E., and D.D. McLean. 2008. *Financial resource management: Sport, tourism, and leisure services.* Champaign, IL: Sagamore Publishing.

Brenner, J. 2007. Overuse injuries, overtraining, and burnout in child and adolescent athletes. *Pediatrics*

119(6): 1242-5. www.pediatrics.org/cgi/content/full/119/6/1242.

Broadway.com. 2009. *Jersey Boys.* www.broadway.com/Jersey-Boys/broadway_show/514165.

Bryson, J.M., and F.K. Alston. 2005. *Creating and implementing your strategic plan: A workbook for public and nonprofit organizations.* 2nd ed. San Francisco: Jossey-Bass.

Burlington Parks and Recreation. 2010. *2010 fall brochure.* www.burlingtonct.us/departments/documents/SpringSummerBrochure2010revised7-8-10.pdf.

Busser, J.A. 2005. Human resource management. In *Management of park and recreation agencies,* ed. B. van der Smissen, M. Moiseichik, and V.J. Hartenburg, 437-67. Ashburn, VA: National Recreation and Park Association.

Byrnes, J. 2009. Creating a higher quality fan experience by preventing aggressive behavior. *Facility Manager.* www.iaam.org/Facility_manager/Pages/2009_Feb_March/OperationsEvents.htm.

California Adult Literacy Professional Development Project. 2010. Framing needs and establishing priorities. www.calpro-online.org/o_guides/sft_res_og/4.asp#theorganizations.

Carmel Clay Parks and Recreation. 2010. *Program guide.* Carmel, IN: Carmel Clay Parks and Recreation.

Carroll, R.B. 2009. Introduction to geodemographics: PRIZM, Claritas, and clusters. http://andreas.com/faq-geodemo3.html.

Carter, K.A., and L.J. Beaulieu. 1992. *Conducting a community needs assessment: Primary data collection techniques.* Gainesville, FL: Florida Cooperative Extension Service.

Centers for Disease Control and Prevention (CDC). 2009. U.S. obesity trends. www.cdc.gov/obesity/data/trends.html.

Charleston County Parks and Recreation Commission. 2010. Overview and qualifications. www.ccprc.com/index.aspx?nid=859.

Chelladurai, P. 2006. *Human resource management in sport and recreation.* 2nd ed. Champaign, IL: Human Kinetics.

Cherry, K. 2009. Kohlberg's theory of moral development: Stages of moral development. http://psychology.about.com/od/developmentalpsychology/a/kohlberg.htm.

Chicago White Sox. 2009. Chicago White Sox tickets. http://chicago.whitesox.mlb.com/ticketing/index.jsp?c_id=cws.

Christ, P. 2009. *Know this: Marketing basics.* Blue Bell, PA: KnowThis Media.

Christiansen, M.L., and H. Vogelsong. 1996. *Play it safe, an anthology of playground safety.* 2nd ed. Arlington, VA: National Recreation and Park Association.

Ciancutti, R.D. 2005. Happy trails. *Parks and Recreation Business* August: 42-3.

City of Asheville, North Carolina. 2010. Home school adventures for (8-17 years old). www.ashevillenc.gov/departments/ParksRCA/default.aspx?id=12726.

City of Duarte. 2010. City of Duarte teen center. www.accessduarte.com/ParksAndRecreation/teencenter.asp.

City of Dublin. 2008. Parks and recreation master plan 2008: City of Dublin, Ohio. http://www.dublin.oh.us/recreation/parks/masterplan.php.

City of Kettering Parks, Recreation and Cultural Arts. 2009. *Fall 2009 activities guide.* Kettering, OH: City of Kettering.

City of Manhattan Beach. 2009. Older adults (55+) bus trips and luncheons on the road. www.citymb.info/Index.aspx?page=1312.

City of Phoenix. 2010. Parks and recreation department. www.phoenix.gov/parks/.

City of Portland. 1998. Bicycle master plan. www.portlandonline.com/shared/cfm/image.cfm?id=40414.

Claritas. 2000. Summary lifestyle descriptions: PRIZM cluster narratives. www.tetrad.com/pub/prices/PRIZM_Clusters.pdf.

Clawson Freeo, S.K. 2009. Crisis communication plan: A PR blue print. www3.niu.edu/newsplace/crisis.html#4.

Cochran, L.J., A.M. Rothschadl, and J. Rudick. 2009. *Leisure programming for baby boomers.* Champaign, IL: Human Kinetics.

Cohen, A. 1997. Keeping track of everything. *Athletic Business* August: 43-6, 48.

Colorado State University. 2009. Mission / vision / values. http://campusrec.colostate.edu/About/6/.

Columbia (Missouri) Parks and Recreation Department. 2010. Capital projects summary. www.gocolumbiamo.com/Finance/Services/Financial_Reports/FY2010_Budget/documents/14_cip_section.pdf.

Columbus Parks and Recreation Department. 2010. *Spring 2010 - early 2011 fun guide.* Columbus, IN: Columbus Parks and Recreation Department.

Commission for Accreditation of Park and Recreation Agencies. 2009. *Commission for Accreditation of Park and Recreation Agencies national accreditation standards.* Ashburn, VA: National Recreation and Park Association.

Committee on Sports Medicine and Fitness and Committee on Injury and Poison Prevention. 2000. Swimming programs for infants and toddlers. *Pediatrics* 105(4): 868.

Congdon, K.G. 2008. Cultivating program audiences. In *Arts and cultural programming: A leisure perspective,* ed. G. Carpenter and D. Blandy, 65-77. Champaign, IL: Human Kinetics.

Cotton, D.J., and J. Wolohan. 2003. *Law for recreation and sport managers.* 3rd ed. Dubuque, IA: Kendall/Hunt.

Crompton, J.L. 1999. *Financing and acquiring park and recreation resources.* Champaign, IL: Human Kinetics.

Crompton, J.L. 2009. Strategies for implementing repositioning of leisure services. *Managing Leisure* 14: 87-111.

Csikszentmihalyi, M. 1990. *Flow: The psychology of optimal experience.* San Francisco: Jossey-Bass.

Csikszentmihalyi, M. 2000. The contribution of flow to positive psychology: Scientific essays in honor of Martin E.P. Seligman. In *The science of optimism and hope,* ed. J.E. Gilham, 387-97. Philadelphia: Templeton Foundation.

Daly, J.W. 1995. *Recreation and sport planning and design.* 2nd ed. Champaign, IL: Human Kinetics.

Dattilo, J. 2002. *Inclusive leisure services: Responding to the rights of people with disabilities.* 2nd ed. State College, PA: Venture.

Destination Marketing Association International. 2009. *DMO organizational and financial profile.* Washington, DC: Destination Marketing Association International.

Dresang, D.L. 2007. *Personnel management in government agencies and nonprofit organizations.* 5th ed. New York: Pearson Longman.

Drumm, A., and A. Moore. 2005. *Ecotourism development: A manual for conservation planners and managers.* 2nd ed. Arlington, VA: The Nature Conservancy.

Edginton, C.R., D.G. DeGraaf, R.B. Dieser, and S.R. Edginton. 2006. *Leisure and life satisfaction: Foundational perspectives.* 4th ed. New York: McGraw-Hill.

Edginton, C.R., S.D. Hudson, and S.V. Lankford. 2001. *Managing recreation, parks, and leisure services.* Champaign, IL: Sagamore Publishing.

Edginton, C.R., and J. Jiang. 2000. Outsourcing: A strategy for improving the quality of leisure services. *Journal of Physical Education, Recreation and Dance* 71(4): 46-9.

Edwards YMCA. 2009. Winter camp registration form. http://www.campedwards.org/images/RegistrationForm09Winter.pdf.

Elk Meadow Lodge and RV Resort. 2009. Resort policies. http://essentialcoloradorv.com/elk-meadow/resort-policies.cfm.

Ellis, M. 1973. *Why people play.* Englewood Cliffs, NJ: Prentice Hall.

Equality Illinois. 2009. Our mission. www.equalityillinois.org/mission.html.

EZFacility. 2010. College and university athletic facility scheduling and intramural management. www.ezfacility.com/colleges_universities.htm.

Fan Trips Travel. 2010. Flexible payment plans. http://fantrips.travel/pages/flexpay.html.

Fort Benning Directorate of Family, Morale, Welfare, and Recreation Outdoor Recreation (ODR) and Equipment Resource Center. 2009. Standard operating procedures (SOP): Equipment rental check-in procedures. www.benningmwr.com/documents/crd/Equipment%20Check-in%20Procedures.pdf.

*Fortune* Magazine. 2010. 100 best companies to work for 2010: SAS. http://money.cnn.com/magazines/fortune/bestcompanies/2010/snapshots/1.html.

Fried, G. 2005. *Managing sport facilities.* Champaign, IL: Human Kinetics.

Friend, G., and S. Zehle. 2009. *Guide to business planning.* New York: Bloomberg Press.

From Mind to Body. 2009. Class description. www.frommindtobody.com/OCschedule.html.

Fullerton, S. 2007. *Sports marketing.* Boston: McGraw-Hill Irwin.

Gabrielsen, M.A. 1987. *Swimming pool: A guide to their planning, design, and operation.* 4th ed. Champaign, IL: Human Kinetics.

Gallahue, D.L., and F.D. Cleland. 2003. *Developmental physical education for all children.* Champaign, IL: Human Kinetics.

Gallahue, D.L., and J.C. Ozmun. 2006. *Understanding motor development: Infants, children, adolescents, adults.* Boston: McGraw-Hill.

Galloway, R. 1999. Desired characteristics of park and recreation executive board members: A Delphi study. PhD diss., Texas A&M University-Commerce.

Getz, D. 1991. *Festivals, special events, and tourism.* New York: Van Nostrand Reinhold.

Gonring, M.P. 1997. Global and local media relations. In *The handbook of strategic public relations,* ed. C.L. Caywood, 63-75. New York: McGraw-Hill.

Gray, D.P., and C.D. McEvoy. 2005. Sport marketing: Strategies and tactics. In *The management of sport: Its foundation and application,* 4th ed., ed. B.L. Parkhouse, 228-55. New York: McGraw-Hill.

Grimm, R., K. Spring, and N. Dietz. 2007. *The health benefits of volunteering: A review of recent research.* Washington, DC: Corporation for National and Community Service Office of Research and Policy Development.

Haines, A. 2001. Hiring a planning consultant: A guide to preparing a request for proposals. http://learningstore.uwex.edu/pdf/G3751.pdf.

Harvard Business Essentials. 2006. *Decision making: 5 steps to better results.* Boston: Harvard Business School Press.

Hawai'i Tourism Authority. 2005. Hawai'i tourism strategic plan 2005-2015. www.hawaiitourismauthority.org/pdf/tsp2005_2015_final.pdf.

Haywood, K.M., and N. Getchell. 2009. *Lifespan motor development.* Champaign, IL: Human Kinetics.

Heathfield, S.M. 2009. Build an organization based on values. http://humanresources.about.com/od/strategicplanning1/a/organizvalues_2.htm.

Henderson, K.A. 2006. *Dimensions of choice: Qualitative approaches to parks, recreation, tourism, sport, and leisure research.* State College, PA: Venture.

Henderson, K.A., and M.D. Bialeschki. 2002. *Evaluating leisure services: Making enlightened decisions.* 2nd ed. State College, PA: Venture.

Herzberg, F. 1968. One more time: How do you motivate employees? *Harvard Business Review* 46(1): 53-62.

Hickerson, B., A. Moore, L. Oakleaf, P.A. James, J. Swanson, and K.A. Henderson. 2008. The role of a senior center in promoting physical activity for older adults. *Journal of Park and Recreation Administration* 26(1): 22-39.

Houston Parks and Recreation Department. 2009. Our parks. www.houstontx.gov/parks/ouparksA-F.html.

Howard, R.A., and C.D. Korver. 2008. *Ethics for the real world.* Boston: Harvard Business Press.

Hronek, B., and J.O. Spengler. 2007. *Legal liability in recreation, sports, and tourism.* 3rd ed. Champaign, IL: Sagamore Publishing.

Hughes, W.L. 1997. The aesthetic effect. *Athletic Business* August: 69-72.

Human Kinetics (Ed.). 2006. *Introduction to recreation and leisure.* Champaign, IL: Human Kinetics.

Hurd, A.R. 2005. Competency development for entry level public park and recreation professionals. *Journal of Park and Recreation Administration* 23: 45-62.

Hurd, A.R., R. Barcelona, and J.T. Meldrum. 2008. *Leisure services management.* Champaign, IL: Human Kinetics.

Hurd, A.R., M.A. Mulvaney, J.R. Rossman, and W. McKinney. 2007. *Official study guide for the certified park and recreation professional exam.* 3rd ed. Arlington, VA: National Recreation and Park Association.

Indiana University Bloomington Recreational Sports. 2009. Mind body summer schedule. Available at www.iurecsports.org.

Indy.com Beta. 2008. YMCA, hospital plan Avon facility. www.indy.com/posts/ymca-hospital-plan-avon-facility.

International Cricket Council. 2007. Rules and regulations. http://icc-cricket.yahoo.net/rules_and_regulations.php.

International Ecotourism Society. 2009. What is ecotourism? www.ecotourism.org/site/c.orLQKXPCLmF/b.4835303/k.BEB9/What_is_Ecotourism__The_International_Ecotourism_Society.htm.

International Olympic Committee. 2007. IOC code of ethics. http://corporate.olympics.com.au/files/38/IOC_Code_of_Ethics_26Feb08.pdf.

Jackson, R. 1997. *Making special events fit in the 21st century.* Champaign, IL: Sagamore Publishing.

Janis, I.L. 1972. *Victims of groupthink: A psychological study of foreign policy decisions and fiascoes.* Boston: Houghton Mifflin.

Jeff Ellis and Associates. 2009. About us. www.jellis.com/about-us.html.

Jewish Community Center of Greater Baltimore. 2009. Fall 2009 guide. www.jcc.org/upimages/Fall-Final%2020-23.pdf.

Jewish Community Center of Greater Baltimore. 2010. Spring 2010 program guide. Baltimore: Jewish Community Center of Greater Baltimore. www.jcc.org/guide/693.

Jewish Community Foundation. 2006. Conflict of interest policy for board and committee members. www.jewishdenver.net/local_includes/downloads/19733.pdf.

Jordan, D.J. 2007. *Leadership in leisure services: Making a difference.* 3rd ed. State College, PA: Venture.

Jordan, D.J., D.G. DeGraaf, and K.H. DeGraaf. 2005. *Programming for parks, recreation, and leisure services: A servant leadership approach.* 2nd ed. State College, PA: Venture.

Josephson Institute. 2009. Making ethical decisions: The six pillars of character. http://josephsoninstitute.org/MED/MED-2sixpillars.html.

Kaner, S., L. Lind, C. Toldi, S. Fisk, and D. Berger. 2007. *Facilitator's guide to participatory decision-making.* 2nd ed. San Francisco: Jossey-Bass.

Kelly, J.R. 1972. Work and leisure: A simplified paradigm. *Journal of Leisure Research* 4: 50-62.

Kingwell, M. 1998. *Better living: In pursuit of happiness from Plato to Prozac.* Toronto: Penguin Books.

Kirotv.com. 2009. Coast Guard hoists injured hiker from Olympic National Park. www.kirotv.com/news/19985217/detail.html.

Knapp, J., and D.D. McLean. 2003. Public service motivation in public parks and recreation. *Parks and Recreation Magazine* 38: 23-9.

Kotler, P., J.T. Bowen, and J.C. Makens. 2010. *Marketing for hospitality and tourism.* 5th ed. Upper Saddle River, NJ: Prentice Hall.

Kouzes, J.M., and B.Z. Posner. 2007. *The leadership challenge.* 4th ed. San Francisco: Wiley.

Kovar, S.K., C.A. Combs, K. Campbell, G.N. Napper-Owen, and V.J. Worrell. 2007. *Elementary classroom teachers as movement educators.* Boston: McGraw-Hill.

Kraus, R., and L.R. Allen. 1988. *Research and evaluation in recreation, parks and leisure studies.* Needham Heights, MA: Allyn & Bacon.

Kraus, R.G., and J.E. Curtis. 2000. *Creative management in recreation, parks, and leisure services.* 6th ed. New York: McGraw-Hill.

Lancaster, R.A. (Ed.). 1983. *Recreation, park and open space standards and guidelines.* Alexandria, VA: National Recreation and Park Association.

LaRue, R.J. 2004. The facility audit. *Parks and Recreation Business* October: 82-5.

LaRue, R.J., and D. Rogers. 2005. Universal and accessible design: Creating facilities that work for all people. In *Facility design and management for health, fitness, physical activity, recreation, and sports facility development,* ed. T.H. Sawyer, 146-54. Champaign, IL: Sagamore Publishing.

Lee, J. 1920. *Play in education.* New York: MacMillan.

L.L. Bean. 2009. About L.L. Bean: Social responsibility. www.llbean.com/outdoorsOnline/conservationAndEnvironment/index.html?nav=ftlink.

MacKinnon, B. 2001. *Ethics: Theory and contemporary issues.* 3rd ed. Belmont, CA: Wadsworth.

Mannell, R., and D. Klieber. 1997. *A social psychology of leisure.* State College, PA: Venture.

Mannell, R., and D. Reid. 1999. Work and leisure. In *Leisure studies: Prospects for the 21st century*, ed. E. Jackson and T. Burton, 151-63. State College, PA: Venture.

Manschot, S., and T. Kerrins. 2009. Building positive inclusion experiences for lifelong recreation customers. *Illinois Parks and Recreation* 40(3): 18-21.

Massanutten Resort. 2009. Classes and activities. www.massresort.com.

Mathis, R.L., and J.H. Jackson. 2008. *Human resource management.* 12th ed. Mason, OH: Thomson South-Western.

Maxwell, J.C. 2005. *Ethics 101: What every leader needs to know.* New York: Center Street.

MayoClinic.com. 2009. Growth plate fractures. www.mayoclinic.com/health/growth-plate-fractures/DS00816.

McCarville, R.E. 2002. *Improving leisure services through marketing action.* Champaign, IL: Sagamore Publishing.

McLean, D.D., J.J. Bannon, and H.R. Gray. 1999. *Leisure resources: Its comprehensive planning.* Champaign, IL: Sagamore Publishing.

McLean, D.D., A.R. Hurd, and N.B. Rogers. 2008. *Recreation and leisure in modern society.* 8th ed. Sudbury, MA: Jones and Bartlett.

McLean, D.J., and D.G. Yoder. 2005. *Issues in recreation and leisure: Ethical decision making.* Champaign, IL: Human Kinetics.

Mecklenberg County Park and Recreation. 2010. Basketball. www.charmeck.org/Departments/Park+and+Rec/Activities/Athletics/Basketball.htm.

Merriam-Webster. 2001. *Merriam-Webster's collegiate dictionary.* 10th ed. Springfield, MA: Merriam-Webster.

Merrick, S., and P. Steffens. 2008. Military family support summary and needs assessment report of findings. www.scribd.com/doc/11610478/SD-ASYMCAfinal-Report-Document-All-Inclusive-With-Cover-Letter.

Micheli, L.J., R. Glassman, and M. Klein. 2000. The prevention of sport injuries in children. *Pediatric and Adolescent Sport Injuries* 19(4): 821-34.

Michigan DNR Parks and Recreation Division. 2009. Sustaining 90 years of excellence: 2009-2019 strategic plan. www.michigan.gov/documents/dnr/COMPLETE_DOCUMENT_Signed_279037_7.pdf.

Middleton, V.T.C., and J. Clark. 2001. *Marketing in travel and tourism.* 3rd ed. Oxford: Butterworth-Heinemann.

Milwaukee Recreation. 2009. Fall 2009 recreation guides. www.milwaukeerecreation.net/activity-guide/youth-teen-activities.pdf.

MindTools. 2009. Using the TOWS matrix. www.mindtools.com/pages/article/newSTR_89.htm.

Mitra, A., and S. Lankford. 1999. *Research methods in parks, recreation, and leisure services.* Champaign, IL: Sagamore Publishing.

Molnar, D.J., and A.J. Rutledge. 1992. *Anatomy of a park.* 2nd ed. Prospect Heights, IL: Waveland Press.

Morgan, D.L. 1998. *Planning focus groups.* Thousand Oaks, CA: Sage Publications.

Motionsoft Club Management Software. 2008. Membership management. www.motionsoft.net.

Mull, R.F., K.G. Bayless, and L.M. Jamieson. 2005. *Recreational sport management.* 4th ed. Champaign, IL: Human Kinetics.

Mull, R.F., B.A. Beggs, and M. Renneisen. 2009. *Recreation facility management: Design, development, operations, and utilization.* Champaign, IL: Human Kinetics.

Mullin, B.J., S. Hardy, and W.A. Sutton. 2007. *Sport marketing.* 3rd ed. Champaign, IL: Human Kinetics.

Municipal Research and Services Center of Washington. 2009. Is it policy or administration? www.mrsc.org/Subjects/Governance/legislative/policyoradmin.aspx.

Nash, J.B. 1953. *Philosophy of recreation and leisure.* Dubuque, IA: Mosby.

National Association for the Education of Young Children. 2009. *Developmentally appropriate practice in early childhood programs serving children from birth through age 8.* Washington, DC: National Association for the Education of Young Children. www.naeyc.org/files/naeyc/file/positions/PSDAP.pdf.

National Institute of Arthritis and Musculoskeletal and Skin Disease. 2007. Growth plate fractures and injuries. www.medicinenet.com/growth_plate_fractures_and_injuries/page2.htm.

National Recreation and Park Association. 2009. National initiatives: Transforming the lives of all people through parks and recreation. www.nrpa.org/partnerprograms/.

National Senior Games Association. 2009. National Senior Games Association official sport rules 2009 Summer National Senior Games - presented by Humana. www.nsga.hangastar.com/ReturnBinary.aspx?Params=584e5b5a445800000001f7.

National Therapeutic Recreation Society. 2001. NTRS code of ethics and interpretive guidelines. www.nrpa.org/uploadedFiles/Connect_and_Share/The_NRPA_Network_(Socnet_Function)/NTRS%20code%20of%20ethics.pdf.

Navy Morale, Welfare, Recreation. 2009. Get on board: A guide on how to do business with Navy MWR. www.mwr.navy.mil/mwrprgms/facdocs/busmwr.pdf.

New York Mets. 2009. Citi Field: Mass transit info. http://newyork.mets.mlb.com/nym/ballpark/directions.jsp.

Noe, R.A., J.R. Hollenbeck, B. Gerhart, and P.M. Wright. 2007. *Fundamentals of human resource management.* 2nd ed. New Delhi: McGraw-Hill.

Northville Parks and Recreation Department. 2007. Northville Community Parks and Recreation master plan 2007-2011. www.northvilleparksandrec.org/RecMasterPlan/MasterPlan2007-2011.pdf.

Oahe Family YMCA. 2009. YMCA character development statement. www.oaheymca.org/default.asp?modId=system&logicId=content&viewId=cms&sectionId=36&parentId=3&subOrderType=title.

Olson, J.R. 1997. *Facility and equipment management.* Champaign, IL: Human Kinetics.

O'Sullivan, E.L., and K.J. Spangler. 1998. *Experience marketing.* State College, PA: Venture.

Otak Team. 2005. City of McCall parks and recreation master plan. www.mccall.id.us/government/committees/Parks_Rec_Advisory/Parks_Rec_Master_Plan.pdf.

Ottawa Parks and Recreation. 2009. Ottawa recreation guide fall-winter 2009-2010. www.ottawa.ca/residents/parks_recreation/programs/guide/index_en.html#P18_964.

Ozmun, J.C., and D.L. Gallahue. 2005. Motor development. In *Adapted physical education,* ed. J.W. Winnick, 343-57. Champaign, IL: Human Kinetics.

Partnership for After School Education. 2009. Competitive analysis. www.pasesetter.com/documents/pdf/turbtimes/Competitive%20Analysis.pdf.

Patton, J.D. 1997. Mission: Control. *Athletic Business* August: 63-8.

Payne, V.G., and L.D. Isaacs. 2008. *Human motor development: A lifespan approach.* 7th ed. Mountain View, CA: Mayfield.

Peterson, J. 2009. 5 amazing eco-tourism destinations. http://planetgreen.discovery.com/travel-outdoors/popular-ecotourism-destinations.html.

Peterson, J.A., and S.J. Tharrett. 1997. *ACSM's health/fitness facility standards and guidelines.* 2nd ed. Champaign, IL: Human Kinetics.

Pfister, R.E., and P.T. Tierney. 2009. *Recreation, event, and tourism businesses: Start-up and sustainable operations.* Champaign, IL: Human Kinetics.

Phillips, L.E. 1996. *Parks: Design and management.* New York: McGraw-Hill.

Phoenix Parks and Recreation Department. 2009. Policy on codes of conduct. www.phoenix.gov/TEAMSPRT/code1006.pdf.

Piaget, J. 1961. *The origins of intelligence in children.* New York: International University Press.

Pitts, H. 2007. Assessing the risks. *Facility Manager.* www.iaam.org/Facility_manager/Pages/2007_Jun_Jul/Feature_2.htm.

The Pittsburgh Channel. 2009. Zambelli CEO talks about worker's July 4th fireworks death. www.thepittsburghchannel.com/news/19965286/detail.html.

Planet Hollywood. 2009. Corporate-company history. www.planethollywoodintl.com/corporate.php.

Pleasant Hill Recreation and Park District. 2009. Clubs and organizations. www.pleasanthillrec.com/Clubs.htm.

Popke, M. 2009. How to keep parking lots safe. *Athletic Business.* www.athleticbusiness.com/articles/article.aspx?articleid=2095&zoneid=18.

Potter, W. 2005. Grounded in safety. *Parks and Recreation Business* August: 24-6.

Pritchard, J. 2009. Debit or credit? Who pays interchange fees? http://banking.about.com/od/checkingaccounts/a/debitvscredit.htm.

Pynes, J.E. 2009. *Human resources management for public and nonprofit organizations: A strategic approach.* 3rd ed. San Francisco: Jossey-Bass.

Recreation and Leisure Services Consultants. 2004. Recreation needs assessment draft #2: Town of Essex, Vermont. www.essex.org/vertical/Sites/%7B60B9D552-E088-4553-92E3-EA2E9791E5A5%7D/uploads/%7BDBFDE2F4-80B9-4EF8-8703-2CEEF5584983%7D.pdf.

REI. 2009. REI's culture and values. www.rei.com/jobs/culture.html.

Reingold, D., and R. Nesbit. 2006. *Volunteer growth in America: A review of trends since 1974.* Washington, DC: Corporation for National and Community Service Office of Research and Policy Development.

Reviere, R., S. Berkowitz, C.C. Carter, and C.G. Ferguson. 1996. *Needs assessment: A creative and practical guide for social scientists.* Washington, DC: Taylor & Francis.

Riddick, C.C., and R.V. Russell. 1999. *Evaluative research in recreation, parks, and sport settings: Searching for useful information.* Champaign, IL: Sagamore Publishing.

Riley, D.D. 2002. *Public personnel administration.* New York: Longman.

River Expeditions. 2010. Frequently asked rafting questions. www.raftinginfo.com/plan/faq.php.

Robert, H.W., W.J. Evans, D.H. Honemann, T.J. Balch, and S.C. Robert. 2000. *Robert's rules of order: Newly revised.* 10th ed. Reading, MA: Perseus.

Rossi, P.H., M.W. Lipsey, and H.E. Freeman. 2004. *Evaluation: A systematic approach.* 7th ed. Thousand Oaks, CA: Sage Publications.

Rossman, J.R. 1983. Participant satisfaction with employee recreation. *Journal of Physical Education, Recreation and Dance* 54(8): 60-2.

Rossman, J.R., and B.E. Schlatter. 2008. *Recreation programming: Designing leisure experiences.* 5th ed. Champaign, IL: Sagamore Publishing.

Russell, R.V. 2009. *Pastimes.* 4th ed. Champaign, IL: Sagamore Publishing.

Russell, R.V., and L.M. Jamieson. 2008. *Leisure program planning and delivery.* Champaign, IL: Human Kinetics.

Sabbach, J. 2010. 110 percent: The measure of our true character. Presentation at the Texas Recreation and Park Society Conference, Frisco, TX, March.

Sacirbey, O. 2009. Everyone in the pool! (Not you, guys). *Religion News Service,* June 17. http://www.religionnews.com/index.php?/rnstext/everyone_in_the_pool_not_you_guys/.

Sawyer, T.H. 2005. *Facility design and management for health, physical activity, recreation, and sports facility development.* 11th ed. Champaign, IL: Sagamore Publishing.

Sawyer, T.H., and O. Smith. 1999. *The management of clubs, recreation, and sport.* Champaign, IL: Sagamore Publishing.

Seidler, T.L. 2006. Facility design and development: Planning and designing safe facilities. *Journal of Physical Education, Recreation and Dance* 77(5): 33-7, 48.

Senior Softball USA. 2010. Senior Softball USA. www.seniorsoftball.com/.

Shalley, W., and A. Barzdukas. 1997. Dive right in. *Athletic Business* March: 41-2, 44-6, 48, 50-1.

Shank, M.D. 2005. *Sport marketing: A strategic perspective.* 2nd ed. Upper Saddle River, NJ: Pearson Prentice Hall.

Siedentop, D. 2004. *Introduction to physical education, fitness and sport.* Boston: McGraw-Hill.

Siegenthaler, K., and K. Riley. 2002. What needs may be: Using nominal groups and the Delphi technique for needs assessment. *Parks and Recreation* 37(12): 58-64.

Silverman, J. 2010. How labor unions work. www.money.howstuffworks.com/labor-union.htm.

Speck, M., and C. Knipe. 2005. *Why can't we get it right? Designing high-quality professional development for standards-based schools.* 2nd ed. Thousand Oaks, CA: Corwin.

Staff Reports. 2009. Shawnee man, 32, dies rescuing drowning child at Chickasaw National Recreation Area. http://newsok.com/shawnee-man-32-dies-rescuing-drowning-child-at-chickasaw-national-recreation-area/article/3381865?custom_click=masthead_topten.

Starbucks Corporation. 2008. Of coffee and community. A brochure available at North American Starbucks Coffee stores.

Starfish Aquatics Institute. 2010. Home page. www.starfishaquatics.org.

Stebbins, R. 1999. Serious leisure. In *Leisure studies: Prospects for the 21st century,* ed. E. Jackson and T. Burton, 69-78. State College, PA: Venture.

Stotlar, D.K. 2005. *Developing successful sport marketing plans.* 2nd ed. Morgantown, WV: Fitness Information Technology.

Straub, J.T. 1998. *The agile manager's guide to delegating work.* Bristol, VT: Velocity Business.

Sutton-Smith, B., and J. Roberts. 1982. Play, games, sports. In *Handbook of cross-cultural psychology: development psychology,* ed. H. Triandis and A. Heron, 425-43. Boston: Allyn & Bacon.

Thompson, D., S.D. Hudson, and H.M. Olsen. 2007. *S.A.F.E. play areas: Creation, maintenance, and renovation.* Champaign, IL: Human Kinetics.

Timberland. 2009. CSR: Environmental stewardship. www.timberland.com/corp/index.jsp?page=env_steward.

Town of Jupiter Parks and Recreation. 2004. Senior softball fun league rules. www.jupiter.fl.us/ParksRecreation/Sports/Senior-Softball-Rules.cfm.

Trask, C. 2006. *It's easy being green: A handbook for earth-friendly living.* Salt Lake City: Gibbs Smith.

Ulrich, D. 2000. *Test of gross motor development-2.* Austin, TX: Pro-Ed.

University of Maine Campus Recreation. 2009. LEED self-guided tour. www.umaine.edu/campusrecreation/pdf/LEED.pdf.

University of New Hampshire Department of Campus Recreation. 2009. Membership and/or eligibility for sport clubs. http://campusrec.unh.edu/media/Club%20Sports/MicrosoftWord-MEMBERSHIPandEligibility.pdf.

U.S. Census Bureau, Population Division. 2009. Annual estimates of the resident population by sex and selected age groups for the United States: April 1, 2000 to July 1, 2008. www.census.gov/popest/national/asrh/NC-EST2008-sa.html.

U.S. Department of Health and Human Services. 2008. *2008 physical activity guidelines for Americans.* Washington, DC: U.S. Department of Health and Human Services.

U.S. Play Coalition. 2010. Home page. http://usplaycoalition.clemson.edu.

van der Smissen, B., M. Moiseichik, and V.J. Hartenburg (Eds.). 2005. *Management of park and recreation agencies.* Ashburn, VA: National Recreation and Park Association.

Walsh, M. 1993. Filter out your pool problems. *Parks and Recreation* July: 58-63.

Wellesley Recreation. 2009. Open gym. www.ci.wellesley.ma.us/Pages/WellesleyMA_Recreation/Open%20Gym.

Wells, M.S., and S. Arthur-Banning. 2008. The logic of youth development: Constructing a logic model of youth development through sport. *Journal of Park and Recreation Administration* 26(2): 189-202.

Wesolowski, M.A., and J.L. Schwarz. 1995. Employee orientation: What employers should know. *Journal of Contemporary Business Issues* 3: 44-54.

Westerville Parks and Recreation Department. 2009. *Westerville Parks and Recreation Department summer 2009.* Westerville, OH: Westerville Parks and Recreation Department.

White, J. 2006. *StarGuard: Best practices for lifeguards.* 3rd ed. Champaign, IL: Human Kinetics.

Yes I Can Basketball. 2009. Home page. www.yesicanbasketball.com.

YMCA of Central Kentucky. 2009. *YMCA of Central Kentucky 2008 annual report.* Lexington, KY: YMCA of Central Kentucky.

YMCA of Greater Charlotte. 2009. Youth recreation basketball. www.ymcacharlotte.org/university/programs/youthsports/basketballhome/basketleague.aspx.

YMCA of Greater Cincinnati. 2009. Character development. www.myy.org/community/cdevelopment.shtml.

YMCA of Southwestern Indiana. n.d. Welcome to the YMCA of Southwestern Indiana. www.ymca.evansville.net.

YMCA of Topeka. 2009. YMCA character values awards. http://topekaymca.org/site/about-us/character-values-award.html.

Zamengo, E. 1995. Spotlight on security. *Parks and Recreation* November: 28-30.

# index

*Note:* The letters *f* and *t* after page numbers indicate figures and tables, respectively.

# about the authors

**Amy R. Hurd, PhD,** is an associate professor in the School of Kinesiology and Recreation at Illinois State University in Normal, where she teaches graduate and undergraduate courses in recreation management, leadership, and marketing. Hurd received her PhD in leisure behavior from Indiana University in 2001. Her research interests focus on management in parks and recreation with specific regard to management competencies.

Hurd has worked in public-sector parks and recreation as a marketing director for the Champaign Park District in Champaign, Illinois. She has also served on the National Recreation and Park Association's American Park and Recreation Society board. She has coauthored *Kraus' Recreation and Leisure in Modern Society,* the *Official Study Guide for the Certified Park and Recreation Professional Examination,* and *Leisure Services Management.*

In her free time, Hurd enjoys biking, kayaking, and hiking. She lives in Normal, Illinois.

**Denise M. Anderson, PhD,** recevied her PhD from the University of Illinois at Urbana-Champaign in 2000. Anderson is currently an associate professor in the department of parks, recreation, and tourism management at Clemson University in South Carolina, where she teaches courses in community recreation and youth development. She also serves as curriculum coordinator for community recreation, sport, and camp management and as chair of the graduate student committee. In 2008 she was named Clemson's Outstanding Woman Faculty Member.

Anderson worked for four years at the Champaign Park District in Champaign, Illinois. She has also served on the board of the National Recreation and Park Association's Society of Park and Recreation Educators.

Anderson lives in Clemson, South Carolina, with her husband, Dan, and her son, Hayden. She enjoys baking, hiking, and boating with her family.

You'll find other outstanding
recreation resources at
**www.HumanKinetics.com**

In the U.S. call . . . . .1.800.747.4457
Australia . . . . . . . . . . 08 8372 0999
Canada. . . . . . . . . 1.800.465.7301
Europe . . . . .+44 (0) 113 255 5665
New Zealand . . . . . . 0800 222 062

 **HUMAN KINETICS**
*The Information Leader in Physical Activity & Health*
P.O. Box 5076 • Champaign, IL 61825-5076